SRA Corrective Reading

Comprehension C Concept Applications

Siegfried Engelmann
Susan Hanner
Phyllis Haddox

 **SRA**

Columbus, OH

SRAonline.com

 SRA

Printed in the United States of America.

Send all inquiries to this address:
SRA/McGraw-Hill
4400 Easton Commons
Columbus, OH 43219

ISBN: 978-0-07-611193-0
MHID: 0-07-611193-8

6 7 8 9 RMN 13 12

The **McGraw·Hill** Companies

Contents

Contents

Lesson Objectives	LESSON 76	LESSON 77	LESSON 78	LESSON 79	LESSON 80
	Exercise	Exercise	Exercise	Exercise	Exercise
Organization and Study Skills					
Main Idea	SB	SB	3	1, SB	
Writing Mechanics: Copying	3	4	4	3	1
Reasoning Strategies					
Deductions	2	WB	WB	WB	WB
Evidence	WB	WB	SB, WB	WB	WB
Rules: Arguments	WB	WB	1	2	
Contradictions		2	SB	SB	
Information Sources/Study Skills					
Reading Comprehension: Words or Deductions				WB	
Interpretation: Maps/Pictures/Graphs			SB	SB	SB
Supporting Evidence					WB
Vocabulary/Language Arts Strategies					
Definitions					SB
Usage					SB
Sentence Combination	SB	3			WB
Editing/Revising	1	1, WB	2, WB	WB	SB, WB
Information Application/ Study Skills					
Directions: Filling Out Forms	WB				
Information Review				WB	
Assessment/Progress Monitoring					
Ongoing: Workcheck	Workcheck	Workcheck	Workcheck	Workcheck	Workcheck
Formal: Mastery Test					MT8

Workbook page 236

Lesson 76 ERRORS W

A Some sentences have redundant parts. A part is redundant if it repeats something that has already been said. In the following sentences, the redundant part is underlined.

The man, who was an adult male, stood on the street corner.

Here's why the underlined part is redundant. If you know that it was a man, you already know that it was an adult male. The underlined words repeat something that has already been said.

• Here's another sentence:

"I will purchase the dress," she said, deciding to buy it

Here's why the underlined part is redundant. If you know that she will purchase the dress, you already know that she has decided to buy it. The underlined words repeat something that has already been said.

• Here's another sentence:

The man, who was an adult male, stood on the street corner.

Explain why the underlined part in the sentence is redundant. Do this by completing the sentence below.

If you know that it was a man, you already know that _it was an adult male_ Ⓐ

• Here's another sentence:

He presented his inquiries in the form of questions.

Explain why the underlined part is redundant. Do this by completing the sentence below.

If you know that he made inquiries, you already know that _he asked questions_ Ⓑ

• Here's another sentence:

The Great Pyramids of Egypt are made of huge stone blocks that are very big.

Explain why the underlined part is redundant. Do this by completing the sentence below.

If you know that the stone blocks are huge, you already know that _they are very big_ Ⓒ

Read each sentence that follows. Explain why the underlined part is redundant by filling in the blanks.

1. In the middle of his speech, he paused by hesitating.

   If you know that he paused, you already know that _he hesitated_

2. He decided to convert his car engine by changing it.

   If you know that he converted his car engine, you already know that _he changed it_

Workbook page 237
Lesson 76

3. The last time I saw Richard was in 1972, and I haven't seen him since then.

   If you know that 1972 was the last time I saw Richard, you already know that _I haven't seen him since then_

4. She sleeps until noon, never getting up before 12.

   If you know that she sleeps until noon, you already know that _she never gets up before 12_

★**B** Read the rule and each piece of evidence. Write a conclusion after each piece of evidence.

Rule. All musical instruments make sound.

Evidence	Conclusion
1. A violin is a musical instrument.	_A violin makes sound._
2. Asters do not make sounds.	_Asters are not musical instruments._
3. Oboes are musical instruments.	_Oboes make sound._
4. A mandolin is a musical instrument.	_A mandolin makes sound._

Note: The circled letters indicate when you ask a question or when you direct the group to respond.

EXERCISE 1

EDITING

1. (Direct the students to find Lesson 76, part A, in the **Workbook**.)
2. (Call on individual students to read up to Ⓒ.)
   Ⓐ Finish the sentence. *It was an adult male.*
   Ⓑ Finish the sentence. *He asked questions.*
   Ⓒ Finish the sentence. *They are very big.*
3. Read the instructions and do the items. (Wait for the students to complete the items.) Let's check your answers. Put an **X** next to any item you miss.
4. (Call on individual students to read each item and the answer.)

EXERCISE 2

DEDUCTIONS

1. (Direct the students to find Lesson 76, part A, in the **Student Book**.)
2. (Call on individual students to read part A.)
   Ⓓ Read rule 1 and evidence A to yourself and get ready to say the whole deduction. ✓
   Say the whole deduction.
   Astringent substances draw things together. Alum is an astringent substance. Therefore, alum draws things together.
   Ⓔ Read rule 1 and evidence B to yourself and get ready to say the whole deduction. ✓
   Say the whole deduction.
   Astringent substances draw things together. Water does not draw things together. Therefore, water is not an astringent substance.

F Read rule 1 and evidence C to yourself and get ready to say the whole deduction. ✓

Say the whole deduction.

Astringent substances draw things together. Paper does not draw things together. Therefore, paper is not an astringent substance.

G Read rule 2 and evidence D to yourself and get ready to say the whole deduction. ✓

Say the whole deduction.

Consumers buy things. John does not buy things. Therefore, John is not a consumer.

H Read rule 2 and evidence E to yourself and get ready to say the whole deduction. ✓

Say the whole deduction.

Consumers buy things. Most Canadians are consumers. Therefore, most Canadians buy things.

I Read rule 2 and evidence F to yourself and get ready to say the whole deduction. ✓

Say the whole deduction.

Consumers buy things. Parrots do not buy things. Therefore, parrots are not consumers.

Lesson
76

Student Book page 146

A For the rules below, some of the relevant evidence tells what something is not or what something does not do.

Rule 1. **Astringent substances draw things together.**
Evidence A. **Alum is an astringent substance.** ⊕
Evidence B. **Water does not draw things together.** ⊖
Evidence C. **Paper does not draw things together.** ⊖

Rule 2. **Consumers buy things.**
Evidence D. **John does not buy things.** ⊖
Evidence E. **Most Canadians are consumers.** ⊕
Evidence F. **Parrots do not buy things.** ⊖

B Write **Part B** in the left margin of your paper. You have two minutes to copy the paragraph below.

Herbivorous animals are well designed for grazing. Their teeth are flat, which is helpful for grinding grass, leaves, and seeds. The eyes of herbivorous animals are positioned so that they can eat and watch out for enemies at the same time.

★**C** Write **Part C** in the left margin of your paper.
Here's the main idea of a passage:

The color of a sunset is not the same as the color of a sunrise.

Read each of the following passages. Then tell whether the main idea describes passage 1, passage 2, or passage 3.

Passage 1. The color of the sky changes because light passes through particles in the air. The basic rule is this: The more particles the light passes through, the greater the change in color of the light. At sunset and sunrise, the light from the sun is close to the horizon; therefore, it must pass through many particles to reach you. That's why the sky appears to be colored.

━━━━━━━━━━━ **EXERCISE 3** ━━━━━━━━━━━

INDEPENDENT WORK

1. **[Optional]** (Direct the students to read the instructions for part B. Give them two minutes to copy the paragraph. Count as errors miscopied words and punctuation. Deduct errors from the number of copied words, and mark the total on the Writing Rate Graph.)

2. Finish the Student Book and Workbook for Lesson 76. ✓

Workcheck

1. Get ready to check your answers starting with Student Book part C. Use a pen to make an **X** next to any item you miss.

2. (Call on individual students to read each item and its answer. Repeat for Workbook items.)

3. (Direct the students to count the number of errors and write the number in the **error** box at the top of the Workbook page.)

4. (Award points and direct students to record their points in Box **W**.)

0 errors	**15 points**
1–2 errors	**12 points**
3–5 errors	**8 points**
6–9 errors	**5 points**

5. (Award any bonus points. Direct the students to total their points and enter the total on the Point Summary Chart.)

6. Show me your work when you've finished correcting it. (When the students show you their corrected work, record their points on your Record Summary Chart.)

Passage 2. There is no atmosphere on the moon, which means that there are no particles in the air for the light to pass through. The sky is therefore black. There can be no sunset on the moon, because the light does not pass through particles. The sky is never colored—it's always black.

Passage 3. During the daytime, the color of the sky on earth is usually blue. However, the color of the sky is different at sunrise from what it is at sunset. The reason is that the earth rotates from west to east. When the earth is moving away from the light of the sun, the light tends to turn red. When the earth is moving toward the light, the light turns blue. Since the earth is turning toward the east, it turns toward the light in the morning and away from the light in the evening. Therefore, at most sunrises, the sky has a bluish color, and at most sunsets, the sky has a reddish color.

The main idea is: **The color of a sunset is not the same as the color of a sunrise.** Does that main idea best fit passage 1, passage 2, or passage 3?

passage 3

C Each argument below breaks one of these rules:

Rule 1. Just because two things happen around the same time doesn't mean one thing causes another thing.
Rule 2. Just because you know about a part doesn't mean you know about the whole thing.
Rule 3. Just because you know about a part doesn't mean you know about another part.
Rule 4. Just because you know about the whole thing doesn't mean you know about every part.
Rule 5. Just because words are the same doesn't mean they have the same meaning.

After each argument below, write the number of the rule the argument breaks.

1. Dan is so bright that he doesn't need a reading lamp in his room. _5_

2. Jerry Thompson is the healthiest man I know. I'll bet his son never gets sick either. _3_

3. I bought these cookies because they must be good for me. After all, they have whole wheat flour in them, and whole wheat flour is good for me. _2_

4. "The reason you fell off the bike and broke your arm," Granny said, "is because you took her bike without asking." _1_

5. Henry Brown is an intelligent, thoughtful government worker. I'll bet the government makes only intelligent, thoughtful decisions. _2_

Workbook page 239 — Lesson 76

D Use the facts to fill out the form.

Facts: Your name is John Woolfe, and you are single. You are applying for a position as a drafting technician. At night you are a second-year student in drafting at Trident College in Franklin Park, Illinois. You are twenty-one years old and have worked summers for the Village of River Grove, Illinois. You draw street improvement and storm sewer plans. Your grades at the college are all A's. Your favorite hobbies are tennis, soccer, and cross-country hiking. The Village of River Grove paid you $8 per hour for your summer work, and your total earnings were $3,000 for the summer. Your father is chief engineer for the Village of River Grove, and your mother runs a dog-grooming business at home.

a. Print your name on line 5.
b. State your father's occupation on line 10.
c. Print your marital status on line 3.
d. On line 2, state what position you want with this company.
e. On line 9, print your age.
f. On line 7, state your qualifications for the job you want.
g. List two hobbies on line 8.
h. State name and address of most recent employer on line 1.
i. On line 6, state your hourly rate of pay and total income on most recent job.
j. On line 11, tell what year you are in college. Give name of college you are attending.
k. State occupation of your mother on line 4.

1. the village of River Grove, Illinois
2. drafting technician
3. single
4. dog grooming
5. John Woolfe
6. $8 per hour; $3,000 for the summer
7. I am a second-year student in drafting at Trident College. During summers I draw street improvement and storm sewer plans.
8. tennis and soccer
9. twenty-one years old
10. chief engineer for the Village of River Grove
11. second-year student at Trident College

Lesson 76 — Workbook page 240

E In the passage below, the verbs **has** and **have** and the verbs **is** and **are** are used incorrectly six times. Cross out each incorrect word. Write the correct word above it.

Anybody that ~~have~~ *has* enough money should visit Florida in the spring. The sand beaches in Florida ~~is~~ *are* very white. Our class ~~are~~ *is* going there again this spring, just as we have done for the last two years. We ~~has~~ *have* terrific volleyball games on the beach. Our team has won almost every game. Anybody who ~~have~~ *has* seen us play would agree that we ~~is~~ *are* the best team.

END OF LESSON 76

Note: The circled letters indicate when you ask a question or when you direct the group to respond.

====== **EXERCISE 1** ======

CONTRADICTIONS

1. (Direct the students to find Lesson 77, part A, in the **Student Book**.)
2. (Call on individual students to read part B.)
   Ⓐ Find the sentence and get ready to read it. ✓
   Which sentence? *Hilldale is the largest town in Hinker County.*
   Ⓑ Figure out the answer. (Wait.)
   What does the map show? *Muckster is the largest town in Hinker County.*

====== **EXERCISE 2** ======

EDITING

1. (Direct the students to find part B.)
2. (Call on individual students to read part B.)
   Ⓒ Finish the sentence. *She went to her house.*
   Ⓓ Finish the sentence. *The production was increased.*
   Ⓔ Finish the sentence. *It was a disaster.*

====== **EXERCISE 3** ======

SENTENCE COMBINATIONS

1. (Direct the students to find part C.)
2. (Call on individual students to read part C.)
   Ⓕ What's the answer? *Change it to a comma.*
   Ⓖ What's the answer? *And.*
   Ⓗ What's the answer? *Change it to a semicolon.*
   Ⓘ What's the answer? *However.*
   Ⓙ What's the answer? *A comma.*
   Ⓚ What's the answer? *Change it to a comma.*
   Ⓛ What's the answer? *But.*

A Here's an argument for where to locate a new business:

Hilldale is the best location for new business in Hinker County. Here's why Hilldale is the best choice:

* Hilldale is located at the intersection of Route 5 and Route 30.
* Hilldale is only sixteen kilometers from Benjamin.
* Hilldale is the largest town in Hinker County.
* Hilldale is only fourteen kilometers from Muckster.

When you consider all these reasons, you see that there could not be a more convenient location for a new business.

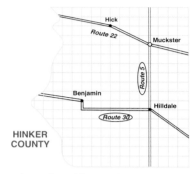

HINKER COUNTY

Each square on the map is two kilometers long and two kilometers wide.
The symbol • means that the city has between 1,000 and 5,000 people.
The symbol ○ means that the city has between 5,000 and 10,000 people.
The symbol ⬭Route 5⬭ means that the road is named Route 5.

Part of the argument is contradicted by the map above. Look at the map and figure out which part. Ⓐ
What does the map show? Ⓑ

B Here's a sentence:
> Before she got home, she stopped at the store <u>and then went to her house.</u>

Explain why the underlined part is redundant. Do this by completing the sentence below.
If you know that she got home, you already know that _____ . Ⓒ

* Here's another sentence:
> Production at the factory was raised <u>when production was increased.</u>

Explain why the underlined part is redundant. Do this by completing the sentence below.
If you know that production at the factory was raised, you already know that _____ . Ⓓ

* Here's another sentence:
> This catastrophe is the worst <u>disaster</u> I've ever seen.

Explain why the underlined part is redundant. Do this by completing the sentence below.
If you know that what happened is a catastrophe, you already know that _____ . Ⓔ

C When you combine sentences with the word **and,** what do you do with the period of the first sentence? Ⓕ
What word follows the comma? Ⓖ
When you combine sentences with the word **however,** what do you do with the period of the first sentence? Ⓗ
What follows the semicolon? Ⓘ
What follows the word **however?** Ⓙ
When you combine sentences with the word **but,** what do you do with the period of the first sentence? Ⓚ
What word follows the comma? Ⓛ

Student Book page 150

D Write **Part D** in the left margin of your paper. You have two minutes to copy the paragraph below.

> Wildlife is made up of wild plants and wild animals. In the last one hundred years, many forms of wildlife have become extinct. Today there are several clubs that have been organized to help protect wildlife that is currently endangered.

★ **E** Write **Part E** in the left margin of your paper.
Here's the main idea of a passage:

> **Changes in weather can affect military battles.**

Read each passage below. Then tell whether the main idea describes passage 1, passage 2, or passage 3.

Passage 1. A few drops of rain at the right time could change the history of the world. In fact, the threat of rain once played an important role in the outcome of a battle. One morning in 1815, Napoleon had planned to attack the British at daybreak, but when daybreak came, the sky was full of clouds. He didn't want to fight in the rain, so he waited. By noon, the sky still hadn't cleared, but Napoleon gave the command to attack. By waiting for the weather, Napoleon had given the British enough time to receive badly needed reinforcements. Napoleon suffered a terrible defeat at this famous battle—the Battle of Waterloo.

Passage 2. A few drops of rain at the right time could change the history of the world. And Dr. Irving Langmuir wanted to figure out how to produce these drops of rain. Dr. Langmuir had been looking for a way to make clouds rain on demand. One day, he left the door to his freezer open. When he realized what he had done, he put a chunk of dry ice into the freezer to cool the freezer down. Later, when he stuck his head in the freezer to retrieve the dry ice, he exhaled, causing hundreds of tiny snowflakes to appear right in front of his face. Dr. Langmuir's discovery led to successful experiments in producing rain from real clouds.

Passage 3. Plutarch, an ancient Greek, noticed that many large military battles were accompanied by rain. He suggested that military battles affect the weather. He said that maybe the gods made it rain because they were angry about all the killing. Other people thought that all of the blood, sweat, and tears shed during a battle were absorbed by the clouds and then rained back down on the battlefield. Still others suggested that it was actually the noise of the battle that caused the rain.

The main idea is: **Changes in weather can affect military battles.**
Does that main idea best fit passage 1, passage 2, or passage 3?
passage 1

Workbook page 241

A Each argument is faulty. Read the arguments and answer the questions.

• Your new plant probably doesn't need much water because my new jade plant only needs to be watered once a week.

1. What does the writer want us to conclude?
   Idea: Your new plant doesn't need much water.
2. How could you show that the argument is faulty?
   Idea: by watering your new plant once a week and seeing if it survives

• Joe takes business classes, so I think I'll ask his advice about the stock market.

3. What does the writer want us to conclude?
   Idea: Joe knows about the stock market.
4. How could you show that the argument is faulty?
   Idea: by seeing if Joe's business classes teach him about the stock market

• Don't loan her anything that you want to get back. She borrowed a book of mine and lost it.

5. What does the writer want us to conclude?
   Idea: She won't return loaned items.
6. How could you show that the argument is faulty?
   Idea: loan her something else and see if she returns it

INDEPENDENT WORK

1. **[Optional]** (Direct the students to read the instructions for part D to themselves. Then give them exactly two minutes to copy the paragraph. Count as errors any miscopied words and punctuation. Deduct these errors from the number of copied words, and mark the total on the Writing Rate Graph.)
2. Finish the Student Book and do the Workbook for Lesson 77. ✓

Workcheck

1. Get ready to check your answers starting with Student Book part E. Use a pen to make an **X** next to any item you miss.
2. (Call on individual students to read each item and its answer. Repeat for Workbook items.)
3. (Direct the students to count the number of errors and write the number in the **error** box at the top of the Workbook page.)
4. (Award points and direct students to record their points in Box **W**.)

0 errors	15 points
1–2 errors	12 points
3–5 errors	8 points
6–9 errors	5 points

5. (Award any bonus points. Direct the students to total their points and enter the total on the Point Summary Chart.)
6. Show me your work when you've finished correcting it. (When the students show you their corrected work, record their points on your Record Summary Chart.)

B Read the rule and each piece of evidence. Write a conclusion after each piece of evidence.

> Rule. **Carnivorous animals eat meat.**

Evidence	Conclusion
1. Horses do not eat meat.	Horses are not carnivorous animals.
2. Cows do not eat meat.	Cows are not carnivorous animals.
3. Felines are carnivorous animals.	Felines eat meat.
4. A deer does not eat meat.	A deer is not a carnivorous animal.

C Read each sentence below. Explain why the underlined part is redundant by filling in the blanks.

1. We'll send to you, without charge, this wonderful gadget <u>as a free gift</u>.

   If you know that it will be sent without charge, you already know that
   it's a free gift

2. If you continue to drive like that, you will destroy your car and <u>ruin it completely</u>.

   If you know that driving like that will destroy your car, you already know that
   it will ruin it completely

3. We are prepared to make a dramatic half-price offer—that is, <u>50 percent off</u>—when you buy our product.

   If you know that the price will be cut in half, you already know that
   it will be 50 percent off

4. "I. . . I. . . I. . . ," he said <u>again and again</u>.

   If you know that he repeated **I** several times, you already know that
   he said it again and again

END OF LESSON 77

A

Student Book page 151

The argument below is faulty because it breaks this rule:

> **Just because the writer presents some choices doesn't mean there aren't other choices.**

Read the rule over to yourself and get ready to say it. Ⓐ
Here's an argument:

> **You should go to college. If you don't, you'll either have to join the army or get a job pumping gas.**

What does the writer want us to conclude? Ⓑ
What choices does the writer use as evidence for this conclusion? Ⓒ
Say the rule that the argument breaks. Ⓓ
Here's how to show that the argument is faulty. Name a choice that the writer doesn't mention. Ⓔ

B

Here's a sentence:
> **These temporary problems <u>will go away in time</u>.**

Explain why the underlined part in the sentence is redundant. Do this by completing the sentence below:
If you know that these problems are temporary, you already know that
_____. Ⓕ

* Here's another sentence:
> **Anybody can see the point I'm trying to make <u>because it is very obvious</u>.**

Explain why the underlined part is redundant. Do this by completing the sentence below:
If you know that anybody can see the point I'm trying to make, you already know that _____. Ⓖ

* Here's another sentence:
> **"I will not take part in this," he said, <u>refusing to get involved</u>.**

Explain why the underlined part is redundant. Do this by completing the sentence below:
If you know that he will not take part, you already know that _____. Ⓗ

Student Book page 152

C

Here are three main ideas:

> **Main idea A. Native Americans stampeded a herd.**
> **Main idea B. Native Americans used poison.**
> **Main idea C. Native Americans waited for game.**

Each main idea fits one of the passages below. After reading all the passages, figure out which main idea goes with each passage.

> **Passage 1.** Native Americans had many ways of obtaining food. One method of hunting buffaloes was particularly clever. Native Americans would get behind a buffalo herd and make a lot of noise. The buffaloes charged forward, running from the noise. The Native Americans then moved the herd in the direction of a cliff. The stampeding buffaloes were unable to stop at the edge of the cliff and plunged to their deaths on the rocks below.

> **Passage 2.** Native Americans had many ways of obtaining food. One Native American method of hunting large game is known as still-hunting. A Native American sat by a pool in a deep forest and waited for animals to come to him. With his bow and arrow ready, he remained perfectly still for hours. Sooner or later, a deer would come within range. Then the Indian would shoot an arrow, killing the deer.

> **Passage 3.** Native Americans had many ways of obtaining food. Some of them picked pokeberries or jack-in-the-pulpits, which are both poisonous plants. Then the people mashed up these plants and dropped them into ponds or slow-moving streams. The poisonous plants killed the fish, which floated to the top. The Native Americans picked the dead fish from the surface of the water and ate them. The poison in the fish didn't bother the people.

* Main idea A is: **Native Americans stampeded a herd.** Which passage does main idea A best fit? Ⓘ

* Main idea B is: **Native Americans used poison.** Which passage does main idea B best fit? Ⓙ

* Main idea C is: **Native Americans waited for game.** Which passage does main idea C best fit? Ⓚ

> **Note:** The circled letters indicate when you ask a question or when you direct the group to respond.

EXERCISE 1
ANALYZING ARGUMENTS

1. (Direct the students to find Lesson 78, part A, in the **Student Book**.)
2. (Call on individual students to read part A.)
   Ⓐ Do it. ✓
   (Call on individual students to say the rule.)
   Ⓑ (Call on a student. Idea: *That you should go to college.*)
   Ⓒ (Call on individual students. Idea: *Going to college; joining the army; pumping gas.*)
   Ⓓ Say it. *Just because the writer presents some choices doesn't mean there aren't other choices.*
   Ⓔ How do you show that the argument is faulty? *Name a choice that the writer doesn't mention.* Name one. (Call on individual students. Ideas: *Taking vocational training classes; working as a clerk in a store.*)

EXERCISE 2
EDITING

1. (Direct the students to find part B.)
2. (Call on individual students to read part B.)
   Ⓕ Finish the sentence. *They will go away in time.*
   Ⓖ Finish the sentence. *It is very obvious.*
   Ⓗ Finish the sentence. *He refuses to get involved.*

EXERCISE 3
MAIN IDEA

1. (Direct the students to find part C.)
2. (Call on individual students to read part C.)
   Ⓘ Which passage? *Passage 1.*
   Ⓙ Which passage? *Passage 3.*
   Ⓚ Which passage? *Passage 2.*

━━━━━ **EXERCISE 4** ━━━━━

INDEPENDENT WORK

1. **[Optional]** (Direct the students to read the instructions for part D to themselves. Then give them exactly two minutes to copy the paragraph. Count as errors any miscopied words and punctuation. Deduct these errors from the number of copied words, and mark the total on the Writing Rate Graph.)

2. Finish the Student Book and do the Workbook for Lesson 78. ✓

Workcheck

1. Get ready to check your answers starting with Student Book part E. Use a pen to make an **X** next to any item you miss.

2. (Call on individual students to read each item and its answer. Repeat for Workbook items.)

> **Answer key for Student Book part E**
> **1.** *The old man laughed at the two people trying to break up the fight.* **2.** *He frowned at the two people trying to break up the fight.*

3. (Direct the students to count the number of errors and write the number in the **error** box at the top of the Workbook page.)

4. (Award points and direct students to record their points in Box **W**.)

0 errors	**15 points**
1–2 errors	**12 points**
3–5 errors	**8 points**
6–9 errors	**5 points**

5. (Award any bonus points. Direct the students to total their points and enter the total on the Point Summary Chart.)

6. Show me your work when you've finished correcting it. (When the students show you their corrected work, record their points on your Record Summary Chart.)

Student Book page 153 — Lesson 78

D Write **Part D** in the left margin of your paper. You have two minutes to copy the paragraph below.

> Some sentences have redundant parts. To figure out if a part is redundant, you need to know what the part means. If you listen closely to ads on radio and television, you'll probably hear a lot of redundant parts.

★ E Write **Part E** in the left margin of your paper. Then number it 1 and 2.

Here is a conclusion:
The old man enjoys watching dogs fighting in his garden.
The evidence is below. Some evidence is contradicted by the picture.

* The old man stopped working on the garden to watch the fight.
* Two other people tried to stop the fight while the old man watched.
* The old man laughed at the two people trying to break up the fight.
* The old man did not use his shovel or his hose to break up the fight.

If you see all these things, you can conclude that the old man likes to watch dogs fighting in his garden.

1. Which evidence is contradicted by the picture?
2. What does the picture show?

Workbook page 243 — Lesson 78

★ A Read each sentence below. Explain why the underlined part is redundant by filling in the blanks.

1. "Okay, everybody out. I don't go any farther," said the bus driver, <u>announcing the end of the journey</u>.

   If you know that the bus driver doesn't go any farther, you already know that

   it's the end of the journey

2. In an unhurried manner, the astronaut stepped <u>slowly</u> onto the planet's surface.

   If you know that the astronaut moved in an unhurried manner, then you already know that

   the astronaut stepped slowly

3. I can't afford that car, <u>because I just don't have enough money</u>.

   If you know that the person can't afford that car, you already know that

   the person doesn't have enough money

4. Her inquiries to the school board were very specific <u>questions</u>.

   If you know that she made inquiries to the school board, then you already know that

   she asked questions

B Read each item. Cross out the irrelevant words in the second piece of evidence, and write the conclusion for each item.

1. Herb teas have no stimulants.
   Mint tea is a ~~sweet, flavorsome~~ herb tea.
   Therefore, mint tea has no stimulants.

2. Some birds lay blue eggs.
   A robin is a ~~common~~ bird ~~in America~~.
   So, maybe a robin lays blue eggs.

3. Islands are surrounded by water.
   Australia is a ~~large~~ island ~~in the Pacific Ocean~~.
   Therefore, Australia is surrounded by water.

END OF LESSON 78

Lesson 79

Student Book page 154

A Here are three main ideas:

> **Main idea A.** Johnny can't read because there's something wrong with his health.
> **Main idea B.** Johnny can't read because of social problems.
> **Main idea C.** Johnny can't read because he was improperly taught.

Each main idea fits one of the passages below. After reading all the passages, figure out which main idea goes with each passage.

> **Passage 1.** It's obvious that Johnny has reading problems. There may be something wrong with his eyes or with his diet. Sometimes children have difficulty seeing the chalkboard because they need glasses. If they can't see the chalkboard, they can't follow the lesson and they don't learn. Or Johnny may be in the habit of skipping breakfast. Children need food for energy during the day. If they don't eat properly, they become tired and don't feel like learning anything.

> **Passage 2.** It's obvious that Johnny has reading problems. Look at his social background. He just moved here from Chicago and is having trouble making friends. If he is lonely or unhappy, he may be unable to concentrate on what the teacher is saying. His older sister has a record of bad grades. I would suggest placing him in a low-performers' group and encouraging him in the use of color crayons. He may have a hidden talent for art.

> **Passage 3.** It's obvious that Johnny has reading problems. However, the main reason is that he was not taught very well. Whoever taught him the alphabet never made sure that Johnny knew the difference between **b** and **d**. Whoever taught him to read never made sure that he read each word properly. But with a lot of work on his part and a lot of work on my part, Johnny will be reading pretty well before the year is over.

- Main idea A is: **Johnny can't read because there's something wrong with his health.** Which passage does main idea A best fit? ⊙
- Main idea B is: **Johnny can't read because of social problems.** Which passage does main idea B best fit? ⊙
- Main idea C is: **Johnny can't read because he was improperly taught.** Which passage does main idea C best fit? ⊙

Student Book page 155

Lesson 79

B The argument below is faulty because it breaks this rule:

> **Just because the writer presents some choices doesn't mean there aren't other choices.**

Read the rule over to yourself and get ready to say it. ⊙
Here's an argument:

> The coal miners are on strike and the country needs coal. There are only two possible solutions—send in the army to take over the mines or sit by while we freeze to death. Personally, I don't want to freeze to death.

What does the writer want us to conclude? ⊙
What choices does the writer use as evidence for this conclusion? ⊙
Say the rule that the argument breaks. ⊙
Here's how to show that the argument is faulty. Name a choice that the writer doesn't mention. ⊙

C Write **Part C** in the left margin of your paper. You have two minutes to copy the paragraph below.

> Here's a rule that is sometimes broken in faulty arguments: Just because the writer presents some choices doesn't mean there aren't other choices. Be careful that you don't break this rule when you write arguments or when you argue with somebody.

Note: The circled letters indicate when you ask a question or when you direct the group to respond.

=== **EXERCISE 1** ===

MAIN IDEA

1. (Direct the students to find Lesson 79, part A, in the **Student Book**.)
2. (Call on individual students to read part A.)
   Ⓐ What passage? *Passage 1.*
   Ⓑ What passage? *Passage 2.*
   Ⓒ What passage? *Passage 3.*

=== **EXERCISE 2** ===

ANALYZING ARGUMENTS

1. (Direct the students to find part B.)
2. (Call on individual students to read part B.)
   Ⓓ Do it. ✓
   (Call on individual students to say the rule.)
   Ⓔ (Call on a student. Idea: *That the army should take over the mines.*)
   Ⓕ (Call on individual students. Ideas: *Having the army take over the mines; freezing to death.*)
   Ⓖ Say it. *Just because the writer presents some choices doesn't mean there aren't other choices.*
   Ⓗ How do you show that the argument is faulty? *Name a choice that the author doesn't mention.* Name one. (Call on individual students. Ideas: *Give the coal miners what they are asking for so that they will go back to work; find other fuel instead of coal.*)

━━━━━━ **EXERCISE 3** ━━━━━━

INDEPENDENT WORK

1. **[Optional]** (Direct the students to read the instructions for part C to themselves. Then give them exactly two minutes to copy the paragraph. Count as errors any miscopied words and punctuation. Deduct these errors from the number of copied words, and mark the total on the Writing Rate Graph.)

2. In Lesson 80, you'll have a test on story facts. The facts that will be tested appear in part E of your Workbook. Study them and make sure that you know them. Now finish the Student Book and do the Workbook for Lesson 79.

Workcheck

1. Get ready to check your answers starting with Student Book part D. Use a pen to make an **X** next to any item you miss.

2. (Call on individual students to read each item and its answer. Repeat for Workbook items.)

3. (Direct the students to count the number of errors and write the number in the **error** box at the top of the Workbook page.)

4. (Award points and direct students to record their points in Box **W.**)

0 errors	15 points
1–2 errors	12 points
3–5 errors	8 points
6–9 errors	5 points

5. (Award any bonus points. Direct the students to total their points and enter the total on the Point Summary Chart.)

6. Show me your work when you've finished correcting it. (When the students show you their corrected work, record their points on your Record Summary Chart.)

Lesson 79

Student Book page 156

★ **D** Write **Part D** in the left margin of your paper. Then number it 1 and 2.

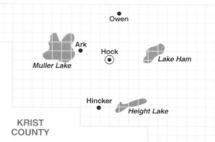

The symbol ● means that the city has between 10,000 and 50,000 people.
The symbol ◉ means that the city has more than 50,000 people.

Although the report doesn't tell exactly where the accident took place, we know that it took place in Krist County. From other information, we can conclude that it took place in Hock. The evidence is below. Some evidence is contradicted by the map.

* The accident took place between two lakes, Lake Ham and Muller Lake.
* The accident took place in the largest city in Krist County.
* The accident took place in the city that is closest to Muller Lake.
* The accident took place near the middle of the county.

1. Which evidence is contradicted by the map?
2. What does the map show?

1. *The accident took place in the city that is closest to Muller Lake.*
2. *The accident took place in the city that is closest to Lake Ham.*

Student Book page 157

Lesson 79

E Write **Part E** in the left margin of your paper. Then number it from 1 to 3. Here are three main ideas:

> **Main idea A. Many Irish came to America.**
> **Main idea B. The Irish and English battled on Easter.**
> **Main idea C. The Republic of Ireland was formed on Easter.**

Each main idea fits one of the passages below. After reading all the passages, figure out which main idea goes with each passage.

> **Passage 1.** Part of Ireland has been ruled by England for hundreds of years. During those centuries, the Irish have often tried to establish their independence. Many Irish people finally left Ireland. They didn't want to pay heavy taxes to English landlords, and the potato famines of the 1840s caused the starvation of hundreds of Irish people. During that time, many Irish sailed from Ireland to America, where they were treated very poorly. NINA was a word often found in job listings. NINA meant "No Irish Need Apply."

> **Passage 2.** Part of Ireland has been ruled by England for hundreds of years. On Easter morning in 1949, Ireland broke its last ties to England and became the Republic of Ireland. Since then, five-sixths of Ireland has been a free country. One-sixth of Ireland is called Northern Ireland and is still part of England. Many bitter, bloody battles for freedom have been fought in Northern Ireland.

> **Passage 3.** Part of Ireland has been ruled by England for hundreds of years. During those centuries, the Irish have often tried to establish their independence. On Easter morning in 1916, two men named Collins and Pearse led a rebellion against the English. The rebellion failed because it was badly organized. Some leaders were sentenced to death by the English. Other rebels were put in jail. The rebellion was called the Easter Rebellion. Although it failed, the rebellion excited most Irish people and increased their anger toward England.

1. Main idea A is: **Many Irish came to America.** Which passage does main idea A best fit? *passage 1*
2. Main idea B is: **The Irish and English battled on Easter.** Which passage does main idea B best fit? *passage 3*
3. Main idea C is: **The Republic of Ireland was formed on Easter.** Which passage does main idea C best fit? *passage 2*

Lesson 79 — Student Book page 158

F Write **Part F** in the left margin of your paper. Then number it from 1 to 4. Look at the graph below. Then answer the questions about what is shown on the graph.

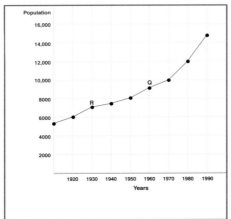

* The letter **Q** shows the population for one year.

1. What year? 1960
2. How many people? About 9,000

* The letter **R** shows the population for one year.

3. What year? 1930
4. How many people? About 7,000

Workbook page 245 — Lesson 79

3. Name three felines.
Ideas: lion, tiger, etc.

4. Do both eyes of a steer see almost the same thing?
no

5. Do both eyes of a wolf see almost the same thing?
yes

6. What is one theory about why carnivorous mammals have two eyes instead of one?
Idea: The simplest explanation is that the animal may lose one eye in battle with another animal. (W) D

7. How are the teeth of a goat different from the teeth of a tiger?
Idea: The teeth of a goat are flat for grinding vegetation; the teeth of a tiger are sharp and pointed for tearing flesh. W (D)

8. Why do carnivorous mammals swallow large chunks of food instead of small bits?
Idea: so that the food will be digested slowly and they won't have to eat as often

B Read each sentence below. Explain why the underlined part is redundant by filling in the blanks.

1. With all this extra corn, we've got more than we can use.
If you know that the corn is extra, you already know that
we have more than we can use

2. Last week's catastrophe was very destructive.
If you know that what happened last week was a catastrophe, you already know that
it was very destructive

3. "There's absolutely nothing I can do for you," she said helplessly.
If you know that there is nothing she can do, you already know that
she is helpless

Workbook page 244 — Lesson 79

ERRORS W

★ **A** Read the passage below and answer the questions. Circle **W** if the question is answered by words in the passage. Circle **D** if the question is answered by a deduction. If you circle **W** for an item, underline the words in the passage that give the answer.

You have read about how herbivorous mammals are well designed for grazing. Their teeth are flat for grinding vegetation, and their eyes permit them to eat and watch for enemies at the same time.

Just as herbivorous mammals are well designed to graze, carnivorous mammals are well designed to hunt, to kill, and to eat the flesh of animals.

The feline family belongs to the group of carnivorous mammals. The house cat is a member of the feline family, along with the leopard, the lion, the tiger, and the jaguar. All are expert killers. The canine family is also carnivorous. The dog is a member of the canine family, which also includes foxes, wolves, and coyotes. These animals do not have the sharp claws of the felines, but the canines are also designed to hunt and kill.

The eyes of a herbivorous mammal permit the animal to see what's on both sides of it at once. A carnivorous mammal does not have to see both sides at once, but it must have a good image of the animal it is hunting. The eyes of a carnivorous mammal look straight ahead so that it can see what its mouth will bite into.

There are different theories about why a carnivorous mammal needs two eyes rather than one. The simplest explanation is that the animal may lose one eye in battle with another animal. Since a carnivorous mammal has two eyes, it can survive the loss of one eye because it needs only one good eye for hunting.

Just as the teeth of herbivorous mammals are designed to grind food, the teeth of carnivorous mammals are designed to tear flesh. The teeth are pointed and sharp, not flat. These teeth do not grind the food into small pieces. Their goal is to tear it into chunks that are just small enough to be swallowed. These chunks are digested more slowly than small bits. Therefore, the carnivore doesn't have to eat as frequently as it would if it swallowed small bits.

1. Tell about two parts of a sheep that are well designed for grazing.
Idea: Its teeth are designed to grind up vegetation, and its eyes are designed to watch for enemies as it eats.

2. Tell about two parts of a jaguar that are well designed for hunting.
Idea: Its teeth are designed to tear flesh, and its eyes are designed to see straight ahead as it pursues an animal. W (D)

Workbook page 246 — Lesson 79

C Read the rule and each piece of evidence. Write a conclusion after each piece of evidence.

Rule. Cactus plants store large amounts of water.

Evidence	Conclusion
1. A prickly pear is a cactus plant.	A prickly pear stores large amounts of water.
2. Spider plants do not store large amounts of water.	Spider plants are not cactus plants.
3. Mescal is a cactus plant.	Mescal stores large amounts of water.

D You will be tested on some facts presented in this lesson. These facts are:

1. The teeth and the eyes of carnivorous mammals are well designed for hunting.
2. The right and the left eye of many carnivorous mammals see nearly the same thing.
3. The teeth of a herbivorous mammal are flat, and the teeth of a carnivorous mammal are pointed.

Study these facts. Repeat them to yourself. Writing these facts may help you to remember them.

E After you finish Lesson 80, you will be tested on facts you have learned. This test will include all the facts presented in Lessons 72–79 and some of the facts from earlier lessons. These facts are:

1. The teeth and the eyes of herbivorous mammals are well designed for grazing.
2. The eyes of herbivorous mammals allow them to eat and to watch out for enemies at the same time.
3. The right and the left eye of many herbivorous mammals see different things.
4. The teeth and the eyes of carnivorous mammals are well designed for hunting.
5. The right and the left eye of many carnivorous mammals see nearly the same thing.
6. The teeth of a herbivorous mammal are flat, and the teeth of a carnivorous mammal are pointed.

END OF LESSON 79

=== **EXERCISE 1** ===
INDEPENDENT WORK

1. **[Optional]** (Direct the students to read the instructions for part A in the **Student Book** to themselves. Then give them exactly two minutes to copy the paragraph. Count as errors any miscopied words and punctuation. Deduct these errors from the number of copied words, and mark the total on the Writing Rate Graph.)

2. Finish the Student Book and do the Workbook for Lesson 80. ✓

Workcheck

1. Get ready to check your answers starting with Student Book part B. Use a pen to make an **X** next to any item you miss.

2. (Call on individual students to read each item and its answer. Repeat for Workbook items.)

3. (Direct the students to count the number of errors and write the number in the **error** box at the top of the Workbook page.)

4. (Award points and direct students to record their points in Box **W**.)

0 errors	15 points
1–2 errors	12 points
3–5 errors	8 points
6–9 errors	5 points

5. (Award any bonus points. Direct the students to total their points and enter the total on the Point Summary Chart.)

6. Show me your work when you've finished correcting it. (When the students show you their corrected work, record their points on your Record Summary Chart.)

Student Book page 159

A Write **Part A** in the left margin of your paper. You have two minutes to copy the paragraph below.

> A carnivorous animal is well designed to hunt other animals. Its teeth are pointed and sharp; therefore, the animal can tear its food into chunks. The eyes of a carnivorous animal look straight ahead so it can see what it is hunting.

★ **B** Write **Part B** in the left margin of your paper. Then number it 1 and 2.

Here is a conclusion:
> **A cat knocked over the plant while it was trying to grab a muffin.**
The evidence is below. Some evidence is contradicted by the picture.

* The man wasn't looking, but the boy clearly saw a cat sitting on the counter.
* There were twelve muffins near the window.
* The plant fell over right below the window.
* The cat had come in through the open window.

We can conclude that the cat wanted to eat a muffin and that it knocked over the plant while trying to get one.

1. Which evidence is contradicted by the picture? *The cat had come in through the open window.*
2. What does the picture show? *There is no open window.*

Student Book page 160

C Here are some words that will be in some editing activities. Test yourself to make sure that you know what the words mean.

affirmed—When you affirm something, you agree with it. Here's a sentence that uses the word **affirmed:**
> The committee voted and affirmed the new regulations.

audibly—When you say something audibly, you say it loud enough for people to hear you. Here's a sentence that uses the word **audibly:**
> She speaks quite audibly, even in a large room.

imitation—Something that is fake is an imitation. Imitation mayonnaise looks like real mayonnaise. Here's a sentence that uses the word **imitation:**
> Her coat is made of imitation fur but it was still very expensive.

remote—A remote area is an area that is far from towns or cities. Very few people live in remote areas. Here's a sentence that uses the word **remote:**
> She settled in a remote part of Alberta because she liked peace and quiet.

Workbook page 247

A Select the right word for combining each pair of sentences that follows. Then write the combined sentence. Remember to punctuate each sentence correctly.

1. Susan did not like her drawing of the horse. It won first prize in the art contest.

      and   however

   Susan did not like her
   drawing of the horse;
   however, it won
   first prize in the art
   contest.

2. Carol got very hungry while watching the movie on television. She made two egg-salad sandwiches.

      and   but

   Carol got very
   hungry while
   watching the movie
   on television, and she
   made two egg-salad
   sandwiches.

3. Alex loves riding on airplanes. He took a train to the meeting in San Francisco.

      so   however

   Alex loves riding on
   airplanes; however,
   he took a train to
   the meeting in
   San Francisco.

4. I avoid that dog. That dog does crazy things.

      who   which

   I avoid that dog,
   which does crazy
   things.

5. I spoke to Marta. Marta is always late for work.

      who   which

   I spoke to Marta,
   who is always late for
   work.

Workbook page 249

D Read the passage below.

> The world's saltiest body of water is the Dead Sea, located between Israel and Jordan. The water of the Dead Sea is about seven times as salty as the water in the Atlantic or the Pacific Ocean. The reason that the Dead Sea is so salty is that it is shrinking. It was once much larger, but it is slowly drying up. The amount of salt that was once contained in a large body of water is now restricted to a very small body of water. There are no fish in the Dead Sea, and plants are very scarce. Salt water is heavier than fresh water. The water of the Dead Sea is so salty that a swimmer cannot sink in it.

• Here's a conclusion:

   The Dead Sea is a good name for this body of water.

1. Does the passage contain evidence to support this conclusion or evidence to refute this conclusion?

   evidence to support
   the conclusion

2. Which sentence contains the evidence?

   There are no fish
   in the Dead Sea,
   and plants are very
   scarce.

• Here's a conclusion:

   Even if you're a poor swimmer, you're probably safe in the Dead Sea.

3. Does the passage contain evidence to support this conclusion or evidence to contradict this conclusion?

   evidence to support
   the conclusion

4. Which sentence contains the evidence?

   The water of the
   Dead Sea is so salty
   that a swimmer
   cannot sink in it.

END OF LESSON 80

Workbook page 248

B Read the rule and each piece of evidence. Write a conclusion after each piece of evidence.

Rule. **Predators kill the animals they eat.**

Evidence	Conclusion
1. Buzzards do not kill the animals they eat.	Buzzards are not predators.
2. Eagles are predators.	Eagles kill the animals they eat.
3. A leopard is a predator.	A leopard kills the animals it eats.
4. Carrion beetles do not kill the animals they eat.	Carrion beetles are not predators.

C Read each sentence that follows. Explain why the underlined part is redundant by filling in the blanks.

1. Before I got to the schoolroom, I stopped at the drugstore <u>and then went to class.</u>

   If you know that I got to the schoolroom, you already know that
   I went to class.

2. We are pleased to announce our first half-price sale—you get <u>50 percent off</u>—when you buy anything in our store.

   If you know that prices will be cut in half, you already know that
   you get 50 percent off

3. He got a temporary job <u>that lasted a short time.</u>

   If you know that his job was temporary, you already know that
   it lasted a short time

4. Those huge, overpopulated cities have <u>too many people in them.</u>

   If you know that the cities are overpopulated, you already know that
   they have too many
   people in them

Mastery Test 8

EXERCISE 1

MASTERY TEST

1. Everybody, find page 446 in your workbook.
   This is a test. You'll do the whole test, and then we'll mark it. If you make no mistakes on the test, you'll earn 20 points. Write the answers to the test items now using your pencil.
2. (After the students complete the items, gather the Workbooks and grade the tests. As you grade each test, record the number of errors the student made on each part of the test in the appropriate box. Record the total number of errors in the **Error** box at the beginning of the test.)
3. (Return the Workbooks to the students.)
4. Raise your hand if you made _____ or more mistakes in part _____.
   (Record the number of students who raise their hand for the part.)

| Key: Part A–2 | Part B–2 | Part C–2 |
| Part D–1 | Part E–2 | Part F–1 |

5. Raise your hand if you made no mistakes on the whole test. Great work. (Award 20 points to the students who made no errors. Award 5 points to students who made 1 or 2 errors.) Record your bonus points in the box marked **MT** at the top of Mastery Test 8.
• (Direct all students to record their points on the Point Summary Chart.)
6. (Record test results on the Group Summary Sheet. Reproducible Summary Sheets are at the back of the Teacher's Guide.)

Mastery Test 8 A B **Workbook page 446**

A Answer each item.

1. Name the two parts of a herbivorous mammal that are well designed for grazing.
   teeth, eyes
2. Do both eyes of a herbivorous animal see almost the same thing?
   no
3. Name the two parts of a carnivorous mammal that are well designed for hunting.
   teeth, eyes
4. Do both eyes of a carnivorous mammal see almost the same thing?
   yes
5. Why do herbivorous mammals have the kind of eyes they have?
   Idea: so they can eat and watch out for enemies at the same time
6. How are the teeth of a herbivorous mammal different from those of a carnivorous mammal?
   Idea: An herbivore's teeth are flat, and a carnivore's teeth are pointed.

B Write the model sentence that means the same thing as each sentence below.

1. Her answer was filled with irrelevant details.
   Her response was replete with extraneous details.
2. They made up a fitting plan.
   They devised an appropriate strategy.
3. By pausing, she lost her chance.
   By hesitating, she lost her opportunity.
4. They changed their Swiss money into Canadian money.
   They converted their Swiss currency into Canadian currency.
5. His directions were unclear and repetitive.
   His directions were ambiguous and redundant.
6. The rule limited their parking.
   The regulation restricted their parking.

Workbook page 447 **Mastery Test 8**

C Look at the graph below. Then answer the questions about what is shown on the graph.

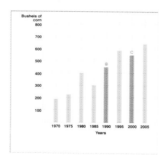

• The letter **B** shows bushels of corn for one year.
1. What year? 1990
2. How many bushels? Idea: about 450

• The letter **C** shows bushels of corn for one year.
3. What year? 2000
4. How many bushels? Idea: about 550

D Select the right word for combining each pair of sentences that follow. Then write the combined sentence. Remember to punctuate each sentence correctly.

1. Police officers need to learn new laws. They go to police school. **therefore** but
   Police officers need to learn new laws; therefore, they go to police school.
2. Cats love Susan. Susan is our animal doctor. **who** which
   Cats love Susan, who is our animal doctor.
3. The mechanic worked all morning on your car. Your car still will not start. so **but**
   The mechanic worked all morning on your car, but your car still will not start.

Workbook page 448

E Read the rule and each piece of evidence. Write a conclusion after each piece of evidence.

Rule: Mammals are warm-blooded.

	Evidence	Conclusion
1.	A salamander is not warm-blooded.	A salamander is not a mammal.
2.	An oryx is a mammal.	An oryx is warm-blooded.
3.	Pythons are not warm-blooded.	Pythons are not mammals.
4.	Sloths are mammals.	Sloths are warm-blooded.

F Read each sentence below. Explain why the underlined part is redundant by filling in the blanks.

1. His responses to the teacher's questions were very specific <u>answers</u>.

   If you know that he gave responses to the teacher's questions, then you already know that _he gave answers_

2. Jean hesitated and <u>paused</u> before she got on the bus.

   If you know that she hesitated, then you already know that _she paused_

3. Before he got to school, he stopped at the store and then <u>went to class</u>.

   If you know that he got to school, then you already know that _he went to class_

EXERCISE 2

TEST REMEDIES

1. (If more than 25% of the students failed a part of the test, provide the remedy specified for that part in the table below. The required Remedy Blackline Master worksheets can be found in Appendix H of the Teacher's Guide.)
2. (All remedies should be completed before beginning the next lesson in the program.)

Test Section	If students made this many errors	Present these tasks: Lesson	Exercise	Remedy Blackline Master	Required Student Book Parts
A	2 or more	Test remedy below		8–A	
B	2 or more	Item 1: 57	1	8–B	Lesson 57–A
		Item 2: 62	2	8–B	Lesson 62–B
		Item 3: 19	1	8–C	Lesson 19–A
		Item 4: 28	3	8–C	Lesson 28–B
		Item 5: 22	1	8–D	Lesson 22–A
		Item 6: 34	2	8–D	Lesson 34–B
C	2 or more	68	2		Lesson 68–B
		69	1		Lesson 69–A
D	1 or more	72	—	8–E	
		73	—	8–F	
E	2 or more	75	—	8–G	
		76	—	8–G	
F	1 or more	76	1	8–H	
		77	1	8–I	Lesson 77–A

> **Note:** The teacher and each student who failed the test will need a copy of Remedy Blackline Master 8–A. The Remedy Blackline Masters can be found in Appendix H of the Teacher's Guide

PART A TEST REMEDY

1. We're going to go over some items from the test. I'll read the items. You'll say the answers. Then you'll write the answers.

2. (Read item 1 in part A of Remedy Blackline Master 8–A.) What's the answer? (Call on a student.)

3. (Repeat step 2 for each remaining item in part A.)

4. (Give each student a copy of Remedy Blackline Master 8–A.) Now you're going to write the answers. Let's see who can get them all correct.

5. (After students complete the items:) Let's check your work. Use your pen to make an **X** next to any item you got wrong.

- (Read the items. Call on individual students to answer each item.)
- Raise your hand if you got all the items correct. Nice work.

END OF MASTERY TEST 8

Lesson Objectives	LESSON 81	LESSON 82	LESSON 83	LESSON 84	LESSON 85
	Exercise	Exercise	Exercise	Exercise	Exercise
Organization and Study Skills					
Main Idea	2, SB	SB	SB	SB	
Writing Mechanics: Copying	4	4	2	2	2
Reasoning Strategies					
Deductions	1, WB	1, WB	WB	WB	
Evidence	WB	WB			
Rules: Arguments	3, WB	3, WB	WB	WB	WB
Contradictions					WB
Information Sources/Study Skills					
Basic Comprehension					SB
Reading Comprehension: Words or Deductions	WB			WB	
Interpretation: Maps/Pictures/Graphs	WB	WB	WB	WB	SB, WB
Vocabulary/Language Arts Strategies					
Definitions		WB			1, WB
Usage		WB			1, WB
Sentence Combination				1	
Editing/Revising		2, WB	1, WB	WB	WB
Information Application/ Study Skills					
Directions: Following					WB
Directions: Writing			WB		
Information Review		WB	WB	WB	
Assessment/Progress Monitoring					
Ongoing: Workcheck	Workcheck	Workcheck	Workcheck	Workcheck	Workcheck

Lesson 81 | ERRORS W | Workbook page 250

A Look at diagram 1.

Diagram 1

You can't see the dots in the diagram, but you can see the circle and the square.

Here's a deduction based on the diagram:

**All the dots are in the circle.
None of the circle is in the square.
So, none of the dots are in the square.**

The diagram below shows that the conclusion is right.

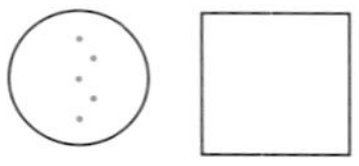

• Look at diagram 2.

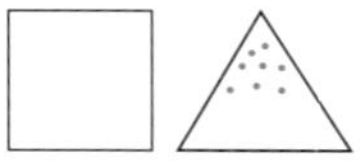

Diagram 2

You can't see the dots in the diagram, but you can see the triangle and the square. Complete the deduction:

**All the dots are in the triangle.
None of the triangle is in the square.** ©

So, _none of the dots are in the square_

Check your conclusion by drawing dots in diagram 2 so that all the dots are in the triangle. ©

• Look at diagram 3.

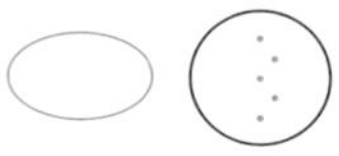

Diagram 3

You can see the dots and the circle, but you can't see the oval. Complete the deduction:

**All the dots are in the circle.
None of the circle is in the oval.** ©

So, _none of the dots are in the oval_

Check your conclusion by drawing an oval in diagram 3 so that none of the circle is in the oval. ©

★ B Read the facts and the items below. If an item is relevant to fact A, write **relevant to fact A**. If an item is relevant to fact B, write **relevant to fact B**. If an item is irrelevant to both facts, write **irrelevant**.

> Fact A. **Freddie is very tall.**
> Fact B. **Freddie is studying landscape gardening.**

1. Freddie's mother is very short.
   irrelevant
2. On the weekends, Freddie works at a lawn and garden shop.
   relevant to fact B
3. Freddie plays on the school basketball team.
   relevant to fact A
4. Freddie reads 400 words per minute.
   irrelevant

Student Book page 161 | Lesson 81

A Here are three main ideas:

> **Main idea A.** The United States fought communism.
> **Main idea B.** Americans were afraid of communism.
> **Main idea C.** Senator Joseph McCarthy was investigated by the Senate.

Each main idea fits one of the passages below. After reading all the passages, figure out which main idea goes with each passage.

> **Passage 1.** In the 1950s, the United States and the former Soviet Union were involved in a "cold war." That means that although the two countries were not actually using guns, the countries were close to being in a shooting war. At the same time, the United States was involved in a shooting war in Korea, where American soldiers were fighting Chinese communists and North Koreans. In 1950, a man named Joseph McCarthy, a United States Senator, became famous when he accused more than fifty employees of the State Department of being communists.

> **Passage 2.** In the 1950s, the United States and the former Soviet Union were involved in a "cold war." Communism produced much anxiety in the United States. If someone accused a person of being communist, others believed that the person was a communist. Many people lost their jobs because Senator Joseph McCarthy said they were communists. Some people even committed suicide. From 1950 to 1954, Senator McCarthy was one of the most powerful people in the United States.

> **Passage 3.** In the 1950s, the United States and the former Soviet Union were involved in a "cold war." That means that although the two countries were not actually using guns, the countries were close to using guns. In 1950, Joseph McCarthy started his own war, accusing many people of being communists. But, by 1954, many Americans were tired of hearing Joe McCarthy accuse people of being communists. In April 1954, McCarthy and his group were investigated by a Senate subcommittee. When asked to prove some of his accusations, McCarthy could provide no real evidence. The Senate criticized McCarthy for not behaving as a senator should behave.

* Main idea A is: **The United States fought communism.** Which passage does main idea A best fit? ©

Note: The circled letters indicate when you ask a question or when you direct the group to respond.

■ EXERCISE 1 ■

DEDUCTIONS

1. (Direct the students to find Lesson 81, part A, in the **Workbook.**)
2. (Call on individual students to read part A.)
   Ⓐ Write the conclusion. ✓
   (Call on a student to read the whole deduction.) *All the dots are in the triangle. None of the triangle is in the square. So, none of the dots is in the square.*
   Ⓑ Do it. ✓(Draw diagram 2 on the board. Call on a student to draw the dots. Acceptable responses must show all the dots in the triangle.)
   Ⓒ Write the conclusion. ✓
   (Call on a student to read the whole deduction.) *All the dots are in the circle. None of the circle is in the oval. So, none of the dots is in the oval.*
   Ⓓ Do it. ✓(Draw diagram 3 on the board. Call on a student to draw the oval. Acceptable responses must show none of the circle in the oval.)

■ EXERCISE 2 ■

MAIN IDEA

1. (Direct the students to find Lesson 81, part A, in the **Student Book.**)
2. (Call on individual students to read part A.)
   Ⓔ Which passage? *Passage 1.*
   Ⓕ Which passage? *Passage 2.*
   Ⓖ Which passage? *Passage 3.*

━━━━━ EXERCISE 3 ━━━━━
ANALYZING ARGUMENTS

1. (Direct the students to find part B.)
2. (Call on individual students to read part B.)
    - **ⓗ** (Call on a student. Idea: *That we should keep all our food in this country.*)
    - **ⓘ** (Call on individual students. Idea: *Sending food to the rest of the world and starving or keeping all the food here.*)
    - **ⓙ** Say it. *Just because the writer presents some choices doesn't mean there aren't other choices.*
    - **ⓚ** What's the answer? *Name a choice that the writer doesn't mention.*
    - **ⓛ** (Call on individual students. Ideas: *Keep some food here and send some to the rest of the world. Stop wasting food here.*)

━━━━━ EXERCISE 4 ━━━━━
INDEPENDENT WORK

1. **[Optional]** (Direct the students to read the instructions for part C. Give them two minutes to copy the paragraph. Count as errors miscopied words and punctuation. Deduct errors from the number of copied words, and mark the total on the Writing Rate Graph.)
2. Finish the Student Book and Workbook for Lesson 81. ✓

Workcheck

1. Get ready to check your answers starting with Student Book part D. Use a pen to make an **X** next to any item you miss.
2. (Call on individual students to read each item and its answer. Repeat for Workbook items.)
3. (Direct the students to count the number of errors and write the number in the **error** box at the top of the Workbook page.)

Student Book page 162

- Main idea B is: **Americans were afraid of communism.** Which passage does main idea B best fit? **ⓒ**
- Main idea C is: **Senator Joseph McCarthy was investigated by the Senate.** Which passage does main idea C best fit? **ⓓ**

B Here's an argument:

> We can send food to the rest of the world or we can keep all the food here and have enough for the people in our country. I don't think we should send food to others while our people starve.

What does the writer want us to conclude? **ⓔ**
What choices does the writer use as evidence for this conclusion? **ⓕ**
Say the rule that the argument breaks. **ⓖ**
To show that the argument is faulty, what do you do? **ⓗ**
Name one. **ⓘ**

C Write **Part C** in the left margin of your paper. You have two minutes to copy the paragraph below.

> The world's saltiest body of water is the Dead Sea. The water of the Dead Sea is about seven times as salty as the water in the Atlantic or Pacific Ocean. The reason that the Dead Sea is so salty is that it is shrinking.

D Write **Part D** in the left margin of your paper. Then number it from 1 to 3. Here are three main ideas:

> **Main idea A.** People worship the moon.
> **Main idea B.** The moon makes people and animals behave strangely.
> **Main idea C.** We keep learning more about what the moon is like.

Each main idea fits one of the passages that follow. After reading all the passages, figure out which main idea goes with each passage.

Student Book page 163

Passage 1. Ever since humans first looked up at the night sky, they have believed that the moon has magical powers. Some people still believe that the best time to plant seeds is at the time of the new moon (when the moon is invisible). Another belief is that the full moon causes strong feelings, such as love or hate. People who lived thousands of years ago wanted to explain the powers of the moon, so they created a moon goddess. People prayed to this goddess. They promised to do favors for the goddess if the goddess would give them a good farming season.

Passage 2. Ever since humans first looked up at the night sky, they have believed that the moon has magical powers. Today, scientists think that there is a certain amount of truth in the old beliefs. Scientists have observed that some animals are more excited during the full moon than they are when the moon is not full. Also, some people have more trouble sleeping during the full moon. In some big cities, more police are assigned to night duty during the time of the full moon. Why? Because there is some evidence that more crimes are committed on those nights.

Passage 3. Ever since humans first looked up at the night sky, they have believed that the moon has magical powers. Today, we know a great deal about what the moon is. We know because we've observed the moon through giant telescopes. We also know because people have actually walked on the moon. In 1969, Neil Armstrong was the first person to do this. Others have followed. Our moon is not the only moon in our solar system. Scientists have predicted that someday astronauts will visit these moons and the planets they circle.

1. Main idea A is: **People worship the moon.** Which passage does main idea A best fit? *passage 1*
2. Main idea B is: **The moon makes people behave strangely.** Which passage does main idea B best fit? *passage 2*
3. Main idea C is: **We keep learning more about what the moon is like.** Which passage does main idea C best fit? *passage 3*

Workbook page 251

Lesson 81

C Read the argument below and answer the questions.

> Here's your choice: sit at home watching television or get out on a Speed motorcycle. Just remember this: you'll have a lot more fun on a Speed.

1. What does the writer want us to conclude?
   Idea: You'll have a lot more fun in life on a Speed motorcycle.

2. What choices does the writer use as evidence for this conclusion?
   Idea: sitting at home watching television or getting out on a Speed motorcycle

3. What rule does the argument break?
   Idea: Just because the writer presents some choices doesn't mean there aren't other choices.

4. To show that the argument is faulty, what do you do?
   Idea: Show that there are other choices than the two that are offered.

5. Name one example.
   Idea: You could have just as much fun going on a boat ride.

D Read the evidence and write the conclusion for each item below.

1. Here's the evidence:

   Some fish have teeth.
   A barracuda is a fish.

   What's the conclusion?
   Maybe a barracuda has teeth.

2. Here's the evidence:

   Fish breathe in water.
   Tadpoles breathe in water.

   What's the conclusion?
   Idea: There is none.

3. Here's the evidence:

   Fish breathe in water.
   Sea lions do not breathe in water.

   What's the conclusion?
   Sea lions are not fish.

---

4. (Award points and direct students to record their points in Box **W**.)

0 errors	15 points
1–2 errors	12 points
3–5 errors	8 points
6–9 errors	5 points

5. (Award any bonus points. Direct the students to total their points and enter the total on the Point Summary Chart.)

6. Show me your work when you've finished correcting it. (When the students show you their corrected work, record their points on your Record Summary Chart.)

Lesson 81

Workbook page 252

E Read the passage below and answer the questions. Circle **W** if the question is answered by words in the passage. Circle **D** if the question is answered by a deduction. If you circle **W** for an item, underline the words in the passage that give the answer.

> From what you have learned about herbivorous mammals and carnivorous mammals, you should be able to draw conclusions about the skulls of some mammals.

Picture 1   Picture 2

> Look at picture 1. The flat teeth in picture 1 tell you that this may be the skull of a herbivorous mammal. So do the holes for the eyes. If the eyes look to the side, the mammal is probably herbivorous. If the eyes look straight ahead, the mammal is probably carnivorous.
>
> The skull of the animal in picture 1 is thin and light. The mammal is probably a fast-running animal whose body is as light as possible. This mammal is not well designed to fight, but with its speed, it can probably outrun most predators.

> Compare the skull of the herbivorous animal with the skull in picture 2. The skull in picture 2 belongs to a carnivorous mammal. The teeth are strong and sharp, built to rip and eat flesh. The eye sockets are facing straight ahead, and the bones around the eyes and top of the skull are very heavy. Look at the thick ridge down the middle of the skull. The skull of this animal is a weapon used in battles with other animals, so it must be thick and strong.
>
> The skull of the animal in picture 1 belongs to a horse. The skull of the animal in picture 2 belongs to a lion. Look at the skull in picture 3.

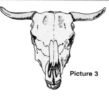

Picture 3

1. Are the eye sockets likely to be those of a carnivore or herbivore?
   a herbivore   W Ⓓ

2. Are the teeth those of a grazing animal or a meat-eating animal?
   a grazing animal   W Ⓓ

3. Is the skull that of a light, fast-moving animal or a heavy animal?
   a light, fast-moving animal

Lesson 81

Workbook page 253

4. Can you figure out what animal the skull belongs to?
   a cow

5. Why do carnivorous mammals have thick, heavy skulls?
   Idea: because their skulls are a weapon used in battles   Ⓦ D

6. How are the teeth of a sheep different from the teeth of a fox?
   Idea: The teeth of a sheep are flat; the teeth of a fox are sharp and pointed.

7. Do both eyes of a horse see almost the same thing?
   no

8. Do both eyes of a coyote see almost the same thing?
   yes

F Look at the diagram.

You can't see the dots in the diagram, but you can see the triangle and the circle.

1. Complete the deduction:

   All the dots are in the triangle.
   None of the triangle is in the circle.

   So, none of the dots are in the circle

2. Check your conclusion by drawing dots in the diagram so that all the dots are in the triangle.

G You will be tested on some facts presented in this lesson. These facts are:

> 1. A cold war happens when two countries are close to being in a shooting war with each other.
>
> 2. In 1969, the first person walked on the moon.

Study these facts. Repeat them to yourself. Writing these facts may help you to remember them.

END OF LESSON 81

Note: The circled letters indicate when you ask a question or when you direct the group to respond.

EXERCISE 1

DEDUCTIONS

1. (Direct the students to find Lesson 82, part A, in the **Workbook**.)
2. (Call on individual students to read part A.)
   Ⓐ Write the conclusion. ✓
   (Call on a student to read the whole deduction.) *All the dots are in the rectangle. None of the rectangle is in the circle. So, none of the dots is in the circle.*
   Ⓑ Do it. ✓
   (Draw diagram 1 on the board. Call on a student to draw the dots. Acceptable responses must show all the dots in the rectangle.)
   Ⓒ Write the conclusion. ✓
   (Call on a student to read the whole deduction.) *All the boxes are in the triangle. None of the triangle is in the oval. So, none of the boxes is in the oval.*
   Ⓓ Do it. ✓
   (Draw diagram 2 on the board. Call on a student to draw the oval. Acceptable responses must show none of the triangle in the oval.)

EXERCISE 2

EDITING

1. (Direct the students to find part B.)
2. (Call on individual students to read part B.)
   Ⓔ What's the answer? *Save our forest animals.*
   Ⓕ Write why the part is redundant. ✓
   (Call on a student to read the completed sentence. Idea: *If you know that we want to preserve wildlife, then you already know that we want to save forest animals.*)
   Ⓖ What's the answer? *Which is made up of parts.*
   Ⓗ Write the answer. (Wait. Call on a student to read the completed sentence. Idea: *If you know that it is a system, then you already know that it is made up of parts.*)

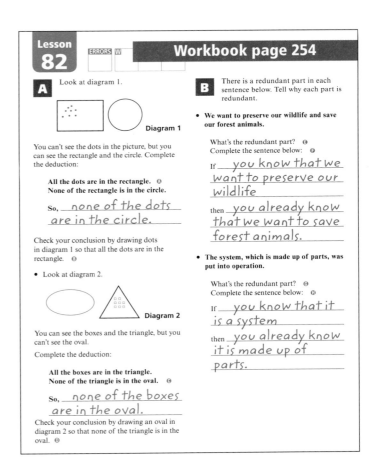

Lesson 82 — **Student Book page 164**

A

Here's an argument:

> "But, Dad, you have to let me stay out past ten o'clock. If you don't, everyone will think I'm a baby or that there's something wrong with me."

What does the writer want us to conclude? **I**
What choices does the writer use as evidence for this conclusion? **J**
Say the rule that the argument breaks. **K**
To show that the argument is faulty, what do you do? **L**
Name one. **M**

B

Write **Part B** in the left margin of your paper. You have two minutes to copy the paragraph below.

> In the 1950s, the United States and the former Soviet Union were involved in a cold war. That means that although the two countries were not actually using guns, the countries were close to being in a shooting war. Many Americans were afraid of communism.

C

Write **Part C** in the left margin of your paper. Then number it from 1 to 3. Here are three main ideas:

> Main idea A. A famous man painted the Mona Lisa.
> Main idea B. The Mona Lisa was stolen.
> Main idea C. The Mona Lisa has a remarkable smile.

Each main idea fits one of the passages that follows. After reading all the passages, figure out which main idea goes with each passage.

> **Passage 1.** The Mona Lisa is one of the most famous paintings in the world. It is a picture of an Italian woman, and it was painted around 1500 by Leonardo da Vinci. One thing that makes the painting so famous is the Mona Lisa's mysterious smile. Many people have theories to explain what is strange about her smile. Some people say that it shows that she's in love, and others say it shows that she is insane.

Student Book page 165 — **Lesson 82**

> **Passage 2.** The Mona Lisa is one of the most famous paintings in the world. For three hundred years, it hung in the Louvre, now a famous museum in Paris. But, in 1911, the museum reported that the Mona Lisa was missing. No one had a clue as to what had happened to it. For two years, detectives were unable to find a single clue. Finally, in 1913, the painting was found in Italy. An Italian worker had stolen it. He said that the Mona Lisa should remain in Italy because it was painted in Italy. In 1914, the Mona Lisa was returned to the Louvre in Paris.

> **Passage 3.** The Mona Lisa is one of the most famous paintings in the world. The man who painted it, Leonardo da Vinci, was one of the most remarkable people who ever lived. He was born in 1452, and he died in 1519. During da Vinci's lifetime, he studied many things. He was an inventor, a musician, and a scientist. He studied the human body and drew plans for airplanes and submarines.

1. Main idea A is: **A famous man painted the Mona Lisa.** Which passage does main idea A best fit? *passage 3*
2. Main idea B is: **The Mona Lisa was stolen.** Which passage does main idea B best fit? *passage 2*
3. Main idea C is: **The Mona Lisa has a remarkable smile.** Which passage does main idea C best fit? *passage 1*

EXERCISE 3
ANALYZING ARGUMENTS

1. (Direct the students to find Lesson 82, part A, in the **Student Book**.)
2. (Call on individual students to read part A.)
   - **I** (Call on a student. Idea: *That the speaker should be allowed to stay out past 10 o'clock.*)
   - **J** (Call on individual students. Idea: *That everyone will think the speaker is a baby; that everyone will think the speaker has something wrong with him or her.*)
   - **K** Say it. *Just because the writer presents some choices doesn't mean there aren't other choices.*
   - **L** What's the answer? *Name a choice that the writer doesn't mention.*
   - **M** (Call on individual students. Ideas: *No one will care if the speaker doesn't stay out past 10 o'clock. Everyone will understand that the speaker has to follow his or her father's rules.*)

EXERCISE 4
INDEPENDENT WORK

1. **[Optional]** (Direct the students to read the instructions for part B to themselves. Then give them exactly two minutes to copy the paragraph. Count as errors any miscopied words and punctuation. Deduct these errors from the number of copied words, and mark the total on the Writing Rate Graph.)
2. Finish the Student Book and Workbook for Lesson 82. ✓

Workcheck

1. Get ready to check your answers starting with Student Book part C. Use a pen to make an **X** next to any item you miss.
2. (Call on individual students to read each item and its answer. Repeat for Workbook items.)
3. (Direct the students to count the number of errors and write the number in the **error** box at the top of the Workbook page.)
4. (Award points and direct students to record their points in Box **W**.)

0 errors	**15 points**
1–2 errors	**12 points**
3–5 errors	**8 points**
6–9 errors	**5 points**

5. (Award any bonus points. Direct the students to total their points and enter the total on the Point Summary Chart.)
6. Show me your work when you've finished correcting it. (When the students show you their corrected work, record their points on your Record Summary Chart.)

Lesson 82 — **Workbook page 256**

E Underline the redundant part in the sentence below. Then explain why the underlined part is redundant by filling in the blanks.

"I will never give up," he said, refusing to surrender.

If _you know that he will never give up_

then _you already know that he refuses to surrender._

F Look at diagram 1.

 Diagram 1

You can see the rectangle and the triangle, but you can't see the boxes.

1. Complete the deduction:

All the boxes are in the triangle.
None of the triangle is in the rectangle.

So, _none of the boxes are in the rectangle._

2. Check your conclusion by drawing boxes in diagram 1 so that all of the boxes are in the triangle.

• Look at diagram 2.

 Diagram 2

You can see the dots and the oval, but you can't see the square.

3. Complete the deduction:

All the dots are in the oval.
None of the oval is in the square.

So, _none of the dots are in the square._

4. Check your conclusion by drawing a square in diagram 2 so that none of the oval is in the square.

Workbook page 255 — **Lesson 82**

C For each item, write a sentence that means the same thing by changing the underlined word or words.

1. His directions were <u>unclear</u> and <u>repetitive</u>.
   His directions were ambiguous and redundant.
2. The cashier <u>paused</u> before accepting their French <u>money</u>.
   The cashier hesitated before accepting their French currency.
3. Her <u>fears</u> had no <u>fitting</u> outlet.
   Her anxieties had no appropriate outlet.
4. They argued that the <u>rule</u> was <u>irrelevant</u>.
   They argued that the regulation was extraneous.

D Read the argument below and answer the questions.

"You must stop skipping classes. If you don't, you'll either flunk out of school or be expelled."

1. What does the writer want us to conclude?
   Idea: You must stop skipping classes.
2. What choices does the writer use as evidence for this conclusion?
   Idea: flunking out of school or getting expelled
3. What rule does the argument break?
   Idea: Just because the writer presents some choices doesn't mean there aren't other choices.
4. To show that the argument is faulty, what do you do?
   Idea: Show that there are other choices than the two that are offered.
5. Name one example.
   Idea: Skip classes and see if you can still get decent grades.

Workbook page 257 — **Lesson 82**

G Read the rule and each piece of evidence. Write a conclusion after each piece of evidence.

Rule. All reptiles are cold-blooded.

Evidence	Conclusion
1. A West Indian gecko is a reptile.	_A West Indian gecko is cold-blooded._
2. The reticulated python is a reptile.	_The reticulated python is cold-blooded._
3. A marten is not cold-blooded.	_A marten is not a reptile._
4. The bee hummingbird is not cold-blooded.	_The bee hummingbird is not a reptile._

H You will be tested on a fact presented in this lesson. This fact is:

Leonardo da Vinci was an inventor, a painter, a musician, and a scientist.

Study this fact. Repeat it to yourself. Writing the fact may help you remember it.

END OF LESSON 82

Lesson 83 | ERRORS W | Workbook page 258

A There is a redundant part in each sentence below. Tell why each part is redundant.

- These real diamonds are not imitation jewels!

What's the redundant part? Ⓐ
Complete the sentence below: Ⓑ

If _you know that the diamonds are real_ then _you already know that they are not imitation jewels_

- "I don't doubt what you say because I believe you."

What's the redundant part? Ⓒ
Complete the sentence below: Ⓓ

If _you know that I don't doubt what you say_ then _you already know that I believe you_

★ B Write the verb **is** or **are** in each blank.

1. The salt in the salt shaker _is_ damp.
2. Special privileges _are_ given to senators.
3. You _are_ the one person I have been looking for.
4. Some of the members of the band _are_ giving a party.
5. Everybody who runs in these races _is_ capable of winning.
6. Members of the club _are_ given a special discount.

C Look at diagram 1.

Diagram 1

You can see the circle and the triangle, but you can't see the boxes.

1. Complete the deduction:

All the boxes are in the circle.
None of the circle is in the triangle.

So, _none of the boxes are in the triangle._

2. Check your conclusion by drawing the boxes in diagram 1 so that all the boxes are in the circle.

Lesson 83 | Student Book page 166

A Write **Part A** in the left margin of your paper. You have two minutes to copy the paragraph below.

> The Mona Lisa is one of the most famous paintings in the world. The man who painted it, Leonardo da Vinci, was one of the most remarkable people who ever lived. He was born in 1452, and he died in 1519.

★ B Write **Part B** in the left margin of your paper. Then number it from 1 to 3.
Here are three main ideas:

Main idea A. Plans were devised to build the coast-to-coast railroad.
Main idea B. The coast-to-coast railroad was finished.
Main idea C. The railroad companies encountered problems.

Each main idea fits one of the passages that follow. After reading all the passages, figure out which main idea goes with each passage.

> **Passage 1.** People in the United States dreamed of building a railroad that would connect the east coast to the west coast. This railroad would enable trains to carry freight, mail, and passengers across the country faster and more safely. But there were some big obstacles in the way of building that railroad—laying tracks over the Rocky Mountains and tunneling through California's High Sierra Mountains. President Lincoln signed the Pacific Railroad Act in 1862. This act provided government money for building the railroad.

> **Passage 2.** People in the United States dreamed of building a railroad that would connect the east coast to the west coast. In 1862, two major railway companies began this great task. The Union Pacific Railroad began in the Midwest and laid track westward toward California. At the same time, the Central Pacific began laying track from California eastward. Both railroad companies encountered great problems. Native Americans often attacked work crews on the Union Pacific. The problems of the Central Pacific were different. The railroad passed through high mountains in California. To make a path for the railroad, tunnels had to be built and cliffs had to be dynamited. Hundreds of workers lost their lives from rock slides and accidental explosions.

Note: The circled letters indicate when you ask a question or when you direct the group to respond.

EXERCISE 1

EDITING

1. (Direct the students to find Lesson 83, part A, in the **Workbook**.)
2. (Call on individual students to read part A.)
   Ⓐ What's the answer? *Are not imitation jewels.*
   Ⓑ Write why the part is redundant. ✓
   (Call on a student to read the completed sentence. Idea: *If you know that the diamonds are real, then you already know that they are not imitation jewels.*)
   Ⓒ What's the answer? *Because I believe you.*
   Ⓓ Write the answer. ✓
   (Call on a student to read the completed sentence. Idea: *If you know that I don't doubt what you say, then you already know that I believe you.*)

EXERCISE 2

INDEPENDENT WORK

1. **[Optional]** (Direct the students to read the instructions for part A in the **Student Book** to themselves. Then give them exactly two minutes to copy the paragraph. Count as errors any miscopied words and punctuation. Deduct these errors from the number of copied words, and mark the total on the Writing Rate Graph.)
2. Finish the Student Book and Workbook for Lesson 83. ✓

Workcheck

1. Get ready to check your answers starting with Student Book part B. Use a pen to make an **X** next to any item you miss.
2. (Call on individual students to read each item and its answer. Repeat for Workbook items.)
3. (Direct the students to count the number of errors and write the number in the error box at the top of the Workbook page.)
4. (Award points and direct students to record their points in Box **W**.)

0 errors	**15 points**
1–2 errors	**12 points**
3–5 errors	**8 points**
6–9 errors	**5 points**

5. (Award any bonus points. Direct the students to total their points and enter the total on the Point Summary Chart.)
6. Show me your work when you've finished correcting it. (When the students show you their corrected work, record their points on your Record Summary Chart.)

Workbook page 259

- Look at diagram 2.

Diagram 2

You can see the dots and the square, but you can't see the oval.

3. Complete the deduction:

   All the dots are in the square.
   None of the square is in the oval.

   So, *none of the dots are in the oval.*

4. Check your conclusion by drawing an oval in diagram 2 so that none of the square is in the oval.

D Read the argument below and answer the questions.

> "We must either destroy Mars or be destroyed by the Martians. I'd rather destroy than be destroyed, wouldn't you?"

1. What does the writer want us to conclude?
   Idea: We must destroy Mars.
2. What choices does the writer use as evidence for this conclusion?
   Idea: If we don't destroy Mars, Martians will destroy us.
3. What rule does the argument break?
   Idea: Just because the writer presents some choices doesn't mean there aren't other choices.
4. To show that the argument is faulty, what do you do?
   Idea: Show that there are other choices than the two the writer offers.
5. Name one example.
   Idea: Don't destroy Mars and see if the Martians destroy us or not.

Student Book page 167

Lesson 83

> **Passage 3.** People in the United States dreamed of building a railroad that would connect the east coast to the west coast. On May 10, 1869, this dream came true. The railroad crews of the Central Pacific and Union Pacific railroads met at Promontory Point, Utah. The long railroad track, begun on opposite sides of the United States, was finally joined. The final spike to be driven into the track was made of pure gold. When that spike was driven in, a great cheer went up. The building of the coast-to-coast railroad had been completed in seven years. The trip between Nebraska and California had taken weeks by stagecoach. Now that same trip could be made in four days.

1. Main idea A is: **Plans were devised to build the coast-to-coast railroad.** Which passage does main idea A best fit? *passage 1*
2. Main idea B is: **The coast-to-coast railroad was finished.** Which passage does main idea B best fit? *passage 3*
3. Main idea C is: **The railroad companies encountered problems.** Which passage does main idea C best fit? *passage 2*

Workbook page 260

Lesson 83

E Underline the redundant part in each sentence below. Then explain why the underlined part is redundant by filling in the blanks.

1. "Yes," she <u>affirmed</u>, pacing the floor.

   If *you know that she said, "Yes"*, then *you already know that she affirmed it*

2. The table was set with a huge variety of <u>many</u> foods.

   If *you know that there's a variety of foods*, then *you already know that there are many foods*

F Each argument below breaks one of these rules:

> **Rule 1.** Just because two things happen around the same time doesn't mean one thing causes the other thing.
>
> **Rule 2.** Just because you know about a part doesn't mean you know about the whole thing.
>
> **Rule 3.** Just because you know about a part doesn't mean you know about another part.
>
> **Rule 4.** Just because you know about the whole thing doesn't mean you know about every part.
>
> **Rule 5.** Just because words are the same doesn't mean they have the same meaning.

After each argument below, write the number of the rule the argument breaks.

1. I know Pat took my purse. She was the last one in the room before I noticed it was missing. *1*
2. You can tell she's a real snob about everything. She doesn't speak to anyone at the office. *2*
3. Sue said to meet her at the riverbank. When it came time to go meet her, I looked up banks in the phone directory and discovered there was no River Bank. She must have gotten her banks confused. *5*

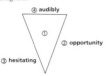

Lesson 83

Workbook page 261
Lesson **83**

4. The record of this company is nearly perfect. Other large corporations have been sued for trying to control the market, for not complying with federal laws, and for using unfair sales tactics. Our company has never been guilty of any of these offenses. We enjoy the record of being a very honorable, honest organization. You know, therefore, that every employee in our company is completely

honorable and honest. _____ *4*

H You will be tested on a fact presented in this lesson. This fact is:

> In 1869, the first coast-to-coast railroad in the United States was completed.

Study this fact. Repeat it to yourself. Writing the fact may help you remember it.

G Write the instructions for this diagram.

④ audibly

①

② opportunity

③ hesitating

1. (what) _Idea: Draw an upside-down triangle._

2. (what and where) _Idea: Write the word opportunity to the right of the triangle._

3. (what and where) _Idea: Write the word hesitating to the left of the triangle._

4. (what and where) _Idea: Write the word audibly above the triangle._

END OF LESSON 83

Student Book page 168

Lesson 84

A When you combine sentences with the word **who** or **which**, what punctuation do you need before **who** or **which**? Ⓐ
When you combine sentences with the word **therefore**, what do you do with the period of the first sentence? Ⓑ
What follows the semicolon? Ⓒ
What follows the word **therefore**? Ⓓ
When you combine sentences with the word **but**, what do you do with the period of the first sentence? Ⓔ
What word follows the comma? Ⓕ

B Write **Part B** in the left margin of your paper. You have two minutes to copy the paragraph below.

> People in the United States dreamed of building a railroad that would connect the east coast to the west coast. Trains would then be able to carry freight, mail, and passengers across the country faster and more safely than any other kind of transportation.

★ C Write **Part C** in the left margin of your paper. Then number it from 1 to 3. Here are three main ideas:

> Main idea A. Oil spills affect people who ship oil.
> Main idea B. Oil spills affect the sea.
> Main idea C. Oil spills affect the people who make their living from the sea.

Each main idea fits one of the passages that follows. After reading all the passages, figure out which main idea goes with each passage.

> **Passage 1.** "Twenty-six million tons of oil were dumped into the sea off the coast of France. Hundreds of birds are dead or dying. We won't be able to save even half of them. The water is poisoned. Fish and plants are dead. The fine white sand on the beaches has turned black. It will be many years before the oil is gone from the water. It will be at least fifty years before sea life returns to normal here."

Student Book page 169

Lesson 84

> **Passage 2.** "Twenty-six million tons of oil were dumped into the sea off the coast of France. My family has fished these waters for two hundred years. I fish for a living like my father and his father before him. Like them, I have to support a family on what I can fish from the sea. But now, I can't fish. That's my fishing boat out there in that black water. See the dead fish floating around it? It will take fifty years before anybody will be able to fish in that sea."

> **Passage 3.** "Twenty-six million tons of oil were dumped into the sea off the coast of France. But it was an accident. Apparently, the ship ran onto some rocks while the captain was talking with someone. The rocks tore holes in the ship, and the oil spilled into the sea. Our company realizes how terrible this is, but we think it could have happened to anybody. Our company will suffer a great deal. Think of the money we lost. Instead of trying to put restrictions on oil companies and oil freighters, we should all work together and stop crying about this unfortunate event."

1. Main idea A is: **Oil spills affect people who ship oil.** Which passage does main idea A best fit? *passage 3*
2. Main idea B is: **Oil spills affect the sea.** Which passage does main idea B best fit? *passage 1*
3. Main idea C is: **Oil spills affect people who make their living from the sea.** Which passage does main idea C best fit? *passage 2*

Note: The circled letters indicate when you ask a question or when you direct the group to respond.

EXERCISE 1
SENTENCE COMBINATIONS

1. (Direct the students to find Lesson 84, part A, in the **Student Book**.)
2. (Call on individual students to read part A.)
   Ⓐ What's the answer? *A comma.*
   Ⓑ What's the answer? *Change it to a semicolon.*
   Ⓒ What's the answer? *Therefore.*
   Ⓓ What's the answer? *A comma.*
   Ⓔ What's the answer? *Change it to a comma.*
   Ⓕ What's the answer? *But.*

EXERCISE 2
INDEPENDENT WORK

1. **[Optional]** (Direct the students to read the instructions for part B to themselves. Then give them exactly two minutes to copy the paragraph. Count as errors any miscopied words and punctuation. Deduct these errors from the number of copied words, and mark the total on the Writing Rate Graph.)

Workcheck

1. Get ready to check your answers starting with Student Book part C. Use a pen to make an **X** next to any item you miss.
2. (Call on individual students to read each item and its answer. Repeat for Workbook items.)
3. (Direct the students to count the number of errors and write the number in the **error** box at the top of the Workbook page.)

4. (Award points and direct students to record their points in Box **W**.)

0 errors	**15 points**
1–2 errors	**12 points**
3–5 errors	**8 points**
6–9 errors	**5 points**

5. (Award any bonus points. Direct the students to total their points and enter the total on the Point Summary Chart.)

6. Show me your work when you've finished correcting it. (When the students show you their corrected work, record their points on your Record Summary Chart.)

Workbook page 263

7. The passage names three types of carnivores. One type is the predator. Fill in the boxes below for the other two types.

- Below the box for predators, list six kinds of predators.
- Below the other two boxes, list two examples of each kind of animal.

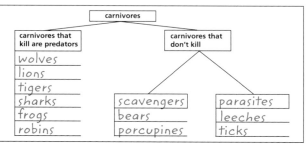

B Each argument below is faulty.

- This club is well liked and it has many friends. Consider the facts. There are 100 members in the club. Each member in the club has at least five friends. Therefore, the club has at least 500 friends.

1. What does the writer want us to conclude?

 Idea: Friends of the members are friends of the club.

2. How could you show that the argument is faulty?

 Idea: Find out what the members' friends think of the club itself.

- I told the man at the cat hospital that I would give no more money to that hospital. He said, "All right. You can give just as much money as you gave before."

3. What does the writer want us to conclude?

 Idea: The man at the cat hospital thought that I didn't want to give more money than I did before.

4. How could you show that the argument is faulty?

 Idea: Show that the phrase "no more money" has more than one meaning.

Workbook page 262

★ **A** Read the passage that follows and answer the questions. Circle **W** if the question is answered by words in the passage. Circle **D** if the question is answered by a deduction. If you circle **W** for an item, underline the words in the passage that give the answer.

Not every carnivorous animal kills. Those that kill are called predators. Wolves, lions, tigers, and sharks are fierce predators. Some other predators may not be as dangerous to people as a shark or a jaguar, but these animals are still predators, which means that they kill so they can eat. Frogs and robins are predators. Frogs eat flies; robins eat worms. The eagle is a predator with good eyesight and very strong claws, which are called talons.

Parasites and scavengers are two types of carnivorous animals that do not kill. Leeches and ticks are parasites. They attach themselves to another animal and suck nourishment from their "host," but they do not kill the host. The host does the work of hunting for food while the parasite feasts on the host. Instead of killing animals, scavengers wait for animals to die or to be killed by predators. After the predators have eaten what they want, the scavengers eat the remains of the animals. Bears are scavengers. So are porcupines, crows, buzzards, hyenas, and jackals.

Remember that carnivorous animals include parasites and scavengers. A parasite attaches itself to a host, and a scavenger waits for an animal to die or be killed by a predator.

1. What do we call carnivores that kill?

 predators Ⓦ D

2. How is a parasite different from a predator?

 Idea: A parasite doesn't kill its food; a predator does. W Ⓓ

3. What do we call the plant or animal that a parasite lives on?

 a host

4. What do scavengers eat?

 Idea: the remains of animals Ⓦ D

5. How are parasites and scavengers the same?

 Idea: They do not kill for their food.

6. How are parasites and scavengers different?

 Idea: Parasites get nourishment from living animals; scavengers get nourishment from dead ones.

Workbook page 264

- This ring contains one of the most precious metals in the world—gold. If it has gold in it, this ring must be one of the most precious rings in the world. Yet, believe it or not, it is yours for only $4.56 plus postage.

5. What does the writer want us to conclude?

 Idea: The ring is one of the most precious in the world.

6. How could you show that the argument is faulty?

 Idea: Find out if the ring is made mostly of gold or whether it's made mostly of less precious metals.

C Look at diagram 1.

Diagram 1

You can't see the dots in the diagram, but **all the dots are in the triangle.**

1. Complete the deduction.

 **All the dots are in the triangle.
 The triangle is in the circle.**

So, _all the dots are in the circle_

2. Draw the dots in diagram 1.

•Look at diagram 2.

Diagram 2

You can't see the dots in the diagram, but **all the dots are in the triangle.**

3. Complete the deduction.

 **All the dots are in the triangle.
 None of the triangle is in the circle.**

So, _none of the dots are in the circle_

4. Draw the dots in diagram 2.

D You will be tested on some facts presented in this lesson. These facts are:

1. Scavengers and parasites are two kinds of carnivores that do not kill.
2. Ticks and leeches are two kinds of parasites.
3. Bears, porcupines, crows, and vultures are scavengers.

Study these facts. Repeat them to yourself. Writing these facts may help you remember them.

Workbook page 265

Lesson 84

E Read the argument below and answer the questions.

> When you graduate from high school, you can either go to college or work at a job you hate for the rest of your life.

1. What does the writer want us to conclude?
   Idea: You should go to college.

2. What choices does the writer use as evidence for this conclusion?
   Idea: going to college or working at a job you hate for the rest of your life

3. What rule does the argument break?
   Idea: Just because the writer presents some choices doesn't mean there aren't other choices.

4. To show that the argument is faulty, what do you do?
   Idea: Show that there are other choices than the two the writer offers.

5. Name one example.
   Idea: Interview people who haven't gone to college, but who enjoy their jobs.

F Underline the redundant part in each sentence that follows. Then explain why the underlined part is redundant by filling in the blanks.

1. I found this toothbrush in a remote part of Africa, <u>far from civilization.</u>
   If you know that it's a remote part of Africa then you already know that it's far from civilization

2. Between 1934 and 1944, <u>a full ten years passed.</u>
   If you know it's between 1934 and 1944 then you already know that a full ten years has passed

3. Everyone could hear the professor, <u>who spoke quite audibly.</u>
   If you know that everyone could hear the professor then you already know that he spoke quite audibly

END OF LESSON 84

Lesson 85

EXERCISE 1

DEFINITIONS

1. (Direct the students to find Lesson 85, part A, in the **Student Book**.)
2. (Call on individual students to read part A.)
   Ⓐ Do it. ✓
   (Call on individual students to say the model sentence.)
   Ⓑ Which word? *Phenomenon.*
   Ⓒ Which word? *Anxiety.*
   Ⓓ Which word? *Exhibited.*
   Ⓔ Say a sentence that means the same thing.
   A strange phenomenon caused the behavior that they exhibited.
   Ⓕ Say a sentence that means the same thing.
   The horror movie caused an outcome of anxiety.

EXERCISE 2

INDEPENDENT WORK

1. [Optional] (Direct the students to read the instructions for part B to themselves. Then give them exactly two minutes to copy the paragraph. Count as errors any miscopied words and punctuation. Deduct these errors from the number of copied words, and mark the total on the Writing Rate Graph.)
2. Finish the Student Book and Workbook for Lesson 85. ✓

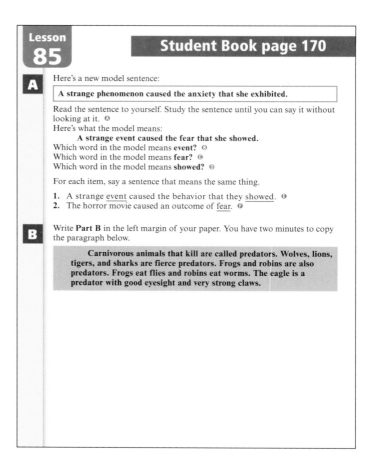

Lesson 85 — Student Book page 170

A

Here's a new model sentence:

> A strange phenomenon caused the anxiety that she exhibited.

Read the sentence to yourself. Study the sentence until you can say it without looking at it. Ⓐ
Here's what the model means:
> A strange event caused the fear that she showed.

Which word in the model means **event**? Ⓑ
Which word in the model means **fear**? Ⓒ
Which word in the model means **showed**? Ⓓ

For each item, say a sentence that means the same thing.

1. A strange <u>event</u> caused the behavior that they <u>showed</u>. Ⓔ
2. The horror movie caused an outcome of <u>fear</u>. Ⓕ

B

Write **Part B** in the left margin of your paper. You have two minutes to copy the paragraph below.

> Carnivorous animals that kill are called predators. Wolves, lions, tigers, and sharks are fierce predators. Frogs and robins are also predators. Frogs eat flies and robins eat worms. The eagle is a predator with good eyesight and very strong claws.

Student Book page 171 — Lesson 85

C

Write **Part C** in the left margin of your paper. Then number it 1 and 2.
Here's a fact:

> The Canadian province of Alberta has four national parks.

1. In what kind of reference book would you look to find evidence to support this fact? *Atlas*
2. Look at the map below. Then write the names of the national parks.
   Wood Buffalo, Jasper, Banff, Waterton Lakes

Workbook page 266

★ **A** Underline the redundant part in each sentence that follows. Then explain why the underlined part is redundant by filling in the blanks.

1. **This opportunity, which represents a real chance, was presented to Mr. Jones.**
   If *you know that this is an opportunity,*
   then *you already know that it represents a real chance* .

2. **"My, goodness," he said as he spoke.**
   If *you know that he said it,*
   then *you already know that he spoke* .

3. **I had my car fixed by a mechanic, who does car work.**
   If *you know that I had my car fixed by a mechanic,*
   then *you already know that the person does car work* .

B Read the argument below and answer the questions.

If you don't cut your hair, you're going to get it caught in a machine someday. Or maybe you'll end up in a pool hall with a bunch of bums.

1. What does the writer want us to conclude?
   Idea: If you don't cut your hair, you'll come to no good.

2. What rule does the argument break?
   Idea: Just because the writer presents some choices doesn't mean there aren't other choices.

3. Show that the argument is faulty.
   Idea: Plenty of people with long hair lead successful lives.

Workbook page 267

C For each item, write a sentence that means the same thing by changing the underlined word or words.

1. A strange <u>event</u> caused the <u>fear</u> that she <u>showed</u>.
   A strange phenomenon caused the anxiety that she exhibited.

2. None of the scientists could explain the <u>event</u>.
   None of the scientists could explain the phenomenon.

3. A total eclipse is an exciting <u>event</u> to see.
   A total eclipse is an exciting phenomenon to see.

4. As the bear approached, Tom's face <u>showed his fear</u>.
   As the bear approached, Tom's face exhibited his anxiety.

D Look at this diagram:

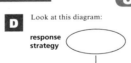

response strategy

The diagram contradicts part of these instructions:

1. Draw an oval.
2. Draw a horizontal line below the oval.
3. Write the word **response** to the left of the oval.
4. Write the word **strategy** below the word **response**.

Circle the instruction that the diagram contradicts.

Draw a new diagram that follows the instructions.

response strategy

Workcheck

1. Get ready to check your answers starting with Student Book part C. Use a pen to make an **X** next to any item you miss.

2. (Call on individual students to read each item and its answer. Repeat for Workbook items.)

3. (Direct the students to count the number of errors and write the number in the **error** box at the top of the Workbook page.)

4. (Award points and direct students to record their points in Box **W.**)

0 errors	**15 points**
1–2 errors	**12 points**
3–5 errors	**8 points**
6–9 errors	**5 points**

5. (Award any bonus points. Direct the students to total their points and enter the total on the Point Summary Chart.)

6. Show me your work when you've finished correcting it. (When the students show you their corrected work, record their points on your Record Summary Chart.)

END OF LESSON 85

Lesson Objectives	LESSON 86	LESSON 87	LESSON 88	LESSON 89	LESSON 90	Fact Game
	Exercise	Exercise	Exercise	Exercise	Exercise	6
Organization and Study Skills						
Main Idea		SB	SB	SB		
Writing Mechanics: Copying	2	3	3	3	1	
Reasoning Strategies						
Deductions	WB	WB		WB	WB	
Evidence				WB	WB	FG
Rules: Arguments	WB	WB	WB	WB	WB	FG
Contradictions	SB					
Inference		1	2	2		
Information Sources/ Study Skills						
Reading Comprehension: Words or Deductions	WB					
Interpretation: Maps/Pictures/Graphs	SB, WB	WB				
Supporting Evidence						FG
Vocabulary/Language Arts Skills						
Definitions	1, WB	2, WB	1, WB	WB	SB, WB	FG
Usage	1, WB	2, WB	1, WB	WB	SB, WB	FG
Sentence Combination		WB	WB	1	SB	FG
Editing/Revising	WB	WB	WB	WB	SB, WB	
Information Application/ Study Skills						
Directions: Filling Out Forms	WB					
Information Review	WB			WB		
Assessment/Progress Monitoring						
Ongoing: Workcheck	Workcheck	Workcheck	Workcheck	Workcheck	Workcheck	
Formal: Mastery Test					MT9	

Lesson 86 — Student Book page 172

A Here's the latest model sentence you learned:

> A strange phenomenon caused the anxiety that she exhibited.

What sentence means the same thing? Ⓐ
What word means **event**? Ⓑ
What word means **fear**? Ⓒ
What word means **showed**? Ⓓ
What's another way of saying,
> A strange event caused the fear that she showed? Ⓔ

B Write **Part B** in the left margin of your paper. You have two minutes to copy the paragraph below.

> Parasites are carnivorous animals that do not kill. They attach themselves to another animal and suck nourishment from their host, but they do not kill the host. The host does the work of hunting for food while the parasite feasts on the host.

Student Book page 173 — Lesson 86

C Write **Part C** in the left margin of your paper. Then number it from 1 to 5. Assume that the picture below is accurate. Examine the picture carefully, and then read the statements below it. Some of the statements contradict what the picture shows.

- Write **contradictory** or **not contradictory** for each statement.
- If a statement contradicts the picture, write what the picture shows.

1. A boy is sitting at a desk looking at a television set.
2. Two books are on the shelf of the television stand.
3. The boy has a cookie in one hand and a pencil in the other hand.
4. There are two books on the desk but only one is open.
5. A glass and a plate of cupcakes are on the desk.

1. *not contradictory*
2. *Contradictory; one book is on the shelf of the television stand.*
3. *not contradictory*
4. *not contradictory*
5. *Contradictory; a glass and a plate of cookies are on the desk.*

Note: The circled letters indicate when you ask a question or when you direct the group to respond.

EXERCISE 1
DEFINITIONS

1. (Direct the students to find Lesson 86, part A, in the **Student Book**.)
2. (Call on individual students to read part A.)
   - Ⓐ Say it. *A strange event caused the fear that she showed.*
   - Ⓑ What word? *Phenomenon.*
   - Ⓒ What word? *Anxiety.*
   - Ⓓ What word? *Exhibited.*
   - Ⓔ Say that sentence another way. *A strange phenomenon caused the anxiety that she exhibited.*

EXERCISE 2
INDEPENDENT WORK

1. **[Optional]** (Direct the students to read the instructions for part B to themselves. Then give them exactly two minutes to copy the paragraph. Count as errors any miscopied words and punctuation. Deduct these errors from the number of copied words, and mark the total on the Writing Rate Graph.)
2. Finish the Student Book and do the Workbook for Lesson 86. ✓

Workcheck

1. Get ready to check your answers starting with Student Book part C. Use a pen to make an **X** next to any item you miss.
2. (Call on individual students to read each item and its answer. Repeat for Workbook items.)
3. (Direct the students to count the number of errors and write the number in the **error** box at the top of the Workbook page.)

4. (Award points and direct students to record their points in Box **W.**)

0 errors	15 points
1–2 errors	12 points
3–5 errors	8 points
6–9 errors	5 points

5. (Award any bonus points. Direct the students to total their points and enter the total on the Point Summary Chart.)

6. Show me your work when you've finished correcting it. (When the students show you their corrected work, record their points on your Record Summary Chart.)

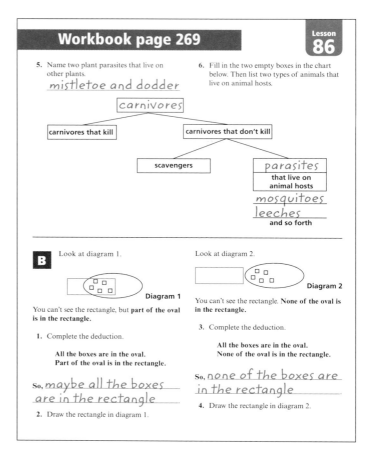

Workbook page 269 — Lesson 86

5. Name two plant parasites that live on other plants.

mistletoe and dodder

6. Fill in the two empty boxes in the chart below. Then list two types of animals that live on animal hosts.

carnivores
├── carnivores that kill
└── carnivores that don't kill
    ├── scavengers
    └── _parasites_ that live on animal hosts
        mosquitoes
        leeches
        and so forth

B Look at diagram 1.

Diagram 1

You can't see the rectangle, but **part of the oval is in the rectangle.**

1. Complete the deduction.

   All the boxes are in the oval.
   Part of the oval is in the rectangle.

So, _maybe all the boxes are in the rectangle_

2. Draw the rectangle in diagram 1.

Look at diagram 2.

Diagram 2

You can't see the rectangle. **None of the oval is in the rectangle.**

3. Complete the deduction.

   All the boxes are in the oval.
   None of the oval is in the rectangle.

So, _none of the boxes are in the rectangle_

4. Draw the rectangle in diagram 2.

Lesson 86 ERRORS W **Workbook page 268**

★ **A** Read the passage that follows and answer the questions. Circle **W** if the question is answered by words in the passage. Circle **D** if the question is answered by a deduction. If you circle **W** for an item, underline the words in the passage that give the answer.

Some parasites are plants and some parasites are animals. Mistletoe is a plant parasite that grows in the tops of trees. Mushrooms are also plant parasites. Still another plant parasite is a flowering plant called dodder, which grows on the stalks of other plants and sucks the sap from them.

Some animal parasites use plant hosts. The mealybug lives off the soft parts of plants. The animal parasites we are most familiar with, however, are animal parasites that use animal hosts. Ticks and mosquitoes are animal parasites that use animal hosts.

Everybody knows how mosquitoes work. They stick a tube into your skin and suck out blood. When they are filled, they fly off. What you may not know about mosquitoes is that only females bite in this manner and that they must get blood from a host before they can lay eggs.

Mosquito bites can be very harmful. In some areas, there are so many mosquitoes that a person could go crazy while trying unsuccessfully to escape from the swarming insects. In addition, some mosquitoes carry deadly diseases, such as malaria and yellow fever.

Just as mosquitoes bother humans, fleas and ticks bother dogs, cats, and other animals. Moose and elk will sometimes

thunder through the forest, trying to run from fleas or stinging flies. Often the animal that is under the attack of insects will not stop running until it reaches a lake or river. It will then dive in to find relief.

One of the most disgusting parasites is the leech, which looks like a large, flat worm, and is able to attach itself to the host's body. Like a mosquito, the leech sucks blood. Turtles sometimes have leeches stuck between their legs and on their chests. Leeches sometimes will attach themselves between a swimmer's toes or around the waistband of a bathing suit.

1. How is a parasite different from a predator?
   Idea: A parasite gets its food from something alive; a predator gets its food from something dead.

2. What do we call the plant or animal that a parasite lives on? _a host_

3. Why do female mosquitoes need blood?
   Idea: so that they can lay their eggs Ⓦ D

4. How do forest animals sometimes escape from fleas and ticks?
   Idea: They run through the forest until they reach a lake or river. Ⓦ D

Lesson 86 **Workbook page 270**

C Underline the redundant part in each sentence below. Then explain why the underlined part is redundant by filling in the blanks.

1. He purchased the bike for his son **by buying it.**
   If _you know that he purchased the bike_
   then _you already know that he bought it_

2. "Yes, yes, yes," she said **repeatedly.**
   If _you know that she said "Yes" several times_
   then _you already know that she repeated it_

3. He encouraged his sister to buy the store **by urging her to purchase it.**
   If _you know that he encouraged her to buy the store_
   then _you already know that he urged her to purchase it_

D For each item, write a sentence that means the same thing by changing the underlined word or words.

1. A strange <u>event</u> caused the <u>fear</u> that she <u>showed</u>.
   A strange phenomenon caused the anxiety that she exhibited.

2. Tom <u>showed fear</u> at the sight of a snake.
   Tom exhibited anxiety at the sight of a snake.

3. The erupting volcano caused an unusual <u>event</u>.
   The erupting volcano caused an unusual phenomenon.

4. The horses <u>showed</u> their <u>fear</u> by rearing.
   The horses exhibited their anxiety by rearing.

Workbook page 271

E Read this: A title is a piece of paper that tells who owns something. When you buy a car, for example, you take title to the car. When you apply for license plates, you must show that you have title to the car. You must also show that you have title to the car when you sell it. Use the facts to fill out the form.

Facts: Your name is Adrian Garner and you are applying for a new driver's license. You were born March 1, 1985, in Sarasota, Florida. You live with your parents, Mr. and Mrs. Guy Garner. Your address is 1440 Temple in Sarasota. You passed both the written and the driving test. Your total score on the road-signs test was 18 out of 20 correct. Your score on the driver-information test was 15 out of 20 correct. You drive a 1995 Ramrod. The license plate number is HL 6747. Plates and title to the car are in your name. The title number is #6009-87-567. The serial number of the car is C320-4687-49. You have good eyesight without glasses. You are 5 feet 8 inches tall, you weigh about 145 pounds, your hair is brown, and your eyes are blue. Your Social Security number is 435-77-3008. Your insurance company is Western Insurance. The insurance policy number is 477-09-89.

State of Florida—Driver's License Application

Name _Adrian Garner_ Age _Response will vary_

Date of birth _March 1, 1985_ Place of birth _Sarasota, Florida_

Present address _1440 Temple, Sarasota, Florida_

Social Security number _435-77-3008_

Is this an application for a new license or a renewal of an old one? old _____ new ✓_

Height _5'8"_ Weight _145_

Hair color _brown_ Eye color _blue_

Eyesight without glasses: good _✓_ poor _____ Eyesight with glasses: good _____ poor _____

Name of insurance company that insures car _Western Insurance_

Insurance policy number _477-09-89_

Workbook page 272

F Each argument below breaks one of these rules:

Rule 1. Just because two things happen around the same time doesn't mean one thing causes the other thing.

Rule 2. Just because you know about a part doesn't mean you know about the whole thing.

Rule 3. Just because you know about a part doesn't mean you know about another part.

Rule 4. Just because you know about the whole thing doesn't mean you know about every part.

Rule 5. Just because words are the same doesn't mean they have the same meaning.

Rule 6. Just because the writer presents some choices doesn't mean there aren't other choices.

After each argument below, write the number of the rule the argument breaks.

1. The introduction of front-wheel drive has caused cars to become smaller. In the 1960s, cars were large and only a few had front-wheel drive. The number of front-wheel drive cars went up and up in the 1970s, and the average car got smaller and smaller. _1_

2. You asked me whether the voters in the west suburb will vote Democratic or Republican. I'll tell you this. The voters in the downtown district voted Democratic. So did the voters in the east suburb. There's no doubt that the voters in the west suburb will vote Democratic. _3_

3. That football team has lost nine games in a row. Their quarterback must be a terrible player. _4_

4. Every time it rains at night, the crickets stop chirping just before the storm. I have observed this trend for twelve years. My chart shows that every time it has rained, the crickets stopped chirping. I know that it will rain tonight because the crickets had been chirping, but they stopped about five minutes ago. _1_

G You will be tested on some facts presented in this lesson. These facts are:

1. **Mistletoe and dodder are parasites that live on plants.**
2. **Fleas, ticks, mosquitoes and leeches are parasites that live on animals.**

Study these facts. Repeat them to yourself. Writing these facts may help you remember them.

END OF LESSON 86

Note: The circled letters indicate when you ask a question or when you direct the group to respond.

━━━━━━━━ **EXERCISE 1** ━━━━━━━━

STATEMENT INFERENCE

1. (Direct the students to find Lesson 87, part A, in the **Student Book**.)
2. (Call on individual students to read up to Ⓖ.)
   Ⓐ What are you going to write if the answer is on the graph? *G.* What are you going to write if the answer is in the passage? *P.* What are you going to write if the answer is both on the graph and in the passage? *GP.*
   Ⓑ Figure out the answer. (Wait.) What's the answer? *A gallon of milk.* Write it. ✓
   Ⓒ What's the answer? *On the graph.* So, what are you going to write? *G.* Do it. ✓
   Ⓓ Figure out the answer. (Wait.) What's the answer? *A large increase in the cost of living.*
   Write it. ✓
   Ⓔ What's the answer? *In the passage.* So, what are you going to write? *P.* Do it. (Wait.)
   Ⓕ Figure out the answer. (Wait.) What's the answer? *$0.12.*
   Write it. ✓
   Ⓖ What's the answer? *On the graph and in the passage.* So, what are you going to write? *GP.* Do it. ✓
3. Do the rest of the items. ✓
   Let's check your answers. Put an **X** next to any item you miss.
4. (Read each item. Call on individual students to answer each item.)

Answer key for Student Book part A
1. *A gallon of milk*   2. *G*   3. Idea: *A large increase in the cost of living*   4. *P*   5. *$0.12*
6. *GP*   7. *A pound of round steak*   8. *G*
9. Idea: *It goes down.*   10. *P*   11. Idea: *So that they can control it*   12. *P*   13. *$1.90*   14. *G*

Student Book page 174

A Read the passage and look at the graph. Then answer the questions. Answers to some of the questions are found in the passage. Answers to other questions are found in the graph. Some answers are found in both the passage and the graph.

> Rising prices can make the dollar less valuable, which means the dollar buys less. In 1890, a dollar could buy three gallons of milk. That same dollar in 1930 bought less than two gallons of milk. In 1890, a pound of round steak cost $.12. In 1930, a pound of round steak cost $.43.
> When the cost of living goes up, the buying power of the dollar goes down. An increase in the cost of living is called inflation. For many years, economists have been trying to explain what causes inflation. They hope that understanding inflation will point the way to controlling it. As the graph shows, inflation is still with us, and it doesn't seem to show any signs of letting up.

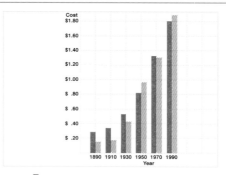

This kind of bar ▉ shows how much one gallon of milk cost.
This kind of bar ▧ shows how much one pound of round steak cost.

Student Book page 175

Write **Part A** in the left margin of your paper. Then number it from 1 to 14. Write the answers to the questions. Some of the questions ask where you found the answer. Use this key:

- Write **G** if the answer is in the graph.
- Write **P** if the answer is in the passage.
- Write **GP** if the answer is in both the graph and the passage. Ⓐ

1. In 1910, which cost more—a gallon of milk or a pound of round steak? Ⓐ
2. Where did you find the answer to question 1? Ⓐ
3. What is inflation? Ⓓ
4. Where did you find the answer to question 3? Ⓐ
5. How much did a pound of round steak cost in 1890? Ⓐ
6. Where did you find the answer to question 5? Ⓖ
7. In 1990, which cost more—a gallon of milk or a pound of round steak?
8. Where did you find the answer to question 7?
9. What happens to the buying power of the dollar when the cost of living increases?
10. Where did you find the answer to question 9?
11. Why do economists want to understand what causes inflation?
12. Where did you find the answer to question 11?
13. How much did a pound of round steak cost in 1990?
14. Where did you find the answer to question 13?

B Here's the latest model sentence you learned:

> A strange phenomenon caused the anxiety that she exhibited.

What sentence means the same thing? Ⓐ
What word means **event**? Ⓐ
What word means **fear**? Ⓐ
What word means **showed**? Ⓐ
What's another way of saying,
   A strange event caused the fear that she showed? Ⓐ

C Write **Part C** in the left margin of your paper. You have two minutes to copy the paragraph below.

> Scavengers are carnivorous animals that do not kill. Instead of killing animals, scavengers wait for animals to die or to be killed by predators. After the predators have eaten what they want, the scavengers eat the remains of the animals.

Student Book page 175

Write **Part A** in the left margin of your paper. Then number it from 1 to 14. Write the answers to the questions. Some of the questions ask where you found the answer. Use this key:

- Write **G** if the answer is in the graph.
- Write **P** if the answer is in the passage.
- Write **GP** if the answer is in both the graph and the passage.

1. In 1910, which cost more—a gallon of milk or a pound of round steak?
2. Where did you find the answer to question 1?
3. What is inflation?
4. Where did you find the answer to question 3?
5. How much did a pound of round steak cost in 1890?
6. Where did you find the answer to question 5?
7. In 1990, which cost more—a gallon of milk or a pound of round steak?
8. Where did you find the answer to question 7?
9. What happens to the buying power of the dollar when the cost of living increases?
10. Where did you find the answer to question 9?
11. Why do economists want to understand what causes inflation?
12. Where did you find the answer to question 11?
13. How much did a pound of round steak cost in 1990?
14. Where did you find the answer to question 13?

B Here's the latest model sentence you learned:

A strange phenomenon caused the anxiety that she exhibited.

What sentence means the same thing?
What word means **event**?
What word means **fear**?
What word means **showed**?
What's another way of saying,
A strange event caused the fear that she showed?

C Write **Part C** in the left margin of your paper. You have two minutes to copy the paragraph below.

Scavengers are carnivorous animals that do not kill. Instead of killing animals, scavengers wait for animals to die or to be killed by predators. After the predators have eaten what they want, the scavengers eat the remains of the animals.

Student Book page 176

D Write **Part D** in the left margin of your paper. Then number it from 1 to 3. Here are three main ideas:

Main idea A. What to do if you get frostbite.
Main idea B. Why we were stranded on the mountain.
Main idea C. You can recognize frostbite.

Each main idea fits one of the passages below. After reading all the passages, figure out which main idea goes with each passage.

Passage 1. Frostbite results from extreme cold. Frostbite most often affects the ears, nose, hands, and feet. At first, a frostbitten body part feels cold and stings. Then it becomes numb, losing all feeling. The frostbitten part may sometimes appear gray or yellow in color, and it will feel extremely cold when you touch it.

Passage 2. Frostbite results from extreme cold. Frostbite most often affects the ears, nose, hands, and feet. Some people mistakenly believe that you should rub the frostbitten body part with snow or ice. This is not only wrong, it is dangerous. If a doctor cannot be reached, the frostbitten part should be warmed slowly in lukewarm water or against a warm part of someone's body, such as between the thighs or under the arm.

Passage 3. It was getting dark, and there was no sign that the snow would let up. The cold northern wind was getting harsher. It was impossible to start a fire in this weather, so we sat huddled together in our tent. This was the third night we had spent here, halfway up Mount McKinley. We were unable to go higher or lower on the mountain because of the foul weather.

1. Main idea A is: **What to do if you get frostbite.** Which passage does main idea A best fit? *passage 2*
2. Main idea B is: **Why we were stranded on the mountain.** Which passage does main idea B best fit? *passage 3*
3. Main idea C is: **You can recognize frostbite.** Which passage does main idea C best fit? *passage 1*

EXERCISE 2

DEFINITIONS

1. (Direct the students to find part B.)
2. (Call on individual students to read part B.)
   - Say it. *A strange event caused the fear that she showed.*
   - What word? *Phenomenon.*
   - What word? *Anxiety.*
   - What word? *Exhibited.*
   - Say that sentence another way. *A strange phenomenon caused the anxiety that she exhibited.*

EXERCISE 3

INDEPENDENT WORK

1. **[Optional]** (Direct the students to read the instructions for part C to themselves. Then give them exactly two minutes to copy the paragraph. Count as errors any miscopied words and punctuation. Deduct these errors from the number of copied words, and mark the total on the Writing Rate Graph.)
2. Finish the Student Book and do the Workbook for Lesson 87. ✓

Workcheck

1. Get ready to check your answers starting with Student Book part D. Use a pen to make an **X** next to any item you miss.
2. (Call on individual students to read each item and its answer. Repeat for Workbook items.)
3. (Direct the students to count the number of errors and write the number in the **error** box at the top of the Workbook page.)

Lesson 87

4. (Award points and direct students to record their points in Box **W**.)

0 errors	**15 points**
1–2 errors	**12 points**
3–5 errors	**8 points**
6–9 errors	**5 points**

5. (Award any bonus points. Direct the students to total their points and enter the total on the Point Summary Chart.)

6. Show me your work when you've finished correcting it. (When the students show you their corrected work, record their points on your Record Summary Chart.)

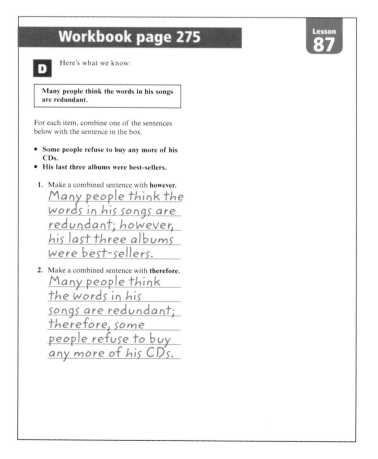

Lesson 87 — Workbook page 274

C Each argument below breaks one of these rules:

Rule 1. Just because two things happen around the same time doesn't mean one thing causes the other thing.
Rule 2. Just because you know about a part doesn't mean you know about the whole thing.
Rule 3. Just because you know about a part doesn't mean you know about another part.
Rule 4. Just because you know about the whole thing doesn't mean you know about every part.
Rule 5. Just because words are the same doesn't mean they have the same meaning.
Rule 6. Just because the writer presents some choices doesn't mean there aren't other choices.

After each argument, write the number of the rule the argument breaks.

1. An officer stopped a man on the freeway for speeding. The man had been traveling at about 85 miles per hour and had been weaving in and out of traffic.
   When the officer began writing the first of three tickets, the man said: "But, officer, you don't understand. I must get home. I left home about an hour ago, and I forgot that I had left my welding torch on in the basement. If somebody doesn't turn it off very soon, it will burn up the house. My wife is in the house. If I don't get home right now, I'm going to lose my home and my wife." _6_

2. Bob said that he'd give me a ring Thursday, and all he did was call me on the phone. I wonder if I should even see him again. _5_

3. I'm sure that she has pretty feet. Her legs and arms are very attractive. _3_

4. Not everybody's going to agree with me, but I don't think Mary Cass is right for the job of union official. I know what others have said. Even the president of the union called Mary a stout supporter of the union. But that's the problem. We don't need a stout supporter. We need somebody who is slim, somebody who can get out there and fight. _5_

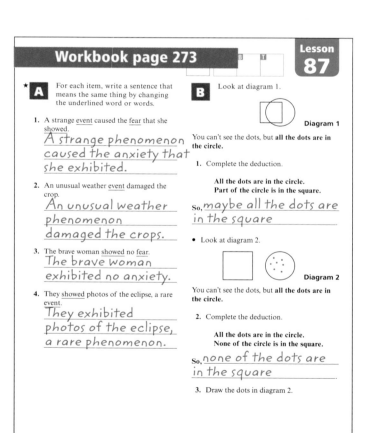

Workbook page 273 — Lesson 87

★ A For each item, write a sentence that means the same thing by changing the underlined word or words.

1. A strange underline{event} caused the underline{fear} that she showed.
   A strange phenomenon caused the anxiety that she exhibited.

2. An unusual weather underline{event} damaged the crop.
   An unusual weather phenomenon damaged the crops.

3. The brave woman underline{showed} no fear.
   The brave woman exhibited no anxiety.

4. They underline{showed} photos of the eclipse, a rare underline{event}.
   They exhibited photos of the eclipse, a rare phenomenon.

B Look at diagram 1.

Diagram 1

You can't see the dots, but **all the dots are in the circle.**

1. Complete the deduction.

   All the dots are in the circle.
   Part of the circle is in the square.

   So, _maybe all the dots are in the square_

• Look at diagram 2.

Diagram 2

You can't see the dots, but **all the dots are in the circle.**

2. Complete the deduction.

   All the dots are in the circle.
   None of the circle is in the square.

   So, _none of the dots are in the square_

3. Draw the dots in diagram 2.

Workbook page 275 — Lesson 87

D Here's what we know:

> Many people think the words in his songs are redundant.

For each item, combine one of the sentences below with the sentence in the box.

• Some people refuse to buy any more of his CDs.
• His last three albums were best-sellers.

1. Make a combined sentence with **however**.
   Many people think the words in his songs are redundant; however, his last three albums were best-sellers.

2. Make a combined sentence with **therefore**.
   Many people think the words in his songs are redundant; therefore, some people refuse to buy any more of his CDs.

END OF LESSON 87

Student Book page 177

A

You learned a model sentence that means:
   A strange event caused the fear that she showed.
Say that model sentence. ⊙
What word in the model sentence means **event**? ⊙
What word in the model sentence means **fear**? ⊙
What word in the model sentence means **showed**? ⊙

B

Read the passage and look at the map on the following page. Then answer
the questions. Answers to some of the questions are found in the passage.
Answers to other questions are found on the map. Some answers are found
both in the passage and on the map.

> For part of the eighteenth and nineteenth centuries, Alaska was owned
> by Russia. In 1867, the United States bought Alaska for $7,200,000, which
> was less than two cents an acre. Alaska did not become a state until
> January 3, 1959, when it became the forty-ninth state to join the United
> States.
>   Alaska is closer to the North Pole than any other state in the United
> States. The town in Alaska that is closest to the North Pole is Barrow,
> which is 300 kilometers north of the Arctic Circle. This means that for
> over half the year, it is daytime in Barrow. The sun comes up in the month
> of April, and it doesn't go down again until September. From April
> through September, the sun never sets. If you went outside at midnight,
> you would see the sun.
>   Alaska has the largest area of any state in the United States. With over
> 1.5 million square kilometers, it has more than twice the area of Texas.
> However, Alaska has the smallest population of any state. In Alaska, there
> is only about one person for every square kilometer. In the state of New
> York, there are over 140 people for every square kilometer.
>   Anchorage is Alaska's largest city. It has a population of 305 thousand
> people. Anchorage is located on Alaska's southern coast, on Cook Inlet.
> About 300 kilometers north of Anchorage is Alaska's tallest mountain,
> Mount McKinley. Mount McKinley has an altitude of 6,194 meters,
> which makes it the tallest mountain in North America.
>   Alaska is a growing state with many natural resources. It has an
> abundance of oil and natural gas. These resources are becoming more and
> more important to the United States.

Student Book page 178

The symbol ● means that the city has under 10,000 people.
The symbol ○ means that the city has between 10,000 and 50,000 people.
The symbol ⊙ means that the city has over 50,000 people.

The symbol (EL 4176) means that the mountain is 4,176 meters high.

Write **Part B** in the left margin of your paper. Then number it from 1 to 14.
Write the answers to the questions. Some of the questions ask where you
found the answer. Use this key:

• Write **M** if the answer is on the map.
• Write **P** if the answer is in the passage.
• Write **MP** if the answer is both on the map and in the passage. ⊙

Note: The circled letters indicate when
you ask a question or when you direct the
group to respond.

━━━━━━━━━━ **EXERCISE 1** ━━━━━━━━━━
DEFINITIONS

1. (Direct the students to find Lesson 88,
   part A, in the **Student Book**.)
2. (Call on individual students to read
   part A.)
   ⒶSay it. *A strange phenomenon caused
   the anxiety that she exhibited.*
   ⒷWhat word? Phenomenon.
   ⒸWhat word? *Anxiety.*
   ⒹWhat word? *Exhibited.*

━━━━━━━━━━ **EXERCISE 2** ━━━━━━━━━━
STATEMENT INFERENCE

1. (Direct the students to find part B.)
2. (Call on individual students to read up
   to Ⓚ.)
   ⒠What are you going to write if the
   answer is on the map? *M.*
   What are you going to write if the
   answer is in the passage? *P.*
   What are you going to write if the
   answer is both on the map and in the
   passage? *MP.*

F Figure out the answer. (Wait.)
What's the answer? *More than 50,000 people.*
Write it. ✓

G What's the answer? *On the map.*
So, what are you going to write? *M.*
Do it. ✓

H Figure out the answer. (Wait.)
What's the answer? *January 3, 1959.*
Write it. ✓

I What's the answer? *In the passage.*
So, what are you going to write? *P.*
Do it. ✓

J Figure out the answer. (Wait.)
What's the answer? *Barrow.*
Write it. ✓

K What's the answer? *On the map and in the passage.*
So, what are you going to write? *MP.*
Do it. ✓

3. Do the rest of the items. ✓
Let's check your answers. Put an **X** next to any item you miss.

4. (Read each item. Call on individual students to answer each item.)

━━━━━━━━ **EXERCISE 3** ━━━━━━━━

INDEPENDENT WORK

1. **[Optional]** (Direct the students to read the instructions for part C to themselves. Then give them exactly two minutes to copy the paragraph. Count as errors any miscopied words and punctuation. Deduct these errors from the number of copied words, and mark the total on the Writing Rate Graph.)

2. Finish the Student Book and do the Workbook for Lesson 88. ✓

Student Book page 179

1. What is the population of Fairbanks? ⊙
2. Where did you find the answer to question 1? ⊕
3. When did Alaska become a state? ⊙
4. Where did you find the answer to question 3? ⊙
5. What town in Alaska is north of the Arctic Circle? ⊙
6. Where did you find the answer to question 5? ⊙
7. Who owned Alaska before the United States?
8. Where did you find the answer to question 7?
9. How tall is Mount McKinley?
10. Where did you find the answer to question 9?
11. What are two important resources in Alaska?
12. Where did you find the answer to question 11?
13. What ocean is north of Barrow?
14. Where did you find the answer to question 13?

C Write **Part C** in the left margin of your paper. You have two minutes to copy the paragraph below.

> Frostbite results from extreme cold. Frostbite most often affects the ears, nose, hands, and feet. At first, a frostbitten body part feels cold and stings. Then it becomes numb, losing all feeling. The frostbitten part may appear gray or yellow in color.

1. More than 50,000 people
2. M
3. January 3, 1959
4. P
5. Barrow
6. MP
7. Russia
8. P
9. 6,194
10. MP
11. Oil and natural gas
12. P
13. The Arctic Ocean
14. M

Student Book page 180

★ **D** Write **Part D** in the left margin of your paper. Then number it from 1 to 3. Here are three main ideas:

> **Main idea A.** Nesting places for bluebirds are disappearing.
> **Main idea B.** Bluebirds are forced out of their nesting places.
> **Main idea C.** People build nesting places for bluebirds.

Each main idea fits one of the passages below. After reading all the passages, figure out which main idea goes with each passage.

> **Passage 1.** Bluebirds are disappearing from North America. One reason is the increased population of sparrows and starlings, which are not native to North America. Sparrows and starlings like to nest in the same places that bluebirds like. Bluebirds are mild-mannered, peaceful animals, so the frisky sparrows find it easy to drive the bluebirds away and move into the stolen homes.

> **Passage 2.** Bluebirds are disappearing from North America. They have always preferred to nest in old fence posts and rotting trees near farms and on the outskirts of towns. As our cities grow larger, most rotten trees are cut down, and metal fence posts have largely replaced the old wooden kind. Consequently, it is getting harder and harder for bluebirds to find proper places to build nests and raise their young. The population of bluebirds is declining steadily.

> **Passage 3.** Bluebirds are disappearing from North America. But as more and more people become concerned, a determined effort to save this friendly bird is growing. People all over the country are building nesting boxes for the bluebirds and mounting them on fence posts and tree trunks. The boxes are designed to keep the larger starlings out, as well as to protect the bluebirds from cold weather and predators. In areas where the boxes are plentiful, the population of bluebirds is starting to increase.

1. Main idea A is: **Nesting places for bluebirds are disappearing.** Which passage does main idea A best fit? *passage 2*
2. Main idea B is: **Bluebirds are forced out of their nesting places.** Which passage does main idea B best fit? *passage 1*
3. Main idea C is: **People build nesting places for bluebirds.** Which passage does main idea C best fit? *passage 3*

Lesson 88 — Workbook page 276

ERRORS [ ] W [ ]

 A Each argument that follows is faulty.

- Our sun is not even two million kilometers across, and Red Giant stars are more than ten million kilometers across. Therefore, Red Giant stars must be brighter than our sun.

1. What does the writer want us to conclude?
   Idea: The larger a star is, the brighter it is.

2. How could you show that the argument is faulty?
   Idea: Show that the sun is brighter, even though it is smaller than Red Giant stars.

- I support the mayor for reelection. He has the experience and knowledge necessary to run our city. Our city government works very well. The mayor is part of the city government, so it follows that he must be doing good work, too.

3. What does the writer want us to conclude?
   Idea: The mayor is doing good work because the city government works very well.

4. How could you show that the argument is faulty?
   Idea: Find out what projects the mayor has been doing and see how effective he or she has been.

- When the cost of raw materials goes up, we have no choice but to raise the price of our cars. Either you let us price our cars however we please, or you destroy the very foundation of our economy. The choice is up to you.

5. What does the writer want us to conclude?
   Idea: If car makers can't price cars however they want to, our country's economy will be destroyed.

6. How could you show that the argument is faulty?
   Idea: Put limitations on how much car makers may charge for their cars and see if our economy is ruined.

Workbook page 277 — Lesson 88

B Underline the redundant part in each sentence below. Then explain why the underlined part is redundant by filling in the blanks.

1. "Yes," she said, agreeing.
   If you know that she said "Yes"
   then you already know that she agreed

2. To change some of her money, she converted it.
   If you know that she changed some money
   then you already know that she converted it

3. "Ouch, that thing hurts," he screamed in pain.
   If you know that he said "Ouch, that thing hurts"
   then you already know that he was in pain

C For each item, write a sentence that means the same thing by changing the underlined word or words.

1. A strange event caused the fear that she showed.
   A strange phenomenon caused the anxiety that she exhibited.

2. An earthquake is a geological event that creates fear.
   An earthquake is a geological phenomenon that creates anxiety.

3. Sam showed no fear when he jumped from the airplane.
   Sam exhibited no anxiety when he jumped from the airplane.

4. A hurricane can be a destructive event.
   A hurricane can be a destructive phenomenon.

Lesson 88 — Workbook page 278

D Select the right word for combining each pair of sentences below. Then write the combined sentence. Remember to punctuate each sentence correctly.

1. Police officers need to learn new laws. They go to police school.
   therefore   but
   Police officers need to learn new laws; therefore, they go to police school.

2. The bank's computer broke down. The bank clerk couldn't tell me the exact amount in my savings account.
   so   however
   The bank's computer broke down, so the bank clerk couldn't tell me the exact amount in my savings account.

3. The newspaper photographer ran out of film. She was unable to take a picture when the building collapsed.
   therefore   however
   The newspaper photographer ran out of film; therefore, she was unable to take a picture when the building collapsed.

4. Don had to return some books. They were overdue.
   who   which
   Don had to return some books, which were overdue.

5. Many people enjoy seeing dolphins perform at water shows. Dolphins seem to enjoy performing tricks for crowds.
   and   but
   Many people enjoy seeing dolphins perform at water shows, and dolphins seem to enjoy performing tricks for crowds.

6. Cats love Susan. Susan is our animal doctor.
   who   which
   Cats love Susan, who is our animal doctor.

END OF LESSON 88

Workcheck

1. Get ready to check your answers starting with Student Book part D. Use a pen to make an **X** next to any item you miss.
2. (Call on individual students to read each item and its answer. Repeat for Workbook items.)
3. (Direct the students to count the number of errors and write the number in the **error** box at the top of the Workbook page.)
4. (Award points and direct students to record their points in Box **W**.)

0 errors	15 points
1–2 errors	12 points
3–5 errors	8 points
6–9 errors	5 points

5. (Award any bonus points. Direct the students to total their points and enter the total on the Point Summary Chart.)
6. Show me your work when you've finished correcting it. (When the students show you their corrected work, record their points on your Record Summary Chart.)

Note: The circled letters indicate when you ask a question or when you direct the group to respond.

EXERCISE 1

STATEMENT INFERENCE

1. (Direct the students to find part A in the **Student Book.**)
2. (Call on individual students to read up to Ⓐ.)
   Ⓐ What are you going to write if the answer is in passage A? *A.* What are you going to write if the answer is in passage B? *B.* What are you going to write if the answer is in both passage A and passage B? *AB.*
   Ⓑ Figure out the answer. (Wait.) What's the answer? *Ike, Pennsylvania.* Write it. ✓
   Ⓒ What's the answer? *In passage A and passage B.* So, what are you going to write? *AB.* Do it. ✓
   Ⓓ Figure out the answer. (Wait.) (Call on individual students. Idea: *They are striking over wage disputes; they want a fair share for doing work that is hard and dangerous; and there is foul-smelling gas.*) Write it. ✓
   Ⓔ Figure out the answer. (Wait.) What's the answer? *At one minute after midnight this morning.*
   Ⓕ What's the answer? *Passage B.* So, what are you going to write? *B.* Do it. ✓
3. Do the rest of the items. ✓
   Let's check your answers. Put an **X** next to any item you miss.

A Read the passages below. Then answer the questions. Answers to some of the questions are found in passage A. Answers to other questions are found in passage B. Some answers are found in both passage A and passage B.

> **Passage A.** A coal strike started in Ike, Pennsylvania, today. Mine workers are striking over wage disputes. Wage negotiations are presently going on between the coal mining companies and the miners' union. The president of Ike Coal Company said in reaction to the strike, "This strike is poorly timed. There's a high demand for coal at this time of year, and we need to work at full capacity. The union is being unfair, undiplomatic, and is not considering the good of the nation as a whole."
> The president of the Ike, Pennsylvania, mine workers' union today said, "The Ike Coal Company has been making larger and larger profits from our work. It's time we got a fair share for doing work that is hard and dangerous."
> The strike is expected to go on for a long time.

> **Passage B.** At one minute after midnight this morning, the mine workers in Ike, Pennsylvania, walked out of their jobs and began a strike that is expected to last for months. The mine workers' union has a large strike fund and can afford to strike for a long time. Negotiations between the coal companies and the union are going on right now, but no one is hopeful that there will be an early end to the strike.
> Jeremy Plob, the president of the striking coal workers' union, said today, "The coal companies have been making larger and larger profits from our work."
> Plob also cites foul-smelling gas in the mines as one reason for the walkout.

Write **Part B** in the left margin of your paper. Then number it from 1 to 9. Write the answers to the questions. Some of the questions ask where you found the answer. Use this key:

* Write **A** if the answer is in passage A.
* Write **B** if the answer is in passage B.
* Write **AB** if the answer is in passage A and passage B. Ⓐ

1. Where is the coal strike taking place? Ⓑ
2. Where did you find the answer to question 1? Ⓒ
3. Why are the coal miners striking? Ⓓ
4. At what time did the strike begin? Ⓔ
5. Where did you find the answer to question 4? Ⓕ
6. Why can the union afford to strike for a long time?
7. Where did you find the answer to question 6?

---

8. Name a coal company that is being struck.
9. Where did you find the answer to question 8?

B When you combine sentences with **who** or **which**, what punctuation do you need before **who** or **which**? Ⓐ
When you combine sentences with the word **so**, what do you do with the period of the first sentence? Ⓑ
What word follows the comma? Ⓒ
When you combine sentences with the word **however**, what do you do with the period of the first sentence? Ⓓ
What follows the semicolon? Ⓔ
What follows the word **however**? Ⓕ

C Write **Part C** in the left margin of your paper. You have two minutes to copy the paragraph below.

> **Bluebirds are disappearing from North America. One reason for this is the increased population of sparrows and starlings, which are not native to North America. Sparrows and starlings like to nest in the same places that bluebirds like—old fence posts and rotting trees.**

D Write **Part D** in the left margin of your paper. Then number it from 1 to 3. Here are three main ideas:

> **Main idea A. Alcoholism is a disease.**
> **Main idea B. People are taught about alcoholism.**
> **Main idea C. Alcoholism is tied to other social problems.**

Each main idea fits one of the passages that follows. After reading all the passages, figure out which main idea goes with each passage.

Student Book page 183

Passage 1. Alcohol abuse is one of the biggest health and social problems in the United States today. There are ten million "problem drinkers" in the United States. Seven million of these people are serious alcoholics who require counseling or medical attention. It has been known for a long time that alcohol abuse leads to serious physical damage. In the last thirty years, though, medical researchers have begun to recognize that alcoholism, like other diseases, can be cured.

Passage 2. Alcohol abuse is one of the biggest health and social problems in the United States today. There are ten million "problem drinkers" in the U.S. Seven million of these people are serious alcoholics who require counseling or medical attention. Many social problems are often associated with alcohol. It is believed that over half of this country's crimes are committed by people who have been drinking. Poverty and family conflicts are also frequently tied to alcohol abuse.

Passage 3. Alcohol abuse is one of the biggest health problems in the United States today. Public education about alcoholism is growing rapidly, as community groups use television and radio to reach the population. Community groups are trying to accomplish two things. First, they want people to recognize that alcoholics are sick, not irresponsible or lazy. Second, they want people to recognize the early signs of alcoholism, so that victims of the disease can get treatment before serious physical or mental damage is done.

1. Main idea A is: **Alcoholism is a disease.** Which passage does main idea A best fit? *passage 1*
2. Main idea B is: **People are taught about alcoholism.** Which passage does main idea B best fit? *passage 3*
3. Main idea C is: **Alcoholism is tied to other social problems.** Which passage does main idea C best fit? *passage 2*

Workbook page 279

B | T

★ **A** For each item, write a sentence that means the same thing by changing the underlined words.

1. They <u>made up</u> a <u>fitting plan</u>.
   They devised an appropriate strategy.

2. She had a <u>chance</u> to present the facts about the <u>frightening event</u>.
   She had an opportunity to present the facts about the frightening phenomenon.

3. Bev experienced <u>fear</u> before she found her missing <u>money</u>.
   Bev experienced anxiety before she found her missing currency.

4. The <u>rule</u> was very <u>unclear</u>.
   The regulation was very ambiguous.

B Read each item. Cross out the irrelevant words in the second piece of evidence, and write the conclusion for each item.

1. Mailing packages costs more than mailing letters.

   Our books are mailed in ~~brown paper~~ packages.

   Therefore, our books cost more to mail than letters.

2. Some periodicals contain advertising.

   Newsmagazines are ~~informative~~ periodicals.

   So, maybe newsmagazines contain advertising.

3. Cold temperatures preserve food.

   Household freezers have ~~unwavering~~ cold temperatures.

   Therefore, household freezers preserve food.

4. (Read each item. Call on individual students to answer each Item.)

> **Answer key for Student Book part A**
> **1.** *Ike, Pennsylvania* **2.** *AB* **3.** *Idea: Over wage disputes; they want a fair share for doing work that is hard and dangerous; there is foul-smelling gas.* **4.** *At one minute after midnight this morning.* **5.** *B* **6.** *Idea: It has a large strike fund.* **7.** *B* **8.** *Ike Coal Company* **9.** *A*

EXERCISE 2
SENTENCE COMBINATIONS

1. (Direct the students to find Lesson 89, part B.)
2. (Call on individual students to read part B.)
   G What's the answer? *A comma.*
   H What's the answer? *Change it to a comma.*
   I What's the answer? *So.*
   J What's the answer? *Change it to a semicolon.*
   K What's the answer? *However.*
   L What's the answer? *A comma.*

EXERCISE 3
INDEPENDENT WORK

1. **[Optional]** (Direct the students to read the instructions for part C to themselves. Then give them exactly two minutes to copy the paragraph. Count as errors any miscopied words and punctuation. Deduct these errors from the number of copied words, and mark the total on the Writing Rate Graph.)
2. In Lesson 90, you'll have a test on story facts. The facts that will be tested appear in part D of your Workbook. Study them and make sure that you know them. Now finish the Student Book and do the Workbook for Lesson 89.

Lesson 89

Workcheck

1. Get ready to check your answers starting with Student Book part D. Use a pen to make an **X** next to any item you miss.
2. (Call on individual students to read each item and its answer. Repeat for Workbook items.)
3. (Direct the students to count the number of errors and write the number in the **error** box at the top of the Workbook page.)
4. (Award points and direct students to record their points in Box **W**.)

0 errors	15 points
1–2 errors	12 points
3–5 errors	8 points
6–9 errors	5 points

5. (Award any bonus points. Direct the students to total their points and enter the total on the Point Summary Chart.)
6. Show me your work when you've finished correcting it. (When the students show you their corrected work, record their points on your Record Summary Chart.)

Lesson 89 — Workbook page 280

C Each argument that follows is faulty.

- Three years ago, I had a bad cough. Dr. Samuel made me take some medicine. It tasted awful, but my cough went away in one day. Later, I had the flu. I had to take a different kind of medicine. It tasted bad too, but the next day I felt fine. My dad has some medicine that is supposed to make hair grow. If this medicine tastes bad, I know it will work and I will have lots of hair tomorrow.

1. What does the writer want us to conclude?
   Idea: If medicine tastes bad, then it will really work.

2. How could you show that the argument is faulty?
   Idea: The next time the writer gets sick, give him or her the good-tasting medicine and see if he or she gets better.

- Would you rather pay $20,000 for this automobile and have something that you will love and all your friends will admire? Or would you prefer to drive that junk you've got now and have everybody think you're a slob?

3. What does the writer want us to conclude?
   Idea: Unless you pay $20,000 for a car, your friends will think you're a slob.

4. How could you show that the argument is faulty?
   Idea: Show the writer a less expensive car that his or her friends will be sure to admire.

- Sue must not have any friends, because she always goes to the movies by herself.

5. What does the writer want us to conclude?
   Idea: She doesn't have any friends.

6. How could you show that the argument is faulty?
   Idea: Find out if Sue goes to the movies alone for some reason other than that she doesn't have any friends.

Workbook page 281 — Lesson 89

D After you finish Lesson 90, you will be tested on facts you have learned. The test will include all the facts presented in Lessons 81–90 and some of the facts from earlier lessons. These facts are:

1. The right and the left eye of many herbivorous mammals see different things.
2. The right and left eye of many carnivorous mammals see nearly the same thing.
3. A cold war happens when two countries are close to being in a shooting war with each other.
4. In 1969, the first person walked on the moon.
5. Leonardo do Vinci was an inventor, a painter, a musician, and a scientist.
6. In 1869, the first coast-to-coast railroad in the United States was completed.
7. Study the chart below. Make sure that you could fill in this chart.

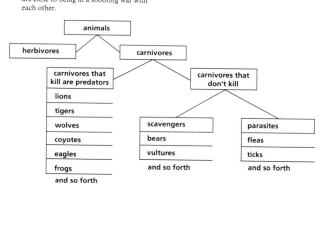

END OF LESSON 89

Student Book page 184

Lesson 90

A Write **Part A** in the left margin of your paper. You have two minutes to copy the paragraph below.

> Alcohol abuse is one of the biggest health and social problems in the United States today. It is believed that over half of this country's crimes are committed by people who have been drinking. Family conflicts are also frequently tied to alcohol abuse.

★ B Write **Part B** in the left margin of your paper. Rewrite the passage below in three or four sentences. Combine consistent sentences with **so** or **therefore**. Combine inconsistent sentences with **but** or **however**. Combine some sentences with **who** or **which**.

> The Federal Trade Commission supervises advertising. It is anxious to hear your complaints. There is a lot of honest, informative advertising. There is also misleading and dishonest advertising. The Federal Trade Commission would like to stop all dishonest advertising. Dishonest advertising is against the law.

C Here are some words that will be in some editing activities. Test yourself to make sure that you know what the words mean.

clarity—Something that has clarity is very clear. A diamond with great clarity is a very clear diamond. Here's a sentence that uses the word **clarity:**
The clarity of his argument answered many questions.

cautious—When you are cautious, you are very careful. Here's a sentence that uses the word **cautious:**
She was a very cautious driver, especially in heavy traffic.

sorrow—Sorrow is sadness. When you are filled with sorrow, you are very sad. Here's a sentence that uses the word **sorrow:**
He showed great sorrow when his dog died.

B—Idea: The Federal Trade Commission supervises advertising; therefore, it is anxious to hear your complaints. There is a lot of honest, informative advertising; however, there is also misleading and dishonest advertising. The Federal Trade Commission would like to stop all dishonest advertising, which is against the law.

Workbook page 282

Lesson 90 **ERRORS** **W**

★ A Each argument that follows breaks one of these rules.

Rule 1. Just because two things happen around the same time doesn't mean one thing causes the other thing.
Rule 2. Just because you know about a part doesn't mean you know about the whole thing.
Rule 3. Just because you know about a part doesn't mean you know about another part.
Rule 4. Just because you know about the whole thing doesn't mean you know about every part.
Rule 5. Just because words are the same doesn't mean they have the same meaning.
Rule 6. Just because the writer presents some choices doesn't mean there aren't other choices.

After each argument that follows, write the number of the rule the argument breaks.

1. Poor Morey. His mother said he seemed to have lost his senses since the accident. Can you imagine not being able to hear, smell, or see? I hope it's not permanent. _5_

2. What kind of a suggestion is that? How could we possibly drop our athletic program? Do you realize that you're talking about St. Francis University, which has a tradition of sports excellence that dates back to Knute Dropley, the first football coach to have a national champion at St. Francis? Do I have to remind you that the very fiber of this university is woven from the principles that are formed on the athletic field and in athletic competition? Athletes are real men and women, strong and knowledgeable about how to share and how to be a member of a working group. If we do away with our athletic program, we will turn out people who are weak and know nothing of what it is like to compete for excellence. _6_

3. The army is not efficient, so we cannot expect Major Schlock to do an efficient job. _4_

4. The Johnsons had a serious fight. Mr. Johnson left this morning with a suitcase, and that's just what happens after married people have a big fight. _2_

B Use the rule in the box and the evidence to answer the questions.

All fires need air.

• **Sam lit a candle.**
1. What's the conclusion?
Idea: Sam's candle needed air.

• **There was a fire in the fireplace.**
2. What's the conclusion?
The fire in the fireplace needed air.

• **There is no air on the moon.**
3. What's the conclusion?
Idea: There are no fires on the moon.

EXERCISE 1
INDEPENDENT WORK

1. **[Optional]** (Direct the students to read the instructions for part A in the **Student Book** to themselves. Then give them exactly two minutes to copy the paragraph. Count as errors any miscopied words and punctuation. Deduct these errors from the number of copied words, and mark the total on the Writing Rate Graph.)
2. Finish the Student Book and do the Workbook for Lesson 90. ✓

Workcheck

1. Get ready to check your answers starting with Student Book part B. Use a pen to make an **X** next to any item you miss.
2. (Call on individual students to read each item and its answer. Repeat for Workbook items.)
3. (Direct the students to count the number of errors and write the number in the **error** box at the top of the Workbook page.)
4. (Award points and direct students to record their points in Box **W**.)

0 errors	15 points
1–2 errors	12 points
3–5 errors	8 points
6–9 errors	5 points

5. (Award any bonus points. Direct to total their points and enter the total on the Point Summary Chart.)
6. Show me your work when you've finished correcting it. (When the students show you their corrected work, record their points on your Record Summary Chart.)

Note: Before presenting lesson 91, present Fact Game Lesson 6.

Workbook page 282

★ **A** Each argument that follows breaks one of these rules:

> **Rule 1.** Just because two things happen around the same time doesn't mean one thing causes the other thing.
> **Rule 2.** Just because you know about a part doesn't mean you know about the whole thing.
> **Rule 3.** Just because you know about a part doesn't mean you know about another part.
> **Rule 4.** Just because you know about the whole thing doesn't mean you know about every part.
> **Rule 5.** Just because words are the same doesn't mean they have the same meaning.
> **Rule 6.** Just because the writer presents some choices doesn't mean there aren't other choices.

After each argument that follows, write the number of the rule the argument breaks.

1. Poor Morey. His mother said he seemed to have lost his senses since the accident. Can you imagine not being able to hear, smell, or see? I hope it's not permanent. _5_

2. What kind of a suggestion is that? How could we possibly drop our athletic program? Do you realize that you're talking about St. Francis University, which has a tradition of sports excellence that dates back to Knute Dropley, the first football coach to have a national champion at St. Francis? Do I have to remind you that the very fiber of this university is woven from the principles that are formed on the athletic field and in athletic competition? Athletes are real men and women, strong and knowledgeable about how to share and how to be a member of a working group. If we do away with our athletic program, we will turn out people who are weak and know nothing of what it is like to compete for excellence. _6_

3. The army is not efficient, so we cannot expect Major Schlock to do an efficient job. _4_

4. The Johnsons had a serious fight. Mr. Johnson left this morning with a suitcase, and that's just what happens after married people have a big fight. _2_

B Use the rule in the box and the evidence to answer the questions.

> All fires need air.

• Sam lit a candle.
1. What's the conclusion?
   Idea: Sam's candle needed air.

• There was a fire in the fireplace.
2. What's the conclusion?
   The fire in the fireplace needed air.

• There is no air on the moon.
3. What's the conclusion?
   Idea: There are no fires on the moon.

Workbook page 284

E Each argument that follows is faulty.

• I think my Aunt Alice is very strange. She's always been a little bit odd. As long as I've known her, she's had a tendency to put things in strange places. She once put a statue of a giant swan on her roof. Another time, she put a little folding table in the back seat of the car. She even put a little tiny television set inside her doghouse.

   When I got the last letter from Aunt Alice, I knew that she had gone too far putting things in strange places. She wrote that she was going to the dentist's office to have a bridge put in her mouth. I don't know if it's a railroad bridge or a bridge for cars, but I do know that poor Aunt Alice has lost her mind.

1. What does the writer want us to conclude?
   Idea: Aunt Alice was having a railroad or traffic bridge put into her mouth.

2. How could you show that the argument is faulty?
   Idea: Look at the bridge in Aunt Alice's mouth and see if it really is a railroad or traffic bridge.

• Primp circuit boards are recognized as the finest in the world. You know that any company that produces such a circuit board must be the world leader in electronic components.

3. What does the writer want us to conclude?
   Idea: The company that makes primp circuit boards is the world leader in electronic components.

4. How could you show that the argument is faulty?
   Idea: Find some of the company's other electronic products and see how they compare with their competitors'.

• J. Paul Getty was an American, and he had more than a billion dollars. John Jackson is an American, so he must be rich too.

5. What does the writer want us to conclude?
   Idea: All Americans are rich.

6. How could you show that the argument is faulty?
   Idea: Find Americans who are not rich.

Workbook page 283

C Underline the redundant part in each sentence below. Then explain why the underlined part is redundant by filling in the blanks.

1. He halted by <u>coming to a complete stop</u>.
   If _you know that he halted_
   then _you already know that he came to a complete stop_

2. She was the kind of employee <u>who worked for somebody</u>.
   If _you know that she was an employee_
   then _you already know that she worked for somebody_

3. That car didn't move <u>as long as it was standing still</u>.
   If _you know that the car didn't move_
   then _you already know that it was standing still_

D For each item, write a sentence that means the same thing by changing the underlined words.

1. A strange <u>event</u> caused the <u>fear</u> that she <u>showed</u>.
   A strange phenomenon caused the anxiety that she exhibited.

2. The crooks had a <u>plan</u> for making <u>money</u>.
   The crooks had a strategy for making currency.

3. He <u>showed</u> his <u>fear</u> when he <u>paused</u>.
   He exhibited his anxiety when he hesitated.

4. His paper was <u>filled</u> with <u>irrelevant</u> facts.
   His paper was replete with extraneous facts.

EXERCISE 1

MASTERY TEST

1. Everybody, find page 449 in your workbook.
- This is a test. You'll do the whole test, and then we'll mark it. If you make no mistakes on the test, you'll earn 20 points. Write the answers to the test items not using your pencil.
2. (After the students complete the items, gather the Workbooks and grade the tests. As you grade each test, record the number of errors the student made on each part of the test in the appropriate box. Record the total number of errors in Error box at the beginning of the test.)
3. (Return the Workbooks to the students.)
4. Raise your hand if you made _____ or more mistakes in part _____.
(Record the number of students who raise their hand for the part.)

> **Key:** Part A–5 Part B–2 Part C–1
> Part D–2

5. Raise your hand if you made no mistakes on the whole test. Great work. (Award 20 points to the students who made no errors. Award 5 points to students who made 1 or 2 errors.)
- Record your points in the box marked **MT** at the top of Mastery Test 9.
- (Direct all students to enter their points on the Point Summary Chart.)
6. (Record test results on the Group Summary Sheet. Reproducible Summary Sheets are at the back of the Teacher's Guide.)

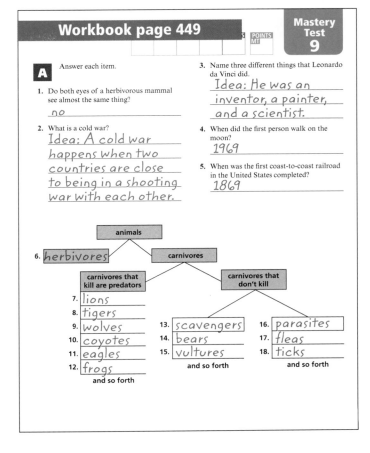

Workbook page 449

A Answer each item.

1. Do both eyes of a herbivorous mammal see almost the same thing?
   no

2. What is a cold war?
   Idea: A cold war happens when two countries are close to being in a shooting war with each other.

3. Name three different things that Leonardo da Vinci did.
   Idea: He was an inventor, a painter, and a scientist.

4. When did the first person walk on the moon?
   1969

5. When was the first coast-to-coast railroad in the United States completed?
   1869

6. animals
   - herbivores
   - carnivores
     - carnivores that kill are predators
       7. lions
       8. tigers
       9. wolves
       10. coyotes
       11. eagles
       12. frogs
       and so forth
     - carnivores that don't kill
       13. scavengers
       14. bears
       15. vultures
       and so forth
       16. parasites
       17. fleas
       18. ticks
       and so forth

Workbook page 450

B Write the model sentence that means the same thing as each sentence below.

1. A strange event caused the fear that she showed.
   A strange phenomenon caused the anxiety that she exhibited.

2. His directions were unclear and repetitive.
   His directions were ambiguous and redundant.

3. The rule limited their parking.
   The regulation restricted their parking.

4. They made up a fitting plan.
   They devised an appropriate strategy.

5. By pausing, she lost her chance.
   By hesitating, she lost her opportunity.

6. They changed their Swiss money into Canadian money.
   They converted their Swiss currency into Canadian currency.

7. Her answer was filled with irrelevant details.
   Her response was replete with extraneous details.

C Here are two main ideas:

Main idea A. **Schools are responsible for a student's education.**
Main idea B. **Students are responsible for their own education.**

Each main idea fits one of the passages below. After reading both passages, figure out which main idea goes with each passage.

Passage 1. The school is being sued for damages, because when Albert graduated, he couldn't read well enough to fill out a job application. But it's not the school's fault that Albert can't read. Albert was one of those students who are incapable of learning. The school gave Albert every opportunity to learn—the same opportunities it gave to other students. Albert didn't take advantage of those opportunities. That doesn't mean that the school is responsible.

Passage 2. The school is being sued for damages, because when Albert graduated, he couldn't read well enough to fill out a job application. The school's responsibility is to teach students how to read, write, and do arithmetic. We don't build schools and hire teachers to babysit kids until they're eighteen. If the schools aren't responsible for the education of children, then let's get rid of the schools.

1. Main idea A is: **Schools are responsible for a student's education.**
   Which passage does main idea A best fit?
   passage 2

Workbook page 451 — Mastery Test 9

2. Main idea B is: **Students are responsible for their own education.**
Which passage does main idea B best fit?

<u>passage 1</u>

D Each argument below is faulty. Read the arguments and the answer the questions.

J. Paul Getty was an American, and he had more than a billion dollars. John Jackson is an American, so he must be rich too.

1. What does the writer want us to conclude?

<u>Idea: All Americans are rich.</u>

2. How could you show that the argument is faulty?

<u>Idea: Find Americans who are not rich.</u>

Joe takes business classes, so I think I'll ask his advice about the stock market.

3. What does the writer want us to conclude?

<u>Idea: Joe knows about the stock market.</u>

4. How could you show that the argument is faulty?

<u>Idea: by seeing if Joe's business classes teach him about the stock market</u>

━━━━━━━ **EXERCISE 2** ━━━━━━━

TEST REMEDIES

1. (If more than 25% of the students failed a part of the test, provide the remedy specified for that part in the table below. The required Remedy Blackline Master worksheets can be found in Appendix H of the Teacher's Guide.)

3. (All remedies should be completed before beginning the next lesson in the program.)

Test Section	If students made this many errors	Present these tasks: Lesson	Exercise	Remedy Blackline Master	Required Student Book Parts
A	5 or more	Test remedy below		9–A, 9–B	
B	2 or more	Item 1: 85	1	9–C	Lesson 85–A
		Item 2: 21	3	9–C	Lesson 21–C
		Item 3: 33	1	9–D	Lesson 33–A
		Item 4: 62	2	9–D	Lesson 62–B
		Item 5: 18	2	9–E	Lesson 18–B
		Item 6: 27	2	9–F	Lesson 27–A
		Item 7: 57	1		Lesson 57–A
C	1 or more	78	3		Lesson 78–C
		79	1		Lesson 79–A and E
D	2 or more	84	—	9–F	
		88	—	9–G	

Note: The teacher and each student who failed the test will need a copy of Remedy Blackline Master 9–A. The Remedy Blackline Masters can be found in Appendix H of the Teacher's Guide.

PART A TEST REMEDY

1. We're going to go over some items from the test. I'll read the items. You'll say the answers. Then you'll write the answers.

2. (Read item 1 in part A of Remedy Blackline Master 9–A) What's the answer? (Call on a student. Ideas: *Invented, painted, was a scientist.*)

3. (Repeat step 2 for items 2–9.)

4. (Give each student a copy of Remedy Blackline Master 9–A.)
   This worksheet shows the chart that was on the test.

5. Touch box 10.
   Everybody, what goes in that box? (Signal.) *Herbivores.*

6. (Repeat step 4 for each remaining box.)

7. Study the chart for a few minutes. Then you'll fill in the empty boxes.

8. (After several minutes:)
   Now you're going to write the answers to all the items in part A. Let's see who can get them all correct.

9. (After students complete the items:)
   Let's check your work. Use your pen to make an **X** next to any item you got wrong.

• (For items 1–9: Read the items. Call on individual students to answer each item.)

• (For chart items:) What goes in box 10? (Call on a student.) *Herbivores.*

• (Repeat for each remaining box.)

• Raise your hand if you got all the items correct. Nice work.

END OF MASTERY TEST 9

Note: Before beginning Lesson 91, present this Fact Game lesson. You will need a pair of dice for every four or five students. Each student needs a pencil and a Workbook.

EXERCISE 1

FACT GAME

1. (Divide the students into groups of four or five. Assign one player in each group to be the monitor. Seat the groups at different tables with a pair of dice.)
2. (Direct the players to open their Workbooks to page 285. Direct the monitors to open their Workbooks to page 285.)
3. You have 20 minutes to play the game. (Circulate as students play. Comment on groups that are playing well.)

Points for Fact Game

1. (At the end of 20 minutes, have all students who earned more than 12 points stand up. Award 5 bonus points to these players.)
2. (Award points to monitors. Monitors receive the same number of points earned by the highest performer in the group.)
3. (Tell the monitor of each game that ran smoothly:) Your group did a good job. Give yourself and each of your players 5 bonus points. ✓
4. Everybody, write your game points in Box FG on your Point Chart. Write your bonus points in the bonus box. ✓

Workbook page 285 — Fact Game 6

| 11 | 12 | 13 | 14 | 15 | 16 | 17 | 18 | 19 | 20 |
| 21 | 22 | 23 | 24 | 25 | 26 | 27 | 28 | 29 | 30 |

2. a. How many days did it take to deliver mail from St. Joseph, Missouri, to Sacramento, California, before the Pony Express?
   b. How long did mail delivery from St. Joseph to Sacramento take with the Pony Express?

3. Combine these sentences with **who** or **which**.

   Josie wants to read this book.
   This book is about training for races.

4. Tell which rule this argument breaks.

   If Jolene is such a great athlete, everyone in her family must be a great athlete.

5. Tell the conclusion for each piece of evidence.

   Rule: **All mammals are warm-blooded.**

   Evidence
   a. Snakes are not warm-blooded.
   b. Polar bears are mammals.

6. Tell the redundant part in each sentence.
   a. They moved to a remote house, far from town.
   b. The diamond, which was very clear, had a lot of clarity.

7. Say the model sentence that means this:

   A strange **event** caused the **fear** that she **showed**.

8. Tell which rule this argument breaks.

   If you don't want to have bad breath, use Rinso Mouthwash.

9. Tell the redundant part in each sentence.
   a. She was filled with sorrow and felt very sad.
   b. He hesitated at the top of the stairs, pausing for a minute.

10. a. Name two parasites that live on plants.
    b. Name three parasites that live on animals.

11. Combine these sentences with **therefore** or **however**.

    All of his clothes were dirty.
    He didn't do any laundry.

12. a. Name the three ingredients that plants need to manufacture their own food.
    b. What do we call animals that eat other animals?

Fact Game Answer Key — Workbook page 480

FACT GAME 5

2. a. Eyes, teeth
   b. No
3. a. Relevant
   b. Irrelevant
4. a. 2000
   b. 450
5. a. 2003
   b. 550
6. Just because you know about a part doesn't mean you know about another part.
7. They devised an appropriate strategy.
8. Just because you know about a whole thing doesn't mean you know about every part.
9. She wants to move that couch, which is very heavy.
10. Just because words are the same doesn't mean they have the same meaning.
11. He wrote a paper about Alice Walker, who is an author.
12. a. Braille
    b. Boycott

FACT GAME 6

2. a. 20 days
   b. 8 days
3. Josie wants to read this book, which is about training for races.
4. Just because you know about a part doesn't mean you know about the whole thing.
5. a. Snakes are not mammals.
   b. Polar bears are warm-blooded.
6. a. Far from town
   b. Had a lot of clarity
7. A strange phenomenon caused the anxiety that she exhibited.
8. Just because the writer presents some choices doesn't mean there aren't other choices.
9. a. Felt very sad
   b. Pausing
10. a. Mistletoe, dodder
    b. Any 3: Fleas, ticks, leeches, mosquitoes
11. All of his clothes were dirty; however, he didn't do any laundry.
12. a. Sunlight, water, carbon dioxide
    b. Carnivorous

Lesson Objectives	LESSON 91	LESSON 92	LESSON 93	LESSON 94	LESSON 95
	Exercise	Exercise	Exercise	Exercise	Exercise
Organization and Study Skills					
Main Idea	2	1	SB	SB	SB
Outlining			SB	SB	SB
Writing Mechanics: Copying	3	2	2	3	4
Reasoning Strategies					
Rules: Arguments	SB			WB	
Contradictions	SB	WB			
Inference	1				
Information Sources/Study Skills					
Basic Comprehension			SB	SB	SB
Interpretation: Maps/Pictures/Graphs	SB	SB		SB	
Supporting Evidence		SB	SB	SB	SB
Vocabulary/Language Arts Strategies					
Definitions	SB		1, WB	2, WB	3, WB
Usage	SB		1, WB	2, WB	3, WB
Editing/Revising	SB, WB	WB	WB	1, WB	1, WB
Comprehension: Meaning from Context					2, WB
Assessment/Progress Monitoring					
Ongoing: Workcheck	Workcheck	Workcheck	Workcheck	Workcheck	Workcheck

A Read the passage and look at the graph below. Then answer the questions on the next page. Answers to some of the questions are found in the passage. Answers to other questions are found in the graph. Some answers are found in both the passage and the graph.

> Ten thousand Americans in California died of scurvy in the year 1849 because they were cut off from a steady source of fresh fruits and vegetables. In the United States today, such an event would be unlikely. Modern machinery and new farming methods have made the land more productive than ever before. In addition, our transportation system makes fresh food available to nearly everyone.
>
> For all the problems that technology has solved, it has also created some problems. Specialized machines are now doing a large part of the hard physical work once done by humans. Automobiles have almost eliminated walking for some people. People's appetites, however, have not decreased as much as their exercise has.
>
> For the first time in history, millions of people are eating far more food than their bodies can use. In western Europe and in North America, excess weight is now recognized as a serious risk to the health of millions of people. Research shows that being as little as 10 percent overweight seriously increases the risk of early death.
>
> The graph shows how an increase in weight is related to early deaths in men. For men who are overweight by 10 percent, the number of early deaths is 13 percent over normal. At 20 percent overweight, the number of early deaths in men is 25 percent over normal. As the graph indicates, the percentage of early deaths increases as the amount that men are overweight increases.

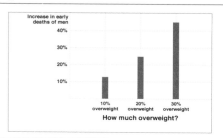

Write **Part A** in the left margin of your paper. Then number it from 1 to 12. Write the answers to the questions. Some of the questions ask where you found the answer. Use this key:

* Write **G** if the answer is in the graph.
* Write **P** if the answer is in the passage.
* Write **GP** if the answer is in both the passage and the graph. ⓐ

1. Tell one good effect of progress. ⓑ
2. Where did you find the answer to question 1? ⓒ
3. Is being extremely overweight more serious than being just a little overweight? ⓓ
4. Where did you find the answer to question 3? ⓔ
5. What's a good way to prevent scurvy? ⓕ
6. Where did you find the answer to question 5? ⓖ
7. As you become more overweight, what happens to your chances of dying?
8. Where did you find the answer to question 7?
9. For men who are 30 percent overweight, what is the expected increase in early deaths?
10. Where did you find the answer to question 9?
11. For men who are 20 percent overweight, what is the expected increase in early deaths?
12. Where did you find the answer to question 11?

B Write **Part B** in the left margin of your paper. Read the passage below.

> You will probably have many job interviews during your life. Knowing how to be interviewed is very important. You will do well on a job interview if you remember certain things. Here are a few pointers to keep in mind when you're being interviewed. First, make sure that your clothes are neat and well pressed. They don't have to be expensive or high-fashion clothes—just clean and ironed. If you look as if you care about yourself, the employer will think you will care about your job. The second thing to remember is to be on time for the interview. If you arrive late, your chances of getting hired are probably pretty small. A third point is to find out as much about the job as you can during the interview. Ask what kind of work you will be doing and what you will be paid. Ask about benefits, such as insurance and vacations. The last thing to remember is to be relaxed during an interview. Many people are so nervous when they are interviewed that the employer thinks they can't do the job. So if you smile, relax, and ask questions, your chances of getting hired are very good.

> **Note:** The circled letters indicate when you ask a question or when you direct the group to respond.

EXERCISE 1

STATEMENT INFERENCE

1. (Direct the students to find Lesson 91, part A, in the **Student Book**.)
2. (Call on individual students to read up to ⓖ.)

   ⓐ What are you going to write if the answer is on the graph? *G.*
   What are you going to write if the answer is in the passage? *P.*
   What are you going to write if the answer is both on the graph and in the passage? *GP.*

   ⓑ Figure out the answer. (Wait.)
   What's the answer? (Idea: *Modern machinery and new farming methods have made the land more productive than ever before; our transportation system makes fresh food available to nearly everyone.*)
   Write it. ✓

   ⓒ What's the answer? *In the passage.* So, what are you going to write? *P.*
   Do it. ✓

   ⓓ Figure out the answer. (Wait.)
   What's the answer? *Yes.* Write it. ✓

   ⓔ What's the answer? *On the graph and in the passage.* So, what are you going to write? *GP.* Do it. ✓

   ⓕ Figure out the answer. (Wait.)
   What's the answer? *Eat fresh fruits and vegetables.* Write it. ✓

   ⓖ What's the answer? *In the passage.* So, what are you going to write? *P.*
   Do it. ✓

3. Do the rest of the items. (Wait for the students to complete the items.) Let's check your answers. Put an **X** next to any item you miss.
4. (Read each item. Call on individual students to answer each item.)

Answer key for Student Book part A
1. *Idea: Modern machinery and new farming methods have made the land more productive than ever before; our transportation system makes fresh food available to nearly everyone.*
2. *P* **3.** *Yes* **4.** *GP* **5.** *Idea: Eat fresh fruits and vegetables.* **6.** *P* **7.** *They increase.* **8.** *GP* **9.** *45 percent* **10.** *G* **11.** *25 percent* **12.** *GP*

━━━━━━ **EXERCISE 2** ━━━━━━
MAIN IDEA
1. (Direct the students to find part B.)
2. (Call on individual students to read part B.)
   ⓗ (Call on three students to name one tip each. Idea: *Arrive on time; find out as much about the job as you can; be relaxed.*)
   ⓘ Copy the main idea and the four points. Raise your hand when you're done. ✓
   (As the students finish, check their work.)
   ⓙ Write the main idea and the three points. Raise your hand when you're done. ✓
   (As the students finish, check their work.)

Answer key for Student Book part B (Ideas:)
I. *What can happen if you write illegibly on a credit application* **A.** *The credit manager may not be able to figure out where you live.* **B.** *The credit manager may not be able to figure out who sent in the form.* **C.** *The credit manager may think you won't take care in repaying the loan.*

Write **Part A** in the left margin of your paper. Then number it from 1 to 12. Write the answers to the questions. Some of the questions ask where you found the answer. Use this key:

* Write **G** if the answer is in the graph.
* Write **P** if the answer is in the passage.
* Write **GP** if the answer is in both the passage and the graph. ⓔ

1. Tell one good effect of progress. ⓕ
2. Where did you find the answer to question 1? ⓖ
3. Is being extremely overweight more serious than being just a little overweight? ⓗ
4. Where did you find the answer to question 3? ⓘ
5. What's a good way to prevent scurvy? ⓙ
6. Where did you find the answer to question 5? ⓚ
7. As you become more overweight, what happens to your chances of dying?
8. Where did you find the answer to question 7?
9. For men who are 30 percent overweight, what is the expected increase in early deaths?
10. Where did you find the answer to question 9?
11. For men who are 20 percent overweight, what is the expected increase in early deaths?
12. Where did you find the answer to question 11?

B Write **Part B** in the left margin of your paper. Read the passage below.

> You will probably have many job interviews during your life. Knowing how to be interviewed is very important. You will do well on a job interview if you remember certain things. Here are a few pointers to keep in mind when you're being interviewed. First, make sure that your clothes are neat and well pressed. They don't have to be expensive or high-fashion clothes—just clean and ironed. If you look as if you care about yourself, the employer will think you will care about your job. The second thing to remember is to be on time for the interview. If you arrive late, your chances of getting hired are probably pretty small. A third point is to find out as much about the job as you can during the interview. Ask what kind of work you will be doing and what you will be paid. Ask about benefits, such as insurance and vacations. The last thing to remember is to be relaxed during an interview. Many people are so nervous when they are interviewed that the employer thinks they can't do the job. So if you smile, relax, and ask questions, your chances of getting hired are very good.

The main idea of the passage you just read is: **What to do on a job interview.**
The author gives four tips on what you should do on a job interview. The first tip is: **Make sure your clothes are clean and neat.** What are the other three tips? ⓛ
Copy the main idea and the four points on your paper just as they appear in the outline below. Label the main idea roman numeral one. To show that the points are under the main idea, indent them and label them **A, B, C,** and **D.**

I. What to do on a job interview
   A. Make sure your clothes are neat and clean.
   B. Arrive on time.
   C. Find out as much about the job as you can.
   D. Be relaxed. ⓜ

Read the passage below.

> Small details are very important when you apply for credit. An important reason that people are not given credit has to do with their handwriting. They write illegibly. The writing may be so poor that the credit manager cannot figure out where the person lives. The credit manager may not even be able to figure out who sent in the form. Sometimes the credit manager looks at the sloppy handwriting and concludes that if the person who is applying for credit does not take care in filling out the form, that person will not take care in repaying the loan.

The main idea of the passage is:
What can happen if you write illegibly on a credit application.
The author makes three points that fall under the main idea. Write the main idea and the three points in outline form. Label the points **A, B,** and **C,** and indent them under the main idea. ⓝ

C Write **Part C** in the left margin of your paper. You have two minutes to copy the paragraph below.

> **Some parasites attach themselves to animals. Other parasites attach themselves to plants. Dodder grows on the stalks of plants and sucks sap from them. Mistletoe is a part-time parasite that grows in the tops of trees and takes nourishment from them.**

Lesson 91 — Student Book page 188

★ **D** Write **Part D** in the left margin of your paper. Then number it 1 and 2. Here's an argument for where not to build a bicycle path.

> The proposed bicycle path should not be built in Goshen Park. Here's why.

- The bicycle path will have to be between four and five meters above the interstate highway to give trucks enough room to pass underneath.
- The interstate highway has four lanes.
- Bicyclists will have to dodge the traffic on the interstate highway.
- The proposed bicycle path will go through Goshen Park and cross the interstate highway.

It is obvious that crossing the interstate highway at Goshen Park will be very dangerous for bicyclists.

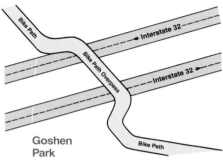

Goshen Park

1. Part of the argument is contradicted by the map. Which part is contradicted?
2. What does the map show?

1. Bicyclist will have to dodge the traffic on the interstate highway.
2. Idea: There will be an overpass for bicycles to cross the interstate highway.

Student Book page 189 — Lesson 91

E Write **Part E** in the left margin of your paper. In the passage below, there are eight underlined words. These words can be replaced with words from the model sentences you have learned. Rewrite the passage using the model-sentence words. Remember to start every sentence with a capital letter and to punctuate each sentence correctly.

> Pat was a mountain climber who had never experienced <u>fear</u>. As she neared the snowcapped mountain, she <u>paused</u>. She checked her route, but the map was <u>unclear</u>. Pat radioed base camp for help, but there was no <u>answer</u>. A light fog in the area <u>limited</u> visibility, but she continued to climb. Soon darkness fell and Pat had missed her last <u>chance</u> to turn back. Pat was lost, and as the night grew colder, she <u>showed fear</u> in her eyes for the first time.

EXERCISE 3

INDEPENDENT WORK

1. **[Optional]** (Direct the students to read the instructions for part C to themselves. Then give them exactly two minutes to copy the paragraph. Count as errors any miscopied words and punctuation. Deduct these errors from the number of copied words, and mark the total on the Writing Rate Graph.)
2. Finish the Student Book and do the Workbook for Lesson 91. ✓

Workcheck

1. Get ready to check your answers starting with **Student Book** part D. Use a pen to make an **X** next to any item you miss.
2. (Call on individual students to read each item and its answer. Repeat for Workbook items.)

> **Answer key for Student Book part E**
> *Pat was a mountain climber who had never experienced anxiety. As she neared the snow-capped mountain, she hesitated. She checked her route, but the map was ambiguous. Pat radioed base camp for help, but there was no response. A light fog in the area restricted visibility, but she continued to climb. Soon darkness fell, and Pat had missed her last opportunity to turn back. Pat was lost, and as the night grew colder, she exhibited anxiety in her eyes for the first time.*

3. (Direct students to count the number of errors and write the number in the error box at top of the Workbook page.)
4. (Award points and direct students to record their points in Box **W**.)

0 errors	15 points
1–2 errors	12 points
3–5 errors	8 points
6–9 errors	5 points

5. (Award any bonus points. Direct the students to total their points and enter the total on the Point Summary Chart.)
6. Show me your work when you've finished correcting it. (When the students show you their corrected work, record their points on your Record Summary Chart.)

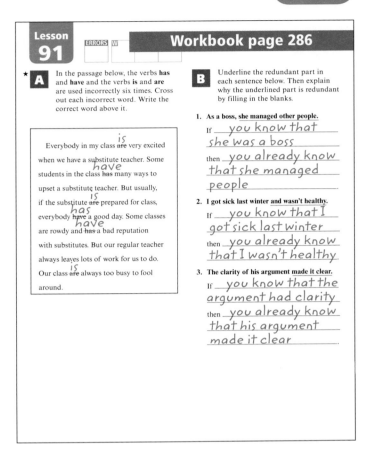

END OF LESSON 91

Lesson
92

Student Book page 190

A Write **Part A** in the left margin of your paper. Read the passage below.

Humans have gained power over all other animals. Humans have controlled the temperature of their environment, making it warm in winter and cool in summer. If humans are hungry, they don't have to go out and kill a deer or a rabbit—they merely go to the store and buy something to eat. How did humans become the most powerful of all? One possible reason for the power of humans is the human brain. The human brain is capable of figuring out problems that would stump any other animal. Another possible reason is that no other animal has hands with four fingers and a thumb that can touch each of the fingers. With these hands, humans made tools with which to kill other animals. Humans made fires to keep warm and shelters to protect themselves. Still another possible reason is that humans have a written language. With written language, humans transmitted ideas and accounts of the past. What one generation learned could be passed on to the next generation through written language.

This sentence expresses the main idea:
There are several possible reasons why humans have gained control over all other animals.
The author gives three points that fall under the main idea. What are those three points? Ⓐ
Write the main idea and the three points in outline form. Label the points **A, B,** and **C,** and indent them under the main idea. Ⓑ

B Write **Part B** in the left margin of your paper. You have two minutes to copy the paragraph below.

There are several reasons why humans have gained power over other animals. The human brain is capable of figuring out problems that other animals couldn't. Humans have four fingers and a thumb that can touch each of the fingers. Humans have a written language.

Student Book page 191

Lesson
92

★**C** Write **Part C** in the left margin of your paper. Then number it from 1 to 6. Read the story and answer the questions. Some of the questions are not answered in this passage, but you should already know the answers.

Not all scavengers are full-time scavengers. Some will kill when they are quite hungry and scavenge when it is more convenient to scavenge. Turtles, crows, and coyotes are part-time scavengers, but the bear is the most famous part-time scavenger. If you leave hot dogs on the grill in bear country, you may have a guest for dinner. You may find that your guest will eat nearly everything that you eat—pancakes, eggs, candy bars, and ice cream. The bear is not fussy. But don't be confused by the bear's willingness to let somebody else do the hunting. Bears can kill. You've probably seen pictures of bears fishing from streams. They make it look easy, but if you've ever tried grabbing a large, strong salmon from a stream, you'll know just how quick and how strong bears are. They can catch small animals that are fairly quick. And if a bear gets angry, it will attack nearly any animal, particularly if the bear is a mother with young cubs.

One of the most powerful bears is the grizzly, which is now nearly extinct. The grizzly is heavier than the black or brown bear. The grizzly is so heavy that it cannot climb trees. But the grizzly bear is like other bears in one important way. If it has a choice of hunting for a meal or taking a meal away from someone else, it will probably stand up on its back legs, make a lot of noise, and act as if it is the rightful owner of the meal!

1. What do scavengers eat?
2. How are parasites and scavengers the same?
3. How are parasites and scavengers different?
4. Name two part-time scavengers.
5. What do we mean when we say that grizzly bears are almost extinct?
6. How is a grizzly bear different from other kinds of bears?

Note: The circled letters indicate when you ask a question or when you direct the group to respond.

--- **EXERCISE 1** ---

MAIN IDEA

1. (Direct the students to find Lesson 92, part A, in the **Student Book**.)
2. (Call on individual students to read part A.)
   Ⓐ (Call on three students to name one reason each. Idea: *The human brain is capable of figuring out problems that other animals couldn't; humans have unique hands; humans have a written language.*)
   Ⓑ Write the main idea and the three points. Raise your hand when you're done. (As the students finish, check their work.)

> **Answer key for Student Book part A   (Ideas:)**
> **I.** *There are several possible reasons why humans have gained control over all other animals.*
>   **A.** *The human brain is capable of figuring out problems that other animals couldn't.*
>   **B.** *Humans have unique hands.*
>   **C.** *Humans have a written language.*

--- **EXERCISE 2** ---

INDEPENDENT WORK

1. **[Optional]** (Direct the students to read the instructions for part B to themselves. Then give them exactly two minutes to copy the paragraph. Count as errors any miscopied words and punctuation. Deduct these errors from the number of copied words, and mark the total on the Writing Rate Graph.)
2. Finish the Student Book and do the Workbook for Lesson 92. ✓

Workcheck

1. Get ready to check your answers starting with Student Book part C. Use a pen to make an **X** next to any item you miss.
2. (Call on individual students to read each item and its answer. Repeat for Workbook items.)

> **Answer key for Student Book part C (Ideas:)**
> **1.** *animals that are already dead* **2.** *They are both carnivores that don't kill to get their food.* **3.** *Parasites attach themselves to their food while it is alive; scavengers wait for their food to be killed or to die before eating it.* **4.** *turtles, crows, coyotes, and bears—any two* **5.** *There are not many grizzly bears still alive.* **6.** *It can't climb trees.*

> **Answer key for Student Book part E**
> *The ranger's expression exhibited his anxiety as he hesitated to observe the progress of the raging fire. The land near the river, once replete with wildlife and trees, was about to be converted into a barren wasteland. The firefighters were waiting anxiously for the ranger to devise a strategy to restrict the spreading fire. The situation was not the least bit ambiguous—they must act soon or lose the opportunity to contain the fire.*

Lesson 92

Student Book page 192

D Write **Part D** in the left margin of your paper. Then number it from 1 to 14. Read the passage and look at the map on the next page. Then write the answers to the questions.

> Sri Lanka is an island. India is the country that is closest to Sri Lanka. Sri Lanka was once the British colony of Ceylon, and gained its independence in 1948. It joined the United Nations in 1955.
>
> Sri Lanka has an area of about 25,600 square miles. Since it has about 18 million people, Sri Lanka is very crowded, with more than 700 people in every square mile. The capital of Sri Lanka is Colombo. Colombo is also Sri Lanka's largest city, with almost a million people.
>
> Sri Lanka exports tea, rubber, and coconut products. These products go mostly to Britain, the United States, Japan, India, and Germany.

Some of the questions below ask where you found the answer. Use this key:

* Write **M** if the answer is on the map.
* Write **P** if the answer is in the passage.
* Write **MP** if the answer is both on the map and in the passage.

1. What ocean surrounds Sri Lanka? the Indian Ocean
2. Where did you find the answer to question 1? M
3. What is Sri Lanka's nearest neighbor? India
4. Where did you find the answer to question 3? MP
5. What are Sri Lanka's most common exports? tea, rubber, coconut products
6. Where did you find the answer to question 5? P
7. On what river is Colombo located? Kelani
8. Where did you find the answer to question 7? M
9. When did Sri Lanka join the United Nations? 1955
10. Where did you find the answer to question 9? P
11. When did Sri Lanka gain independence? 1948
12. Where did you find the answer to question 11? P
13. What is the capital of Sri Lanka? Colombo
14. Where did you find the answer to question 13? MP

Student Book page 193

Lesson 92

E

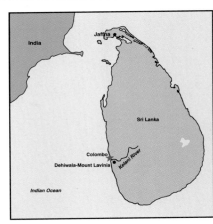

The symbol ★ means that the city is the capital of the country.

Write **Part E** in the left margin of your paper. In the passage below, the underlined words can be replaced with words from the model sentences you have learned. Rewrite the passage using the model-sentence words. Remember to start every sentence with a capital letter and to punctuate each sentence correctly.

> The ranger's expression showed his fear as he paused to observe the progress of the raging fire. The land near the river, once filled with wildlife and trees, was about to be changed into a barren wasteland. The fire fighters were waiting anxiously for the ranger to make up a plan to limit the spreading fire. The situation was not the least bit unclear—they must act soon or lose the chance to contain the fire.

3. (Direct the students to count the number of errors and write the number in the **error** box at the top of the Workbook page.)

4. (Award points and direct students to record their points in Box **W**.)

0 errors	**15 points**
1–2 errors	**12 points**
3–5 errors	**8 points**
6–9 errors	**5 points**

5. (Award any bonus points. Direct the students to total their points and enter the total on the Point Summary Chart.)

6. Show me your work when you've finished correcting it. (When the students show you their corrected work, record their points on your Record Summary Chart.)

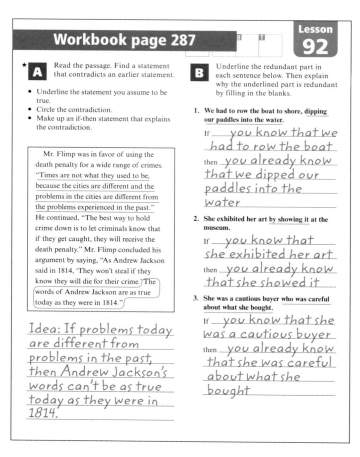

Workbook page 287

★ **A** Read the passage. Find a statement that contradicts an earlier statement.

- Underline the statement you assume to be true.
- Circle the contradiction.
- Make up an if-then statement that explains the contradiction.

> Mr. Flimp was in favor of using the death penalty for a wide range of crimes. "Times are not what they used to be, because the cities are different and the problems in the cities are different from the problems experienced in the past." He continued, "The best way to hold crime down is to let criminals know that if they get caught, they will receive the death penalty." Mr. Flimp concluded his argument by saying, "As Andrew Jackson said in 1814, 'They won't steal if they know they will die for their crime.' The words of Andrew Jackson are as true today as they were in 1814."

Idea: If problems today are different from problems in the past, then Andrew Jackson's words can't be as true today as they were in 1814.

B Underline the redundant part in each sentence below. Then explain why the underlined part is redundant by filling in the blanks.

1. We had to row the boat to shore, dipping our paddles into the water.

   If _you know that we had to row the boat_ then _you already know that we dipped our paddles into the water_

2. She exhibited her art by showing it at the museum.

   If _you know that she exhibited her art_ then _you already know that she showed it_

3. She was a cautious buyer who was careful about what she bought.

   If _you know that she was a cautious buyer_ then _you already know that she was careful about what she bought_

END OF LESSON 92

Note: The circled letters indicate when you ask a question or when you direct the group to respond.

A

Here are some words that we use to tell how often something happens:

- **Usually** means **most of the time.**
- **Occasionally** means **once in a while.**
- **Rarely** means **almost never.**

What word means **most of the time?**
What word means **once in a while?** Ⓑ
What word means **almost never?** Ⓒ

Here's a sentence with a word that means she did it most of the time:
    She <u>usually</u> went to the store.
Say the sentence with a word that means she did it most of the time. Ⓓ
Say the sentence with a word that means she did it once in a while. Ⓔ
Say the sentence with a word that means she almost never did it. Ⓕ

Write **Part A** in the left margin of your paper. Then number it from 1 to 3. For each item, write a sentence that uses the word **usually, occasionally,** or **rarely.**

1. The girl (most of the time) rode her bike to school. *usually*
2. Those hunters (almost never) shot any ducks. *rarely*
3. (Once in a while) that dog comes onto our porch. *occasionally*

B

Write **Part B** in the left margin of your paper. You have two minutes to copy the paragraph below.

> Not all scavengers are full-time scavengers. Some will kill when they are quite hungry and scavenge when it is more convenient to scavenge. Turtles, crows, and coyotes are part-time scavengers, but the bear is the most famous part-time scavenger.

EXERCISE 1

DEFINITIONS

1. (Direct the students to find Lesson 93, part A, in the **Student Book**.)
2. (Call on individual students to read up to Ⓕ.)
   - Ⓐ What word? *Usually.*
   - Ⓑ What word? *Occasionally.*
   - Ⓒ What word? *Rarely.*
   - Ⓓ Say it. *She usually went to the store.*
   - Ⓔ Say it. *She occasionally went to the store.*
   - Ⓕ Say it. *She rarely went to the store.*
3. Read the instructions and do the items. ✓ Let's check your answers. Put an **X** next to any item you miss.
4. (Read each item. Call on individual students to answer each item.)

EXERCISE 2

INDEPENDENT WORK

1. **[Optional]** (Direct the students to read the instructions for part B to themselves. Then give them exactly two minutes to copy the paragraph. Count as errors any miscopied words and punctuation. Deduct these errors from the number of copied words, and mark the total on the Writing Rate Graph.)
2. Finish the Student Book and do the Workbook for Lesson 93. ✓

Workcheck

1. Get ready to check your answers starting with Student Book part C. Use a pen to make an **X** next to any item you miss.
2. (Call on individual students to read each item and its answer. Repeat for Workbook items.)

Student Book page 195

★ **C** Write **Part C** in the left margin of your paper. Read the passage below.

When you hear a piece of music, you may listen for the sound of each instrument, or you may listen to the sound of all the instruments blended together. In an orchestra, there are four major sections of sound. The first section is the woodwinds, and it contains instruments such as oboes and clarinets. The woodwind instruments are some of the earliest instruments ever devised by humans. The second section of the orchestra contains the stringed instruments, such as violins and cellos. Another section is the brass section, which contains horns such as trumpets, French horns, and tubas. The last section is one you are all familiar with. The percussion section contains such instruments as drums, chimes, and clashing cymbals. This section maintains the rhythm of a piece of music. The next time you listen to a CD or attend a concert, try to listen to each separate section of the orchestra. You will learn a lot about how the different sounds of the instruments blend together.

This sentence expresses the main idea:
There are four major types of instruments in an orchestra.
The author makes four points that fall under the main idea. Write the main idea and the four points in outline form. Label the points **A, B, C,** and **D,** and indent them under the main idea.

D Write **Part D** in the left margin of your paper. Then number it from 1 to 12. Read the passages that follow. Then write the answers to the questions.

Passage A. Diamonds are now being mined from the ocean floor. Most of the diamonds from the ocean are of a higher quality than those from land. All of the undersea mining is done with huge vacuum cleaners that suck the gravel off the ocean floor. Every ton of gravel yields about one carat in diamonds. But there are some disadvantages to ocean mining. When the gravel is removed, the creatures that live there are disturbed. Then the processed gravel is dumped back into the sea, leaving huge brown clouds of silt and sand in the water. By the time the mining is done, the environment is no longer suitable for many of the ocean animals.

Student Book page 196

Passage B. Diamonds are being mined from the floor of the ocean. This practice has been questioned by some leading economists. They contend that the practice presents two serious problems. The first is the damage to the underwater environment. Vacuuming material from the bottom of the ocean disturbs the underwater life as far as eight kilometers from the mining site.
The second problem is the value of diamonds. According to the economists, the major mines in Africa could mine diamonds at ten times their present rate if they wished. They do not mine at this rate, however, because the value of diamonds would drop. A diamond valued at $1,000 would not be as rare as it is now, and the price might drop to $100. The mines produce diamonds at a slow rate so that the value of diamonds stays high. But what will happen if large amounts of diamonds are mined from the ocean floor? The value of diamonds will drop and everyone will suffer, including the ocean miners. They will have to work hard to mine gems that are not very valuable.

Some of the questions below ask where you found the answer. Use this key:

- Write **A** if the answer is found in passage A.
- Write **B** if the answer is found in passage B.
- Write **AB** if the answer is found in both passage A and passage B.

1. What kind of mining is being done on the ocean floor?
2. Where did you find the answer to question 1?
3. How are ocean diamonds different from land diamonds?
4. Where did you find the answer to question 3?
5. Why do diamond mines produce diamonds at a slow rate?
6. Where did you find the answer to question 5?
7. How many carats of diamonds does one ton of ocean gravel yield?
8. Where did you find the answer to question 7?
9. How does the vacuuming process affect sea creatures?
10. Where did you find the answer to question 9?
11. What will happen to the value of diamonds if large amounts of diamonds are mined from the ocean floor?
12. Where did you find the answer to question 11?

Answer key for Student Book part C (Ideas:)

I. *There are four major types of instruments in an orchestra.*
  A. *Woodwind*
  B. *Stringed*
  C. *Brass*
  D. *Percussion*

Answer key for Student Book part D
1. Idea: *Diamond mining* **2.** *AB*
3. Idea: *They are of a higher quality.* **4.** *A*
5. Idea: *So that their value stays high* **6.** *B* **7.** *One*
8. *A* **9.** Idea: *It disturbs their environment so that it is no longer suitable for them to live in.* **10.** *A*
11. Idea: *The value of diamonds will drop.* **12.** *B*

3. (Direct the students to count the number of errors and write the number in the **error** box at the top of the Workbook page.)
4. (Award points and direct students to record their points in Box **W.**)

0 errors	15 points
1–2 errors	12 points
3–5 errors	8 points
6–9 errors	5 points

5. (Award any bonus points. Direct the students to total their points and enter the total on the Point Summary Chart.)
6. Show me your work when you've finished correcting it. (When the students show you their corrected work, record their points on your Record Summary Chart.)

Workbook page 288

★ **A** Write the verb **has** or **have** in each blank.

1. Nobody with brains _has_ any reason to worry.

2. Some players on the team _have_ gotten their tickets already.

3. You _have_ a good opportunity to be first in line.

4. The rain in those four counties _has_ ruined all the crops.

5. Wrestlers on the squad _have_ to do a lot of push-ups.

6. One of the vacationers _has_ more than one boat.

B Underline the redundant part in each sentence below. Then explain why the underlined part is redundant by filling in the blanks.

1. The music created a sad mood, <u>filling us with a feeling of sorrow.</u>

If _you know that the music created a sad mood_

then _you already know that it filled us with a feeling of sorrow_

2. He was no longer afraid <u>when he lost his fear.</u>

If _you know that he was no longer afraid_

then _you already know that he lost his fear_

3. They devised a new sales strategy <u>by making up a new sales plan.</u>

If _you know that they devised a new sales strategy_

then _you already know that they made up a new sales plan_

Workbook page 289

C Noreen sometimes has trouble using the words **who** and **which**. Below is a report she wrote. Cross out the words **who** and **which** if they are used incorrectly. Write the correct word above every crossed-out word.

People ~~which~~ *who* climb mountains are often very interesting. Some of the most interesting mountain climbers are people ~~which~~ *who* climb for a living. These people are called Sherpas, and they live near very high mountains, ~~who~~ *which* are both dangerous and beautiful. These mountains, which are called the Himalayas, have many peaks over 25,000 feet high. The Sherpas guide visitors who come to climb the Himalayas. They often accompany the climbers ~~which~~ *who* hire them to tops of mountains. Mount Everest, ~~who~~ *which* is the highest mountain in the world, was first climbed by a person who was a Sherpa.

D Rewrite each sentence below, using the word **usually, occasionally,** or **rarely.**

1. The girl (almost never) went to football games.

   The girl rarely went to football games.

2. (Once in a while) Tom likes to study.

   Occasionally, Tom likes to study.

3. It (almost never) rains in the desert.

   It rarely rains in the desert.

4. (Most of the time) Lynn and Ann walk home together.

   Usually, Lynn and Ann walk home together.

END OF LESSON 93

Student Book page 197

A

There is a redundant part in each sentence below.

* **The ambiguity of the situation was increased by the unclearness of what was happening.**
What's the redundant part? Ⓐ
Why is that part redundant? Ⓑ
* **At a rapid pace, she moved quickly.**
What's the redundant part? Ⓒ
Why is that part redundant? Ⓓ

B

Here are some words that we use to tell how often something happens:

* **Usually** means **most of the time.**
* **Occasionally** means **once in a while.**
* **Rarely** means **almost never.**

What word means **most of the time?** Ⓔ
What word means **once in a while?** Ⓕ
What word means **almost never?** Ⓖ
 Here's a sentence with a word that means we do it almost never: **We rarely go jogging in the morning.**
Say the sentence with a word that means we do it almost never. Ⓗ
Say the sentence with a word that means we do it once in a while. Ⓘ
Say the sentence with a word that means we do it most of the time. Ⓙ

Write **Part B** in the left margin of your paper. Then number it from 1 to 3. For each item, write a sentence that uses the word **usually, occasionally,** or **rarely.**

1. Tilly is home (once in a while) by 4 o'clock. *occasionally*
2. Chad (almost never) watches television. *rarely*
3. They (once in a while) play tennis after school. *occasionally*

C

Write **Part C** in the left margin of your paper. You have two minutes to copy the paragraph below.

You will probably have many job interviews during your life. When you go for an interview, remember to dress neatly, arrive on time, ask questions, and be relaxed. If you remember these things, your chances of getting hired will be much better.

Note: The circled letters indicate when you ask a question or when you direct the group to respond.

═══════ **EXERCISE 1** ═══════

EDITING

1. (Direct the students to find Lesson 94, part A, in the **Student Book**.)
2. (Call on individual students to read part A.)
   Ⓐ What's the answer? *The unclearness of what was happening.*
   Ⓑ (Call on a student. Idea: *If the situation was ambiguous, you already know that what was happening was unclear.*)
   Ⓒ What's the answer? Quickly.
   Ⓓ (Call on a student. Idea: *If you know that she moved at a rapid pace, you already know that she moved quickly.*)

═══════ **EXERCISE 2** ═══════

DEFINITIONS

1. (Direct the students to find part B.)
2. (Call on individual students to read part B.)
   Ⓔ What word? *Usually.*
   Ⓕ What word? *Occasionally.*
   Ⓖ What word? *Rarely.*
   Ⓗ Say it. *We rarely go jogging in the morning.*
   Ⓘ Say it. *We occasionally go jogging in the morning.*
   Ⓙ Say it. *We usually go jogging in the morning.*
3. Read the instructions and do the items. ✓ Let's check your answers. Put an **X** next to any item you miss.
4. (Read each item. Call on individual students to answer each item.)

EXERCISE 3

INDEPENDENT WORK

1. **[Optional]** (Direct the students to read the instructions for part C to themselves. Then give them exactly two minutes to copy the paragraph. Count as errors any miscopied words and punctuation. Deduct these errors from the number of copied words, and mark the total on the Writing Rate Graph.)

2. Finish the Student Book and do the Workbook for Lesson 94. ✓

Workcheck

1. Get ready to check your answers starting with Student Book part D. Use a pen to make an **X** next to any item you miss.

2. (Call on individual students to read each item and its answer. Repeat for Workbook items.)

Answer key for Student Book part D (Ideas:)
I. *There are three basic types of cheese.*
  A. *Hard cheese*
  B. *Semisoft cheese*
  C. *Soft cheese*

Answer key for Student Book part E
1. *$19,000* **2.** *P* **3.** *Idea: Her job* **4.** *GP*
5. *Idea: Insurance policies, Social Security* **6.** *P*
7. *$15,000* **8.** *P* **9.** *Idea: House payments* **10.** *GP*
11. *Idea: House payments, food, new clothes, car payments, and miscellaneous items* **12.** *GP*

★ **D**   Write **Part D** in the left margin of your paper. Read the passage below.

> Probably one of the oldest meals in human history is bread and cheese. If you are interested in experimenting with cheeses, remember that there are three basic types. Hard cheeses, which include Swiss and cheddar, are very popular in the United States. Semisoft cheeses include Muenster, Gouda, and mozzarella. Mozzarella is good for cooking, since it melts easily and blends well with other flavors. It is a cheese you eat in pizza and many other Italian dishes. Soft cheeses are often eaten for dessert. Soft cheeses include Camembert and Brie. These cheeses have an edible "crust," which adds to their unique flavor. The next time you're too full for a dessert like pie or ice cream, try a wedge of Camembert—you may be pleasantly surprised.

This sentence expresses the main idea: **There are three basic types of cheese.** The author makes three points that fall under the main idea. Write the main idea and the three points in outline form. Label the points **A**, **B**, and **C**, and indent them under the main idea.

E   Write **Part E** in the left margin of your paper. Then number it from 1 to 12. Read the passage and look at the graphs on the next page. Then write the answers to the questions.

> Like most adults, Sharon receives income every year. Her income for last year was $19,000. Not everybody receives income in the same way that Sharon does. Some people receive income from insurance policies. Sharon doesn't. Some people have Social Security income. Sharon doesn't. Sharon receives most of her income from her job. She works as a secretary and earns $15,000 per year.
> Sharon's income is shown in graph 1. The largest part is from her secretarial job. The smaller parts of the graph show that Sharon receives money from her stocks and from renting out her garage. Graph 2 shows what Sharon does with her income. The largest part shows that she spends the greatest amount of her money on house payments. Her other expenses are for food, new clothes, car payments, and miscellaneous items.

Graph 1. Income   Graph 2. Expenses

Some of the questions below ask where you found the answer. Use this key:

- Write **G** if the answer is in one of the graphs.
- Write **P** if the answer is in the passage.
- Write **GP** if the answer is both in a graph and in the passage.

1. What was Sharon's income last year?
2. Where did you find the answer to question 1?
3. Where does most of Sharon's income come from?
4. Where did you find the answer to question 3?
5. What are some other kinds of income besides the ones Sharon has?
6. Where did you find the answer to question 5?
7. How much does Sharon make at her job?
8. Where did you find the answer to question 7?
9. What is Sharon's largest expense?
10. Where did you find the answer to question 9?
11. Name all the things that Sharon spends her money on.
12. Where did you find the answer to question 11?

Lesson 94 — Workbook page 290

ERRORS W

★ **A** Rewrite each sentence below, using the word **usually, occasionally,** or **rarely.**

1. Our baseball team (almost never) wins.
   Our baseball team rarely wins.

2. (Once in a while) Sarah likes to sing.
   Occasionally, Sarah likes to sing.

3. Tom is (most of the time) a good student.
   Tom is usually a good student.

B Underline the redundant part in each sentence that follows. Then explain why the underlined part is redundant.

1. I found his repetitive statements redundant.
   Idea: If you know that his statements were repetitive, then you already know that they were redundant.

2. I know that we've made progress because we have moved forward.
   Idea: If you know that we've made progress, then you already know that we have moved forward.

3. He had the kind of bird that has wings, feathers, and two legs.
   Idea: If you know that he had a bird, then you already know that the bird had wings, feathers, and two legs.

C Each argument that follows is faulty.

We know that our mayor belongs to the Zeep Club, a club which does not allow black people or women to be members. We can hardly expect the mayor to give all people equal consideration in the course of his duties. We should elect someone new to run our city.

1. What does the author want us to conclude?
   Idea: The mayor should be replaced because of his membership in the Zeep Club.

Workbook page 291 — Lesson 94

2. How could you show that the argument is faulty?
   Idea: Find out whether or not the mayor gives all people equal consideration in the course of his duties.

I can prove beyond any doubt that Abraham Lincoln was never president of the United States. In the mid-1800s, when he was supposed to be president, there were over thirty million people in the United States. There was only one president. The chance of any one person being president was 1 in 30 million. When the odds get this small, we can say there is just about no chance of any one person being president. Therefore, Lincoln could not have been president.

3. What does the author want us to conclude?
   Idea: Abraham Lincoln's chances of being president were so small that he couldn't have been president.

Good steaks are rare these days. You shouldn't order yours well done.

4. What does the author want us to conclude?
   Idea: Good steaks are hard to come by; therefore, you should eat them only slightly cooked.

5. How could you show that the argument is faulty?
   Idea: Show that part of the evidence has more than one meaning.

3. (Direct the students to count the number of errors and write the number in the **error** box at the top of the Workbook page.)
4. (Award points and direct students to record their points in Box **W**.)

0 errors	**15 points**
1–2 errors	**12 points**
3–5 errors	**8 points**
6–9 errors	**5 points**

5. (Award any bonus points. Direct the students to total their points and enter the total on the Point Summary Chart.)
6. Show me your work when you've finished correcting it. (When the students show you their corrected work, record their points on your Record Summary Chart.)

END OF LESSON 94

Note: The circled letters indicate when you ask a question or when you direct the group to respond.

EXERCISE 1

EDITING

1. (Direct the students to find Lesson 95, part A, in the **Student Book**.)
2. (Call on individual students to read part A.)
   - Ⓐ What's the answer? *That did not agree with each other.*
   - Ⓑ (Call on a student. Idea: *If his argument was full of inconsistent parts, you already know that the parts did not agree with each other.*)

EXERCISE 2

MEANING FROM CONTEXT

1. (Direct the students to find part B.)
2. (Call on individual students to read part B.)
   - Ⓒ What does **notorious** probably mean? *Well known.*
   - Ⓓ (Call on a student. Idea: *Because parts of the passage contradict the idea that notorious means kind.*)
   - Ⓔ (Call on a student. Idea: *His crimes were notorious for their daring and success.*)
   - Ⓕ What does **magnanimous** probably mean? *Generous.*
   - Ⓖ (Call on students. Ideas: *Her magnanimous behavior wins her many friends.*)
   - Ⓗ What does **malaise** probably mean? *A feeling of depression.*
   - Ⓘ (Call on a student. Ideas: *One rainy Sunday, a deep malaise engulfed me, making me feel sad without knowing exactly why.*)

Lesson 95

Student Book page 200

A

There is a redundant part in the sentence below.

- **His argument was full of inconsistent parts that did not agree with each other.**

What's the redundant part? ⊖
Why is that part redundant? ⊖

B

Each passage below contains a word you may not know.

> Jesse James was a <u>notorious</u> outlaw, wanted in several states for robbery and murder. His crimes were notorious for their daring and success. As he held up more and more banks, he became more notorious. Hundreds of articles and books were written about him. He became so notorious that many other outlaws began to imitate him.

Notorious probably means:

a velvety texture   well known   pudgy   kind ⊖

How do you know that **notorious** does not mean **a velvety texture?** We know this because parts of the passage contradict the idea that **notorious** means **a velvety texture.** The passage indicates that Jesse James was a notorious outlaw, and a person is not usually described as having a velvety texture.

How do you know that **notorious** does not mean **pudgy?** Because parts of the passage contradict the idea that **notorious** means **pudgy.** The passage indicates that his crimes were notorious for their daring and success.

How do you know that **notorious** does not mean **kind?** ⊖
Find a sentence in the passage that contradicts the idea that **notorious** means **kind.** ⊖
Here's another passage:

> She is so <u>magnanimous</u> that she would give her last dollar to a friend or her last bit of food to a hungry dog. Her magnanimous behavior wins her many friends. Sometimes I am afraid that she is too magnanimous and that people might try to take advantage of her.

Magnanimous probably means:

a form of cabbage   generous   stingy ⊖

Find a sentence in the passage that contradicts the idea that **magnanimous** means **stingy.** ⊖

Student Book page 201

Lesson 95

Here's another passage:

> One rainy Sunday, a deep <u>malaise</u> engulfed me, making me feel sad without knowing exactly why. I was restless and dissatisfied, wanting to cry, but I had no reason to weep. I had a family, a home, a job—what caused this malaise? I was alone and lonely, and I felt that I belonged to nothing and to no one.

Malaise probably means:

mayonnaise mixed with lemon   a feeling of cheerfulness
a feeling of depression ⊖

Find a sentence in the passage that contradicts the idea that **malaise** means **a feeling of cheerfulness.** ⊖

C

You learned some words that tell how often something happens.
What word means **almost never?** ⊖
What word means **once in a while?** ⊖
What word means **most of the time?** ⊖

Here's a sentence: **They <u>usually</u> went to the movies.**
Say that sentence with a word that means they went once in a while. ⊖
Say that sentence with a word that means they went most of the time. ⊖
Say that sentence with a word that means they almost never went. ⊖

Write **Part C** in the left margin of your paper. Then number it from 1 to 3. For each item, write a sentence that uses the word **usually, occasionally,** or **rarely.**

1. He (almost never) eats in a restaurant.   *rarely*
2. (Most of the time) she does her laundry on Saturday.   *usually*
3. The Chan family (almost never) takes a vacation.   *rarely*

D

Write **Part D** in the left margin of your paper. You have two minutes to copy the paragraph below.
Here's another passage:

> **There are three basic types of cheese. The group of hard cheeses includes Swiss and cheddar. The group of semisoft cheeses includes Muenster, Gouda, and mozzarella. The last group of cheeses is the soft cheeses, including Camembert and Brie.**

Student Book page 201

Here's another passage:

> One rainy Sunday, a deep <u>malaise</u> engulfed me, making me feel sad without knowing exactly why. I was restless and dissatisfied, wanting to cry, but I had no reason to weep. I had a family, a home, a job—what caused this malaise? I was alone and lonely, and I felt that I belonged to nothing and to no one.

Malaise probably means:

mayonnaise mixed with lemon   a feeling of cheerfulness
a feeling of depression ⓔ

Find a sentence in the passage that contradicts the idea that **malaise** means **a feeling of cheerfulness.** ⓕ

C You learned some words that tell how often something happens.
What word means **almost never?** ⓖ
What word means **once in a while?** ⓗ
What word means **most of the time?** ⓘ

Here's a sentence: They <u>usually</u> went to the movies.
Say that sentence with a word that means they went once in a while. ⓙ
Say that sentence with a word that means they went most of the time. ⓚ
Say that sentence with a word that means they almost never went. ⓛ

Write **Part C** in the left margin of your paper. Then number it from 1 to 3. For each item, write a sentence that uses the word **usually, occasionally,** or **rarely.**

1. He (almost never) eats in a restaurant. *rarely*
2. (Most of the time) she does her laundry on Saturday. *usually*
3. The Chan family (almost never) takes a vacation. *rarely*

D Write **Part D** in the left margin of your paper. You have two minutes to copy the paragraph below.
Here's another passage:

> There are three basic types of cheese. The group of hard cheeses includes Swiss and cheddar. The group of semisoft cheeses includes Muenster, Gouda, and mozzarella. The last group of cheeses is the soft cheeses, including Camembert and Brie.

Student Book page 202

★ **E** Write **Part E** in the left margin of your paper. Read the passage below.

> Because desert animals don't have many opportunities to drink water, they need desert plants. These plants provide the animals with both food and water. To protect themselves from the animals that feed on them, these plants have developed some strange defenses. One is thorns. If you've ever seen a prickly pear cactus, you know how hard it is to touch one without getting thorns in your hand. The leaves of other plants contain sour and sometimes poisonous juices. Still other plants do not have appetizing leaves—only leathery stems that tempt very few animals. These unattractive physical characteristics prevent desert animals from eating certain desert plants.

This sentence expresses the main idea: **Desert plants have ways to defend themselves.** The author makes three points that fall under the main idea. Write the main idea and the three points in outline form. Label the points **A, B,** and **C,** and indent them under the main idea.

F Write **Part F** in the left margin of your paper. Then number it 1 and 2. Here's a fact: **The fins of whales do not have the same name as the fins of fish.**

1. In what kind of reference book would you look to find evidence to support this fact? *an encyclopedia*
2. Read the passage below and write the name for the fins of whales. *flukes*

> When we study bones of ancient animals, we discover that the whale was once a land animal. Because whales used the sea for their food, their bodies changed over the centuries so that they were better adapted to live in the water. Their front legs became little flippers while their back legs became fins, called flukes. Today, whales do not live on land; in fact, they cannot live on land. Their skeletons could not support the weight of their bodies. If a whale is washed up on shore, it may die simply because its body is so heavy that its lungs collapse. When a whale's lungs collapse, the whale cannot breathe and it dies.

===== **EXERCISE 3** =====

DEFINITIONS

1. (Direct the students to find part C.)
2. (Call on individual students to read up to ⓞ.)
   ⓙ What word? *Rarely.*
   ⓚ What word? *Occasionally.*
   ⓛ What word? *Usually.*
   ⓜ Say it. *They occasionally went to the movies.*
   ⓝ Say it. *They usually went to the movies.*
   ⓞ Say it. *They rarely went to the movies.*
3. Read the instructions and do the items. ✓ Let's check your answers. Put an **X** next to any item you miss.
4. (Read each item. Call on individual students to answer each item.)

===== **EXERCISE 4** =====

INDEPENDENT WORK

1. **[Optional]** (Direct the students to read the instructions for part D to themselves. Then give them exactly two minutes to copy the paragraph. Count as errors any miscopied words and punctuation. Deduct these errors from the number of copied words, and mark the total on the Writing Rate Graph.)
2. Finish the Student Book and do the Workbook for Lesson 95. ✓

Workcheck

1. Get ready to check your answers starting with Student Book part E. Use a pen to make an **X** next to any item you miss.
2. (Call on individual students to read each item and its answer. Repeat for Workbook items.)

Answer key for Student Book part E (Ideas:)
I. *Desert plants have ways to defend themselves.*
  A. *Some have thorns.*
  B. *Some have sour or poisonous juices in their leaves.*
  C. *Some have leathery and unattractive stems.*

3. (Direct the students to count the number of errors and write the number in the **error** box at the top of the Workbook page.)

4. (Award points and direct students to record their points in Box **W.**)

0 errors	15 points
1–2 errors	12 points
3–5 errors	8 points
6–9 errors	5 points

5. (Award any bonus points. Direct the students to total their points and enter the total on the Point Summary Chart.)

6. Show me your work when you've finished correcting it. (When the students show you their corrected work, record their points on your Record Summary Chart.)

END OF LESSON 95

ERRORS W **Workbook page 292**

★ **A** The passage below contains a word you may not know. Read the passage and answer the questions.

The owner of the house felt that windows are very important, so you can understand why the house was so well fenestrated. The fenestration, which had been laid out by an architect who loved stained glass, allowed much light and air into all the rooms. When the sunlight came through the stained glass, the rooms shone with the glory of colored light.

1. Circle the answer.

Fenestration probably means:

ceiling
light
(the arrangement of windows)

2. Write any sentence from the passage that contradicts the idea that **fenestration** means **light.**

The fenestration, which had been laid out by an architect who loved stained glass, allowed much light and air into all the rooms.

B Underline the redundant part in each sentence that follows. Then explain why the underlined part is redundant.

1. He bought the kind of automobile that is designed to take people from one place to another.

Idea: If you know he bought an automobile, then you already know that it takes people from one place to another.

2. My apartment had been robbed, and some of my things had been stolen.

Idea: If you know that my apartment had been robbed, then you already know that some of my things had been stolen.

3. He was a salesperson who sold things.

Idea: If you know that he was a salesperson, then you already know that he sold things.

Workbook page 293

C Rewrite each sentence below, using the word **usually, occasionally,** or **rarely.**

1. Ron (once in a while) likes to watch television.

Ron occasionally likes to watch television.

2. He (almost never) brushes his teeth.

He rarely brushes his teeth.

3. Oranges are (most of the time) sweet and juicy.

Oranges are usually sweet and juicy.

Lesson Objectives

Lesson Objectives	LESSON 96 Exercise	LESSON 97 Exercise	LESSON 98 Exercise	LESSON 99 Exercise	LESSON 100 Exercise
Organization and Study Skills					
Main Idea	SB	SB	2, SB	SB	SB
Outlining			SB	SB	SB
Writing Mechanics: Copying	3	3	3	2	1
Reasoning Strategies					
Evidence					WB
Rules: Arguments	2	2, WB			
Statements: Ought	2	WB	WB		WB
Contradictions			1	1	SB
Information Sources/Study Skills					
Reading Comprehension: Words of Deductions	WB				
Supporting Evidence				WB	SB
Vocabulary/Language Arts Strategies					
Definitions	WB		WB	WB	SB, WB
Usage	WB		WB	WB	SB, WB
Editing/Revising	WB	WB	WB	WB	WB
Comprehension: Meaning from Context	1	1	WB	WB	
Information Application/ Study Skills					
Information Review	WB		WB	WB	
Assessment/Progress Monitoring					
Ongoing: Workcheck	Workcheck	Workcheck	Workcheck	Workcheck	Workcheck
Formal: Mastery Test					MT10

Lesson

96

Student Book page 203

A

Each passage below contains a word you may not know.

> Sherry was in an ebullient mood, joking and singing while she worked. The people around her were infected with her ebullience and started laughing and playing. Sherry grinned ebulliently, a wide-toothed grin of such joy that even the boss stopped yelling at everyone and slunk back into his office.

Ebullient probably means: **sad**   **joyful**   **purple** ⊖
  Find a sentence in the passage that contradicts the idea that **ebullient** means **sad.** ⊖
  Find a sentence in the passage that contradicts the idea that **ebullient** means **purple.** ⊕
  Here's another passage:

> My mother taught me that it was uncouth to chew with my mouth open. She claimed that it was a disgusting sight. Since then I have been angered by other people who are uncouth enough to talk while they eat. People with beautiful manners delight me; unfortunately, there seem to be many more people with uncouth habits, particularly at the dinner table.

Uncouth probably means:

understandable   **a box**   **graceful**   **vulgar** ⊕

  Find a sentence in the passage that contradicts the idea that **uncouth** means **understandable.** ⊖
  Find a sentence in the passage that contradicts the idea that **uncouth** means **a box.** ⊖
  Find a sentence in the passage that contradicts the idea that **uncouth** means **graceful.** ⊕

B

Some statements tell what we should do or what ought to happen. These statements often contain the word **ought** or **should.** These statements tell how things ought to be, so they are called **statements of ought.** Here are some statements of ought:

* People should not go near the ocean during a bad storm.
* You should obey your parents.
* You ought to get enough sleep and exercise.

> **Note:** The circled letters indicate when you ask a question or when you direct the group to respond.

════ EXERCISE 1 ════

MEANING FROM CONTEXT

1. (Direct the students to find Lesson 96, part A, in the **Student Book**.)
2. (Call on individual students to read part A.)

   🅐 What does **ebullient** probably mean? *Joyful.*

   🅑 (Call on a student. Ideas: *Sherry was in an ebullient mood, joking and singing while she worked.*)

   🅒 (Call on a student. Idea: *The people around her were infected with her ebullience and started laughing and playing.*)

   🅓 What does **uncouth** probably mean? *Vulgar.*

   🅔 (Call on a student. Idea: *Since then, I have been angered by other people who are uncouth enough to talk while they eat.*)

   🅕 (Call on a student. Idea: *My mother taught me that it was uncouth to chew with my mouth open.*)

   🅖 (Call on a student. Idea: *Since then, I have been angered by other people who are uncouth enough to talk while they eat.*)

EXERCISE 2
ANALYZING ARGUMENTS

1. (Direct the students to find part B.)
2. (Call on individual students to read part B.)
   Ⓗ What kind of statement? *Statement of fact.*
   Ⓘ What kind of statement? *Statement of fact.*
   Ⓙ What kind of statement? *Statement of ought.*
   Ⓚ What kind of statement? *Statement of ought.*
   Ⓛ What kind of statement? *Statement of ought.*
   Ⓜ What kind of statement? *Statement of fact.*
   Ⓝ What kind of statement? *Statement of fact.*
   Ⓞ What kind of statement? *Statement of ought.*
   Ⓟ What kind of statement? *Statement of fact.*
   Ⓠ What kind of statement? *Statement of ought.*
   Ⓡ What kind of statement? *Statement of ought.*
   Ⓢ What kind of statement? *Statement of fact.*
   Ⓣ What kind of statement? *Statement of fact.*
   Ⓤ What kind of statement? *Statement of ought.*

EXERCISE 3
INDEPENDENT WORK

1. **[Optional]** (Direct the students to read the instructions for part C to themselves. Then give them exactly two minutes to copy the paragraph. Count as errors any miscopied words and punctuation. Deduct these errors from the number of copied words, and mark the total on the Writing Rate Graph.)
2. Finish the Student Book and do the Workbook for Lesson 96. ✓

Student Book page 203 — Lesson 96

A Each passage below contains a word you may not know.

> Sherry was in an <u>ebullient</u> mood, joking and singing while she worked. The people around her were infected with her ebullience and started laughing and playing. Sherry grinned ebulliently, a wide-toothed grin of such joy that even the boss stopped yelling at everyone and slunk back into his office.

Ebullient probably means: sad   joyful   purple   ⓐ
   Find a sentence in the passage that contradicts the idea that **ebullient** means **sad**. ⓑ
   Find a sentence in the passage that contradicts the idea that **ebullient** means **purple**. ⓒ
   Here's another passage:

> My mother taught me that it was <u>uncouth</u> to chew with my mouth open. She claimed that it was a disgusting sight. Since then I have been angered by other people who are uncouth enough to talk while they eat. People with beautiful manners delight me; unfortunately, there seem to be many more people with uncouth habits, particularly at the dinner table.

Uncouth probably means:

   understandable   a box   graceful   vulgar   ⓓ

   Find a sentence in the passage that contradicts the idea that **uncouth** means **understandable**. ⓔ
   Find a sentence in the passage that contradicts the idea that **uncouth** means **a box**. ⓕ
   Find a sentence in the passage that contradicts the idea that **uncouth** means **graceful**. ⓖ

B Some statements tell what we should do or what ought to happen. These statements often contain the word **ought** or **should**. These statements tell how things ought to be, so they are called **statements of ought**. Here are some statements of ought:

* People should not go near the ocean during a bad storm.
* You should obey your parents.
* You ought to get enough sleep and exercise.

Student Book page 204 — Lesson 96

Some statements simply tell what is or what happens. These are not statements of ought. They are **statements of fact**. Statements of fact do **not** tell how things ought to be. They tell how things are. Here are some statements of fact:

* Nearly half of the people in Canada go to the doctor once a year.
* On the average, people who get enough sleep and exercise live three years longer than people who don't.
* Children who obey their parents usually don't get into as much trouble.
* In Peru, seven people were drowned in the surf because they went near the ocean during a bad storm.

Tell whether each statement below is a **statement of ought** or a **statement of fact**.
1. He went swimming. ⓐ
2. He wanted to go swimming. ⓑ
3. We should go swimming. ⓒ
4. People ought to eat the right kinds of food. ⓓ
5. We should outlaw nuclear power. ⓔ
6. He exercised every day. ⓕ
7. Exercising makes the body stronger. ⓖ
8. You ought to exercise. ⓗ
9. Smoking is dangerous to your health. ⓘ
10. People shouldn't smoke. ⓙ
11. Cars with bigger engines should be outlawed. ⓚ
12. Cars with bigger engines burn more gas than cars with smaller engines. ⓛ
13. Many people throw garbage along the highway. ⓜ
14. We ought to stop people from throwing garbage along the highway. ⓝ

C Write **Part C** in the left margin of your paper. You have two minutes to copy the paragraph below.

> Desert plants provide desert animals with both food and water. To protect themselves from the animals that feed on them, many desert plants have developed some strange defenses. Some of these defenses are sharp thorns, poisonous or sour juices, and leathery stems.

Student Book page 205

Lesson 96

D Write **Part D** in the left margin of your paper. Then number it from 1 to 3.
Here are three main ideas:

> Main idea A. Living things protect themselves from desert sun.
> Main idea B. Some living things can produce water from fat.
> Main idea C. Living things can sleep through dry spells.

Each main idea fits one of the passages below. After reading all the passages, figure out which main idea goes with each passage.

Passage 1. There are many ways in which living things adapt to a desert environment. During the months when there is almost no water to be found, many animals hibernate. This means that they curl up in a safe place and sleep for a long period of time. Because they are sleeping and using very little energy, fat in the animals' bodies can last a long time. Some animals can hibernate for many weeks without becoming weak. When water becomes more plentiful, they wake up and resume an active life.

Passage 2. There are many ways in which living things adapt to a desert environment. The camel is an interesting example of how desert creatures survive without much water. When a camel eats and drinks, extra food is stored in its hump in the form of fat. Later, when there is nothing to eat or drink, the fat in this hump is digested by the camel. As the fat is digested, hydrogen is released. As the camel breathes, oxygen from the air combines with the hydrogen. The combination of these two elements is H_2O—water!

Passage 3. There are many ways in which living things adapt to a desert environment. Human beings have developed many different ways to cope with the heat of the harsh sun. For example, members of a certain tribe in Australia wear very little clothing. They do most of their hunting for food in the early morning hours and at dusk, when the sun is not so hot. In the daytime, they sleep in holes dug in the ground, or rest in the shade of trees. Tribes in the Sahara Desert survive in a very different fashion. To protect themselves from the blistering heat, they wrap themselves with many layers of clothing. Using clothes for insulation works well as long as you don't work too hard.

1. Which passage does main idea A best fit? *passage 3*
2. Which passage does main idea B best fit? *passage 2*
3. Which passage does main idea C best fit? *passage 1*

Workcheck

1. Get ready to check your answers starting with Student Book part D. Use a pen to make an **X** next to any item you miss.
2. (Call on individual students to read each item and its answer. Repeat for Workbook items.)
3. (Direct the students to count the number of errors and write the number in the **error** box at the top of the Workbook page.)
4. (Award points and direct students to record their points in Box **W**.)

0 errors	15 points
1–2 errors	12 points
3–5 errors	8 points
6–9 errors	5 points

5. (Award any bonus points. Direct the students to total their points and enter the total on the Point Summary Chart.)
6. Show me your work when you've finished correcting it. (When the students show you their corrected work, record their points on your Record Summary Chart.)

Lesson 96

96 ERRORS W **Workbook page 294**

A Read the passage below and answer the questions. Circle **W** if the question is answered by words in the passage. Circle **D** if the question is answered by a deduction. If you circle **W** for an item, underline the words in the passage that give the answer.

<u>Any living thing is called an organism.</u> Some organisms, such as a monkey or an oak tree, are very complicated. Other organisms are very small and simple. Some are so small that we cannot see them without using a strong magnifying glass. Millions of these small organisms live in our bodies. The picture shows what you might see if you looked at a speck of saliva through a microscope. Some of the organisms you see have hairs and move like worms. Others are shaped like spirals. Still others look like little disks.

Different types of organisms live in different parts of our body. They perform different jobs. If we didn't have some types of organisms in our blood, our body couldn't fight diseases. When unwanted organisms get in the blood, the organisms that protect the body fight them and try to get rid of them. Other organisms help us digest different kinds of food.

These tiny organisms are also found outside the body. A drop of water from a lake is loaded with such organisms. If the water is clean, there are fewer organisms than there are in polluted or dirty water.

Polluted water makes people sick, because it contains organisms that can overpower the organisms in the body. When these outside organisms win, the person gets sick. Often, the person will develop a fever. Drugs, such as penicillin, contain very strong organisms that can usually overpower the outside organisms.

1. What do we call any living thing?
<u>an organism</u> (W) D
2. Which has more organisms in it, tap water or sewer water?
<u>sewer water</u> W (D)
3. Why is polluted water dangerous to people?
<u>Idea: It contains organisms that can overpower organisms in the body and make people sick.</u>
4. How does penicillin work?
<u>Idea: It contains very strong organisms that can overpower the organisms that are making a person sick.</u>

Workbook page 295

5. Fill in the empty box below.

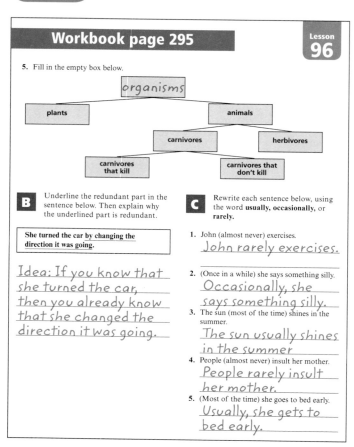

B Underline the redundant part in the sentence below. Then explain why the underlined part is redundant.

> She turned the car <u>by changing the direction it was going.</u>

Idea: If you know that she turned the car, then you already know that she changed the direction it was going.

C Rewrite each sentence below, using the word **usually, occasionally,** or **rarely.**

1. John (almost never) exercises.
   John rarely exercises.

2. (Once in a while) she says something silly.
   Occasionally, she says something silly.

3. The sun (most of the time) shines in the summer.
   The sun usually shines in the summer

4. People (almost never) insult her mother.
   People rarely insult her mother.

5. (Most of the time) she goes to bed early.
   Usually, she gets to bed early.

Workbook page 297

E In the passage below, the verbs **has** and **have** are used incorrectly five times. Cross out each incorrect word. Write the correct word above it.
There are also three redundant parts in the passage below. Cross out each redundant part.

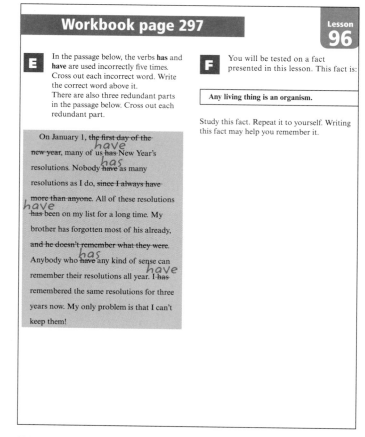

On January 1, ~~the first day of the new year,~~ many of us *have* ~~has~~ New Year's resolutions. Nobody *has* ~~have~~ as many resolutions as I do, ~~since I always have more than anyone.~~ All of these resolutions *have* ~~has~~ been on my list for a long time. My brother has forgotten most of his already, ~~and he doesn't remember what they were.~~ Anybody who *has* ~~have~~ any kind of sense can remember their resolutions all year. I *have* ~~has~~ remembered the same resolutions for three years now. My only problem is that I can't keep them!

F You will be tested on a fact presented in this lesson. This fact is:

> Any living thing is an organism.

Study this fact. Repeat it to yourself. Writing this fact may help you remember it.

END OF LESSON 96

Workbook page 296

D Each passage that follows contains a word you may not know. Read each passage and answer the questions.

- Sue has a habit of doing and saying the most <u>malapropos</u> things, embarrassing everyone around her. For instance, we all went bowling the other night. The red velvet evening gown she wore, which she tripped on all night, was quite malapropos. Some of the things she says are also malapropos. When her sister showed off her newborn baby, Sue said, "That little thing is bald and ugly." Her sister didn't think that was the right thing to say.

1. Circle the answer. **Malapropos** probably means:
   (inappropriate)   intelligent   lazy

2. Write any sentence from the passage that contradicts the idea that **malapropos** means **intelligent.**

   Idea: Sue has a habit of doing and saying the most malapropos things, embarrassing everyone around her.

- The handsome musketeer had such <u>panache</u> that all the ladies loved him. The way he swept off his hat and kissed their hands, the dashing way he had of leaping onto his horse and galloping off—these things thrilled the ladies at court. He always had a witty remark and was never afraid. Other young soldiers tried to copy his panache.

3. Circle the answer. **Panache** probably means:
   pancake   greediness   (a dashing charm)

4. Write any sentence from the passage that contradicts the idea that **panache** means **pancake.**

   Idea: The way he swept off his hat and kissed their hands, the dashing way he had of leaping onto his horse and galloping off — these things thrilled the ladies at court.

Lesson 97 — Student Book page 206

A The passage below contains a word you may not know.

> That rich old man is so penurious that he saves his broken shoelaces and uses them for dental floss. He wouldn't loan a dime to his best friend. His house is falling apart, but he refuses to spend money on fixing it up. What good is all his money if he's too penurious to spend it?

Penurious probably means: **generous**   **handkerchief**   **stingy** Ⓐ

Find a sentence in the passage that contradicts the idea that **penurious** means **generous**. Ⓑ

Find a sentence in the passage that contradicts the idea that **penurious** means **handkerchief**. Ⓒ

B Statements of ought always tell how things ought to be. Statements of fact simply tell what is true.

Tell whether each statement below is a **statement of ought** or a **statement of fact.**

* Their goal was to climb the mountain.
  What kind of statement? Ⓓ
* We should climb that mountain.
  What kind of statement? Ⓔ
* They ought to stop at Mike's house after school.
  What kind of statement? Ⓕ
* They were supposed to stop at Mike's house after school.
  What kind of statement? Ⓖ
* They stopped at Mike's house after school.
  What kind of statement? Ⓗ

C Write **Part C** in the left margin of your paper. You have two minutes to copy the paragraph below.

> Any living thing is called an organism. Some organisms are so small that we cannot see them without using a strong magnifying glass. Different types of organisms live in different parts of our body and they perform different jobs for us.

Note: The circled letters indicate when you ask a question or when you direct the group to respond.

=== EXERCISE 1 ===
MEANING FROM CONTEXT

1. (Direct the students to find Lesson 97, part A, in the **Student Book**.)
2. (Call on individual students to read part A.)
   Ⓐ What does **penurious** probably mean? *Stingy.*
   Ⓑ (Call on a student. Idea: *He wouldn't loan a dime to his best friend.*)
   Ⓒ (Call on a student. Idea: *That rich old man is so penurious that he saves his broken shoelaces and uses them for dental floss.*)

=== EXERCISE 2 ===
ANALYZING ARGUMENTS

1. (Direct the students to find part B.)
2. (Call on individual students to read part B.)
   Ⓓ What's the answer? *Statement of fact.*
   Ⓔ What's the answer? *Statement of ought.*
   Ⓕ What's the answer? *Statement of ought.*
   Ⓖ What's the answer? *Statement of fact.*
   Ⓗ What's the answer? *Statement of fact.*

=== EXERCISE 3 ===
INDEPENDENT WORK

1. **[Optional]** (Direct the students to read the instructions for part C to themselves. Then give them exactly two minutes to copy the paragraph. Count as errors any miscopied words and punctuation. Deduct these errors from the number of copied words, and mark the total on the Writing Rate Graph.)
2. Finish the Student Book and do the Workbook for Lesson 97. ✓

Workcheck

1. Get ready to check your answers starting with Student Book part D. Use a pen to make an **X** next to any item you miss.

2. (Call on individual students to read each item and its answer. Repeat for Workbook items.)

3. (Direct the students to count the number of errors and write the number in the **error** box at the top of the Workbook page.)

4. (Award points and direct students to record their points in Box **W**.)

0 errors	**15 points**
1–2 errors	**12 points**
3–5 errors	**8 points**
6–9 errors	**5 points**

5. (Award any bonus points. Direct the students to total their points and enter the total on the Point Summary Chart.)

6. Show me your work when you've finished correcting it. (When the students show you their corrected work, record their points on your Record Summary Chart.)

Student Book page 207

D Write **Part D** in the left margin of your paper. Then number it from 1 to 3.
Here are three main ideas:

> **Main idea A. Plants respond to noise around them.**
> **Main idea B. Plants are different from animals.**
> **Main idea C. Plants protect themselves from predators.**

Each main idea fits one of the passages below. After reading all the passages, figure out which main idea goes with each passage.

Passage 1. Plants differ greatly from animals. For instance, animals, including human beings, breathe in oxygen and exhale carbon dioxide. Plants do just the opposite—they "breathe in" carbon dioxide and "exhale" oxygen. Plants are also the only living things that can make their own food, using sunlight, water, and carbon dioxide.

Passage 2. Plants differ greatly from other living things, but there is one danger they share with almost all other forms of life—predators. Some desert plants have developed spikes and thick outer fibers to discourage animals from eating them. Many plants, such as walnut and filbert trees, drop seeds that are protected by hard outer shells. Like all other living things, plants have developed their own survival skills.

Passage 3. Plants differ greatly from animals. They don't have eyes, and they don't talk, bark, crawl, or run. They don't seem to have much in common with animals, but recently scientists have made some interesting discoveries. They have found that plants grow poorly when exposed to harsh, jarring music, and they grow well when exposed to soothing music. This indicates that plants respond to sound. Plants may not be able to see, touch, smell, or taste, but they can "hear."

1. Main idea A is: **Plants respond to noise around them.** Which passage does main idea A fit best? _passage 3_
2. Main idea B is: **Plants are different from animals.** Which passage does main idea B fit best? _passage 1_
3. Main idea C is: **Plants protect themselves from predators.** Which passage does main idea C fit best? _passage 2_

Workbook page 298

A Write whether each statement below is a **statement of ought** or a **statement of fact.**

1. Lula ought to get a job.
   statement of ought
2. Lula wants to get a job.
   statement of fact
3. People shouldn't drive after they've drunk alcohol.
   statement of ought
4. People who drive after drinking alcohol often have accidents.
   statement of fact

B Each argument that follows breaks one of these rules:

> **Rule 1.** Just because two things happen around the same time doesn't mean one thing causes the other thing.
> **Rule 2.** Just because you know about a part doesn't mean you know about the whole thing.
> **Rule 3.** Just because you know about a part doesn't mean you know about another part.
> **Rule 4.** Just because you know about the whole thing doesn't mean you know about every part.
> **Rule 5.** Just because words are the same doesn't mean they have the same meaning.
> **Rule 6.** Just because the writer presents some choices doesn't mean there aren't other choices.

After each argument below, write the number of the rule the argument breaks.

1. Nitrogen helps the soil, and Burno Insecticide not only kills unwanted insects but contains nitrogen. Therefore, Burno Insecticide is good for your soil. _2_

2. I'm afraid that Frank is becoming an alcoholic. You know that alcoholics don't eat very much. Well, Frank has eaten almost nothing in the last three days. _1_

3. Look at the group of people who smoke more than one package of cigarettes a day. The people in this group will not live as long as the people who do not smoke. The average life expectancy of smokers is four years less than the average of the nonsmoking group. My aunt Sarah smokes more than one package of cigarettes a day. You know what that means? She will not live as long as the average person who does not smoke. _4_

4. Remember this: The constitution of the United States guarantees citizens the right to own guns. These guns were needed when the nation was young. Guns were used for hunting and for protecting property and loved ones. Now the government is talking about preventing people from owning guns. Guns are part of the freedom that we are guaranteed. Take away our guns and you take away our freedom. So, the question is simple: Do we have guns, or are we to become slaves of the government? _6_

Workbook page 299

C Underline the redundant part in the sentence below. Then explain why the underlined part is redundant.

The soldier returned <u>by coming back home</u>.

Idea: If you know that the soldier returned, then you already know that the soldier came back home.

D Each passage that follows contains a word you may not know. Read each passage and answer the questions.

• My <u>fubsy</u> mother really should go on a diet. In fact, most of my family is fubsy. We were raised on meat and potatoes, and it shows. My dad and brother are the only thin ones—all the rest of us need to lose at least ten pounds. It's no fun to be fubsy.

1. Circle the answer.
   Fubsy probably means:

   skinny   old   (fat)

2. Write any sentence from the passage that contradicts the idea that **fubsy** means **skinny**.

   Idea: My fubsy mother really should go on a diet.

• Little <u>niggling</u> details drive me crazy. Take paper clips, for instance. I'm always losing them, and a niggling thing like that costs me hours of time. Another niggling detail I sometimes forget is to replace the cap on the toothpaste tube. It seems strange that such tiny details can sometimes cause so many problems.

3. Circle the answer.
   Niggling probably means:

   (petty or small)   important   blue

4. Write any sentence from the passage that contradicts the idea that **niggling** means **important**.

   Idea: It seems strange that such tiny details can sometimes cause so many problems.

Workbook page 300

• When he told her boss that she wasn't good at her job and that she was a slob, he <u>maligned</u> her very badly. And he was quite wrong. But his maligning remarks resulted in her being fired. She's suing him now, and I'll bet she wins the case. Maybe next time he'll think twice about saying nasty things about people.

5. Circle the answer.
   Malign probably means:

   cheer someone up
   talk to a boss
   (speak badly about someone)

6. Write any sentence from the passage that contradicts the idea that **malign** means **cheer someone up.**

   Idea: When he told her boss that she wasn't good at her job and that she was a slob, he maligned her very badly.

E Rewrite each sentence that follows, using the word **usually, occasionally,** or **rarely.**

1. My brother (almost never) goes to bed early.

   My brother rarely goes to bed early.

2. (Once in a while) Fred goes to the movies.

   Occasionally, Fred goes to the movies.

3. We (most of the time) eat our biggest meal in the evening.

   We usually eat our biggest meal in the evening.

4. The woman (almost never) ate a large dinner.

   The woman rarely ate a large dinner.

5. (Most of the time) our football team wins.

   Usually, our football team wins.

F You will be tested on a fact presented in this lesson. This fact is:

> Plants are different from animals in several ways: (a) plants "breathe in" carbon dioxide; (b) plants "exhale" oxygen; and (c) plants make their own food.

Study the fact. Repeat it to yourself. Writing this fact may help you remember it.

END OF LESSON 97

Student Book page 208

A Written accounts about an event don't always agree. The two accounts below tell about the same event. The accounts contradict each other on an important point. When you read these accounts, look for the contradiction.

Passage 1. Last night, the police were on the scene of an accident as it happened. The police car was behind a black sedan at a four-way intersection. A blue sedan failed to stop, skidded through the intersection, and sailed into the black sedan, inflicting serious damage to both vehicles. Almost before the two drivers could step from their cars, Officer Jeffrey Daniels had his ticket pad in hand. Fortunately, nobody was injured; however, Officer Daniels wasted no time in issuing two tickets to Sidney Grapp, driver of the blue vehicle. One ticket was for failing to stop at a stop sign, and the other was for driving without proper control of the vehicle. According to city officials, Officer Daniels now holds the record for issuing tickets quickly. The accident occurred at 9:34 p.m., and the tickets were issued by 9:37 p.m. This record may stand for some time.

Passage 2. Last night, a blue sedan drove past a stop sign. As the sedan crossed the intersection, the driver slammed on the brakes and the car nearly came to a stop before hitting a black sedan. The driver of the blue sedan slowly stepped from his car to assess the damage. He commented that the only damage to the black sedan was a little scratch in the side of the car and a dented hubcap. The driver of the blue sedan then looked at his own vehicle. The front bumper, the grill, and the hood were badly dented. The damages amounted to over $1000. The driver of the blue sedan was later ticketed for $100 because he had failed to stop at a stop sign.

These accounts contradict each other on one big point. What point is that? ⊙

Write **Part A** in the left margin of your paper. Then number it from 1 to 12. Answer each question. Some of the questions ask where you found an answer. Write **passage 1, passage 2,** or **passages 1 and 2** for these questions.

1. At what time did the accident take place?
2. Where did you find the answer to question 1?
3. How many dollars' worth of damage did the blue sedan suffer?
4. Where did you find the answer to question 3?
5. Which vehicle was at fault?
6. Where did you find the answer to question 5?
7. What parts of the blue sedan were damaged?
8. Where did you find the answer to question 7?
9. Who was in the car behind the black sedan?
10. Where did you find the answer to question 9?
11. How did the police officer set a record?
12. Where did you find the answer to question 11?

Note: The circled letters indicate when you ask a question or when you direct the group to respond.

=== **EXERCISE 1** ===

CONTRADICTIONS

1. (Direct the students to find Lesson 98, part A, in the **Student Book**.)
2. (Call on individual students to read up to Ⓐ.)
   Ⓐ (Call on a student. Idea: *How much damage the black sedan suffered.*)
3. Read the instructions and do the items. ✓ Let's check your answers. Put an **X** next to any item you miss.
4. (Read each item. Call on individual students to answer each item.)

Answer key for Student Book part A
1. *9:34 P.M.*   2. *Passage 1*   3. *Over $1,000*
4. *Passage 2*   5. *The blue sedan*   6. *Passages 1 and 2*   7. *Idea: The front bumper, the grill, and the hood*   8. *Passage 2*   9. *Idea: A policeman*
10. *Passage 1*   11. *Idea: By issuing tickets so quickly* 12. *Passage 1*

Student Book page 209

B Write **Part B** in the left margin of your paper. Read the passage below.

All animals need water. A camel can drink up to 100 liters of water in a few minutes. The grasshopper mouse drinks very little, obtaining most of its water from the insects it eats. There are three basic ways in which animals can obtain water. The first and most obvious way is to drink it. A human being working in the heat of a desert must drink a lot of water—about eight liters a day! A second way of obtaining water is through food. The grasshopper mouse eats insects, which may be up to 85 percent water. Some animals can derive all the water they need from plants. A third way to obtain water is to manufacture it, as the camel does.

This sentence expresses the main idea:
Animals obtain water in different ways.
The author makes three points that fall under the main idea. What are those three points? ⊙

Write the main idea and the three points in outline form. Label the points **A, B,** and **C,** and indent them under the main idea. ⊖

C Write **Part C** in the left margin of your paper. You have two minutes to copy the paragraph below.

Plants don't seem to have much in common with animals, but recently scientists have made some interesting discoveries. They found that plants grow poorly when exposed to harsh, jarring music, and that they grow well when exposed to soothing music.

━━━━━ EXERCISE 2 ━━━━━

MAIN IDEA

1. (Direct the students to find part B.)
2. (Call on individual students to read part B.)

   Ⓑ (Call on three students to name one point each. Idea: *Some drink it; some get it through food; some manufacture it themselves.*)

   Ⓒ Write the main idea and the three points. Raise your hand when you're done. ✓

> **Answer key for Student Book part B** (Ideas:)
> **I.** *Animals obtain water in different ways.*
>   **A.** *Some animals drink their water.*
>   **B.** *Some animals get their water from food.*
>   **C.** *Some animals manufacture water.*

━━━━━ EXERCISE 3 ━━━━━

INDEPENDENT WORK

1. **[Optional]** (Direct the students to read the instructions for part C to themselves. Then give them exactly two minutes to copy the paragraph. Count as errors any miscopied words and punctuation. Deduct these errors from the number of copied words, and mark the total on the Writing Rate Graph.)
2. Finish the Student Book and do the Workbook for Lesson 98. ✓

Student Book page 209

Ⓑ Write **Part B** in the left margin of your paper. Read the passage below.

> All animals need water. A camel can drink up to 100 liters of water in a few minutes. The grasshopper mouse drinks very little, obtaining most of its water from the insects it eats. There are three basic ways in which animals can obtain water. The first and most obvious way is to drink it. A human being working in the heat of a desert must drink a lot of water—about eight liters a day! A second way of obtaining water is through food. The grasshopper mouse eats insects, which may be up to 85 percent water. Some animals can derive all the water they need from plants. A third way to obtain water is to manufacture it, as the camel does.

This sentence expresses the main idea:
   Animals obtain water in different ways.
The author makes three points that fall under the main idea. What are those three points? ⊕

Write the main idea and the three points in outline form. Label the points **A, B,** and **C,** and indent them under the main idea. ⊕

Ⓒ Write **Part C** in the left margin of your paper. You have two minutes to copy the paragraph below.

> **Plants don't seem to have much in common with animals, but recently scientists have made some interesting discoveries. They found that plants grow poorly when exposed to harsh, jarring music, and that they grow well when exposed to soothing music.**

Student Book page 210

★ Ⓓ Write **Part D** in the left margin of your paper. Read the passage below.

> When the Old West was being settled, there were no cars, airplanes, trains, or buses. People devised several ways to haul supplies, passengers, and mail between the east coast and the west coast. The "bull train" was one early type of transportation. It was an ordinary train of wagons pulled by oxen. Bull trains hauled freight from Missouri to California, a distance of about 2,000 miles. The stagecoaches were another means of transporting freight and people. Six horses pulled a stage at a rate of about five miles an hour. Bull trains took about two months to haul freight between Missouri and California, while stagecoaches took several weeks to make the same journey. The Pony Express was another early form of transportation. A rider rode his horse at a dead run for a short distance and then exchanged his tired horse for a fresh one. In this way, it took the mail only eight days to get across the country. Perhaps the least-known means of early transportation in the United States was camels. The camels were well suited to hauling things between Texas and California. Americans were familiar with horses, mules, and oxen, but they couldn't figure out how to deal with camels, so many camels were turned loose in the desert.

This sentence expresses the main idea:
   There were several means of transportation in the Old West.
The author makes four points that fall under the main idea. Write the main idea and the four points in outline form. Label the points **A, B, C,** and **D,** and indent them under the main idea.

Workcheck

1. Get ready to check your answers starting with Student Book part D. Use a pen to make an **X** next to any item you miss.

2. (Call on individual students to read each item and its answer. Repeat for Workbook items.)

Answer key for Student Book part D (Ideas:)

I. *There were several means of transportation in the Old West.*

  A. *The bull train*
  B. *The stagecoach*
  C. *The Pony Express*
  D. *The camel*

---

3. (Direct the students to count the number of errors and write the number in the **error** box at the top of the Workbook page.)

4. (Award points and direct students to record their points in Box **W.**)

0 errors	**15 points**
1–2 errors	**12 points**
3–5 errors	**8 points**
6–9 errors	**5 points**

5. (Award any bonus points. Direct the students to total their points and enter the total on the Point Summary Chart.)

6. Show me your work when you've finished correcting it. (When the students show you their corrected work, record their points on your Record Summary Chart.)

Workbook page 301 — Lesson 98

★ A Rewrite each sentence below, using the word **usually, occasionally,** or **rarely.**

1. Our basketball team (almost never) loses a game.
   <u>Our basketball team rarely loses a game.</u>

2. I (most of the time) go to the movies on a Saturday.
   <u>I usually go to the movies on Saturday.</u>

3. She likes to stay at home (once in a while).
   <u>She likes to stay at home occasionally.</u>

4. Most people (almost never) go ice-skating in the summer.
   <u>Most people rarely go ice-skating in the summer.</u>

5. (Most of the time) Jane goes to the grocery store after work.
   <u>Usually, Jane goes to the grocery store after work.</u>

B In the passage below, the verbs **was** and **were** are used incorrectly six times. Cross out each incorrect word. Write the correct word above it.

There are also three redundant parts in the passage below. Cross out each redundant part.

Last summer I ~~were~~ *was* camping up at Gold Lake with my best friend, ~~who I like better than any other pal.~~ I had never been camping before, so she ~~were~~ *was* showing me how to do everything, ~~since it was a new experience for me.~~ We pitched the tent and gathered firewood. She ~~were~~ *was* up there to go fishing, so we went down to the river, ~~which were~~ *was* near our campsite. While we ~~was~~ *were* down there, she taught me how to cast a line out into the water. We caught trout for dinner ~~and cooked them up for our evening meal.~~ It ~~were~~ *was* tons of fun.

C Write whether each statement below is a **statement of ought** or a **statement of fact.**

1. The death penalty is being used again in several states.
   <u>statement of fact</u>

2. We should outlaw the death penalty.
   <u>statement of ought</u>

3. Canada depends heavily on oil imports.
   <u>statement of fact</u>

4. Mike likes to go to the game.
   <u>statement of fact</u>

Lesson 98 — Workbook page 302

D Each passage contains a word you may not know. Read each passage and answer the questions.

• They took the prisoner in for interrogation. He was taken to the interrogation room, where three officers began to question him. The interrogation consisted of thousands of questions asked over and over by the officers.

1. Circle the answer.
   Interrogation probably means:
   sleeping   eating   (questioning)

2. Write any sentence from the passage that contradicts the idea that **interrogation** means **sleeping.**
   <u>Idea: The interrogation consisted of thousands of questions asked over and over by the officers.</u>

• She tenaciously held onto her position in the argument. Everybody tried to attack what she said, but she would not give an inch. She fought back. She was so tenacious that the people who tried to attack her argument finally got tired and gave up. She won the argument because she was so tenacious.

3. Circle the answer.
   Tenacious probably means:
   tenderness   timid   (stubborn)

4. Write any sentence from the passage that contradicts the idea that **tenacious** means **to be timid.**
   <u>Idea: Everybody tried to attack her, but she would not give an inch.</u>

• His problem was that he was too loquacious. In fact, he never shut up. He talked all the time, day and night. He was so loquacious that people would avoid him. They couldn't stand to hear him talk, talk, talk, talk, talk.

5. **Loquacious** probably means:
   (talkative)   lazy   shy   skinny

6. Write any sentence from the passage that contradicts the idea that **loquacious** means **shy.**
   <u>Idea: In fact, he never shut up.</u>

E Underline the redundant part in the sentence below. Then explain why the underlined part is redundant.

The little girl raced down the street on a tricycle <u>with three wheels.</u>

<u>Idea: If you know that it is a tricycle, then you already know that it has three wheels.</u>

END OF LESSON 98

> **Note:** The circled letters indicate when you ask a question or when you direct the group to respond.

EXERCISE 1

CONTRADICTIONS

1. (Direct the students to find Lesson 99, part A, in the **Student Book**.)
2. (Call on individual students to read up to **Ⓐ**.)
   Ⓐ (Call on a student. Idea: *What was thrown into the fountain to produce the bubbles.*)
3. Read the instructions and do the items. ✓ Let's check your answers. Put an **X** next to any item you miss.
4. (Read each item. Call on individual students to answer each item.)

> **Answer key for Student Book part A**
> **1.** *Idea: In City Park* **2.** *Passage 1* **3.** *Idea: Caused a traffic jam and a two-car accident* **4.** *Passages 1 and 2* **5.** *129 Hilyard Avenue* **6.** *Passage 2* **7.** *Idea: He saw the students carrying a box of laundry detergent.* **8.** *Passage 1* **9.** *Idea: They were arrested and released on bail.* **10.** *Passages 1 and 2* **11.** *$200* **12.** *Passages 1 and 2*

EXERCISE 2

INDEPENDENT WORK

1. **[Optional]** (Direct the students to read the instructions for part B to themselves. Then give them exactly two minutes to copy the paragraph. Count as errors any miscopied words and punctuation. Deduct these errors from the number of copied words, and mark the total on the Writing Rate Graph.)
2. In Lesson 100, you'll have a test on story facts. The facts that will be tested appear in part E of your Workbook. Study them and make sure that you know them. Now, finish the Student Book and do the Workbook for Lesson 99. ✓

Student Book page 211

A The two accounts below contradict each other on an important point. Make sure you find that contradiction when you read the accounts.

> **Passage 1.** Two college students were arrested yesterday for throwing soap into a fountain. The students were arrested near the fountain, which is in City Park. The fountain overflowed with bubbles, which drifted into the streets and caused traffic jams. The students were apprehended by a quick-thinking police officer.
> "I spotted them right away," said Officer Blub. "They were carrying a big box of laundry detergent."
> The students were released on $200 bail.

> **Passage 2.** Traffic became snarled yesterday when hundreds of bubbles drifted into the streets. A two-car accident occurred near City Park as a direct result of the bubbles. One of the cars was carrying three dozen eggs, which smashed all over the inside of the vehicle. The driver, Mrs. Mooch of 129 Hilyard Avenue, was very upset.
> "Eggs don't come cheap these days," she sobbed.
> The bubbles came from a nearby fountain. Apparently, two students had dumped an unknown chemical substance into the fountain. The students were arrested. Later, they were released on $200 bail.

These accounts contradict each other on one big point. What point is that? **Ⓐ**

Write **Part A** in the left margin of your paper. Then number it from 1 to 12. Answer each question. Some of the questions ask where you found an answer. Write **passage 1, passage 2,** or **passages 1 and 2** for these questions.

1. Where was the fountain?
2. Where did you find the answer to question 1?
3. What did the bubbles do?
4. Where did you find the answer to question 3?
5. Where does Mrs. Mooch live?
6. Where did you find the answer to question 5?
7. How did the police officer know who committed the crime?
8. Where did you find the answer to question 7?
9. What happened to the students?
10. Where did you find the answer to question 9?
11. How much bail did the students have to pay?
12. Where did you find the answer to question 11?

Lesson 99

Lesson 99 — Student Book page 212

B Write **Part B** in the left margin of your paper. You have two minutes to copy the paragraph below.

> All animals need water to stay alive. Some animals drink the water that they need. Some animals get the water they need from food that contains lots of water. That food may be plants or animals. Some animals, like the camel, manufacture their own water.

★ C Write **Part C** in the left margin of your paper. Read the passage below.

> Here are a few tips on how to grow a vegetable garden. First, you must prepare the land. This preparation involves digging it up and mixing the earth with fertilizer. The second step is to plant your seeds. Space the seeds so that the plants will have room to grow. Most seeds will take only a few days to sprout. When you see the sprouted seedlings, the third step is to "mulch" the garden. Lay down straw or hay between the seedlings. This protective mulch will stop weeds from growing around your plants. Now your garden is on its way. The last thing you must remember is to water the garden daily. If enough water is available, water your garden in the early morning and evening. Soon you'll have plenty of vegetables for the table!

This sentence expresses the main idea:
Growing a vegetable garden involves several important steps.
The author makes four points that fall under the main idea. Write the main idea and the four points in outline form. Label the points **A, B, C,** and **D,** and indent them under the main idea.

Workbook page 303 — Lesson 99

★ A Each passage contains a word you may not know. Read each passage and answer the questions.

• I liked that suntan lotion except that it was very <u>unctuous</u>. In fact, when I put it on, I felt like a greased pig. The lotion was so unctuous that sand stuck to me and I had trouble getting it off. I think I prefer a lotion that is less unctuous.

1. Circle the answer.
Unctuous probably means:

(oily)   pleasant   yellow   warm

2. Write any sentence from the passage that contradicts the idea that **unctuous** means **yellow.**

Idea: The lotion was so unctuous that sand stuck to me and I had trouble getting it off.

• When the sun is beating down in the desert, you might see something that looks like a lake off in the distance. This is an <u>illusion</u>, because the lake isn't really there. An illusion of a lake is caused by heat waves. Many thirsty people in the desert have wandered after illusions of cool water only to find hills of dry sand.

3. Circle the answer. **Illusion** probably means:

laughter
solid substance
gold or silver
(something that doesn't exist)

4. Write any sentence from the passage that contradicts the idea that **illusion** means **solid substance.**

Idea: This is an illusion because the lake isn't really there.

• It is useless to discuss anything with him because all of his arguments are obviously <u>fallacious</u>. The conclusions he comes up with are always wrong. For instance, he said his neighbors were criminals, just because he saw a cop car outside their home. Actually, his neighbors had called the police themselves, because they had been robbed. I have no patience with his fallacious reasoning.

5. Circle the answer.
Fallacious probably means:

(full of error)
full of fear
frisky
serious

6. Write any sentence from the passage that contradicts the idea that **fallacious** means **serious.**

Idea: For instance, he said his neighbors were criminals, just because he saw a cop car outside their home.

WORKCHECK

1. Get ready to check your answers starting with Student Book part C. Use a pen to make an **X** next to any item you miss.
2. (Call on individual students to read each item and its answer. Repeat for Workbook items.)

> **Answer key for Student Book part C (Ideas:)**
> I. *Growing a vegetable garden involves several important steps.*
>   **A.** *Preparing the land*
>   **B.** *Planting the seeds*
>   **C.** *Mulching the garden*
>   **D.** *Watering the garden daily*

3. (Direct students to count the number of errors and write the number in the **error** box at the top of the Workbook page.)
4. (Award points and direct students to record their points in Box **W.**)

0 errors	15 points
1–2 errors	12 points
3–5 errors	8 points
6–9 errors	5 points

5. (Award any bonus points. Have the students total their points and enter the total on the Point Summary Chart.)
6. Show me your work when you've finished correcting it. (When the students show you their corrected work, record their points on your Record Summary Chart.)

Lesson 99 — Workbook page 304

B Read the passage below.

> Ancient Egyptian legend tells of a time when the world was all water. The water receded, leaving a tall hill of sand. A magic bird rose up from the center of the hill, soared into the sky, and became the sun.
>
> Ancient Egyptian kings believed that when they died, they would join the sun and rise and set with it forever. They had huge pyramids built over their graves so that after they died, the trip to the sun would be easier. To an ancient Egyptian, the pyramid was a symbol of the creation of the world as well as a stairway to the sun.

- Here's a conclusion:

  The ancient Egyptians believed in an afterlife.

1. Does the passage contain evidence to support this conclusion or evidence to contradict this conclusion?

   evidence to support this conclusion

2. Write a sentence that contains the evidence.

   (Either:) They had huge pyramids built over their graves so that after they died, the trip to the sun would be easier.
   Ancient Egyptians believed that when they died, they would join the sun and rise and set with it forever.

- Here's another conclusion:

  The Egyptians did not believe in magic.

3. Does the passage contain evidence to support this conclusion or evidence to contradict this conclusion?

   evidence to contradict this conclusion

4. Which sentence contains the evidence?

   A magic bird rose up from the center of the hill, soared into the sky, and became the sun.

- Here's another conclusion:

  A pyramid had no special meaning to the ancient Egyptians.

5. Does the passage contain evidence to support this conclusion or evidence to contradict this conclusion?

   evidence to contradict this conclusion

6. Which sentence contains the evidence?

   To an ancient Egyptian, the pyramid was a symbol of the creation of the world as well as a stairway to the sun.

Workbook page 305 — Lesson 99

- Here's another conclusion:

  Pyramids served as tombs.

7. Does the passage contain evidence to support this conclusion or evidence to contradict this conclusion?

   evidence to support this conclusion

8. Which sentence contains the evidence?

   They had huge pyramids built over their graves so that after they died, the trip to the sun would be easier.

C Underline the redundant part in the sentence below. Then explain why the underlined part is redundant.

Matt hated his job and didn't like his occupation.

Idea: If you know that he hated his job, then you already know that he didn't like his occupation.

D Rewrite each sentence below, using the word **usually, occasionally,** or **rarely.**

1. Ann likes to take a long walk (once in a while).

   Ann likes to take a long walk occasionally.

2. Our radio (almost never) works.

   Our radio rarely works.

3. (Most of the time) he drinks milk with his breakfast.

   Usually, he drinks milk with his breakfast.

4. (Once in a while) my car runs smoothly.

   Occasionally, my car runs smoothly.

5. The school is (most of the time) closed on Saturday.

   The school is usually closed on Saturday.

Lesson 99 — Workbook page 306

E After you finish Lesson 100, you will be tested on facts you have learned. The test will include the facts presented in Lessons 96 and 97 and some of the facts from earlier lessons. These facts are:

1. Any living thing is an organism.
2. The eyes of herbivorous mammals allow them to eat and to watch out for enemies at the same time.
3. The teeth of a herbivorous mammal are flat, and the teeth of a carnivorous mammal are pointed.
4. Plants are different from animals in several ways: (a) plants "breathe in" carbon dioxide; (b) plants "exhale" oxygen; and (c) plants make their own food.
5. Study the chart below. Make sure that you can fill in this chart.

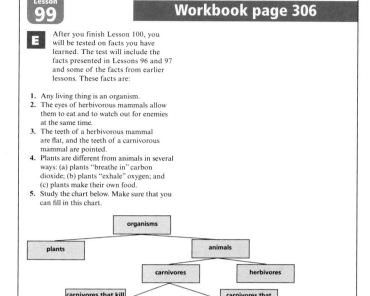

END OF LESSON 99

Student Book page 213

A Write **Part A** in the left margin of your paper. You have two minutes to copy the paragraph below.

> Ancient Egyptian kings believed that when they died, they would join the sun and rise and set with it forever. They had huge pyramids built over their graves so that after they died, the trip to the sun would be easier.

★**B** Write **Part B** in the left margin of your paper. Read the passage below.

> Canadians enjoy many forms of recreation. Each year thousands of Canadians fish through the ice when the lakes and rivers freeze. Entire fishing villages seem to spring up in areas where the ice is safe. Another very popular sport in Canada is ice hockey. Each year, thousands of Canadians watch or play ice hockey. There are many professional and amateur hockey teams in Canada. Canadians also enjoy the sport of Canadian football. This game is very similar to football that is played in the United States, except Canadian football teams have twelve players instead of eleven. Another form of recreation that Canadians enjoy is sport fishing. People fish for salmon in salt water and for trout in fresh water. These are just a few of the many kinds of recreation that Canadians enjoy.

This sentence expresses the main idea:
There are many forms of recreation in Canada.
The author makes four points that fall under the main idea. Write the main idea and the four points in outline form. Label the points **A, B, C,** and **D,** and indent them under the main idea.

Student Book page 214

C Write **Part C** in the left margin of your paper. Then number it from 1 to 9. The two accounts below contradict each other on an important point. Make sure you find that contradiction when you read the accounts.

> **Passage 1.** The eclipse will take place at 2:40 P.M. on Monday, July 5. The moon will be directly between the sun and the earth, blocking the sun. This is called a total solar eclipse. The sun will actually disappear for more than two minutes. Stars will come out, and the earth will be in darkness in the middle of the afternoon. You are cautioned not to look directly at the sun during the eclipse, because this may cause blindness. The next eclipse in this area will not take place until the year 2017.

> **Passage 2.** All those wishing to view the last eclipse until the year 2017 will want to be outside at around 2:40 P.M. on Monday, July 5. The earth will be directly between the moon and the sun, causing total darkness over an area of about 2,000 square miles. The eclipse will be seen in all of North America, but it will last the longest when viewed from the midwest part of the United States.

Answer each question below. Some of the questions ask where you found an answer. Write **passage 1, passage 2,** or **passages 1 and 2** for these questions.

1. These passages contradict each other on one big point. What point is that?
2. What is a solar eclipse?
3. Where did you find the answer to question 2?
4. Where will the eclipse last the longest?
5. Where did you find the answer to question 4?
6. When will the next eclipse happen?
7. Where did you find the answer to question 6?
8. What is the date of the eclipse?
9. Where did you find the answer to question 8?

1. Idea: the position of the moon during an eclipse
2. Idea: when the moon has moved directly between the sun and Earth, thus blocking the sun
3. passage 1
4. Idea: in the midwestern part of the United States
5. passage 2
6. 2017
7. passages 1 and 2
8. on July 5
9. passages 1 and 2

═══════════ **EXERCISE 1** ═══════════

INDEPENDENT WORK

1. **[Optional]** (Direct the students to read the instructions for part A in the **Student Book** to themselves. Then give them exactly two minutes to copy the paragraph. Count as errors any miscopied words and punctuation. Deduct these errors from the number of copied words, and mark the total on the Writing Rate Graph.)
2. Finish the Student Book and Workbook for Lesson 100. ✓

Workcheck

1. Get ready to check your answers starting with Student Book part B. Use a pen to make an **X** next to any item you miss.
2. (Call on individual students to read each item and its answer. Repeat for Workbook items.)

> **Answer key for Student Book part B (Idea:)**
> I. *There are many forms of recreation in Canada.*
>   **A.** *Ice fishing*
>   **B.** *Ice hockey*
>   **C.** *Football*
>   **D.** *Sport fishing*

3. (Direct the students to count the number of errors and write the number in the **error** box at the top of the Workbook page.)
4. (Award points and direct the students to record their points in Box **W.**)

0 errors	**15 points**
1–2 errors	**12 points**
3–5 errors	**8 points**
6–9 errors	**5 points**

5. (Award any bonus points. Direct the students to total their points and enter the total on the Point Summary Chart.)
6. Show me your work when you've finished correcting it. (When the students show you their corrected work, record their points on your Record Summary Chart.)

Student Book page 215

D

Here are some words that will be in some editing activities. Test yourself to make sure that you know what the words mean.

rogue—An animal that is a rogue is an animal that travels by itself and is usually mean. Here's a sentence that uses the word **rogue:**

The elk was a rogue that avoided other animals.

sanctioned—When you sanction something, you approve of it. Here's a sentence that uses the word **sanctioned:**

He sanctioned her decision to move to another city.

scrupulous—A person who is scrupulous is a person who pays a lot of attention to details. Here's a sentence that uses the word **scrupulous:**

She is a scrupulous bookkeeper.

somnolent—When you are somnolent, you are sleepy. Here's a sentence that uses the word **somnolent:**

After eating a big meal, I always feel somnolent.

Workbook page 307

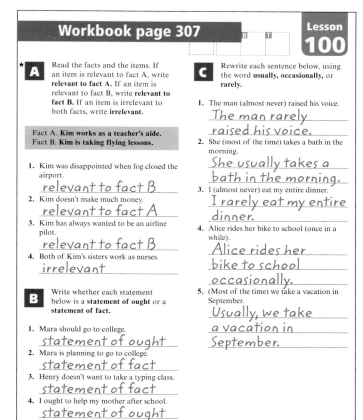

A

Read the facts and the items. If an item is relevant to fact A, write **relevant to fact A.** If an item is relevant to fact B, write **relevant to fact B.** If an item is irrelevant to both facts, write **irrelevant.**

Fact A. **Kim works as a teacher's aide.**
Fact B. **Kim is taking flying lessons.**

1. Kim was disappointed when fog closed the airport.
   relevant to fact B
2. Kim doesn't make much money.
   relevant to fact A
3. Kim has always wanted to be an airline pilot.
   relevant to fact B
4. Both of Kim's sisters work as nurses.
   irrelevant

B

Write whether each statement below is a **statement of ought** or a **statement of fact.**

1. Mara should go to college.
   statement of ought
2. Mara is planning to go to college.
   statement of fact
3. Henry doesn't want to take a typing class.
   statement of fact
4. I ought to help my mother after school.
   statement of ought

C

Rewrite each sentence below, using the word **usually, occasionally,** or **rarely.**

1. The man (almost never) raised his voice.
   The man rarely raised his voice.
2. She (most of the time) takes a bath in the morning.
   She usually takes a bath in the morning.
3. I (almost never) eat my entire dinner.
   I rarely eat my entire dinner.
4. Alice rides her bike to school (once in a while).
   Alice rides her bike to school occasionally.
5. (Most of the time) we take a vacation in September.
   Usually, we take a vacation in September.

END OF LESSON 100

━━━━━ **EXERCISE 1** ━━━━━

MASTERY TEST

1. Everybody, find page 452 in your workbook.
   - This is a test. If you make no mistakes on the test, you'll earn 20 points. Write the answers to the test items now using your pencil.
2. (After the students complete the items, gather the workbooks and grade the tests. As you grade each test, record the number of errors the student made on each part of the test in the appropriate box. Record the total number of errors in the **Error** box at the beginning of the test.)
3. (Return the workbooks to the students.) Raise your hand if you made _____ or more mistakes in part _____. (Record the number of students who raise their hand for the part.)

> **Key:** Part A–5 Part B–2 Part C–2
> Part D–2 Part E–2 Part F–1 Part G–2

4. Raise your hand if you made no mistakes. Great work. (Award 20 points to the students who made no errors. Award 5 points to students who made 1 or 2 errors.)
   Record your points in the box marked **MT** at the top of Mastery Test 10.
   - (Direct all students to enter their points on the Point Summary Chart.)
6. (Record test results on the Group Summary Sheet. Reproducible Summary Sheets are at the back of the Teacher's Guide.)

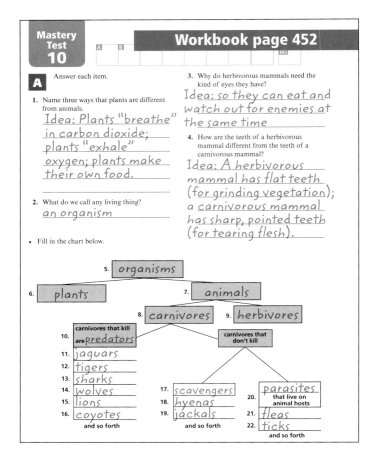

Mastery Test 10 — Workbook page 452

A Answer each item.

1. Name three ways that plants are different from animals.
   Idea: Plants "breathe" in carbon dioxide; plants "exhale" oxygen; plants make their own food.

2. What do we call any living thing?
   an organism

- Fill in the chart below.

5. organisms
6. plants
7. animals
8. carnivores
9. herbivores
10. carnivores that kill are predators
11. jaguars
12. tigers
13. sharks
14. wolves
15. lions
16. coyotes
   and so forth
17. scavengers
18. hyenas
19. jackals
   and so forth
   carnivores that don't kill
20. parasites that live on animal hosts
21. fleas
22. ticks
   and so forth

3. Why do herbivorous mammals need the kind of eyes they have?
   Idea: so they can eat and watch out for enemies at the same time

4. How are the teeth of a herbivorous mammal different from the teeth of a carnivorous mammal?
   Idea: A herbivorous mammal has flat teeth (for grinding vegetation); a carnivorous mammal has sharp, pointed teeth (for tearing flesh).

Workbook page 453 — Mastery Test 10

B Write the model sentence that means the same thing as each sentence below.

1. By pausing, she lost her chance.
   By hesitating, she lost her opportunity.

2. His directions were unclear and repetitive.
   His directions were ambiguous and redundant.

3. They changed their Swiss money into Canadian money.
   They converted their Swiss currency into Canadian currency.

4. The rule limited their parking.
   The regulation restricted their parking.

5. Her answer was filled with irrelevant details.
   Her response was replete with extraneous details.

6. They made up a fitting plan.
   They devised an appropriate strategy.

7. A strange event caused the fear that she showed.
   A strange phenomenon caused the anxiety that she exhibited.

C Read the passage below.

> Here are a few tips on how to grow a vegetable garden. First, you must prepare the land. This preparation involves digging it up and mixing the earth with fertilizer. The second step is to plant your seeds. Space the seeds so that the plants will have room to grow. Most seeds will take only a few days to sprout. When you see the sprouted seedlings, the third step is to "mulch" the garden. Lay down straw or hay between the seedlings. This protective mulch will stop weeds from growing around your plants. Now your garden is on its way. The last thing you must remember is to water the garden daily. If enough water is available, water your garden in the early morning and evening. Soon you'll have plenty of vegetables for the table!

This sentence expresses the main idea: **Growing a vegetable garden involves several important steps.** The author makes four points that fall under the main idea. Write the four points under the main idea.

I. Growing a vegetable garden involves several important steps.
   A. preparing the land
   B. planting the seeds
   C. mulching the garden
   D. watering the garden daily

Workbook page 454

Mastery Test 10

D Each argument below breaks one of these rules:

Rule 1: Just because two things happen around the same time doesn't mean one thing causes the other thing.

Rule 2: Just because you know about a part doesn't mean you know about the whole thing.

Rule 3: Just because you know about a part doesn't mean you know about another part.

Rule 4: Just because you know about a whole thing doesn't mean you know about every part.

Rule 5: Just because words are the same doesn't mean they have the same meaning.

Rule 6: Just because the writer presents some choices doesn't mean there aren't other choices.

After each argument below, write the number of the rule the argument breaks.

1. If the National Food Corporation is earning a huge profit, you can bet that every employee of that company is rich. _4_

2. He is so far in debt that he even has a bill on his cap. _5_

3. I'll never go to that theater again. The last movie I saw there was awful. _3_

4. I really enjoy spending time with Jolene. I'm sure I'll have a good time with the rest of her family. _2_

E Rewrite each sentence below, using the word **usually**, **occasionally**, or **rarely**.

1. She (almost never) eats french fries.
   She rarely eats french fries.

2. The boys (most of the time) play soccer after school.
   The boys usually play soccer after school.

3. Teresa and her sister (almost never) go to the movies.
   Theresa and her sister rarely go to the movies.

4. Their dog (once in a while) chases cats.
   Their dog occasionally chases cats.

EXERCISE 2

TEST REMEDIES

1. (If more than 25% of the students failed a part of the test, provide the remedy specified for that in the table on the next page. The required Remedy Blackline Master worksheets can be found in Appendix H of the Teacher's Guide.)

2. (All remedies should be completed before beginning the next lesson in the program.)

Workbook page 455

Mastery Test 10

F Underline the redundant part in each sentence below. Then explain why the underlined part is redundant.

1. The woman, who was an adult female, walked into the restaurant.
   Idea: If you know that she's a woman, then you already know she's an adult female.

2. The new skyscraper has huge windows that are very big.
   Idea: If you know that the windows are huge, then you already know that they are big.

3. His anxiety and his fear kept him from taking the trip.
   Idea: If you know that he had anxiety, then you already know that he had fear.

G Write whether each sentence below is a **statement of ought** or a **statement of fact**.

1. Lila should get more exercise.
   statement of ought

2. Lila ought to start playing tennis.
   statement of ought

3. Mia plays tennis every day.
   statement of fact

4. Mia should drink more water when she plays tennis.
   statement of ought

Note: The teacher and each student who failed the test will need a copy of Remedy Blackline Master 10–A. The Remedy Blackline Masters can be found in Appendix H of the Teacher's Guide.

PART A TEST REMEDY

1. We're going to go over some items from the test. I'll read the items. You'll say the answers. Then you'll write the answers.
2. (Read item 1 in part A of Remedy Blackline Master 10–A.) What's the answer? (Call on a student.) *No.*
3. (Repeat step 2 for items 2–8.)
4. (Give each student a copy of Remedy Blackline Master 10–A.)
   This worksheet shows the chart that was on the test.
5. Touch box 9.
   Everybody, what goes in this box? (Signal.) *Organisms.*

6. (Repeat step 4 for each remaining box.)
7. Study the chart for a few minutes. Then you'll fill in the empty boxes.
8. (After students complete the items:) Now you're going to write the answers to all the items in part A. Let's see who can get them all correct.
9. (After students complete the items:) Let's check your work. Use your pen to make an **X** next to any item you got wrong.
   - (For items 1–8: Read the items. Call on individual students to answer each item.)
   - (For the chart items:) What goes in box 9? (Call on a student.) *Organisms.*
   - (Repeat for each remaining box.)
   - Raise your hand if you got all the items correct. Nice work.

END OF MASTERY TEST 10

Test Section	If students made this many errors	Present these tasks: Lesson	Exercise	Remedy Blackline Master	Required Student Book Parts
A	5 or more	Test remedy below		10–A, 10–B	
B	2 or more	Item 1: 18	2	10–C	Lesson 18–B
		Item 2: 21	3	10–D	Lesson 21–C
		Item 3: 27	2	10–D	Lesson 27–A
		Item 4: 33	1	10–E	Lesson 33–A
		Item 5: 57	1	10–E	Lesson 57–A
		Item 6: 62	2	10–F	Lesson 62–B
		Item 6: 85	1	10–F	Lesson 85–A
C	2 or more	91	2		Lesson 91–B
		92	1		Lesson 92–A
D	2 or more	86	—	10–G	
		87	—	10–H	
E	2 or more	93	1		Lesson 93–A
		94	2		Lesson 94–B
F	1 or more	94	1	10–I	Lesson 94–A
		95	1	10–I	Lesson 95–A
G	2 or more	96	2		Lesson 96–B
		97	2	10–J	Lesson 97–B

Lesson Objectives	LESSON 101 Exercise	LESSON 102 Exercise	LESSON 103 Exercise	LESSON 104 Exercise	LESSON 105 Exercise	Fact Game 7
Organization and Study Skills						
Main Idea	1, SB	SB	SB	SSB		
Outlining		SB				
Writing Mechanics: Copying	4	4	2	4	3	
Reasoning Strategies						
Deductions	WB					
Evidence	WB					
Rules: Arguments				3	1, 2	
Statements: Ought			WB		WB	FG
Contradictions	SB	3	SB	2	SB, WB	
Inference	2	2				
Information Sources/ Study Skills						
Interpretation: Maps/Pictures/Graphs			SB, WB	SB	WB	FG
Supporting Evidence	SB		SB	SB	SB	FG
Vocabulary/Language Arts Skills						
Definitions	3, WB	1, WB	1, WB	1, WB	WB	FG
Usage	3, WB	1, WB	1, WB	1, WB	WB	FG
Editing/Revising	WB	WB	WB	WB	WB	FG
Comprehension: Meaning from Context				WB	WB	
Information Application/ Study Skills						
Directions: Writing			WB			
Directions: Filling Out Forms				WB		
Assessment/Progress Monitoring						
Ongoing: Workcheck	Workcheck	Workcheck	Workcheck	Workcheck	Workcheck	

Lesson
101

Student Book page 216

A Here are three main ideas:

- **Why so many people are overweight**
- **Why so many people don't walk much anymore**
- **Why so many people are lonely**

One of the main ideas fits the passage below. Read the passage.

There have never been as many overweight people in the United States as there are today. The biggest reason is that people do not exercise as much as they used to. Machines have taken over most of the hard physical labor once done by humans. Because many people have cars, they almost never walk. In addition, people in the United States find it easier than ever to obtain all the food they want. In the past, good food was obtained only by hard physical work on the family farm or ranch. Today, it is easy to purchase more food than your body needs. Some people eat to forget their problems. Lonely, nervous, or unhappy people often eat five or six times a day simply to make themselves feel better.

Which main idea fits the passage you just read? Ⓐ
The author makes three points that fall under the main idea. What are those three points? Ⓑ

B The description below tells about the city shown in one of the maps on the next page. Read the description and then answer the questions.

This map shows a section of downtown Brownsville consisting of twelve square blocks. The colored regions represent surface area that is devoted to cars: parking lots, streets, filling stations, and garages. The heavy broken line represents the route the new elevated train will take. The light broken lines represent subway routes. Notice that more than half the surface area of this busy section of town is devoted to cars. It is also interesting to note that there is not a single park in this area.

Which map does the description tell about? Ⓒ
Which words in the description let you know that map B is not the one that is described? Ⓓ
Which words in the description let you know that map A is not the one that is described? Ⓔ
Which words in the description let you know that map D is not the one that is described? Ⓕ

Student Book page 217

Lesson
101

A

B

C

D

> **Note:** The circled letters indicate when you ask a question or when you direct the group to respond.

EXERCISE 1

MAIN IDEA

1. (Direct the students to find Lesson 101, part A, in the **Student Book**.)
2. (Call on individual students to read part A.)
   - Ⓐ Say the correct main idea. *Why so many people are overweight.*
   - Ⓑ (Call on three students to name one point each. Ideas: *People do not exercise as much as they used to. People find it easier than ever to obtain all the food they want. Some people eat to forget their problems.*)

EXERCISE 2

STATEMENT INFERENCE

1. (Direct the students to find part B.)
2. (Call on individual students to read part B.)
   - Ⓒ Which map? *Map C.*
   - Ⓓ Figure out the answer. (Wait.) Which words? *There is not a single park in this area.*
   - Ⓔ Figure out the answer. (Wait.) Which words? *Consisting of twelve square blocks.*
   - Ⓕ Figure out the answer. (Wait.) Which words? *The light broken lines represent subway routes.*

EXERCISE 3

DEFINITIONS

1. (Direct the students to find part C.)
2. (Call on individual students to read part C.)
   - **G** Do it. ✓
     (Call on individual students to say the model sentence.)
   - **H** Which word? *Contended.*
   - **I** Which word? *Valid.*
   - **J** Which word? *Motives.*
   - **K** Which word? *Concealing.*
   - **L** Which word? *Data.*
   - **M** Say a sentence that means the same thing. *The judge contended that she had valid motives for her decision.*
   - **N** Say a sentence that means the same thing. *Tom was concealing the data from his boss.*

EXERCISE 4

INDEPENDENT WORK

1. **[Optional]** (Direct the students to read the instructions for part D to themselves. Then give them exactly two minutes to copy the paragraph. Count as errors any miscopied words and punctuation. Deduct these errors from the number of copied words, and mark the total on the Writing Rate Graph.)
2. Finish the Student Book and do the Workbook for Lesson 101. ✓

Workcheck

1. Get ready to check your answers starting with Student Book part E. Use a pen to mark an **X** next to any item you miss.
2. (Call on individual students to read each item and its answer. Repeat for Workbook items.)

Student Book page 218

C Here's a new model sentence:

> The major contended that he had valid motives for concealing the data.

Read the sentence to yourself. Study the sentence until you can say it without looking at it. ⊕
Here's what the model means:
> The major argued that he had sound reasons for hiding the facts.

Which word in the model means **argued?** ⊕
Which word in the model means **sound?** ⊕
Which word in the model means **reasons?** ⊕
Which word in the model means **hiding?** ⊕
Which word in the model means **facts?** ⊕

For each item, say a sentence that means the same thing.
1. The judge <u>argued</u> that she had <u>sound reasons</u> for her decision. ⊕
2. Tom was <u>hiding</u> the <u>facts</u> from his boss. ⊕

D Write **Part D** in the left margin of your paper. You have two minutes to copy the paragraph below.

> People in Canada have many forms of recreation. Some Canadians go ice fishing. Many people watch or play ice hockey. Still others like to watch or play Canadian football. Some Canadians enjoy sport fishing—both saltwater fishing and freshwater fishing.

★E Write **Part E** in the left margin of your paper. Then number it from 1 to 11. The two accounts below contradict each other on an important point. Make sure you find that contradiction when you read the accounts.

Passage 1. An art theft was reported Sunday morning. The report was made by Count Radcliff, who owns a large collection of paintings. According to the count, the thieves broke into a skylight above the gallery and lowered themselves to the floor by rope. They stole a number of paintings and escaped through the back door. Sergeant Snorkle, who is in charge of the investigation, said that the burglar alarm had been disconnected.

Passage 2. A valuable collection of pictures painted by the Spanish artist Goya was stolen from Count Radcliff Saturday night. The chief investigating officer, Sergeant Snorkle, says that it could have been an "inside job," meaning that the burglars may have been aided by someone living inside the house. The count speculates that the burglars entered the house by breaking down the back door. The paintings were insured for ten million dollars.

Student Book page 219

Answer each question below. Some of the questions ask where you found an answer. Write **passage 1, passage 2,** or **passages 1 and 2** for these questions.

1. These passages contradict each other on one big point. What point is that?
2. What was stolen?
3. Where did you find the answer to question 2?
4. What happened to the burglar alarm?
5. Where did you find the answer to question 4?
6. What is an "inside job"?
7. Where did you find the answer to question 6?
8. When was the robbery reported?
9. Where did you find the answer to question 8?
10. Who was in charge of the investigation?
11. Where did you find the answer to question 10?

F Write **Part F** in the left margin of your paper.
Here are three main ideas:

- Wildflowers are disappearing.
- Flowers are nice to smell.
- Most flowers have sepals, petals, stamens, and a pistil.

One of the main ideas fits the passage below. Read the passage.

> Nearly all flowers have four basic parts. At the base of the flower, around the outside, are small, green, leaflike parts called sepals. Sepals protect the bud when the flower is still young. Above the sepals are the petals. The petals give the flower its color and odor. In many flowers, they also produce nectar, which helps attract bees. Near the center of the petals there is a ring of stamens, which produce the pollen necessary for plant reproduction. Right at the center of the flower is the pistil, a sticky shaft to which pollen adheres. The pistil is where the seeds develop.

Write the main idea that fits the passage. List the four points that fall under the main idea in outline form. Don't forget to indent and label the four points.

Lesson 101 · Workbook page 308

A In the passage below, the verbs **has** and **have** are used incorrectly six times.
Cross out each incorrect word. Write the correct word above it.
There are three redundant parts in the passage below. Cross out each redundant part.

> This city ~~have~~ *has* the best bus system in Canada, ~~better than any you will find for miles around~~. All you ~~has~~ *have* to know is the bus number, where you are going, and when the bus arrives. (Each bus route ~~have~~ *has* its own printed schedule ~~that shows when the buses arrive and depart.~~) Everybody ~~have to has~~ *has have* correct change because the driver doesn't make change on the bus. Children and those over fifty-five years old ~~has~~ *have* special fares, ~~and they pay a different fare from that paid by other people.~~

B Read the evidence and write the conclusion for each item.

1. Here's the evidence:

   Each part of the nervous system responds to electric current.
   A lightbulb responds to electric current.

   What's the conclusion?
   Idea: There is none.

2. Here's the evidence:

   Things that spill oil are fire hazards.
   Beached tankers spill oil.

   What's the conclusion?
   Beached tankers are fire hazards.

3. Here's the evidence:

   All dogs are canines.
   An albatross is not a canine.

   What's the conclusion?
   An albatross is not a dog.

Workbook page 309 · Lesson 101

C For each item, write a sentence that means the same thing by changing the underlined words.

1. The major argued that he had <u>sound</u> <u>reasons</u> for <u>hiding</u> the <u>facts</u>.
   The major contended that he had valid motives for concealing the data.

2. Tim's <u>reasons</u> for stealing tires were not <u>sound</u>.
   Tim's motives for stealing tires were not valid.

3. The police were <u>hiding</u> the <u>facts</u> regarding the crime.
   The police were concealing the data regarding the crime.

4. Were they trying to <u>hide</u> their real <u>reasons</u> for raising prices?
   Were they trying to conceal their real motives for raising prices?

5. The lawyer will <u>argue</u> that his client's <u>reasons</u> are <u>sound</u>.
   The lawyer will contend that his client's motives are sound.

3. (Direct the students to count the number of errors and write the number in the **error** box at the top of the Workbook page.)

4. (Award points and direct students to record their points in Box **W**.)

0 errors	**15 points**
1–2 errors	**12 points**
3–5 errors	**8 points**
6–9 errors	**5 points**

5. (Award any bonus points. Direct the students to total their points and enter the total on the Point Summary Chart.)

6. Show me your work when you've finished correcting it. (When the students show you their corrected work, record their points on your Record Summary Chart.)

END OF LESSON 101

Note: The circled letters indicate when you ask a question or when you direct the group to respond.

EXERCISE 1

DEFINITIONS

1. (Direct the students to find Lesson 102, part A, in the **Student Book**.)
2. (Call on individual students to read part A.)

   🅐 Say it. *The major argued that he had sound reasons for hiding the facts.*

   🅑 What word? *Contended.*

   🅒 What word? *Valid.*

   🅓 What word? *Motives.*

   🅔 What word? *Concealing.*

   🅕 What word? *Data.*

   🅖 Say that sentence another way. *The major contended that he had valid motives for concealing the data.*

EXERCISE 2

STATEMENT INFERENCE

1. (Direct the students to find part B.)
2. (Call on individual students to read part B.)

   🅗 Which graph? *Graph A.*

   🅘 Figure out the answer. (Wait.) Which words? *Three hours of rain during the night greatly reduced the level of carbon monoxide.*

   🅙 Figure out the answer. (Wait.) Which words? *The level of carbon monoxide is very high in the midmorning and late afternoon hours.*

   🅚 Figure out the answer. (Wait.) Which words? *During a period of twenty-four hours.*

Lesson
102

Student Book page 220

A Here's the latest model sentence you learned:

> **The major contended that he had valid motives for concealing the data.**

What sentence means the same thing? ⊙
What word means **argued**? ⊙
What word means **sound**? ⊙
What word means **reasons**? ⊙
What word means **hiding**? ⊙
What word means **facts**? ⊙
What's another way of saying,

> **The major argued that he had sound reasons for hiding the facts?** ⊙

B The description below and one of the graphs on the next page tell about the carbon monoxide in Center City. Read the description and then answer the questions.

> Carbon monoxide is a poisonous gas found in automobile exhaust. The graph shows the amount of carbon monoxide in Center City's air during a period of twenty-four hours. Notice that the level of carbon monoxide is very high in the midmorning and late afternoon hours, when traffic through the city is heaviest. The graph also shows that three hours of rain during the night greatly reduced the level of carbon monoxide.

Which graph does the description tell about? ⊙
Which words in the description let you know that graph C is not the one that is described? ⊙
Which words in the description let you know that graph D is not the one described? ⊙
Which words in the description let you know that graph B is not the one described? ⊙

Student Book page 221   **Lesson 102**

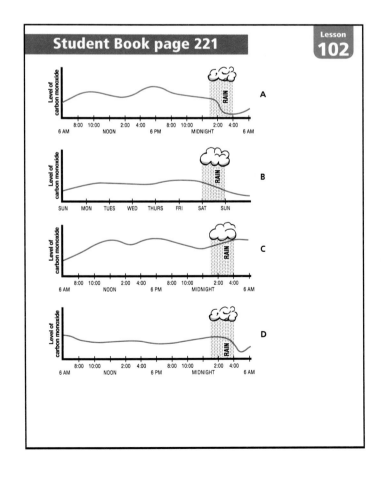

Lesson 102 — Student Book page 222

C The two accounts below contradict each other on two small points. Make sure you find those contradictions when you read the accounts.

> **Passage 1.** The circus rolled into town last night, with a long caravan of elephants bringing up the rear. The director of the circus, B. B. Barney, said that tents would be set up for business by Friday afternoon. Price of admission is $3.00 for children and $5.00 for adults. The circus features trapeze acts, lion taming, bareback riding, clowns, and a freak show. There are more animals this year than ever—zebras, lions, elephants, and even a dancing bear! Hot dogs, peanuts, and cotton candy will be sold in separate booths. Madam Sarah will read your palm and tell your fortune for $1.00.

> **Passage 2.** The circus is back in town! All children wanting to attend the circus need $3.50 for the entry fee. There aren't as many animals as there were last year; however, there is a dancing bear from Russia that should provide a good show. The circus director, Mr. Barney, said that the circus will open on Friday. Food will be sold at the circus, and a fortuneteller will be on hand to tell your future for only $1.00. Come one, come all, to the show you won't forget!

These accounts contradict each other on two small points. What are they? ⊕

Write **Part C** in the left margin of your paper. Then number it from 1 to 8. Answer each question. Some of the questions ask where you found an answer. Write **passage 1, passage 2,** or **passages 1 and 2** for these questions.

1. What kind of bear does the circus own? *a dancing bear*
2. Where did you find the answer to question 1? *passages 1 and 2*
3. What does Madam Sarah do? *Idea: sell fortunes*
4. Where did you find the answer to question 3? *passage 1*
5. How much does it cost to get your fortune told? *$1.00*
6. Where did you find the answer to question 5? *passages 1 and 2*
7. When will the circus open? *Friday*
8. Where did you find the answer to question 7? *passages 1 and 2*

D Write **Part D** in the left margin of your paper. You have two minutes to copy the paragraph below.

> Statements of ought are statements that tell what we should do or what ought to happen. Statements of ought often contain the word "ought," "should," or "shouldn't." Here is a statement of ought: You ought to go to school every day.

Student Book page 223 — Lesson 102

★ **E** Write **Part E** in the left margin of your paper.

Here are three main ideas:
* A food chain involves plants, herbivores, carnivores, and decomposers.
* Decomposers break down dead plants and animals.
* Herbivores eat plants.

One of the main ideas fits the passage below. Read the passage.

> All food chains start with plants, which make their own food from sunlight, water, carbon dioxide, and minerals in the soil. Herbivores, such as rabbits, mice, and many types of insects, are the next link in the chain. They obtain all their food from plants. Carnivores come next in the food chain. Cats, dogs, and predatory birds, such as hawks and falcons, are some of the animals that obtain food from the flesh of other animals. Decomposers, which break down dead plant and animal material, form the last link in the food chain. As plant and animal material is decomposed, minerals are returned to the soil and become food for the next generation of plants.

Write the main idea that fits the passage. List the four points that fall under the main idea in outline form. Don't forget to indent and label the four points.

EXERCISE 3

CONTRADICTIONS

1. (Direct the students to find part C.)
2. (Call on individual students to read up to ⓛ.)
   ⓛ (Call on two students to name one point each. Ideas: *Price of admission, and how many animals are in the circus.*)
3. Read the instructions and do the items. ✓ Let's check your answers. Put an **X** next to any item you miss.
4. (Read each item. Call on individual students to answer each item.)

EXERCISE 4

INDEPENDENT WORK

1. **[Optional]** (Direct the students to read the instructions for part D to themselves. Then give them exactly two minutes to copy the paragraph. Count as errors any miscopied words and punctuation. Deduct these errors from the number of copied words, and mark the total on the Writing Rate Graph.)
2. Finish the Student Book and do the Workbook for Lesson 102. ✓

Workcheck

1. Get ready to check your answers starting with Student Book part E. Use a pen to make an **X** next to any item you miss.

2. (Call on individual students to read each item and its answer. Repeat for the Workbook items.)

> **Answer key for Student Book part E**
> **I.** *A food chain involves plants, herbivores, carnivores, and decomposers.*
> **A.** *Idea: Plants make their own food.*
> **B.** *Idea: Herbivores eat plants.*
> **C.** *Idea: Carnivores eat herbivores and other animals.*
> **D.** *Idea: Decomposers break down dead plant and animal material.*

3. (Direct the students to count the number of errors and write the number in the **error** box at the top of the Workbook page.)

4. (Award points and direct students to record their points in Box **W**.)

0 errors	15 points
1–2 errors	12 points
3–5 errors	8 points
6–9 errors	5 points

5. (Award any bonus points. Direct the students to total their points and enter the total on the Point Summary Chart.)

6. Show me your work when you've finished correcting it. (When the students show you their corrected work, record their points on your Record Summary Chart.)

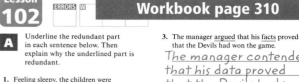

Lesson 102 ERRORS W **Workbook page 310**

★ **A** Underline the redundant part in each sentence below. Then explain why the underlined part is redundant.

1. Feeling sleepy, the children were somnolent after lunch.
Idea: If you know that the children were feeling sleepy, then you already know that they were somnolent.

2. The elephant was a rogue that traveled alone.
Idea: If you know that the elephant was a rogue, then you already know that it traveled alone.

B For each item, write a sentence that means the same thing by changing the underlined words.

1. The major argued that he had sound reasons for hiding the facts.
The major contended that he had valid motives for concealing the data.

2. What reasons does Helen have for hiding her love from Tom?
What motives does Helen have for concealing her love from Tom?

3. The manager argued that his facts proved that the Devils had won the game.
The manager contended that his data proved that the Devils had won the game.

4. The spy was hiding the secret facts in a brown bag.
The spy was concealing the secret data in a brown bag.

C In the passage below, the verbs **is** and **are** are used incorrectly five times. Cross out each incorrect word. Write the correct word above it. There are **two** redundant parts in the passage below. Cross out each redundant part.

Almost every country ~~are~~ *is* famous for a particular dish. Italy ~~are~~ *is* famous for its spaghetti, and Germany is famous for its sausages. The United States has become well known for several dishes. For instance, hamburgers originated in the United States, ~~where they were made for the first time.~~ Hamburgers ~~is~~ *are* popular all over the world, ~~and people in many places like to eat them.~~ Hush puppies, which ~~is~~ *are* balls of fried cornmeal, ~~is~~ *are* popular in the southern states.

END OF LESSON 102

Lesson 103

Student Book page 224

A

Here's the latest model sentence you learned:

> The major contended that he had valid motives for concealing the data.

What sentence means the same thing? Ⓐ
What word means **argued**? Ⓑ
What word means **sound**? Ⓒ
What word means **reasons**? Ⓓ
What word means **hiding**? Ⓔ
What word means **facts**? Ⓕ
What's another way of saying,
> The major argued that he had sound reasons for hiding the facts? Ⓖ

B

Write **Part B** in the left margin of your paper. You have two minutes to copy the paragraph below.

> Statements of fact tell what is or what happens. They do not tell how things ought to be. They tell how things are. Here is a statement of fact: Most of the people in Canada live along the southern border of the country.

★C

Write **Part C** in the left margin of your paper. Then number it from 1 to 9. The two accounts below contradict each other on an important point. Make sure you find that contradiction when you read the accounts.

Passage 1. An accident report was filed today in the 87th Police Precinct. The report was turned in by Officer Kucharski, who was at the scene when the incident occurred. According to the report, Mrs. Bernstein was dusting her windowsill overlooking Thirteenth Avenue when she accidentally tipped over a flowerpot. The flowerpot fell two stories, and it landed on the head of Ambassador Nittnek, a visiting dignitary from eastern Siberia. The ambassador was rushed to the hospital, where doctors determined that he had a minor concussion. The ambassador contended that the incident was a plot to make him appear foolish. United States officials calmed the ambassador, and Mrs. Bernstein was fined $500.

Passage 2. Ambassador Nittnek, who is visiting the United States from eastern Siberia, suffered a slight injury today when a flowerpot fell on his head. An alert police officer spotted the incident and called an ambulance. Apparently, the flowerpot was thrown from the window of Mrs. Bernstein, a widow who lives at Thirteenth and Tulip. Officer Kucharski interviewed Mrs. Bernstein, who said that Ambassador Nittnek was responsible for the death of her husband. The ambassador was reported in good condition, with only a minor concussion.

Note: The circled letters indicate when you ask a question or when you direct the group to respond.

EXERCISE 1

DEFINITIONS

1. (Direct the students to find Lesson 103, part A, in the **Student Book**.)
2. (Call on individual students to read part A.)
   Ⓐ Say it. *The major argued that he had sound reasons for hiding the facts.*
   Ⓑ What word? *Contended.*
   Ⓒ What word? *Valid.*
   Ⓓ What word? *Motives.*
   Ⓔ What word? *Concealing.*
   Ⓕ What word? *Data.*
   Ⓖ Say that sentence another way. *The major contended that he had valid motives for concealing the data.*

EXERCISE 2

INDEPENDENT WORK

1. **[Optional]** (Direct the students to read the instructions for part B to themselves. Then give them exactly two minutes to copy the paragraph. Count as errors any miscopied words and punctuation. Deduct these errors from the number of copied words, and mark the total on the Writing Rate Graph.)
2. Finish the Student Book and do the Workbook for Lesson 103. ✓

Workcheck

1. Get ready to check your answers starting with Student Book part C. Use a pen to mark an **X** next to any item you miss.
2. (Call on individual students to read each item and its answer. Repeat for the Workbook items.)

Answer key for Student Book part C
1. Idea: *How the flowerpot fell* 2. *Officer Kucharski* 3. *Passage 1* 4. Idea: *That it was a plot to make him appear foolish* 5. *Passage 1*
6. Idea: *That Ambassador Nittnek was responsible for the death of her husband*
7. *Passage 2* 8. Idea: *A minor concussion*
9. *Passages 1 and 2*

Answer key for Student Book part D
I. *Why wolves are disappearing*
   A. Idea: *Areas of wilderness are disappearing.*
   B. Idea: *There's not enough food for wolves to eat.*
   C. Idea: *Ranchers and farmers have been killing wolves to protect their livestock.*

Answer key for Student Book part E
1. *Island B* 2. *Nobody lives on this island.*
3. Idea: *A small stream runs through the middle of the banana grove.*

3. (Direct the students to count the number of errors and write the number in the **error** box at the top of the Workbook page.)
4. (Award points and direct students to record their points in Box **W**.)

0 errors	**15 points**
1–2 errors	**12 points**
3–5 errors	**8 points**
6–9 errors	**5 points**

5. (Award any bonus points. Direct the students to total their points and enter the total on the Point Summary Chart.)
6. Show me your work when you've finished correcting it. (When the students show you their corrected work, record their points on your Record Summary Chart.)

Answer each question below. Some of the questions ask where you found an answer. Write **passage 1**, **passage 2**, or **passages 1 and 2** for these questions.

1. These passages contradict each other on one big point. What point is that?
2. Who reported the accident?
3. Where did you find the answer to question 2?
4. What did the ambassador say about the incident?
5. Where did you find the answer to question 4?
6. What did Mrs. Bernstein say about the incident?
7. Where did you find the answer to question 6?
8. What kind of injury does the ambassador have?
9. Where did you find the answer to question 8?

D Write **Part D** in the left margin of your paper.

Here are three main ideas:
* **Why wilderness areas are disappearing**
* **Why wolves are disappearing**
* **How to shoot, trap, or poison a wolf**

One of the main ideas fits the passage below. Read the passage.

> Wolves travel in packs of ten to fifteen members that roam over large expanses of wilderness. One pack may cover an area of almost 5,000 square miles. Since there are fewer and fewer places where such large wilderness areas still exist, wolves are disappearing from our land. As the open land disappears, so does the wild game on which wolves survive. This lack of food is the second reason wolves are disappearing. Many wolves have moved up into Canada and Alaska to find more food. Finally, ranchers and farmers, in an effort to protect their livestock, have shot, trapped, and poisoned thousands of wolves. Except for those wolves in Alaska, a small population of wolves in Minnesota is the last of these animals in the United States.

Write the main idea that fits the passage. List the three points that fall under the main idea in outline form. Don't forget to indent and label the three points.

E Write **Part E** in the left margin of your paper. Then number it from 1 to 3. The description below and one of the maps tell about an island. Read the description and then answer the questions.

The map shows an island in the South Pacific. Nobody lives on this island. A huge banana grove covers the southern third of the island. A small stream runs from its source, a spring at the center of the island, through the middle of the banana grove and into the ocean.

1. Which island does the description tell about?
2. Which words in the description let you know that island A is not the one that is described?
3. Which words in the description let you know that island D is not the one that is described?

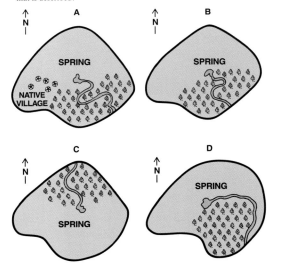

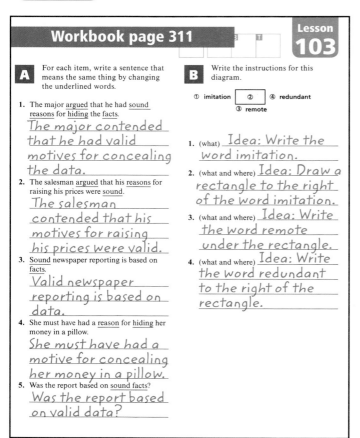

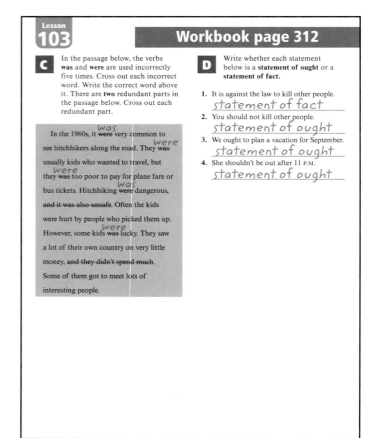

Workbook page 311

A For each item, write a sentence that means the same thing by changing the underlined words.

1. The major argued that he had sound reasons for hiding the facts.

   The major contended that he had valid motives for concealing the data.

2. The salesman argued that his reasons for raising his prices were sound.

   The salesman contended that his motives for raising his prices were valid.

3. Sound newspaper reporting is based on facts.

   Valid newspaper reporting is based on data.

4. She must have had a reason for hiding her money in a pillow.

   She must have had a motive for concealing her money in a pillow.

5. Was the report based on sound facts?

   Was the report based on valid data?

B Write the instructions for this diagram.

① imitation   ②   ④ redundant
         ③ remote

1. (what) *Idea: Write the word imitation.*

2. (what and where) *Idea: Draw a rectangle to the right of the word imitation.*

3. (what and where) *Idea: Write the word remote under the rectangle.*

4. (what and where) *Idea: Write the word redundant to the right of the rectangle.*

Workbook page 312

C In the passage below, the verbs **was** and **were** are used incorrectly five times. Cross out each incorrect word. Write the correct word above it. There are **two** redundant parts in the passage below. Cross out each redundant part.

In the 1960s, it ~~were~~ *was* very common to see hitchhikers along the road. They ~~was~~ *were* usually kids who wanted to travel, but they ~~was~~ *were* too poor to pay for plane fare or bus tickets. Hitchhiking ~~were~~ *was* dangerous, ~~and it was also unsafe.~~ Often the kids were hurt by people who picked them up. However, some kids ~~was~~ *were* lucky. They saw a lot of their own country on very little money, ~~and they didn't spend much.~~ Some of them got to meet lots of interesting people.

D Write whether each statement below is a **statement of ought** or a **statement of fact.**

1. It is against the law to kill other people.

   statement of fact

2. You should not kill other people.

   statement of ought

3. We ought to plan a vacation for September.

   statement of ought

4. She shouldn't be out after 11 P.M.

   statement of ought

END OF LESSON 103

Note: The circled letters indicate when you ask a question or when you direct the group to respond.

A You learned a model sentence that means:
> **The major argued that he had sound reasons for hiding the facts.**

Say that model sentence. ⊙
What word in the model sentence means **argued**? ⊙
What word in the model sentence means **sound**? ⊙
What word in the model sentence means **reasons**? ⊙
What word in the model sentence means **hiding**? ⊙
What word in the model sentence means **facts**? ⊙

─────────── **EXERCISE 1** ───────────

DEFINITIONS

1. (Direct the students to find Lesson 104, part A, in the **Student Book**.)
2 (Call on individual students to read part A.)

Ⓐ Say it. *The major contended that he had valid motives for concealing the data.*

Ⓑ What word? *Contended.*

Ⓒ What word? *Valid.*

Ⓓ What word? *Motives.*

Ⓔ What word? *Concealing.*

Ⓕ What word? *Data.*

─────────── **EXERCISE 2** ───────────

CONTRADICTIONS

Note: You will need a reference book that tells about the history of calendars.

1. (Direct the students to find part B.)
2. (Call on individual students to read part B.)

Ⓖ (Call on two students to name one point each. Ideas: *Passage 1, the new year for all calendars has always begun in January; passage 2, the Hebrew new year is in the fall. Passage 1, the Roman calendar originally had twelve months; passage 2, the original Roman calendar had ten months.*)

Ⓗ I'll read what it says in this reference book about calendars. (**Read the relevant passages.**) Which of the passages that you read earlier is accurate—passage 1 or passage 2? *Passage 2.*

B The two passages below contradict each other on two important points. Make sure you find those contradictions when you read the passages.

Passage 1. The new year for all calendars has always begun in January. The Roman calendar originally had twelve months and began with January. The Egyptian calendar also had twelve months. There were some problems with the original Roman calendar, but most of these were resolved by Julius Caesar, who adjusted the length of the months so that the year was 365 days. Julius Caesar also introduced a leap year every four years. In a leap year, there is an extra day.

The names of some of the months from the early Roman calendar are with us today—September, October, November, and December. These names mean the seventh month, eighth month, ninth month, and tenth month. Julius Caesar renamed the fifth month after himself—July. The ruler who followed as his successor, Augustus Caesar, renamed the sixth month after himself—August.

Passage 2. A calendar is a way of dividing up time so that people can keep track of time in the same way. Throughout history, there have been several different calendars. For example, one day is the amount of time it takes for the earth to turn around one time. A year, which is 365 days long, is the amount of time it takes for the earth to travel around the sun one time.

Different calendars have divided up the days of the year in different ways. The original Roman calendar had ten months—January and February were added to the calendar many centuries later. The Egyptian calendar had twelve months of thirty days each, with five days tacked on to the end of the year. The Hebrew calendar has twelve months of twenty-nine or thirty days each and occasionally adds a thirteenth month to make the calendar come out evenly. The Hebrew new year is in the fall to coincide with the estimated date of Creation.

The passages contradict each other on two important points. What are those points? ⊙
Let's look up **calendar** in a dictionary or encyclopedia and find out which passage is accurate. ⊙

Lesson 104 — Student Book page 228

C Each sentence below has two possible meanings. One is the meaning that the author intends. The other meaning is an unintended meaning.

- **Everybody around the racetrack cheered as the man beat the greyhound dog.**

Here's the intended meaning of the sentence:
   The man ran faster than the dog.
Here's the unintended meaning of the sentence:
   The man hit the dog.
The two meanings are possible because one word in the sentence can have two meanings. Which word is that? **①**

Here's another sentence:

- **When the final buzzer sounded, the Vikings were on top of the Braves.**

What's the intended meaning of the sentence? **①**
What's the unintended meaning? **①**
Which words are involved in the two meanings? **①**

D Write **Part D** in the left margin of your paper. You have two minutes to copy the paragraph below.

> Family structure varies from country to country. Most people in the United States and Canada are part of a nuclear family. This means that husband, wife, and children live together in their own living space, usually in a house or an apartment.

★ E Write **Part E** in the left margin of your paper. Then number it 1 and 2. The description below tells about one of the graphs. Read the description and then answer the questions.

The graph shows the use of electrical power in Center City. The solid line shows how much power business and industry use. The broken line shows how much power is used by private homes. Although you might expect power use to be high in the winter, the graph shows that power use is actually higher in the summer, when people use air conditioners. The graph also shows that business and industry use more power than individual homes, except during the cold winter months.

Student Book page 229 — Lesson 104

1. Which graph does the description tell about?
2. Which words in the description let you know that graph D is not the one that is described?

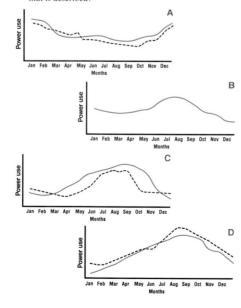

═══ EXERCISE 3 ═══
ANALYZING ARGUMENTS

1. (Direct the students to find part C.)
2. (Call on individual students to read part C.)
   ① Which word? *Beat.*
   ① (Call on a student. Idea:*The Vikings team had a higher score than the Braves.*)
   ⑩ (Call on a student. Idea:*The Vikings were on the Braves.*)
   ① Which words? *On top of.*

═══ EXERCISE 4 ═══
INDEPENDENT WORK

1. **[Optional]** (Direct the students to read the instructions for part D to themselves. Then give them exactly two minutes to copy the paragraph. Count as errors any miscopied words and punctuation. Deduct these errors from the number of copied words, and mark the total on the Writing Rate Graph.)
2. Finish the Student Book and do the Workbook for Lesson 104. ✓

Workcheck

1. Get ready to check your answers starting with Student Book part E. Use a pen to mark an **X** next to any item you miss.
2. (Call on individual students to read each item and its answer. Repeat for the Workbook items.)

> **Answer key for Student Book part E**
> **1.** *Graph C* **2.** *Business and industry use more power than individual homes.*

Answer key for Student Book part F

I. *People are vegetarians for several reasons.*
A. *Idea: Some people don't like the taste of meat.*
B. *Idea: Some people believe that eating meat is unhealthy.*
C. *Idea: Some people think that killing animals is immoral.*
D. *Idea: Some people think that the world food shortage makes it bad policy to eat meat.*

3. (Direct the students to count the number of errors and write the number in the **error** box at the top of the Workbook page.)

4. (Award points and direct students to record their points in Box **W.**)

0 errors	**15 points**
1–2 errors	**12 points**
3–5 errors	**8 points**
6–9 errors	**5 points**

5. (Award any bonus points. Direct the students to total their points and enter the total on the Point Summary Chart.)

6. Show me your work when you've finished correcting it. (When the students show you their corrected work, record their points on your Record Summary Chart.)

Lesson 104

Student Book page 230

F Write **Part F** in the left margin of your paper.

Here are three main ideas:
- **People are vegetarians for several reasons.**
- **A vegetarian diet can decrease heart disease.**
- **Few meat eaters would kill their own meat.**

One of the main ideas fits the passage below. Read the passage.

> A vegetarian is a person who eats no meat, fish, or poultry. There are over three million vegetarians in the United States alone. They can be divided into four different groups, according to their reasons for not eating meat. Some people are vegetarians simply because they don't like the taste of meat. Other people believe that eating meat is unhealthy. The American Medical Association has published a report saying that a vegetarian diet could possibly eliminate over 90 percent of the heart disease in the United States. Some vegetarians say that killing animals is immoral. They claim that very few meat eaters would be willing to kill a cow with their own hands, skin it, bleed it, and prepare it to be eaten. A fourth group of vegetarians claims that the world food shortage makes it bad policy to eat meat. We use 75 percent of the corn, barley, oats, and soybeans we produce to feed cattle. If these grains were fed directly to humans, much less land would be wasted on livestock, more food could be produced, and fewer people would go hungry. Whatever their individual reasons, the number of vegetarians is growing rapidly.

Write the main idea that fits the passage. List the four points that fall under the main idea in outline form. Don't forget to indent and label the four points.

Workbook page 313 **Lesson 104**

A For each item, write a sentence that means the same thing by changing the underlined word or words.

1. The major argued that he had sound reasons for hiding the facts.
   The major contended that he had valid motives for concealing the data.

2. Did Art have a sound excuse for hiding his laundry?
   Did Art have a valid excuse for concealing his laundry?

3. How can you argue that you won when you're hiding the truth?
   How can you contend that you won when you're concealing the truth?

4. His report was filled with useless facts.
   His report was filled with useless data.

B Each sentence below has two possible meanings. Read each sentence and answer the questions.

- **She told the tailor to mind his business.**

1. What's the intended meaning of the sentence?
   Idea: She told the tailor not to interfere in her business.

2. What's the unintended meaning?
   Idea: She told the tailor to take care of his business.

3. Which word is involved in the two meanings?
   mind

- **She said, "Your brother is on the phone. Make him get off it."**

4. What's the intended meaning of the sentence?
   Idea: Your brother is using the phone. Make him hang up.

5. What's the unintended meaning?
   Idea: Your brother is sitting on the phone. Make him get himself up from it.

6. Which words are involved in the two meanings?
   on, off

C Read this:

A lease is an agreement to pay for the use of
an apartment or house or car for a set length of time.

Use the facts to fill out the form.

Facts: **Your name is Sarah Templeton and you are applying to rent a new apartment. You currently live with your parents at 1617 Augusta in Oak Park, Illinois. Your social security number is 443-76-9008. Your present phone number is 383-0907. You work as a cashier in Kenwood's Drug Store at 123 Oak Park Mall. Your pay is $7 an hour and you make $1,100 a month. Your expenses are $500 a month. Your father is a painter for New Era Construction Company in Oak Park, and your mother is a salesperson in a small novelty shop in the mall. Your parents live together, and their combined earnings are $38,000 a year. The person who knows you best is Mr. Jim Rowe, who is your supervisor at Kenwood's. His phone number is 434-6758. The bank where you cash your paycheck is Oak Park Trust, 1345 Ridgeland Avenue, in Oak Park. You wish to sign a one-year lease. You have no pets, and you don't own a waterbed.**

Application for Apartment Rental

Name ___Sarah Templeton___ Phone number ___383-0907___

Address ___1617 Augusta___ ___Oak Park___ ___Illinois___
                                    City   State

Employment ___Kenwood's Drug Store___ Reference ___Mr. Jim Rowe___
                        Company name

___123 Oak Park Mall___ Phone ___434-6758___
            Address

Hourly rate of pay ___$7.00___ Earnings per month ___$1,100___

Parents' address ___1617 Augusta___ ___Oak Park___ ___Illinois___
                                              City   State

Occupation of father ___painter___ Occupation of mother ___salesperson___

Current monthly expenses ___$500___ Bank where you do business ___Oak Park Trust___

Lease desired: (1 year) 2 years 3 years (Circle one)

Do you wish to keep pets in the apartment? Yes _____ No __√__

Do you own a waterbed? Yes _____ No __√__

END OF LESSON 104

Note: The circled letters indicate when you ask a question or when you direct the group to respond.

A The sentence below has two possible meanings.
   He said, "My new record is really groovy."
   What's the intended meaning of the sentence? ⓐ
   What's the unintended meaning? ⓑ
   Which word is involved in the two meanings? ⓒ

B Some statements tell about numbers or statistics. If a statement tells that most people do a certain thing, it is a statement of fact. If a statement tells that most people should do a certain thing, it is a statement of ought.

• **Everybody agreed that murder is evil.**
That statement is a statement of fact. It tells what everybody agreed about.

• **Everybody should agree that murder is evil.**
That statement is a statement of ought. It tells what everybody should agree about.

• **Almost all of the participants thought that young people should not marry when they are in high school.**
This statement is a statement of fact. It tells what most of the participants thought should happen, not what should happen.
Tell whether each statement below is a **statement of ought** or a **statement of fact.**

• **Nearly all of the members thought that the club president should go to the convention.**
What kind of statement? ⓓ

• **The club president should go to the convention.**
What kind of statement? ⓔ

C Write **Part C** in the left margin of your paper. You have two minutes to copy the paragraph below.

> When the western part of the United States was first being settled, there were no cars, trains, planes, or buses. People devised other ways to haul supplies, passengers, and mail. Bull trains, the Pony Express, stagecoaches, and camels were used as transportation.

════════ **EXERCISE 1** ════════

ANALYZING ARGUMENTS

1. (Direct the students to find Lesson 105, part A, in the **Student Book.**)
2. (Call on individual students to read part A.)
   ⓐ (Call on a student. Idea: *He likes his new record a lot.*)
   ⓑ (Call on a student. Idea: *His new record has grooves.*)
   ⓒ Which word? *Groovy.*

════════ **EXERCISE 2** ════════

ANALYZING ARGUMENTS

1. (Direct the students to find part B.)
2. (Call on individual students to read part B.)
   ⓓ What's the answer? *Statement of fact.*
   ⓔ What's the answer? *Statement of ought.*

════════ **EXERCISE 3** ════════

INDEPENDENT WORK

1. **[Optional]** (Direct the students to read the instructions for part C to themselves. Then give them exactly two minutes to copy the paragraph. Count as errors any miscopied words and punctuation. Deduct these errors from the number of copied words, and mark the total on the Writing Rate Graph.)
2. Finish the Student Book and do the Workbook for Lesson 105. ✓

Student Book page 232

★ **D** Write **Part D** in the left margin of your paper. Then number it from 1 to 10. The two accounts below contradict each other on an important point. Make sure you find that contradiction when you read the accounts.

> **Passage 1.** Alobovia and Torania have been involved in a cold war for the last six years. The heads of these two countries have been discussing their conflicts this week at a meeting in Furgon. People all over the world are anxiously waiting for the outcome of these peace talks. At the end of today's session, the prime minister of Alobovia held a press conference. He reported that the peace talks were going very well. He is hopeful that by the end of the week, Alobovia and Torania will settle their differences. He refused to give specific details of the meetings, saying that worldwide knowledge of the details might threaten the success of the talks.

> **Passage 2.** The heads of two European countries are meeting this week in Furgon. The prime ministers of Torania and Alobovia are discussing their conflicts, which have been the basis for a cold war between the two countries for the last six years. At the end of today's session, the prime minister of Alobovia held a news conference. He denied reports that the peace talks were going well and indicated that he thought it would be some time before Alobovia and Torania would come to some agreement on their conflicts. The prime minister of Torania refused to comment on the situation.

Student Book page 233

Answer each question below. Some of the questions ask where you found an answer. Write **passage 1**, **passage 2**, or **passages 1 and 2** for these questions.

1. These passages contradict each other on one big point. What point is that?
2. What is a cold war?
3. How long have Alobovia and Torania been involved in a cold war?
4. Where did you find the answer to question 3?
5. Why are the prime ministers meeting?
6. Where did you find the answer to question 5?
7. What did the prime minister of Torania say about the meetings?
8. Where did you find the answer to question 7?
9. Why didn't the prime minister of Alobovia give details of the meetings?
10. Where did you find the answer to question 9?

1. Idea: how the peace talks are going
2. Idea: when two countries are close to using their guns on each other
3. for six years
4. passages 1 and 2
5. Idea: to discuss their conflicts
6. passages 1 and 2
7. Idea: nothing
8. passage 2
9. Idea: He thought that worldwide knowledge of the details might threaten the success of the talks.
10. passage 1

Workcheck

1. Get ready to check your answers starting with Student Book part D. Use a pen to make an **X** next to any item you miss.
2. (Call on individual students to read each item and its answer. Repeat for Workbook items.)
3. (Direct the students to count the number of errors and write the number in the **error** box at the top of the Workbook page.)
4. (Award points and direct students to record their points in Box **W**.)

0 errors	**15 points**
1–2 errors	**12 points**
3–5 errors	**8 points**
6–9 errors	**5 points**

5. (Award any bonus points. Direct the students to total their points and enter the total on the Point Summary Chart.)
6. Show me your work when you've finished correcting it. (When the students show you their corrected work, record their points on your Record Summary Chart.)

Note: Before presenting Lesson 106, present Fact Game Lesson 7

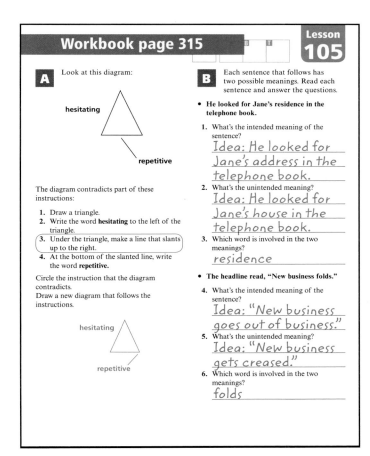

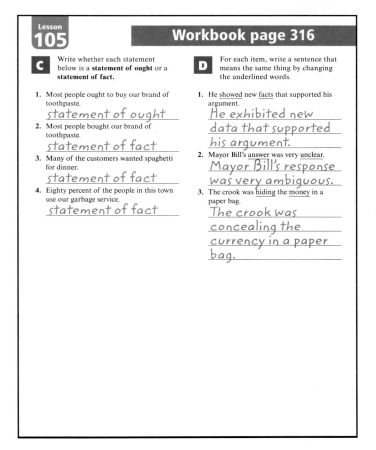

Workbook page 315

A Look at this diagram:

hesitating

repetitive

The diagram contradicts part of these instructions:

1. Draw a triangle.
2. Write the word **hesitating** to the left of the triangle.
3. Under the triangle, make a line that slants up to the right.
4. At the bottom of the slanted line, write the word **repetitive.**

Circle the instruction that the diagram contradicts.
Draw a new diagram that follows the instructions.

hesitating

repetitive

B Each sentence that follows has two possible meanings. Read each sentence and answer the questions.

• **He looked for Jane's residence in the telephone book.**

1. What's the intended meaning of the sentence?
Idea: He looked for Jane's address in the telephone book.

2. What's the unintended meaning?
Idea: He looked for Jane's house in the telephone book.

3. Which word is involved in the two meanings?
residence

• **The headline read, "New business folds."**

4. What's the intended meaning of the sentence?
Idea: "New business goes out of business."

5. What's the unintended meaning?
Idea: "New business gets creased."

6. Which word is involved in the two meanings?
folds

Workbook page 316

C Write whether each statement below is a **statement of ought** or a **statement of fact.**

1. Most people ought to buy our brand of toothpaste.
statement of ought

2. Most people bought our brand of toothpaste.
statement of fact

3. Many of the customers wanted spaghetti for dinner.
statement of fact

4. Eighty percent of the people in this town use our garbage service.
statement of fact

D For each item, write a sentence that means the same thing by changing the underlined words.

1. He showed new facts that supported his argument.
He exhibited new data that supported his argument.

2. Mayor Bill's answer was very unclear.
Mayor Bill's response was very ambiguous.

3. The crook was hiding the money in a paper bag.
The crook was concealing the currency in a paper bag.

END OF LESSON 105

Lesson 105   **105**

Workbook page 317

|21|22|23|24|25|26|27|28|29|30|

AFTER LESSON 105

2. a. In what year did the first person walk on the moon?
   b. In what year was the first coast-to-coast railroad in the United States completed?

3. a. What do we call any living thing?
   b. Name 3 scavengers.

4. Tell the redundant part in each sentence.
   a. He concealed the money by hiding it.
   b. This weapon, which is lethal, could kill someone.

5. Fill in each blank with **has** or **have.**

   a. Players on that team ▪▪▪ practice every day.

   b. Nobody in those houses ▪▪▪ a TV set.

6. Say each sentence below, using **rarely, usually,** or **occasionally.**
   a. He (almost never) likes to eat pizza.
   b. She goes to the movies (once in a while).

7. Say the model sentence that means this:

   > The major **argued** that he had **sound reasons** for **hiding** the **facts.**

8. Tell whether each statement is a **statement of fact** or a **statement of ought.**
   a. People who smoke should try to quit.
   b. Many people die each year from problems related to smoking.

9. a. Name the earliest-known close relative of the modern horse.
   b. What do we call a species that is nearly extinct?

10. Combine these sentences with **so** or **but.**

    > He wants to buy a new bike.
    > He is saving all his money.

11. Look at the map and answer these questions.
    a. How many countries border Bolivia?
    b. Name those countries.

12. Brazil is bordered by five countries. Look at the map and name those countries.

Workbook page 481

Fact Game Answer Key

FACT GAME 7

2. a. 1969
   b. 1869

3. a. Organism
   b. Any 3: Bears, porcupines, crows, vultures

4. a. By hiding it
   b. Could kill someone

5. a. Players on that team have practice every day.
   b. Nobody in those houses has a TV set.

6. a. He rarely likes to eat pizza.
   b. She goes to the movies occasionally.

7. The major contended that he had valid motives for concealing the data.

8. a. Statement of ought
   b. Statement of fact

9. a. Eohippus
   b. Endangered

10. He wants to buy a new bike, so he is saving all his money.

11. a. 5
    b. Brazil, Peru, Chile, Argentina, Paraguay

12. Peru, Bolivia, Paraguay, Argentina, Uruguay

FACT GAME 8

2. a. grazing
   b. hunting

3. Just because you know about a part doesn't mean you know about another part.

4. a. 5 years
   b. 3 meters

5. a. 7 years
   b. 6 meters

6. a. The dog was especially happy to see its owner.
   b. Summers in Arizona are especially hot.

7. a. The animals ate the food.
   b. The vehicles stopped in front of the buildings.

8. a. She is a particularly good singer.
   b. It rains a lot here, particularly in the winter.

9. Just because you know about a whole thing doesn't mean you know about every part.

10. a. Ecology
    b. Paragraphos

11. She is going to the movies with Pete, who is her neighbor.

12. a. Green plants
    b. pointed, flat

Note: Before beginning Lesson 106, present this Fact Game Lesson. You will need a pair of dice for every four or five students. Each student needs a pencil and Workbook.

EXERCISE 1

FACT GAME

1. (Divide the students into groups of four or five. Assign one player in each group to be the monitor. Seat the groups at different tables with a pair of dice.)
2. (Direct the players to open their Workbooks to page 317. Direct the monitors to open their Workbooks to page 481.)
3. You have 20 minutes to play the game. (Circulate as students play. Comment on groups that are playing well.)

Points for Fact Game

1. (At the end of 20 minutes, have all students who earned more than 12 points stand up. Award 5 bonus points to these players.)
2. (Award points to monitors. Monitors receive the same number of points earned by the highest performer in the group.)
3. (Tell the monitor of each game that ran smoothly:) Your group did a good job. Give yourself and each of your players 5 bonus points. ✓
4. Everybody, write your game points in Box FG on your Point Chart. Write your bonus points in the bonus box. ✓

Lesson Objectives	LESSON 106	LESSON 107	LESSON 108	LESSON 109	LESSON 110
	Exercise	Exercise	Exercise	Exercise	Exercise
Organization and Study Skills					
Main Idea	SB	SB	SB	SB	SB
Outlining			SB	SB	SB
Writing Mechanics: Copying	3	3	Ind. Work	3	1
Reasoning Strategies					
Deductions		WB		WB	WB
Rules: Arguments	1	1	1	2	
Statements: Ought		WB		WB	WB
Contradictions	SB			1	
Inference	2	2	3		
Information Sources/Study Skills					
Basic Comprehension					SB
Reading Comprehension: Words or Deductions				WB	
Supporting Evidence	SB			SB	SB
Vocabulary/Language Arts Strategies					
Definitions		SB	SB		SB
Usage		SB	SB		SB
Sentence Combination			2		
Editing/Revising	WB	SB, WB	SB		WB
Comprehension: Meaning from Context	WB	WB		WB	WB
Information Application/ Study Skills					
Information Review					
Assessment/Progress Monitoring					
Ongoing: Workcheck	Workcheck	Workcheck	Workcheck	Workcheck	Workcheck
Formal: Mastery Test					MT11

Note: The circled letters indicate when you ask a question or when you direct the group to respond.

━━━━━━━━ **EXERCISE 1** ━━━━━━━━
ANALYZING ARGUMENTS

1. (Direct the students to find Lesson 106, part A, in the **Student Book**.)
2. (Call on individual students to read part A.)

Ⓐ What's the answer? *It must be a statement of ought.*

Ⓑ Study it and get ready to say it. (Wait. Call on individual students to say the whole deduction without looking at it.)

Ⓒ What's the answer? *It must be a statement of ought.*

Ⓓ Figure it out and get ready to say it. (Wait. Call on a student to say the missing rule. Idea: *You should do things that let you stay in good health.*)

Ⓔ Think about it and get ready to say it. (Wait. Call on individual students to say the whole deduction without looking at it.)

Ⓕ What's the answer? *A statement of ought.*

Ⓖ What's the answer? *It must be a statement of ought.*

Ⓗ Figure it out and get ready to say it. (Wait. Call on a student to say the missing rule. Idea: *You should do things that let you get smart.*)

Ⓘ Think about it and get ready to say it. (Wait. Call on individual students to say the whole deduction without looking at it.)

Student Book page 234

A Some arguments end with a conclusion that is a statement of ought. Here's a rule about conclusions that are statements of ought:

> **If the conclusion is a statement of ought, the rule at the beginning of the deduction must be a statement of ought.**

- Here's a valid deduction:
  > **You ought to do what your mother tells you to do.**
  > **Your mother tells you to do your homework.**
  > **Therefore, you ought to do your homework.**

  The conclusion is a statement of ought and the rule at the beginning of the deduction is a statement of ought. The deduction is valid.

- Here's a deduction with the rule missing:
  > **If you stay slim, you'll live longer.**
  > **Therefore, you should stay slim.**

  The conclusion is a statement of ought, so what do you know about the rule at the beginning of the deduction? Ⓐ
  Here's that rule: **You should do things that let you live longer.**
  Say the whole deduction. Ⓑ

- Here's another deduction with the rule missing:
  > **If you exercise, you'll stay in good health.**
  > **Therefore, you ought to exercise.**

  The conclusion is a statement of ought, so what do you know about the missing rule? Ⓒ
  Figure out the missing rule. Ⓓ
  Say the whole deduction. Ⓔ

- Here's another deduction with the rule missing:
  > **If you work hard at your studies, you'll get smart.**
  > **Therefore, you should work hard at your studies.**

  What kind of statement is the conclusion? Ⓕ
  So what do you know about the missing rule? Ⓖ
  Figure out the missing rule. Ⓗ
  Say the whole deduction. Ⓘ

Student Book page 235

Lesson 106

B The description below tells about one of the words listed below. Read the description and then answer the questions.

The word you're looking for is made by combining two common root words. One of the root words is fact, which means **make**. (The word **factory** means **a place where you make something**.) The other common root word is man, which means **hand**. (**Manually**, meaning **by hand**, and **manicure**, which is **a beauty treatment for your hands**, both contain the root word man.)

The word you're looking for, containing both fact and man, used to mean **handmade**. It means something different today.

manipulated   malefactor   manufactured   manuscript

Which word does the description tell about? ⓙ
Which words in the description let you know that **manipulated** is not the word that is described? ⓚ
Which words in the description let you know that **manuscript** is not the word that is described? ⓛ
Which words in the description let you know that **malefactor** is not the word that is described? ⓜ

C Write **Part C** in the left margin of your paper. You have two minutes to copy the paragraph below.

Some statements tell about numbers or statistics. If a statement tells that most people do a certain thing, it is a statement of fact. If a statement tells that most people should do a certain thing, it is a statement of ought.

Lesson 106

Student Book page 236

★ **D** Write **Part D** in the left margin of your paper. Then number it from 1 to 3. Here are three main ideas:

Main idea A. Some children have many "parents."
Main idea B. Americans live in nuclear families.
Main idea C. Housing is scarce in many parts of the world.

Each main idea fits one of the passages below. After reading all the passages, figure out which main idea goes with each passage.

Passage 1. Family structure varies from country to country. Most people in the United States and Canada are part of a "nuclear" family. This means that husband, wife, and children live together. They usually live in their own living space, such as a house or an apartment. In the nuclear family, the husband and wife provide food and shelter for their children until the children are old enough to take care of themselves.

Passage 2. Family structure varies from country to country. Some societies "share" their children. This means that the children consider any adult in the tribe as their parent. They can sleep at a different house or eat meals with a different "family" when they want to. In this way, children benefit from many different adults. A child who has a talent for art can spend lots of time with an adult who knows about art. A child who likes to build things can learn skills from an adult who also likes to build.

Passage 3. Family structure varies from country to country. In the United States and Canada, most children leave home by the time they are twenty-one. They have their own jobs and their own apartments. In much of Europe and Asia, however, housing is hard to find and very expensive. Most children keep living with their parents for a long time, even after they marry. In many countries, it is not unusual to find great-grandparents, grandparents, parents, and children all living together under one roof.

1. Main idea A is: **Some children have many "parents."** Which passage does main idea A fit best? *passage 2*
2. Main idea B is: **Americans live in nuclear families.** Which passage does main idea B fit best? *passage 1*
3. Main idea C is: **Housing is scarce in many parts of the world.** Which passage does main idea C fit best? *passage 3*

EXERCISE 2

STATEMENT INFERENCE

1. (Direct the students to find part B.)
2. (Call on individual students to read part B.)
   ⓙ Which word? *Manufactured.*
   ⓚ Figure out the answer. (Wait.) Which words? (Ideas: *One of the root words is fact.*)
   ⓛ Figure out the answer. (Wait.) Which words? *(Ideas: One of the root words is fact.)*
   ⓜ Figure out the answer. (Wait.) Which words? (Ideas: *This word, containing both fact and man . . .*)

EXERCISE 3

INDEPENDENT WORK

1. **[Optional]** (Direct the students to read the instructions for part C to themselves. Then give them exactly two minutes to copy the paragraph. Count as errors any miscopied words and punctuation. Deduct these errors from the number of copied words, and mark the total on the Writing Rate Graph.)
2. Finish the Student Book and do the Workbook for Lesson 106. ✓

Workcheck

1. Get ready to check your answers starting with Student Book part D. Use a pen to make an **X** next to any item you miss.
2. (Call on individual students to read each item and its answer. Repeat for Workbook items.)
3. (Direct the students to count the number of errors and write the number in the **error** box at the top of the Workbook page.)

4. (Award points and direct students to record their points in Box **W.**)

0 errors	15 points
1–2 errors	12 points
3–5 errors	8 points
6–9 errors	5 points

5. (Award any bonus points. Direct the students to total their points and enter the total on the Point Summary Chart.)

6. Show me your work when you've finished correcting it. (When the students show you their corrected work, record their points on your Record Summary Chart.)

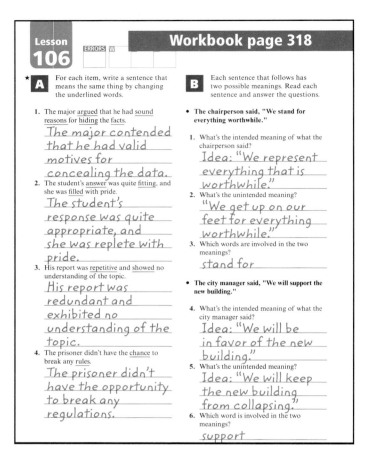

Workbook page 318

Lesson 106 ERRORS W

★ **A** For each item, write a sentence that means the same thing by changing the underlined words.

1. The major <u>argued</u> that he had <u>sound</u> <u>reasons</u> for <u>hiding</u> the facts.
   The major contended that he had valid motives for concealing the data.

2. The student's <u>answer</u> was quite <u>fitting</u>, and she was <u>filled</u> with pride.
   The student's response was quite appropriate, and she was replete with pride.

3. His report was <u>repetitive</u> and <u>showed</u> no understanding of the topic.
   His report was redundant and exhibited no understanding of the topic.

4. The prisoner didn't have the <u>chance</u> to break any <u>rules</u>.
   The prisoner didn't have the opportunity to break any regulations.

B Each sentence that follows has two possible meanings. Read each sentence and answer the questions.

• The chairperson said, "We stand for everything worthwhile."

1. What's the intended meaning of what the chairperson said?
   Idea: "We represent everything that is worthwhile."

2. What's the unintended meaning?
   "We get up on our feet for everything worthwhile."

3. Which words are involved in the two meanings?
   stand for

• The city manager said, "We will support the new building."

4. What's the intended meaning of what the city manager said?
   Idea: "We will be in favor of the new building."

5. What's the unintended meaning?
   Idea: "We will keep the new building from collapsing."

6. Which word is involved in the two meanings?
   support

Student Book page 237 Lesson 106

E Write **Part E** in the left margin of your paper. Then number it from 1 to 9. The two accounts below contradict each other on an important point. Make sure you find that contradiction when you read the accounts.

Passage 1. The National Forest Service today reported a wolf attack that occurred in a national park in Minnesota. "These attacks are occurring quite frequently these days," said a Forest Service employee. "The wolves have become very quick to attack because the wilderness areas where they live and feed are being destroyed." The largest population of wolves left in the United States, outside of Alaska, is in Minnesota, and consists of about 1200 wolves. The state of Minnesota has labeled wolves an endangered species and is trying to protect them.

Passage 2. The National Forest Service reported that a man had been attacked by a wolf in a national park in Minnesota late last night. Ranger Thompson, who reported the attack, told reporters: "This attack is a very rare incident. Wolves have never been known to attack a human. We are afraid that the public will overreact to this event, and will start killing wolves. Since wolves are already an endangered species, any all-out attacks on wolves could wipe them from the face of the Earth."

Answer each question below. Some of the questions ask where you found an answer. Write **passage 1, passage 2,** or **passages 1 and 2** for these questions.
1. These passages contradict each other on one big point. What point is that?
2. Why are wolves becoming quick to attack?
3. Where did you find the answer to question 2?
4. Name the person who reported the attack.
5. Where did you find the answer to question 4?
6. Why is it important to protect wolves?
7. Where did you find the answer to question 6?
8. In what state did the attack occur?
9. Where did you find the answer to question 8?

1. Idea: whether wolf attacks are occurring frequently or rarely
2. Idea: because the wilderness areas where they live are being destroyed
3. passage 1
4. Ranger Thompson
5. passage 2
6. Idea: because they are an endangered species
7. passages 1 and 2
8. Minnesota
9. passages 1 and 2

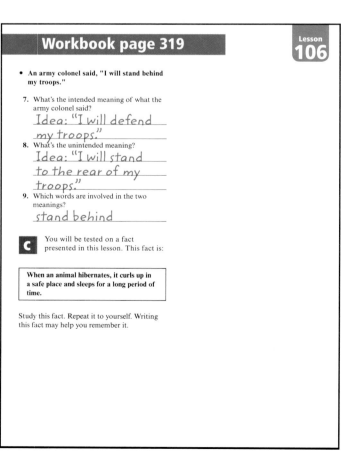

Workbook page 319 Lesson 106

• An army colonel said, "I will stand behind my troops."

7. What's the intended meaning of what the army colonel said?
   Idea: "I will defend my troops."

8. What's the unintended meaning?
   Idea: "I will stand to the rear of my troops."

9. Which words are involved in the two meanings?
   stand behind

C You will be tested on a fact presented in this lesson. This fact is:

> When an animal hibernates, it curls up in a safe place and sleeps for a long period of time.

Study this fact. Repeat it to yourself. Writing this fact may help you remember it.

END OF LESSON 106

Student Book page 238

A Some arguments end with a conclusion that is a statement of ought. Here's a rule about conclusions that are statements of ought:

> If the conclusion is a statement of ought, the rule at the beginning of the deduction must be a statement of ought.

Here's a valid deduction:

> You shouldn't do things that are against the law.
> Stealing things is against the law.
> Therefore, you shouldn't steal things.

The conclusion is a statement of ought and the rule at the beginning of the deduction is a statement of ought. The deduction is valid.

* Here's a deduction with the rule missing:

> Your mother tells you to do your homework.
> Therefore, you ought to do your homework.

The conclusion is a statement of ought, so what do you know about the rule at the beginning of the deduction? Ⓐ
Here's that rule: **You should do what your mother tells you to do.**
Say the whole deduction. Ⓑ

* Here's another deduction with the rule missing:

> Smoking is bad for you.
> Therefore, you shouldn't smoke.

The conclusion is a statement of ought, so what do you know about the missing rule? Ⓒ
Figure out the missing rule. Ⓓ
Say the whole deduction. Ⓔ

* Here's another deduction with the rule missing:

> If you exercise, you'll stay in good health.
> Therefore, you ought to exercise.

What kind of statement is the conclusion? Ⓕ
So what do you know about the missing rule? Ⓖ
Figure out the missing rule. Ⓗ
Say the whole deduction. Ⓘ

Note: The circled letters indicate when you ask a question or when you direct the group to respond.

=== **EXERCISE 1** ===

ANALYZING ARGUMENTS

1. (Direct the students to find Lesson 107, part A, in the **Student Book**.)
2. (Call on individual students to read part A.)

   Ⓐ What's the answer? *It must be a statement of ought.*

   Ⓑ Study it and get ready to say it. (Wait. Call on individual students to say the whole deduction without looking at it.)

   Ⓒ What's the answer? *It must be a statement of ought.*

   Ⓓ Figure it out and get ready to say it. (Wait. Call on a student to say the missing rule. Idea: *You shouldn't do things that are bad for you.*)

   Ⓔ Think about it and get ready to say it. (Wait. Call on individual students to say the whole deduction without looking at it.)

   Ⓕ What's the answer? *A statement of ought.*

   Ⓖ What's the answer? *It must be a statement of ought.*

   Ⓗ Figure it out and get ready to say it. (Wait. Call on a student to say the missing rule. Idea: *You should do things that let you stay in good health.*)

   Ⓘ Think about it and get ready to say it. (Wait. Call on individual students to say the whole deduction without looking at it.)

━━━━━━━━━━ **EXERCISE 2** ━━━━━━━━━━

STATEMENT INFERENCE

1. (Direct the students to find part B.)
2. (Call on individual students to read up to ⓚ.)
   ⓙ What's the answer? *Passage 2.*
   ⓚ (Call on a student. Idea:*The Life of John James Audubon.*)
3. Read the instructions and do the items. (Wait for the students to complete the items.) Let's check your answers. Put an **X** next to any item you miss.
4. (Read each item. Call on individual students to answer each item.)

> **Answer key for Student Book part B**
> **1.** *1803; passage 1* **2.** *Idea: Helps protect wildlife, publishes information about birds, and gives lectures about wildlife and wildlife protection; passages 1 and 2* **3.** *1905; passage 2* **4.** *Idea: To paint all the species of birds in North America; passage 1* **5.** *John James Audubon; passages 1 and 2*

━━━━━━━━━━ **EXERCISE 3** ━━━━━━━━━━

INDEPENDENT WORK

1. **[Optional]** (Direct the students to read the instructions for part C to themselves. Then give them exactly two minutes to copy the paragraph. Count as errors any miscopied words and punctuation. Deduct these errors from the number of copied words, and mark the total on the Writing Rate Graph.)
2. Finish the Student Book and do the Workbook for Lesson 107. ✓

Student Book page 239 — Lesson 107

B Some written passages give more facts about a particular subject than other passages. The two passages below tell something about the Audubon Society. Read both passages and find out which passage gives more facts about the Audubon Society.

> **Passage 1.** John James Audubon came to America in 1803. He was a talented dancer, flute player, violinist, and artist. More than anything, however, he loved the natural world of plants and animals. His biggest ambition was to paint all the species of birds in North America. Although he was poor for many years, his dedication kept him going. Within fifteen years of coming to America, he was well known and his paintings were loved in both Europe and America. It is no wonder that the Audubon Society, a society dedicated to the protection of wildlife, took the name of John James Audubon.

> **Passage 2.** Starting in 1886, many small groups devoting themselves to the appreciation and protection of birdlife sprang up in the United States. In 1905, these local societies banded together into a nationwide society that took its name from the great naturalist John James Audubon. Today, the Audubon Society is involved in many different activities. Congress gets help from the society in drafting new laws for protecting wildlife. The society publishes large amounts of information about birds, and it has a staff of lecturers who travel around the country talking about wildlife and wildlife protection.

Which passage tells more about the Audubon Society? ⓔ
The other passage gives more facts about something else.
What does it tell more about? ⓕ

Write **Part B** in the left margin of your paper. Then number it from 1 to 5.

Answer each question. **Then write whether the question is answered by passage 1, passage 2, or passages 1 and 2.**

1. When did John James Audubon come to America?
2. What does the Audubon Society do?
3. When was the Audubon Society formed?
4. What was John James Audubon's biggest ambition?
5. Who is the Audubon Society named after?

Lesson 107 — **Student Book page 240**

C Write **Part C** in the left margin of your paper. You have two minutes to copy the paragraph below.

> During the months when there is almost no water to be found in the desert, many desert animals hibernate. Some animals can hibernate for many weeks without becoming weak. When water becomes more plentiful, they wake up and resume an active life.

★ **D** Write **Part D** in the left margin of your paper. Rewrite the passage below using words you have learned to replace the underlined words. Remember to start every sentence with a capital letter and to punctuate each sentence correctly.

> Bongo <u>almost never</u> exercised. <u>Most of the time</u> he sat at home and watched television. <u>Once in a while</u> he slept, but not for long. Bongo's mother thought that he should get more exercise. Bongo's greatest <u>fear</u> was that his mother would <u>limit</u> his television time. Bongo's mother <u>made up</u> a plan to help him exercise. She <u>changed</u> the television into an exercise machine. Now Bongo is <u>filled</u> with joy as he exercises and watches television.

E Write **Part E** in the left margin of your paper. Then number it from 1 to 3. Here are three main ideas:

> **Main idea A. Progress creates problems.**
> **Main idea B. Progress leads to more food production.**
> **Main idea C. Progress doesn't always lead to more profits.**

Each main idea fits one of the passages that follow. After reading all the passages, figure out which main idea goes with each passage.

Workcheck

1. Get ready to check your answers starting with Student Book part D. Use a pen to mark an **X** next to any item you miss.
2. (Call on individual students to read each item and its answer. Repeat for Workbook items.)

> **Answer key for Student Book part D** *Bongo rarely exercised. Usually he sat at home and watched television. Occasionally he slept, but not for long. Bongo's mother thought that he should get more exercise. Bongo's greatest anxiety was that his mother would restrict his television time. Bongo's mother devised a strategy to help him exercise. She converted the television into an exercise machine. Now Bongo is replete with joy as he exercises and watches television.*

3. (Direct the students to count the number of errors and write the number in the **error** box at the top of the Workbook page.)
4. (Award points and direct students to record their points in Box **W**.)

0 errors	**15 points**
1–2 errors	**12 points**
3–5 errors	**8 points**
6–9 errors	**5 points**

5. (Award any bonus points. Direct the students to total their points and enter the total on the Point Summary Chart.)
6. Show me your work when you've finished correcting it. (When the students show you their corrected work, record their points on your Record Summary Chart.)

Student Book page 241

Passage 1. Progress in modern science has greatly changed living styles. Eating habits have changed because more food is available. New strains of wheat and corn have been developed that produce more grain per acre than ever before. Farmers are equipped with machinery that makes it possible for fewer people to do more work and also increase productivity. Improvements in the transportation and distribution systems have made vegetables of good quality available to nearly everyone.

Passage 2. Progress in modern science has greatly changed living styles. As machines have taken over the tasks once performed by the muscles of people, physical exercise has decreased. Many people spend the entire workday sitting down, and the automobile has practically eliminated walking. Unfortunately, many people who exercise very little are eating more food than ever. When people regularly eat more food than their body uses, they gradually become overweight. Excess weight, which is a cause of heart disease, diabetes, and emotional problems, is more common now than ever before in history.

Passage 3. "Progress in modern science has greatly changed the way I run my farm. Twenty years ago, I produced less than half of what I do now, and I worked nearly twice as much. New machinery has made it possible for three of us to do what would have been done by a dozen people in 1950. Unfortunately, even though we can produce a lot more, our profits are still quite small. Machinery, fertilizer, feed for the animals, and taxes are all more expensive than ever, and yet we still sell our crops at a very low price. Even with all the modern advancements, it is difficult to make a good living on a farm."

1. Main idea A is: **Progress creates problems.** Which passage does main idea A best fit? *passage 2*
2. Main idea B is: **Progress leads to more food production.** Which passage does main idea B best fit? *passage 1*
3. Main idea C is: **Progress doesn't always lead to more profits.** Which passage does main idea C best fit? *passage 3*

Workbook page 320

 A Each sentence that follows has two possible meanings. Read each sentence and answer the questions.

- **That solution seems very simple to me.**

1. What's the intended meaning of the sentence?
   Idea: The solution to the problem seems very simple to me.
2. What's the unintended meaning?
   Idea: The liquid mixture seems very simple to me.
3. Which word is involved in the two meanings?
   solution

- **They found the used-car salesman to be very slippery.**

4. What's the intended meaning of the sentence?
   Idea: They found the used-car salesman to be very devious.

5. What's the unintended meaning?
   Idea: They found the used-car salesman to be very greasy.
6. Which word is involved in the two meanings?
   slippery

- **In the end, he received a series of rabies shots.**

7. What's the intended meaning of the sentence?
   Idea: Finally, he received a series of rabies shots.
8. What's the unintended meaning?
   Idea: He received a series of rabies shots in his buttocks.
9. Which words are involved in the two meanings?
   in the end

Workbook page 321

B Underline the redundant part in each sentence below. Then explain why the underlined part is redundant.

1. He sanctioned her action, <u>approving of what she did.</u>

   Idea: If you know that he sanctioned her action, then you already know that he approved of what she did.

2. She was scrupulous about her work, <u>attending carefully to every detail.</u>

   Idea: If you know that she was scrupulous about her work, then you already know that she attended carefully to every detail.

3. The project was <u>completely</u> finished.

   Idea: If you know that the project was finished, then you already know that it was completed.

C You will be tested on a fact presented in this lesson. This fact is:

> **Inflation means that prices keep going up.**

Study this fact. Repeat it to yourself. Writing this fact may help you remember it.

END OF LESSON 107

Note: The circled letters indicate when you ask a question or when you direct the group to respond.

═══ EXERCISE 1 ═══
STATEMENT INFERENCE

1. (Direct the students to find Lesson 108, part A, in the Student Book.)
2. (Call on individual students to read up to Ⓑ.)
   Ⓐ What's the answer? *Passage 1.*
   Ⓑ Figure out which main idea fits passage 2. (Wait.)
   Which main idea? *Main idea C.*
3. Read the instructions and do the items. (Wait for the students to complete the items.) Let's check your answers. Put an **X** next to any item you miss.
4. (Read each item. Call on individual students to answer each item.)

Answer key for Student Book part A
1. *Idea: A fine red grit; passage 2* **2.** *Yes; passage 1* **3.** *Idea: It was left behind by a spaceship centuries earlier; passage 2* **4.** *90 degrees below zero; passage 1* **5.** *Idea: The temperature gets very hot during the day and very cold at night, there isn't enough oxygen to support humans; passage 1*

A Some written passages give more facts about a particular subject than other passages. The two passages below tell something about Mars. Read both passages and find out which passage gives more facts about Mars.

> **Passage 1.** In 1881, an Italian astronomer published a book of drawings that he had made during a five-year study of Mars. His drawings showed a complicated network of straight lines that he called channels. Enthusiastic observers concluded that Mars was inhabited by an advanced civilization that used the channels to distribute water around the planet's surface. As more information has been gathered, however, it has become more and more unlikely that there is any life on Mars. Martian days have temperatures as high as 80 degrees Celsius, and at night the temperature plunges to 90 degrees below zero. The Martian atmosphere is very thin and contains only a trace of oxygen, not enough to support humans. Scientists now believe that there is water on the surface of Mars. .

> **Passage 2.** For three days, Fred had roamed the rust-colored Martian desert. He was the lone survivor of a savage battle between the crew of an interplanetary ore freighter and a band of pirates from the asteroid belt. The fine red grit of the desert had worked its way into the joints of his spacesuit, so that even his smallest gestures sent squeaks through the tightly woven metallic fiber. Fred was very thirsty, and he was wandering around the desert just to keep occupied. Suddenly he spotted a large container, a 300-liter water tank that had been left by a spaceship centuries before. Fred jumped up and down and clapped his hands, his suit scraping and squeaking like a puppet with squeaky joints.

Which passage tells more about Mars? Ⓐ
Which of the following main ideas fits passage 2?

* Main idea A. **Fred's spacesuit squeaks.**
* Main idea B. **Fred is alone.**
* Main idea C. **Fred finds water.** Ⓑ

Write **Part A** in the left margin of your paper. Then number it from 1 to 5.

Answer each question. Then write whether the question is answered by **passage 1, passage 2,** or **passages 1 and 2.**

1. What kind of soil is on Mars?
2. Is there any water on the surface of Mars?
3. Where did Fred's water tank come from?
4. How cold does it get on Mars at night?
5. Name two reasons why people can't live on Mars.

EXERCISE 2

ANALYZING ARGUMENTS

1. (Direct the students to find part B.)
2. (Call on individual students to read part B.)
   - **C** What's the answer? *It must be a statement of ought.*
   - **D** Study it and get ready to say it. (Wait. Call on individuals to say the whole deduction without looking at it.)
   - **E** What's the answer? *It must be a statement of ought.*
   - **F** Think about it and get ready to say it. (Wait. Call on a student to say the missing rule. Idea: *You shouldn't do things that are bad for you.*)
   - **G** Study it and get ready to say it. (Wait. Call on individuals to say the whole deduction without looking at it.)
   - **H** What's the answer? *A statement of ought.*
   - **I** What's the answer? *It must be a statement of ought.*
   - **J** Figure it out and get ready to say it. (Wait. Call on a student to say the missing rule. Idea: *You ought to do things that help you stay in good health.*)
   - **K** Think about it and get ready to say it. (Wait. Call on individuals to say the whole deduction without looking at it.)

EXERCISE 3

SENTENCE COMBINATIONS

1. (Direct the students to find part C.)
2. (Call on individual students to read part C.)
   - **L** What's the answer? *Change it to a semicolon.*
   - **M** What's the answer? *Therefore.*
   - **N** What's the answer? *A comma.*
   - **O** What's the answer? *A comma.*
   - **P** What's the answer? *Change it to a semicolon.*
   - **Q** What's the answer? *However.*
   - **R** What's the answer? *A comma.*

Student Book page 243

Lesson 108

B Some arguments end with a conclusion that is a statement of ought. Here's a rule about the conclusions that are statements of ought:

> **If the conclusion is a statement of ought, the rule at the beginning of the deduction must be a statement of ought.**

- Here's a valid deduction:
  You should do everything that lets you live longer.
  If you avoid fatty foods, you'll live longer.
  Therefore, you should avoid fatty foods.
The conclusion is a statement of ought, and the rule at the beginning of the deduction is a statement of ought. The deduction is valid.

- Here's a deduction with the rule missing:
  If you work hard at your studies, you'll get smart.
  Therefore, you should work hard at your studies.
The conclusion is a statement of ought, so what do you know about the rule at the beginning of the deduction? **C**
Here's that rule: **You should do things that will help you get smart.**
Say the whole deduction. **D**

- Here's another deduction with the rule missing:
  Smoking is bad for you.
  Therefore, you shouldn't smoke.
The conclusion is a statement of ought, so what do you know about the missing rule? **E**
Figure out the missing rule. **F**
Say the whole deduction. **G**

- Here's another deduction with the rule missing:
  If you exercise, you'll stay in good health.
  Therefore, you ought to exercise.
What kind of statement is the conclusion? **H**
So what do you know about the missing rule? **I**
Figure out the missing rule. **J**
Say the whole deduction. **K**

Lesson 108

Student Book page 244

C When you combine sentences with the word **therefore,** what do you do with the period of the first sentence? **L**
What follows the semicolon? **M**
What follows the word **therefore?** **N**
When you combine sentences with **who** or **which,** what punctuation do you need before **who** or **which?** **O**
When you combine sentences with the word **however,** what do you do with the period of the first sentence? **P**
What follows the semicolon? **Q**
What follows the word **however?** **R**

D Write **Part D** in the left margin of your paper. You have two minutes to copy the paragraph below.

> **Progress in modern science has greatly changed our farming methods. New strains of wheat and corn have been developed that produce more grain per acre than ever before. New machinery makes it possible for fewer people to do more work.**

★ E Write **Part E** in the left margin of your paper. Rewrite the passage below using words you have learned to replace the underlined words. Remember to start every sentence with a capital letter and to punctuate each sentence correctly.

> <u>Most of the time</u> Dullsville is a quiet town, but last year a spaceship flew over and dropped some American <u>money</u>. This <u>event changed</u> everyone into a millionaire. No one lost <u>this chance</u> to buy things. The people <u>almost never</u> thought about who the money belonged to. One day the spaceship returned and the people were filled with <u>fear</u>. A creature stepped out of the ship and <u>showed</u> a giant gun. As the people screamed, the creature <u>paused</u>, then shot <u>money</u> from the gun. No one screams now, and there are no <u>rules</u> to stop the creature from shooting anyone.

Student Book page 245

F Write **Part F** in the left margin of your paper.
Here are three main ideas:

- The Sahara Desert has lots of sandstorms.
- A desert can be formed in several ways.
- Plants need water to live.

One of the main ideas fits the passage below. Read the passage.

One-seventh of the earth's land is covered by deserts. These hot, dry areas are usually formed in one of three ways. In some parts of the world, high air pressure makes rain an impossibility. Deserts usually result from lack of rain. Without water, few plants can live. This sets the scene for a second factor in creating a desert: erosion. With no plants to hold down the earth, the wind blows the earth away. The sandstorms of the Sahara Desert are famous. A third factor can also make a desert: humans. If there are too many people living on an area of land with too many animals, they can strip the land of all its vegetation. When they do that, erosion sets in and the area can become a wasteland. This happened in the midwestern United States in the 1930s. Certain areas became known as "dust bowls" because of the dust storms that swept the countryside. Many farmers had to give up their farms, which had turned into dry, wasted land.

Write the main idea that fits the passage. List the three points that fall under the main idea in outline form. Don't forget to indent and label the three points.

1. A desert can be formed in several ways.
2. Idea: from lack of rain
3. Idea: fom erosion
4. Idea: by humans who strip the land of vegetation

EXERCISE 4

INDEPENDENT WORK

1. **[Optional]** (Direct the students to read the instructions for part D to themselves. Then give them exactly two minutes to copy the paragraph. Count as errors any miscopied words and punctuation. Deduct these errors from the number of copied words, and mark the total on the Writing Rate Graph.)
2. Finish the Student Book and do the Workbook for Lesson 108. ✓

Workcheck

1. Get ready to check your answers starting with Student Book part E. Use a pen to mark an **X** next to any item you miss.
2. (Call on individual students to read each item and its answer. Repeat for Workbook items.)

> **Answer key for Student Book part E** *Usually Dullsville is a quiet town, but last year a spaceship flew over and dropped some American currency. This phenomenon converted everyone into a millionaire. No one lost this opportunity to buy things. The people rarely thought about who the money belonged to. One day the spaceship returned and the people were filled with anxiety. A creature stepped out of the ship and exhibited a giant gun. As the people screamed, the creature hesitated, and then shot currency from the gun. No one screams now, and there are no regulations to stop the creature from shooting anyone.*

3. (Direct the students to count the number of errors and write the number in the **error** box at the top of the Workbook page.)

4. (Award points and direct students to record their points in Box **W.**)

0 errors	**15 points**
1–2 errors	**12 points**
3–5 errors	**8 points**
6–9 errors	**5 points**

5. (Award any bonus points. Direct the students to total their points and enter the total on the Point Summary Chart.)

6. Show me your work when you've finished correcting it. (When the students show you their corrected work, record their points on your Record Summary Chart.)

Lesson 108 ERRORS W **Workbook page 322**

★ A In the passage below, the verbs **has** and **have** are used incorrectly five times. Cross out each incorrect word. Write the correct word above it. There are three redundant parts in the passage below. Cross out each redundant part.

This year our soccer team ~~have~~ *has* won every game so far, ~~beating every team we've played~~. The coaches ~~has~~ *have* helped a lot with our offense. Most of the player ~~has~~ *have* done a good job on defense, especially me. Some members of the team ~~has~~ *have* been playing soccer for only a couple of years, but they do all right ~~considering that they haven't played the game for more than two years~~. Our best player is from England. He ~~have~~ *has* been scoring about two goals a game. Nobody's legs are more powerful than his, ~~which are more powerful than anyone else's~~.

B In each deduction below, the rule is missing. Read each deduction and then answer the questions.

• If you stay slim, you'll live longer. Therefore, you should stay slim.

1. What kind of statement is the conclusion?
   <u>statement of ought</u>
2. So, what do you know about the missing rule?
   <u>It must be a statement of ought.</u>
3. Write the missing rule.
   <u>Idea: You should do things that help you live longer.</u>

• If you work hard at your studies, you'll get smart. Therefore, you should work hard at your studies.

4. What kind of statement is the conclusion?
   <u>statement of ought</u>
5. So, what do you know about the missing rule?
   <u>It must be a statement of ought.</u>
6. Write the missing rule.
   <u>Idea: You should do things that help you get smart.</u>

Workbook page 323 **Lesson 108**

C Each sentence that follows has two possible meanings. Read each sentence and answer the questions.

• The ghost felt he needed somebody to lift his spirits.

1. What's the intended meaning of the sentence?
   <u>Idea: The ghost felt he needed somebody to put him in a better mood.</u>
2. What's the unintended meaning?
   <u>Idea: The ghost felt he needed somebody to raise up other supernatural beings.</u>
3. Which word is involved in the two meanings?
   <u>spirits</u>

• For three years, quarterback Bosse carried the entire team.

4. What's the intended meaning of the sentence?
   <u>Idea: For three years, quarterback Bosse has played so much better than the rest of the team that the team still has been able to win.</u>

5. What's the unintended meaning?
   <u>Idea: For three years, Bosse has physically picked up the entire team and carried it around.</u>
6. Which word is involved in the two meanings?
   <u>carried</u>

• He decided to run for the office of mayor.

7. What's the intended meaning of the sentence?
   <u>Idea: He decided to try to get elected as mayor.</u>
8. What's the unintended meaning?
   <u>Idea: He decided to move quickly towards the mayor's office.</u>
9. Which words are involved in the two meanings?
   <u>run for</u>

END OF LESSON 108

Student Book page 246

A The two passages below contradict each other on two important points. Make sure you find those contradictions when you read the passages.

Passage 1. In size, Canada is the third largest country in the world. It is a very rich country, even though large areas of its northern part are nearly impossible to live in. Canada is divided into ten provinces, the largest of which are Quebec and Ontario.

The first person from Europe to visit what is now Canada was a sailor named John Cabot, who reached Canada in 1497. Cabot returned to England with stories about the great numbers of fish that lived in the ocean off the coast of Canada. His stories tempted many British fishermen to go to Canada and begin new lives. The ancestors of about 50 percent of Canadian citizens came from Britain; the ancestors of 30 percent came from France.

Today, fishing is still the most important source of income for the coastal provinces. Since Canada has more lakes and inland waters than any other country in the world, freshwater fishing is important to Canada.

Passage 2. Most citizens of Canada live in a narrow belt along the southern border of that country, where the climate is milder. The ancestors of nearly all Canadian citizens came from Britain. The people who originally came to Canada were looking for gold because they had heard stories of great gold deposits. These stories were started by a man named John Cabot, who was the first person known to have visited Canada. Today, gold mining is still a good source of income for Canada, and many other kinds of minerals are also mined. For example, Canada mines about one-half of the world's total supply of asbestos, which is used to manufacture fireproof objects.

The passages contradict each other on two important points. What are those points? Ⓐ

Let's look up **Canada** in a dictionary or encyclopedia and find out which passage is accurate. Ⓑ

Note: The circled letters indicate when you ask a question or when you direct the group to respond.

━━━━━━━ **EXERCISE 1** ━━━━━━━
CONTRADICTIONS

Note: For this exercise, you will need a reference book that tells about the history of Canada.

1. (Direct the students to find Lesson 109, part A, in the **Student Book**.)
2. (Call on individual students to read part A.)
   Ⓐ (Call on two students to name one point each. Ideas: *Passage 1 says that John Cabot went back to England and told stories about the great numbers of fish in Canadian waters; passage 2 says that Cabot went back to England and told stories about great gold deposits. Passage 1 says that about 50 percent of the ancestors were from Britain; passage 2 says that the ancestors of nearly all Canadians came from Britain.*)
   Ⓑ I'll read what it says in this reference book about Canada. (**Read the relevant passages.**) Which of the passages that you read earlier is accurate—passage 1 or passage 2? *Passage 1.*

EXERCISE 2

ANALYZING ARGUMENTS

1. (Direct the students to find part B.)
2. (Call on individual students to read part B.)
   - **C** What's the answer? *It must be a statement of ought.*
   - **D** What's the answer? *A statement of fact.*
   - **E** What's the answer? *A statement of ought.*
   - **F** What's the answer? *No.*
   - **G** (Call on a student. Idea: *When the conclusion is a statement of ought, the rule must be a statement of ought.*)
   - **H** What's the answer? *A statement of ought.*
   - **I** What's the answer? *Yes.*
   - **J** (Call on a student. Idea: *The rule is a statement of ought and the conclusion is a statement of ought.*)
   - **K** What's the answer? *A statement of ought.*
   - **L** What's the answer? *Yes.*
   - **M** (Call on a student. Idea: *The rule is a statement of ought and the conclusion is a statement of ought.*)
   - **N** What's the answer? *A statement of fact.*
   - **O** What's the answer? *No.*
   - **P** (Call on a student. Idea: *When the conclusion is a statement of ought, the rule must be a statement of ought.*)

EXERCISE 3

INDEPENDENT WORK

1. **[Optional]** (Direct the students to read the instructions for part C to themselves. Then give them exactly two minutes to copy the paragraph. Count as errors any miscopied words and punctuation. Deduct these errors from the number of copied words, and mark the total on the Writing Rate Graph.)

Student Book page 247

Lesson 109

B If the conclusion of a deduction is a statement of ought, what do you know about the rule at the beginning of the deduction? **e**

A deduction is not valid or correct if the conclusion is an ought statement and the rule at the beginning of the deduction is not an ought statement.

Below are several deductions. Figure out whether each deduction is valid.

- Here's the first deduction:
  Nearly 90 percent of the people preferred beef.
  Beef is available at nearly every supermarket.
  Therefore, you ought to choose beef.
  What kind of statement does the deduction begin with? **o**
  What kind of statement is the conclusion? **e**
  Is the deduction valid? **e**
  Explain. **o**

- Here's another deduction:
  We should stand up for what we believe.
  John believes that the school day should be made longer.
  Therefore, John should stand up for making a longer school day.
  What kind of statement does the deduction begin with? **o**
  Is the deduction valid? **o**
  Explain. **o**

- Here's another deduction:
  Suspected criminals should have fair trials.
  Jake is a suspected criminal.
  Therefore, Jake should have a fair trial.
  What kind of statement does the deduction begin with? **o**
  Is the deduction valid? **o**
  Explain. **o**

- Here's another deduction:
  Aluminum can be recycled.
  Pop cans are made of aluminum.
  Therefore, pop cans should be recycled.
  What kind of statement does the deduction begin with? **o**
  Is the deduction valid? **o**
  Explain. **o**

Lesson 109

Student Book page 248

C Write **Part C** in the left margin of your paper. You have two minutes to copy the paragraph below.

> Some arguments end with a conclusion that is a statement of ought. A deduction that ends with a statement of ought is valid or correct only if the rule at the beginning of the deduction is also a statement of ought.

★ **D** Write **Part D** in the left margin of your paper.
Here are three main ideas:

- Some eating plans can be dangerous.
- Vegetarian eating plans are very popular.
- There's more than one popular eating plan for staying healthy.

One of the main ideas fits the passage below. Read the passage.

> Doctors usually recommend a balanced diet of meat, grains, vegetables, and fruit. They insist that if you eat a little bit of each of these foods daily, you will lose weight and stay healthy. Many people follow other kinds of eating plans, and they insist that they feel healthier than they ever felt before. One of these plans is a high-protein diet. On this plan, you avoid fruit, bread, potatoes, and all forms of sugar. You eat only meat, cheese, eggs, and some vegetables. This plan is less popular than it used to be, but some people still follow it. Another popular plan is a vegetarian plan. On this plan, you do not eat meat. You eat only vegetables and whole grains such as bulgur and brown rice. Some vegetarians include cheese, yogurt, and eggs in their diet. Many people claim that these foods keep them healthy. Some people claim that fasting cleans out their bodies and makes them feel better. When you fast, you eat nothing at all. Some people fast one day a week; others fast three days in a row each month. Many doctors think it is bad to fast. Although there are many other eating plans that claim to make you healthy, most people now think that a regular balanced diet is best.

Write the main idea that fits the passage. List the four points that fall under the main idea in outline form. Don't forget to indent and label the four points.

Student Book page 249 — Lesson 109

E Write **Part E** in the left margin of your paper. Then number it from 1 to 7. The two passages below both tell something about coffee. Read both passages and find out which passage gives more facts about the effects of coffee.

Passage 1. Coffee is one of the most popular beverages in the United States. It comes from the small beans of the coffee plant, which is grown commercially in South America. The flavor of a coffee bean depends on many things, including the time of harvest, how long the bean was roasted, and how the coffee is prepared. Coffee contains caffeine, a bitter drug that disagrees with some people. However, coffee manufacturers have discovered a way of removing the caffeine from the bean. According to some people, decaffeinated coffee has a flavor that is less bitter than regular coffee.

Passage 2. Coffee is one of the most popular beverages in the United States. The mild "lift" that most coffee drinkers associate with coffee is caused by caffeine, the most widely used stimulant in the world. A normal dose of caffeine from a single cup of coffee relieves drowsiness and muscular fatigue and stimulates the thought processes. Used in large amounts (more than five cups of coffee a day), caffeine can cause insomnia, restlessness, and irritability, and may contribute to the development of ulcers and high blood pressure.

1. Which passage tells more about the effects of coffee?
2. The other passage gives more facts about something else. What does it tell more about?

   Answer each question below. Then write whether the question is answered by **passage 1, passage 2,** or **passages 1 and 2.**

3. What is coffee made from?
4. If you drink too much coffee, what may the caffeine do to you?
5. The flavor of coffee beans depends on several things. Name two.
6. What is caffeine?
7. What is decaffeinated coffee?

Workbook page 324 — Lesson 109

ERRORS W

A Read each deduction and write the answers to the questions.

- We shouldn't damage our ears.
  Listening to extremely loud music damages our ears.
  Therefore, we shouldn't listen to extremely loud music.

1. What kind of statement does the deduction begin with?
   statement of ought

2. Is the deduction valid? _yes_
3. Explain.
   Idea: The deduction begins and ends with a statement of ought, so it's a valid deduction.

- Coyotes kill chickens and sheep.
  We like chickens and sheep.
  Therefore, we should kill coyotes.

4. What kind of statement does the deduction begin with?
   statement of fact

5. Is the deduction valid? _no_
6. Explain.
   Idea: The deduction does not begin and end with a statement of ought, so it's not a valid deduction.

B Read the passage and answer the questions. Circle **W** if the question is answered by words in the passage. Circle **D** if the question is answered by a deduction. If you circle **W** for an item, underline the words in the passage that give the answer.

Some things will rot if they are left in the air. Another word for **rot** is **decompose.** Things that decompose start out as one material and turn into another material. Rocks do not decompose, nor does water. Leaves decompose and turn into a soggy mass that no longer looks like leaves. When animals decompose, their flesh becomes rotten. If they decompose long enough, they will become shriveled.

Tiny organisms are responsible for much of the change that occurs when matter decomposes. These organisms are called decomposers. They are very small plants that have no chlorophyll; therefore, they cannot convert sunlight into food. They get their food by eating the flesh or waste material of other organisms.

When you read about decomposers, you may think they are nothing but filthy little organisms, but think of what the world would be like if there were no decomposers. Leaves from hundreds of years ago would be piled on the ground along with remains of other plants. The bodies of dead animals and their waste material would be piled hundreds of kilometers high.

The decomposers do more than rid the world of this dead matter. As they eat the remains of the animals, they give off waste matter that is high in nitrogen. Nitrogen helps plants grow, so the decomposers actually help many things live.

---

2. In Lesson 110, you'll have a test on story facts. The facts that will be tested appear in part E of your Workbook. Study them and make sure that you know them. Now, finish the Student Book and do the Workbook for Lesson 109. ✓

Workcheck

1. Get ready to check your answers starting with Student Book part D. Use a pen to mark an **X** next to any item you miss.
2. (Call on individual students to read each item and its answer. Repeat for Workbook items.)

Answer key for Student Book part D
I. *There's more than one popular eating plan for staying healthy.*
A. *Idea: A balanced plan consisting of meat, grains, vegetables, and fruit*
B. *Idea: A high-protein plan consisting of meat, cheese, eggs, and some vegetables*
C. *Idea: A vegetarian plan consisting of vegetables and whole grains*
D. *Idea: Fasting, which is eating no food at all*

Answer key for Student Book part E
1. *Passage 2* **2.** *Idea: What coffee is* **3.** *Coffee beans; passage 1* **4.** *Idea: It may cause insomnia, restlessness, irritability, ulcers, and high blood pressure; passage 2* **5.** *Idea: The time of harvest, how long the bean was roasted, and how the coffee was prepared (any two); passage 1* **6.** *Idea: A bitter drug that is a widely used stimulant; passages 1 and 2* **7.** *Idea: Coffee from which the caffeine has been removed; passage 1*

3. (Direct the students to count the number of errors and write the number in the **error** box at the top of the Workbook page.)

4. (Award points and direct students to record their points in Box **W.**)

0 errors	**15 points**
1–2 errors	**12 points**
3–5 errors	**8 points**
6–9 errors	**5 points**

5. (Award any bonus points. Direct the students to total their points and enter the total on the Point Summary Chart.)

6. Show me your work when you've finished correcting it. (When the students show you their corrected work, record their points on your Record Summary Chart.)

Lesson 109

Workbook page 326

C Each passage that follows contains a word you may not know. Read each passage and answer the questions.

- The soil here is so fecund that plants grow ten feet tall. You can scatter corn seeds on top of the ground, and two months later you'll have cornstalks taller than you are. The fecundity of this soil is amazing. This ground grows everything from watermelons to strawberries as big as your fist.

1. Circle the answer.
   Fecund probably means:
   painful   fierce   (fertile)   barren

2. Write any sentence from the passage that contradicts the idea that **fecund** means **barren.**
   Idea: The soil here is so fecund that plants grow ten feet tall.

- She always spoke deprecatingly about her former husband. She pointed out his faults and weaknesses, and she had no kind words for him. Her friends learned to stop asking her about him, because she never missed a chance to deprecate him in public. There was no doubt that she despised him and blamed him for all her troubles.

3. Circle the answer.
   Deprecate probably means:
   nervous
   to express approval of
   (to express disapproval of)
   sweetly

4. Write any sentence from the passage that contradicts the idea that **deprecate** means **sweetly.**
   Idea: She pointed out his faults and weaknesses, and she had no kind words for him.

- He extolled her beauty in poems and songs. He extolled her to his friends by speaking of her grace and her kindness, her wisdom and her generosity. He seemed unable to say anything but good about her. According to him, she was the best at everything.

5. Circle the answer.
   Extol probably means:
   eat   speak evil of   listen   (praise)

6. Write any sentence from the passage that contradicts the idea that **extol** means **speak evil of.**
   Idea: He seemed unable to say anything but good about her.

D You will be tested on a fact presented in this lesson. This fact is:

> **Plants that do not have chlorophyll are decomposers.**

Study this fact. Repeat it to yourself. Writing this fact may help you remember it.

Workbook page 325

Lesson 109

1. Why can't decomposers convert sunlight into food?
   Idea: because they don't contain chlorophyll (W) D

2. How do decomposers get their food?
   Idea: They get their food by eating the flesh or waste material of other organisms. (W) D

3. Are decomposers plants, or are they animals?
   plants (W) D

4. How do decomposers help plants?
   Idea: They give off waste material that is high in nitrogen, which helps plants grow.

5. What would the world look like if there were no decomposers?
   Idea: The remains of dead plants and animals would be piled hundreds of kilometers high.

6. What's another word for rot?
   decompose

7. Why is nitrogen important to a tree?
   Idea: Because it helps a tree grow. W (D)

8. Fill in the chart below. List three types of plants that have chlorophyll. Fill in the name for the plants that do not have chlorophyll.

```
                    plants
                   /      \
   plants with chlorophyll   plants without chlorophyll
   oak tree                  are called decomposers
   rosebush
   grass
```

Workbook page 327

Lesson 109

E After you finish Lesson 10, you will be tested on facts you have learned. The test will include all of the facts presented in Lessons 106–109, and some of the facts from earlier lessons. These facts are:

1. Any living thing is an organism.
2. Living things are designed to keep living.
3. Plants are different from animals in several ways: (a) plants "breathe in" carbon dioxide; (b) plants "exhale" oxygen; and (c) plants make their own food.
4. When an animal hibernates, it curls up in a safe place and sleeps for a long time.
5. Inflation means that prices keep going up.
6. Study the chart below. Make sure that you can fill in this chart.

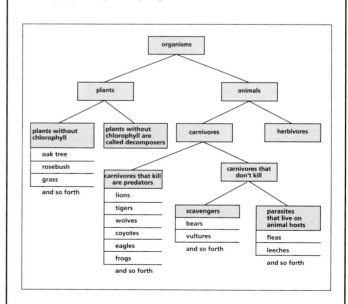

END OF LESSON 109

Student Book page 250

Lesson
110

A

Write **Part A** in the left margin of your paper. You have two minutes to copy the paragraph below.

> Decomposers are very small plants that have no chlorophyll; therefore, they cannot convert sunlight into food. Decomposers get their food by eating the flesh or waste material of other organisms. As decomposers eat, they give off material that is high in nitrogen.

★ **B**

Write **Part B** in the left margin of your paper.
Here are three main ideas:

> • **Canada has several kinds of industry.**
> • **Canada is one of the largest wheat-growing areas in the world.**
> • **Much of Canada is covered by forests.**

One of the main ideas fits the passage below. Read the passage.

> Canada is a rich country, with many ways for people to earn a living. Agriculture is the primary industry. Some areas of Canada form one of the largest wheat-growing areas in the world. Other field crops include oats, barley, rye, and sugar beets. Some farms raise beef cattle; others raise dairy cattle. Still others raise chickens. Mineral mining is another important industry in Canada. Canada makes a lot of money from the minerals that are mined, which include gold, silver, copper, asbestos, and uranium. The last major industry in Canada is manufacturing. Since over one-third of Canada's land is covered by forests, most of Canada's manufactured products are forest products. Pulp and paper are the most important forest products.

Write the main idea that fits the passage. List the three points that fall under the main idea in outline form. Don't forget to indent and label the three points.

Student Book page 251

Lesson
110

C

Write **Part C** in the left margin of your paper. Then number it from 1 to 6. The two passages below tell something about gardening. Read both passages and find out which passage gives more facts about how to garden.

> **Passage 1.** Having your own vegetable garden is probably easier than you think. First you should find out when the growing season in your area starts and when it ends. Some seeds can be planted early in the season (when the weather is still cold). For other seeds, you must wait for warmer weather. Generally, you can tell how good your soil is by the amount of vegetation already growing in it. If the weeds and grass are green and grow fast, the soil will probably support vegetables well. Before you plant, remove all the unwanted plants or rocks, and then break the soil up with a spade. For more information on gardening, read a book about gardening or talk to people who have good vegetable gardens.

> **Passage 2.** Gardening is a popular pastime all over the world. People everywhere grow their own fruits, vegetables, and flowers. Some people make a business of selling their flowers or produce. Others, who garden as a hobby, say that they like the good taste of fresh produce and the satisfaction of seeing things grow. Most gardeners agree that nothing matches the pleasure of seeing months of effort finally produce a harvest of tasty fruits and vegetables. In China, there is an old saying: "If you want to be happy all year long, be a gardener."

1. Which passage tells more about how to garden?
2. The other passage gives more facts about something else. What does it tell more about?

Answer each question below. Then write whether the question is answered by **passage 1, passage 2,** or **passages 1 and 2.**

3. How could you get more information on gardening?
4. Name two things you should do before you plant your garden.
5. What do hobby gardeners like about gardening?
6. How can you tell whether your soil is good enough to support your garden?

EXERCISE 1

INDEPENDENT WORK

1. **[Optional]** (Direct the students to read the instructions for part A in the **Student Book** to themselves. Then give them exactly two minutes to copy the paragraph. Count as errors any miscopied words and punctuation. Deduct these errors from the number of copied words, and mark the total on the Writing Rate Graph.)
2. Finish the Student Book and Workbook for Lesson 110. ✓

Workcheck

1. Get ready to check your answers starting with Student Book part B. Use a pen to make an **X** next to any item you miss.
2. (Call on individual students to read each item and its answer. Repeat for Workbook items.)
3. (Direct the students to count the number of errors and write the number in the **error** box at the top of the Workbook page.)
4. (Award points and direct students to record their points in Box **W.**)

0 errors	15 points
1–2 errors	12 points
3–5 errors	8 points
6–9 errors	5 points

5. (Award any bonus points. Direct the students to total their points and enter the total on the Point Summary Chart.)
6. Show me your work when you've finished correcting it. (When the students show you their corrected work, record their points on your Record Summary Chart.)

Student Book page 252

D Here are some words that will be in some editing activities. Test yourself to make sure that you know what the words mean.

indolent—An indolent person is a lazy person. Here's a sentence that uses the word **indolent**:

She was fired from her job because she was so indolent.

lethal—Something that is lethal is capable of killing living things. Most bug sprays and cleaning compounds are lethal. So are guns, bombs, and many vehicles. Here's a sentence that uses the word **lethal**:

The story told about a man who was murdered with a lethal weapon.

preceding—A preceding event is an event that happened before another event. Here's a sentence that uses the word **preceding**:

I think that his latest strategy for traffic control is much better than his preceding one.

vital—Something that is vital is necessary. Workers are vital to the operation of a factory. Here's a sentence that uses the word **vital**:

Food is vital for survival.

Workbook page 329

C Each sentence that follows has two possible meanings. Read each sentence and answer the questions.

- **When Jack went out dancing, he was dressed to kill.**

1. What's the intended meaning of the sentence?
   Idea: When Jack went out dancing, he was dressed very nicely.

2. What's the unintended meaning?
   Idea: When Jack went out dancing, he was dressed to commit a murder.

3. Which words are involved in the two meanings?
   dressed to kill

- **It was now Rick's turn to step into his dad's shoes.**

4. What's the intended meaning of the sentence?
   Idea: It was now Rick's turn to take on his dad's responsibilities.

5. What's the unintended meaning?
   Idea: It was now Rick's turn to put his dad's shoes on.

6. Which words are involved in the two meanings?
   step into his dad's shoes

- **She was the brightest student in the class.**

7. What's the intended meaning of the sentence?
   Idea: She was the smartest student in the class.

8. What's the unintended meaning?
   Idea: She glowed more than anyone else in the class.

9. Which word is involved in the two meanings?
   brightest

END OF LESSON 110

Workbook page 328

★ A Read each deduction and write the answers to the questions.

- High-rise buildings are very impressive.
  More people than ever before are living in high-rise buildings.
  Therefore, we ought to build more high-rise buildings.

1. What kind of statement does the deduction begin with?
   statement of fact

2. Is the deduction valid? _no_

3. Explain.
   Idea: The deduction does not begin and end with a statement of ought, so it's not a valid deduction.

- The United States uses more oil than any other country.
  Huge oil tankers bring the oil to the United States from other countries.
  Therefore, we should build more huge oil tankers.

4. What kind of statement does the deduction begin with?
   statement of fact

5. Is the deduction valid? _no_

6. Explain.
   The deducation does not begin and end with a statement of ought, so it's not a valid deduction.

B Jim sometimes has trouble using the words **who** and **which**. Below is a letter that he wrote to his friend Ted. Cross out the words **who** and **which** if they are used incorrectly. Write the correct word above every crossed-out word.

Dear Ted,

I have a friend ~~who~~ who would like to meet you. He knows ~~which~~ you are because my sister told him that you run for the Rockets Track Club. He lives in Alton, ~~who~~ which is near Parkvale. His favorite sport, which is track, is very popular in Alton. He knows which lane each runner must run in at the local track meets. He has several friends who used to run for your track team. The team they run for, which is called the Flying Pizzas, has some world-class runners. The people who sponsor the Flying Pizzas give a free pizza to any athlete who comes in first. Who knows, maybe you will win a pepperoni pizza, which is the grand prize. Let me know where you plan to stay when you run in Alton, and I'll tell my friend to look for you. His name is Randy, which is a nice name.

Jim

EXERCISE 1

MASTERY TEST

1. Everybody, find page 456 in your workbook.
   - This is a test. If you make no mistakes on the test, you'll earn 20 points. Write the answers to the test items now using your pencil.

2. (After the students complete the items, gather the workbooks and grade the tests. As you grade each test, record the number of errors the student made on each part of the test in the appropriate box. Record the total number of errors in the **Error** box at the beginning of the test.)

3. (Return the workbooks to the students.) Raise your hand if you made ____ or more mistakes in ____.
   (Record the number of students who raise their hand for the part.)

> **Key: Part A–4   Part B–3   Part C–1**
> **Part D–2   Part E–1   Part F–3**

4. Raise your hand if you made no mistakes on the whole test. Great work. (Award 20 points to the students who made no errors. Award 5 points to students who made 1 or 2 errors.)
   - Record your points in the box marked **MT** at the top of Mastery Test 11.
   - (Direct all students to enter their points on the Point Summary Chart.)

5. (Record test results on the Group Summary Sheet. Reproducible Summary Sheets are at the back of the Teacher's Guide.)

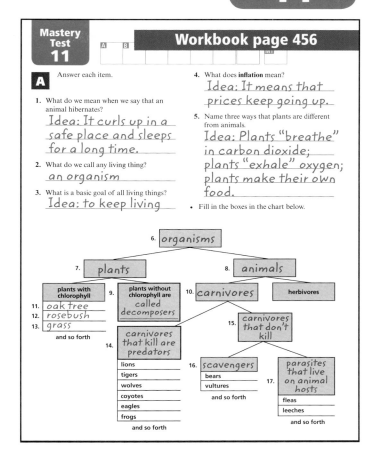

Passage 2. The National Forest Service reported that a man had been attacked by a wolf in a national park in Minnesota late last night. Ranger Thompson, who reported the attack, told reporters: 'This attack is a very rare incident. Wolves have never been known to attack a human. We are afraid that the public will overreact to this event and will start killing wolves. Since wolves are already an endangered species, any all-out attacks on wolves could wipe them from the face of the earth."

- These passages contradict each other on one big point. What is that point?

  Idea: Whether wolf
  attacks are occurring
  frequently or rarely.

 D Here are three main ideas:

- **Some animals manufacture the water they need.**
- **Animals obtain water in different ways.**
- **What different animals eat**

All animals need water. A camel can drink up to 100 liters of water in a few minutes. The grasshopper mouse drinks very little, obtaining most of its water from the insects it eats. There are three basic ways in which animals can obtain water. The first and most obvious way is to drink it. A human being working in the heat of a desert must drink a lot of water — about 2 gallons a day! A second way of obtaining water is through food. The grasshopper mouse eats insects, which may be up to 80% water. Some animals can derive all the water they need from plants. A third way to obtain water is to manufacture it, as the camel does.

Write the main idea that fits the passage. List the three points that fall under the main idea in outline form. Don't forget to indent and label the three points.

I. Animals obtain water
in different ways.
  A. Idea: Some animals
    drink their water.
  B. Some animals get
    their water from
    food.
  C. Some animals
    manufacture water.

F In the passage below, the verbs **has** and **have** and **is** and **are** are used incorrectly six times. Cross out each incorrect word. Write the correct word above it.
There are also three redundant parts in the passage. Draw a line through the redundant parts.

Everybody in my class, ~~all the boys and~~
~~all the girls~~, ~~are~~ very excited when we ~~has~~ *have*
is
a substitute teacher ~~to take the place of~~
~~our regular teacher~~. Some students in the
class have many ways to upset a substitute
teacher. But usually, if the substitute ~~are~~ *is*
has
prepared for class, everybody ~~have~~ a good
day. Some classes are noisy ~~and loud~~ and
have
~~has~~ a bad reputation with substitutes. But
our regular teacher always leaves lots of
work for us to do. Our class ~~are~~ always *is*
too busy to fool around.

E The description below tells about the city shown in one of the maps. Read the description and then answer the questions.

This map shows a section of downtown Brownsville consisting of twelve square blocks. The heavy broken line shows the route the new elevated train will take. The light broken lines represent subway lines. The parks in this area are also shown. The shaded regions represent surface area that is devoted to cars: parking lots, streets, gas stations, and garages. Notice that more than half the surface area of this busy section of town is devoted to cars.

1. Which map does the description tell about?
   B

2. Which words in the description let you know that map D is not the one that is described?
   The parks in this area
   are also shown.

3. Which words in the description let you know that map C is not the one that is described?
   consisting of twelve
   square blocks

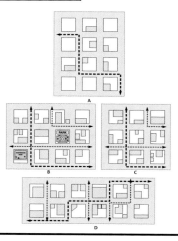

━━━━━━━━━ **EXERCISE 2** ━━━━━━━━━

TEST REMEDIES

1. (If more than 25% of the students failed a part of the test, provide the remedy specified for that part in the table below. The required Remedy Blackline Master worksheets can be found in Appendix H of the Teacher's Guide.)

2. (All remedies should be completed before beginning the next lesson in the program.)

Test Section	If students made this many errors	Present these tasks: Lesson	Exercise	Remedy Blackline Master	Required Student Book Parts
A	4 or more	Test remedy below		11–A, 11–B	
B	3 or more	Item 1: 22	1	11–C	Lesson 22–A
		Item 2: 57	1	11–C	Lesson 57–A
		Item 3: 101	3	11–D	Lesson 101–C
		Item 4: 19	1	11–D	Lesson 19–A
		Item 5: 34	2	11–E	Lesson 34–B
		Item 6: 86	1	11–E	Lesson 86–A
		Item 7: 28	3	11–F	Lesson 28–B
		Item 8: 63	1	11–F	Lesson 63–A
C	1 or more	98	1		Lesson 98–A
		99	1		Lesson 99–A
D	2 or more Part D = 4 Items	101	1		Lesson 101–A and F
		102	—		Lesson 102–E
E	1 or more	102	2		Lesson 102–B
		103	—		Lesson 103–E
F	3 or more Part F = 9 Items	101	—	11–G	
		102	—	11–G	

> **Note:** The teacher and each student who failed the test will need a copy of Remedy Blackline Masters 11–A and 11–B. The Remedy Blackline Masters can be found in Appendix H of the Teacher's Guide

PART A TEST REMEDY

1. We're going to go over some items from the test. I'll read the items. You'll say the answers. Then you'll write the answers.
2. (Read item 1 in part A of Remedy Blackline Master 11–A.) What's the answer? (Call on a student. Idea: *To keep Irving.*)
3. (Repeat step 2 for items 2–7.)
4. (Give each student a copy of Remedy Blackline Masters 11–B.)
   This worksheet shows the chart that was on the test.
5. Touch box 8.
   Everybody, what goes in that box? (Signal.) *Organisms.*
6. (Repeat step 4 for each remaining box.)
7. Study the chart for a few minutes. Then you'll fill in the empty boxes.
8. (After several minutes:) Now you're going to write the answers to all the items in part A. Let's see who can get them all correct.
9. (After students complete the items:) Let's check your work. Use your pen to make an **X** next to any item you got wrong.
- (For items 1–7: Read the items. Call on individual students to answer each item.)
- (For the chart items:) What goes in box 8? (Call on a student.) *Organisms.*
- (Repeat for each remaining box.)
- Raise your hand if you got all the items correct. Nice work.

END OF MASTERY TEST 11

Lesson Objectives	LESSON 111	LESSON 112	LESSON 113	LESSON 114	LESSON 115
	Exercise	Exercise	Exercise	Exercise	Exercise
Organization and Study Skills					
Main Idea	SB	2	3	SB	SB
Outlining	SB				
Specific-General		WB	WB	WB	WB
Writing Mechanics: Copying	2	3	4	2	2
Reasoning Strategies					
Deductions	WB	WB			WB
Evidence		WB			
Rules: Arguments			1, 2	1	
Statements: Ought	WB	WB			WB
Contradictions	SB	SB	SB		1
Information Sources/Study Skills					
Interpretation: Maps/Pictures/Graphs	SB				
Supporting Evidence	SB	SB	SB	SB	
Vocabulary/Language Arts Strategies					
Definitions	1, WB	1, WB	WB	SB	SB
Usage	1, WB	1, WB	WB	SB	SB
Editing/Revising	WB	WB	WB	SB	SB
Comprehension: Meaning from Context			WB	WB	
Information Application/ Study Skills					
Information Review				WB	
Assessment/Progress Monitoring					
Ongoing: Workcheck	Workcheck	Workcheck	Workcheck	Workcheck	Workcheck

Lesson 111

> **Note:** The circled letters indicate when you ask a question or when you direct the group to respond.

EXERCISE 1

DEFINITIONS

1. (Direct the students to find Lesson 111, part A, in the **Student Book**.)
2. (Call on individual students to read part A.)
   Ⓐ Say it with **especially**.
   She was especially happy that evening.
   Ⓑ Say it with **especially**.
   His hand was especially sore after the game.
   Ⓒ Say it with **especially**.
   The bugs were especially bothersome that evening.
   Ⓓ Say it with **especially**.
   Jack was especially tired after the party.
   Ⓔ Say it with **especially**.
   Your eyes look especially green in this light.

EXERCISE 2

INDEPENDENT WORK

1. **[Optional]** (Direct the students to read the instructions for part B to themselves. Then give them exactly two minutes to copy the paragraph. Count as errors any miscopied words and punctuation. Deduct these errors from the number of copied words, and mark the total on the Writing Rate Graph.)
2. Finish the Student Book and do the Workbook for Lesson 111. ✓

Workcheck

1. Get ready to check your answers starting with Student Book part C. Use a pen to make an **X** next to any item you miss.
2. (Call on individual students to read each item and its answer. Repeat for Workbook items.)

> **Answer key for Student Book part C**
> **I.** *Canada and the United States are the same in many ways.*
>   **A.** *Idea: Both are in North America.*
>   **B.** *Idea: Both are large countries.*
>   **C.** *Idea: Both extend from the Atlantic to the Pacific.*
>   **D.** *Idea: Both border on the Great Lakes.*
>   **E.** *Idea: Both contain part of Niagara Falls.*

Student Book page 253 Lesson 111

A The word **especially** can often be used in place of the words **really** and **very**. Say these sentences with the word **especially**:

- She was very happy that evening. Ⓐ
- His hand was really sore after the game. Ⓑ
- The bugs were very bothersome that evening. Ⓒ
- Jack was really tired after the party. Ⓓ
- Your eyes look very green in this light. Ⓔ

B Write **Part B** in the left margin of your paper. You have two minutes to copy the paragraph below.

> There are several steps involved in growing a vegetable garden. First, prepare the land. Second, plant the seeds, spacing them so that the young plants will have room to grow. Next, mulch the seedlings with hay or straw. Last, water the garden.

★ **C** Write **Part C** in the left margin of your paper.
Here are three main ideas:

> - The countries of Canada and the United States are in North America.
> - The United States and Canada are interesting.
> - Canada and the United States are the same in many ways.

One of the main ideas fits the passage below. Read the passage.

> Canada is in North America. So is the United States. Canada is a large country, much larger than most of the countries in Europe. The United States is also a large country. Canada extends from the Atlantic Ocean to the Pacific Ocean. So does the United States. One of Canada's boundaries cuts through the Great Lakes. The United States shares this boundary. Part of Niagara Falls is in Canada. Part is in the United States.

Write the main idea that fits the passage. List the five points that fall under the main idea in outline form. Don't forget to indent and label the five points.

Lesson
111

Student Book page 254

D Write **Part D** in the left margin of your paper. Then number it from 1 to 11. The two accounts below contradict each other on an important point. Make sure you find that contradiction when you read the accounts.

Passage 1. The skiing industry, which is a major source of income for our state, is in trouble. For the last several years, an absence of snow has seriously affected the income of our ski resorts. We interviewed Bob Rasmussen, owner of Blue Mountain Ski Resort, to find out just how serious the situation has become.

"All I can say is that we're in trouble right now," Mr. Rasmussen told reporters. "But it's ridiculous to think that this situation will continue. I figure that next year we'll have the heaviest snowfall we've had in the last five years. That should more than make up for the money we've lost in the last few seasons."

Passage 2. Our state is in serious financial trouble. Senator Frisbee predicts some heavy taxes on the citizens if we can't solve our money problems. One of the biggest reasons for this economic slump is the dry spell we've been having. Because of the lack of snowfall, the skiing industry has not been attracting many customers. The loss of income from this industry is a serious problem for the state. When interviewed about the problem, Senator Frisbee stated: "All we can do is hope for snow. According to owners of the ski resorts, it may be several years before we have a good snowfall. In the meantime, we must tighten our belts and consent to more taxes than we are used to paying."

Answer the questions. Some of the questions ask where you found an answer. Write **passage 1, passage 2,** or **passages 1 and 2** for these questions.

1. These passages contradict each other on one big point. What point is that?
2. Why is the skiing industry losing money?
3. Where did you find the answer to question 2?
4. Why does the state suffer when the skiing industry is in a slump?
5. Where did you find the answer to question 4?
6. What kind of income does Bob Rasmussen predict for the skiing industry next year?
7. Where did you find the answer to question 6?

Student Book page 255

Lesson
111

8. What kind of income does Senator Frisbee predict for the skiing industry next year?
9. Where did you find the answer to question 8?
10. How does Senator Frisbee expect to make up for the money the state is losing?
11. Where did you find the answer to question 10?

E Write **Part E** in the left margin of your paper. Then number it from 1 to 4. The description below tells about one of the organisms listed. Read the description and then answer the questions.

This thing is an organism that you can see without a magnifying glass. The organism is a carnivore, but it does not kill. The organism lives on a host—more specifically, it lives on an animal host.

tree   lion   sheep   vulture   mistletoe   flea

1. Which organism does the description tell about?
2. Which words in the description let you know that a lion is not the organism that is described?
3. Which words in the description let you know that a vulture is not the organism that is described?
4. Which words in the description let you know that a tree is not the organism that is described?

Answer key for Student Book part D
1. *Idea: When there will be a good snowfall*
2. *Idea: Because there isn't enough snow to attract tourists* **3.** *Passages 1 and 2* **4.** *Idea: Because the loss of income from the skiing industry is affecting the state's economy*
5. *Passages 1 and 2* **6.** *Idea: A good income*
7. *Passage 1* **8.** *Idea: A poor income*
9. *Passage 2* **10.** *Idea: By increasing the taxes of the citizens of the state* **11.** *Passage 2*

Answer key for Student Book part E **1.** *A flea*
2. *Idea: The organism is a carnivore, but it does not kill.* **3.** *Idea: The organism lives on a host.*
4. *Idea: The organism is a carnivore.*

Answer key for Student Book part F
1. *Contradictory; Borel and Lisck are countries by the sea.* **2.** *Contradictory; Manx has between 50,000 and 100,000 people.* **3.** *Not contradictory*
4. *Not contradictory* **5.** *Not contradictory*
6. *Contradictory; Mount Fromm is a mountain in Ogshaw that is 3,000 meters high.*

3. (Direct the students to count the number of errors and write the number in the **error** box at the top of the Workbook page.)
4. (Award points and direct students to record their points in Box **W**.)

0 errors	15 points
1–2 errors	12 points
3–5 errors	8 points
6–9 errors	5 points

5. (Award any bonus points. Direct the students to total their points and enter the total on the Point Summary Chart.)
6. Show me your work when you've finished correcting it. (When the students show you their corrected work, record their points on your Record Summary Chart.)

Lesson 111

Student Book page 256

F Write **Part F** in the left margin of your paper. Then number it from 1 to 6. Assume that the map below is accurate. Examine the map carefully and then read the statements below it. Some of the statements contradict what the map shows.

- Write **contradictory** or **not contradictory** for each statement.
- If a statement contradicts the map, write what the map shows.

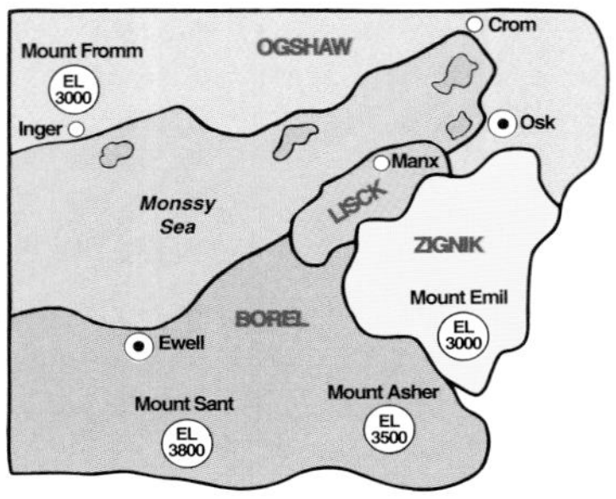

The symbol ○ means that the city has between 50,000 and 100,000 people.
The symbol ⦿ means that the city has more than 100,000 people.
The symbol (EL 3800) means that the mountain is 3,000 meters high.
The area that is shaded like this ░ is a sea.

1. Borel, Zignik, and Lisck are all countries by the sea.
2. The city of Manx lies in Lisck and has more than 100,000 people.
3. Ogshaw and Borel are both neighbors of Zignik.
4. The islands in the Monssy Sea are near the coast of Ogshaw.
5. Zignik is larger than Lisck.
6. Mount Fromm is a mountain in Ogshaw that is 3,500 meters high.

Workbook page 331

Lesson 111

C Underline the redundant part in each sentence below. Then explain why the underlined part is redundant.

1. She nibbled at the cheese, taking small bites.
   Idea: If you know that she nibbled at the cheese, then you already know that she took small bites.
2. For a lazy person, he was very indolent.
   Idea: If you know that he was a lazy person, then you already know that he was very indolent.
3. The fire was burning.
   Idea: If you already know that it was a fire, then you already know that it was burning.

Workbook page 330

Lesson 111 ERRORS W

★ **A** Read each deduction and write the answers to the questions.

- **We should try to lower the crime rate. Good police enforcement lowers the crime rate. Therefore, we should insist on good police enforcement.**

1. What kind of statement does the deduction begin with?
   statement of ought
2. Is the deduction valid? yes
3. Explain. Idea: The deduction begins and ends with a statement of ought, so it's a valid deduction.

- **Digger High has the best basketball team in the state. Digger High spends more money on basketball than our high school does. Therefore, our high school should spend more money on basketball.**

4. What kind of statement does the deduction begin with?
   statement of fact
5. Is the deduction valid? no
6. Explain. Idea: The deduction does not begin and end with a statement of ought, so it's not a valid deduction.

B Write each sentence below with the word **especially**.

1. She was really happy on her birthday.
   She was especially happy on her birthday.
2. The lake is very full in the spring.
   The lake is especially full in the spring.
3. The ground was very soggy after the storm.
   The ground was especially soggy after the storm.

END OF LESSON 111

Student Book page 257

Lesson
112

A The word **especially** can often be used in place of the words **really** and **very**. Say these sentences with the word **especially**:

* That math test was really hard. Ⓐ
* She is a very attractive woman. Ⓑ
* This camera is really fun to use. Ⓒ

B To make a statement more general, you use the names of larger classes. Here's a statement:

> **The fourteen-year-old boy walked into the little coffee shop.**

You can make the statement more general by using the name of a larger class for each underlined part.
Here's a more general statement:

> **The teenager walked into the store.**

Here's a statement that is even more general:

> **The person walked into the building.**

* Here's a new statement:
  > **That cocker spaniel is curled up in a red station wagon.**

Make up a more general statement by using the name of a larger class for each underlined part. Ⓓ

* Here's a new statement:
  > **Oranges are often put in fruit crates.**

Make up a more general statement by using the name of a larger class for each underlined part. Ⓔ

* Here's a new statement:
  > **Sheep, goats, cows, horses, and deer on my farm like to eat grass and bushes.**

Make up a more general statement by using the name of a larger class for each underlined part. Ⓕ

C Write **Part C** in the left margin of your paper. You have two minutes to copy the paragraph below.

> She always spoke deprecatingly about her former husband. She pointed out his faults and weaknesses, and she had no kind words about him. Her friends learned to stop asking her about him, because she never missed a chance to deprecate him in public.

Note: The circled letters indicate when you ask a question or when you direct the group to respond.

=== **EXERCISE 1** ===

DEFINITIONS

1. (Direct the students to find Lesson 112, part A, in the **Student Book**.)
2. (Call on individual students to read part A.)
   Ⓐ Say it with **especially**.
   That math test was especially hard.
   Ⓑ Say it with **especially**.
   She is an especially attractive woman.
   Ⓒ Say it with **especially**.
   This camera is especially fun to use.

=== **EXERCISE 2** ===

MAIN IDEA

1. (Direct the students to find part B.)
2. (Call on individual students to read part B.)
   Ⓓ (Call on individual students. Ideas: *That dog is curled up in a car. That dog is curled up in a vehicle.*)
   Ⓔ (Call on individual students. Ideas: *Fruits are often put in boxes.*)
   Ⓕ (Call on individual students. Ideas: *Animals on my farm like to eat plants. Herbivores on my farm like to eat plants.*)

=== **EXERCISE 3** ===

INDEPENDENT WORK

1. **[Optional]** (Direct the students to read the instructions for part C to themselves. Then give them exactly two minutes to copy the paragraph. Count as errors any miscopied words and punctuation. Deduct these errors from the number of copied words, and mark the total on the Writing Rate Graph.)
2. Finish the Student Book and do the Workbook for Lesson 112. ✓

Lesson
112

Workcheck

1. Get ready to check your answers starting with Student Book part D. Use a pen to make an **X** next to any item you miss.

2. (Call on individual students to read each item and its answer. Repeat for Workbook items.)

Answer key for Student Book part D
1. *Idea: Whether or not a circus animal is still on the loose*   **2.** *At about 10 P.M.*   **3.** *Passage 1*
4. *Idea: In Bessie MacDonald's car*   **5.** *Passage 1*
6. *Idea: By giving it a tranquilizer*   **7.** *Passage 1*
8. *Idea: Call 223-4195 and report its location.*
9. *Passage 2*   **10.** *Falling tree limbs*   **11.** *Passage 1*

Answer key for Student Book part E
1. *A rosebush*   **2.** *This thing is an organism.*
3. *It has chlorophyll.*   **4.** *It is a plant.*

---

3. (Direct the students to count the number of errors and write the number in the **error** box at the top of the Workbook page.)

4. (Award points and direct students to record their points in Box **W.**)

0 errors	**15 points**
1–2 errors	**12 points**
3–5 errors	**8 points**
6–9 errors	**5 points**

5. (Award any bonus points. Direct the students to total their points and enter the total on the Point Summary Chart.)

6. Show me your work when you've finished correcting it. (When the students show you their corrected work, record their points on your Record Summary Chart.)

Lesson 112

★ **D** Write **Part D** in the left margin of your paper. Then number it from 1 to 11. The two accounts below contradict each other on an important point. Make sure you find that contradiction when you read the accounts.

Passage 1. During the lightning storm last night, some animals escaped from the circus. Falling tree limbs apparently damaged some of the cages, and several lions got out. Zebras and elephants were reported wandering around in the downtown shopping mall at about 10 P.M. last night. Bessie MacDonald, of 122 West Blakely, said that she found an upset ocelot hiding in the backseat of her car. Ms. MacDonald called the police, who gave the animal a tranquilizer and took it back to the circus grounds. Circus attendants rounded up the rest of the animals and had them safely back in cages by midnight.

Passage 2. If you happen to see a lion wandering around downtown, don't panic. One escaped from the circus last night and is believed to be somewhere in the downtown area. If you see the beast, call 223-4195 and report its location.
During the storm last night, several animals managed to escape from the circus. Circus attendants thought they had rounded up all the animals, but later discovered that one lion was still missing. Citizens are cautioned not to take walks alone and to watch their children carefully until the lion is caught. The animal won't attack unless it is teased. Circus officials hope that they can get the lion back unharmed.

Answer each question below. Some of the questions ask where you found an answer. Write **passage 1, passage 2,** or **passages 1 and 2** for these questions.

1. These passages contradict each other on one big point. What point is that?
2. When did the animals escape from the circus?
3. Where did you find the answer to question 2?
4. Where was an ocelot found?
5. Where did you find the answer to question 4?
6. How did the police calm the ocelot?
7. Where did you find the answer to question 6?
8. What are you supposed to do if you see the missing animal?
9. Where did you find the answer to question 8?
10. What caused the damaged cages?
11. Where did you find the answer to question 10?

E Write **Part E** in the left margin of your paper. Then number it from 1 to 4. The description below tells about one of the things listed. Read the description and then answer the questions.

This thing is an organism. It is a plant that grows in many places. It has chlorophyll, so it can make its own food. It produces flowers, which can be many colors. The stems of the plants have thorns, which help protect the plant from predators.

book   apple tree   horse   rosebush   decomposer   pumpkin vine

1. Which thing does the description tell about?
2. Which words in the description let you know that a book is not the thing that is described?
3. Which words in the description let you know that a decomposer is not the thing that is described?
4. Which words in the description let you know that a horse is not the thing that is described?

Lesson 112 | Workbook page 332

ERRORS W

★ **A** After each statement, write a statement that is more general by using the name of a larger class for each underlined part.

1. <u>Lobster, clams, and sea bass</u> are served at <u>Barney's Diner</u>.
   Idea: Seafood is served at the restaurant.

2. <u>Sparrows and pigeons</u> often perch on that <u>tall, gray skyscraper</u>.
   Idea: Birds often perch on that building.

B Write each sentence below with the word **especially**.

1. The dog was very glad to come into the house.
   The dog was especially glad to come into the house.

2. The dog was really wet and muddy.
   The dog was especially wet and muddy.

3. Victoria Island is a very popular tourist spot.
   Victoria Island is an especially popular tourist spot.

C Read each deduction and write the answers to the questions.

• We should fail all students who do not perform well.
Students who do not perform well score less than 95 percent on tests.
Therefore, we should fail all students who score less than 95 percent on all tests.

1. What kind of statement does the deduction begin with?
   statement of ought

2. Is the deduction valid? yes

3. Explain. Idea: The deduction begins and ends with a statement of ought, so, it's a valid deduction.

• Beethoven's Ninth Symphony may be the most famous symphony ever written.
Many people have not heard Beethoven's Ninth Symphony.
Therefore, these people should listen to Beethoven's Ninth Symphony.

4. What kind of statement does the deduction begin with?
   statement of fact

5. Is the deduction valid? no

6. Explain. Idea: The deduction does not begin and end with a statement of ought, so, it's not a valid deduction.

Workbook page 333 | Lesson 112

D Read the rule and each piece of evidence. Write a conclusion after each piece of evidence.

> Rule. Parasites grow, feed, and live on other animals.

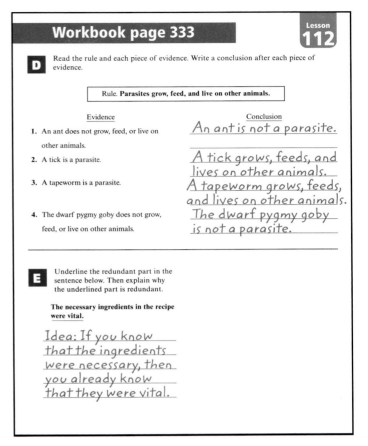

Evidence	Conclusion
1. An ant does not grow, feed, or live on other animals.	An ant is not a parasite.
2. A tick is a parasite.	A tick grows, feeds, and lives on other animals.
3. A tapeworm is a parasite.	A tapeworm grows, feeds, and lives on other animals.
4. The dwarf pygmy goby does not grow, feed, or live on other animals.	The dwarf pygmy goby is not a parasite.

E Underline the redundant part in the sentence below. Then explain why the underlined part is redundant.

The <u>necessary</u> ingredients in the recipe were vital.

Idea: If you know that the ingredients were necessary, then you already know that they were vital.

END OF LESSON 112

Note: The circled letters indicate when you ask a question or when you direct the group to respond.

A

In the item below, the underlined sentence has two possible meanings. The sentence that follows the underlined sentence makes it clear which meaning is intended.

> **The boy ate the cake on the table.** His mother told him to get down when she saw him there.

What are the two possible meanings of the underlined sentence? Ⓐ
Which is the intended meaning? Ⓑ

B

Many arguments about what we should do begin with **statements of ought.** If the argument draws a conclusion about what somebody ought to do, what do you know about the rule at the beginning of the argument? Ⓒ
Read the argument below.

> One of our most basic beliefs is that we should be fair to all, regardless of race, color, or creed. When we look at the courts, however, we are shocked. The courts are not fair to all. The courts have one standard for the wealthy and another standard for the poor. The courts sentence poor people for committing minor crimes. However, the courts do not treat wealthy people in the same way. If we remain consistent with our basic belief, we must conclude that we should change the courts.

What conclusion does the author draw? Ⓓ
Here are the last two parts of a deduction that is based on the author's argument:

> **The courts are not fair to all.**
> **Therefore, we should change the courts.**

The conclusion is an **ought statement.** So, what do you know about the rule at the beginning of the deduction? Ⓔ
Figure out the missing rule. Ⓕ
Say the whole deduction that summarizes the author's argument. Ⓖ
The argument is valid, but you may not agree with it. Do you agree with the rule that we should be fair to all? Ⓗ
What do you think that rule is supposed to mean? Ⓘ

EXERCISE 1

ANALYZING ARGUMENTS

1. (Direct the students to find Lesson 113, part A, in the **Student Book.**)
2. (Call on individual students to read part A.)
   Ⓐ (Call on two students to name one meaning each. Idea: *The boy was on the table; the cake was on the table.*)
   Ⓑ (Call on a student. Idea: *The boy was on the table.*)

EXERCISE 2

ANALYZING ARGUMENTS

1. (Direct the students to find part B.)
2. (Call on individual students to read part B.)
   Ⓒ (Call on a student. Idea: *It must be a statement of ought.*)
   Ⓓ (Call on a student. Idea: *We should change the courts.*)
   Ⓔ (Call on a student. Idea: *It must be a statement of ought.*)
   Ⓕ Figure it out. (Wait. Call on a student. Idea: *Things should be fair to all, or we should change things that are not fair to all.*)
   Ⓖ (Call on a student.) *We should change things that are not fair to all* [or another acceptable rule].
   The courts are not fair to all.
   Therefore, we should change the courts.
   Ⓗ (Call on individual students.)
   Ⓘ (Call on individual students. Accept reasonable responses.)

Student Book page 261

C Here's a statement:
    The <u>wrench</u> is made of <u>steel</u>.
Make up a more general statement by using the name of a larger class for
each underlined part. ❻

• Here's a new statement:
    The <u>woodpecker</u> jumped on the <u>recliner</u>.
Make up a more general statement by using the name of a larger class for
each underlined part. ❼

• Here's a new statement:
    **The <u>fat little man</u> went into the <u>bank</u> with a fistful of <u>pennies,
nickels, dimes, and quarters</u>.**
Make up a more general statement by using the name of a larger class for
each underlined part. ❽

D Write **Part D** in the left margin of your paper. You have two minutes to copy
the paragraph below.

> He extolled her beauty in poems and songs. He extolled her to
> his friends by speaking of her grace, her kindness, and her wisdom.
> He seemed unable to say anything but good things about her.
> According to him, she was the best at everything.

Student Book page 262

★ **E** Write **Part E** in the left margin of your paper. Then number it from 1 to 8.
The two passages below tell something about the effects of aspirin. Read
both passages and find out which passage gives more facts about the effects
of aspirin.

> **Passage A.** Doctors recommend aspirin more than any other pain
> reliever. In studies with cancer patients, aspirin was more reliably effective
> than a dozen other pain relievers, including some powerful narcotics. One
> side effect of aspirin is that it reduces your blood's ability to clot. People
> who take aspirin regularly may have trouble stopping small cuts from
> bleeding.

> **Passage B.** Do you have occasional headaches or muscle pains? You
> know by now that doctors recommend aspirin more than any other pain
> reliever you can buy. But did you know that some aspirins are stronger
> than others? PainZip tablets have twice the amount of aspirin contained in
> other brands, so you get the kind of pain relief you need.
>   Remember—for headaches, get PainZip aspirin.

Answer each question below. Some of the questions ask where you found
an answer. Write **passage A, passage B,** or **passages A and B** for these
questions.

1. Which passage tells more about the effects of aspirin?
2. The other passage gives more facts about something else. What does it tell
more about?
3. What do doctors recommend most for pain relief?
4. Where did you find the answer to question 3?
5. What could happen if you take aspirin regularly and cut yourself?
6. Where did you find the answer to question 5?
7. What does aspirin do to your blood?
8. Where did you find the answer to question 7?

1. passage A
2. PainZip tablets
3. asprin
4. passages A and B
5. Idea: You might have trouble stopping the bleeding.
6. passage A
7. Idea: It reduces the blood's ability to clot.
8. passage A

MAIN IDEA

1. (Direct the students to find part C.)
2. (Call on individual students to read part C.)
   - ❿ (Call on individual students. Ideas: *The tool is made of metal. The object is made of a hard material.*)
   - ⓚ (Call on individual students. Ideas: *The large bird jumped on the chair. The bird jumped on the furniture.*)
   - ⓛ (Call on individual students. Ideas: *The man went into the building with a fistful of change. The person went into the building with a fistful of money.*)

INDEPENDENT WORK

1. **[Optional]** (Direct the students to read the instructions for part D to themselves. Then give them exactly two minutes to copy the paragraph. Count as errors any miscopied words and punctuation. Deduct these errors from the number of copied words, and mark the total on the Writing Rate Graph.)
2. Finish the Student Book and do the Workbook for Lesson 113. ✓

Workcheck

1. Get ready to check your answers starting with Student Book part E. Use a pen to make an **X** next to any item you miss.
2. (Call on individual students to read each item and its answer. Repeat for Workbook items.)
3. (Direct the students to count the number of errors and write the number in the **error** box at the top of the Workbook page.)

4. (Award points and direct students to record their points in Box **W.**)

0 errors	**15 points**
1–2 errors	**12 points**
3–5 errors	**8 points**
6–9 errors	**5 points**

5. (Award any bonus points. Direct the students to total their points and enter the total on the Point Summary Chart.)

6. Show me your work when you've finished correcting it. (When the students show you their corrected work, record their points on your Record Summary Chart.)

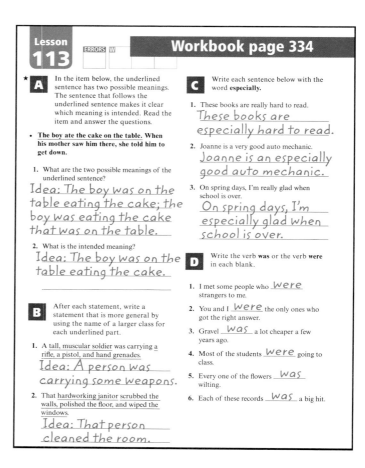

Lesson 113   ERRORS   W

Workbook page 334

★ **A** In the item below, the underlined sentence has two possible meanings. The sentence that follows the underlined sentence makes it clear which meaning is intended. Read the item and answer the questions.

- **The boy ate the cake on the table.** When his mother saw him there, she told him to get down.

1. What are the two possible meanings of the underlined sentence?
   Idea: The boy was on the table eating the cake; the boy was eating the cake that was on the table.

2. What is the intended meaning?
   Idea: The boy was on the table eating the cake.

B After each statement, write a statement that is more general by using the name of a larger class for each underlined part.

1. A tall, muscular soldier was carrying a rifle, a pistol, and hand grenades.
   Idea: A person was carrying some weapons.

2. That hardworking janitor scrubbed the walls, polished the floor, and wiped the windows.
   Idea: That person cleaned the room.

C Write each sentence below with the word **especially.**

1. These books are really hard to read.
   These books are especially hard to read.

2. Joanne is a very good auto mechanic.
   Joanne is an especially good auto mechanic.

3. On spring days, I'm really glad when school is over.
   On spring days, I'm especially glad when school is over.

D Write the verb **was** or the verb **were** in each blank.

1. I met some people who _were_ strangers to me.

2. You and I _were_ the only ones who got the right answer.

3. Gravel _was_ a lot cheaper a few years ago.

4. Most of the students _were_ going to class.

5. Every one of the flowers _was_ wilting.

6. Each of these records _was_ a big hit.

END OF LESSON 113

Student Book page 263 — Lesson 114

A Many arguments about what we should do begin with statements of ought. If the argument draws a conclusion about what somebody ought to do, what do you know about the rule at the beginning of the argument? Ⓐ

Read the argument below.

> Many rules have lived with us for thousands of years. They couldn't have lived this long unless they carried a message that remains important to humans.
>
> One of these rules is: Honor your father and your mother. What this means is that you should respect your parents and do what they tell you to do.
>
> I am your father. And even though you are thirty years old and have a tough time making money, I'm telling you this: Give me a thousand dollars. That's what you should do.

What conclusion does the argument draw? Ⓑ

Here are the last two parts of a deduction that is based on the argument:
Your father tells you to give him a thousand dollars.
You should give your father a thousand dollars.

The conclusion is an ought statement. So, what do you know about the rule at the beginning of the deduction? Ⓒ
Figure out the missing rule. Ⓓ
Say the whole deduction that summarizes the argument. Ⓔ

The argument is valid, but you may not agree with it. Do you agree with the rule that we should do what our parents tell us to do? Ⓕ
What do you think that rule is supposed to mean? Ⓖ

B Write **Part B** in the left margin of your paper. You have two minutes to copy the paragraph below.

> Doctors recommend aspirin more than any other pain reliever. In studies with cancer patients, aspirin was more reliably effective than a dozen other pain relievers, including some powerful narcotics. One side effect of aspirin is that it reduces your blood's ability to clot.

★ C Write **Part C** in the left margin of your paper. Then number it from 1 to 3.
Here are three main ideas:

> Main idea A. A balance of food exists in the desert.
> Main idea B. Humans change a desert into farmland.
> Main idea C. Humans make a desert.

Note: The circled letters indicate when you ask a question or when you direct the group to respond.

=== **EXERCISE 1** ===

ANALYZING ARGUMENTS

1. (Direct the students to find Lesson 114, part A, in the **Student Book**.)
2. (Call on individual students to read part A.)
   Ⓐ (Call on a student. Idea: *It must be a statement of ought.*)
   Ⓑ (Call on a student. Idea: *He should give his father a thousand dollars.*)
   Ⓒ (Call on a student. Idea: *It must be a statement of ought.*)
   Ⓓ Figure it out. (Wait. Call on a student. Idea: *You should do what your father or mother tells you to do.*)
   Ⓔ (Call on a student.) *You should do what your father or mother tells you to do* [or another acceptable rule]. *Your father tells you to give him a thousand dollars. You should give your father a thousand dollars.*
   Ⓕ (Call on individual students.)
   Ⓖ (Call on individual students. Accept reasonable responses.)

=== **EXERCISE 2** ===

INDEPENDENT WORK

1. **[Optional]** (Direct the students to read the instructions for part B to themselves. Then give them exactly two minutes to copy the paragraph. Count as errors any miscopied words and punctuation. Deduct these errors from the number of copied words, and mark the total on the Writing Rate Graph.)
2. Finish the Student Book and do the Workbook for Lesson 114. ✓

Workcheck

1. Get ready to check your answers starting with Student Book part C. Use a pen to make an **X** next to any item you miss.
2. (Call on individual students to read each item and its answer. Repeat for Workbook items.)

Answer key for Student Book part D *Lee is worried because usually her dog, Sammy, is noisy. There is an especially valid motive for her anxiety—her landlord has a regulation that does not allow tenants to have dogs. She doesn't want to get evicted, so she has devised a strategy: as soon as she gets an opportunity, she is going to have Sammy converted into a cat.*

Answer key for Student Book part E
1. *Passage B* **2.** *Rats are both dangerous and helpful to humans.* **3.** *Idea: They are used in laboratories to study human diseases.*
4. *Passage A* **5.** *Idea: They destroy crops; they carry diseases; they will attack humans (any two)*
6. *Passage A* **7.** *Idea: They can climb a brick wall; they can swim half a mile; they can tread water for three days and nights; they can survive being flushed down the toilet; they can gnaw through lead pipes; they can fall five stories to the ground and walk away unharmed (any three)*
8. *Passage B*

3. (Direct the students to count the number of errors and write the number in the **error** box at the top of the Workbook page.)

Lesson 114 — Student Book page 264

Each main idea fits one of the passages below. After reading all the passages, figure out which main idea goes with each passage.

Passage 1. Deserts are interesting places. Some desert areas of Australia are a good example. One hundred years ago, these desert areas didn't exist. In 1859, Australians imported twenty-four rabbits from England and released them on a ranch. Rabbits had no natural enemies in Australia, so within forty years, the rabbits had multiplied into millions. At that time, Australians raised many sheep, which eat the same plants that rabbits eat. Together, the sheep and rabbits stripped much of southern Australia of all vegetation. Without grass roots to hold down the earth, wind blew the earth away. Once green prairie grass was plentiful there, but now there is only sand and dust storms. A land that once fed sheep is now dry and empty.

Passage 2. Deserts are interesting places. Some desert plants produce as many as one and a half billion seeds per year. Most of these seeds are eaten by insects and small animals like rabbits. In turn, the rabbits and other small animals that eat seeds are eaten by larger animals, such as bobcats, eagles, and wolves. If you removed the plants that produce seeds, you would be taking food from the small animals that feed on these seeds. And if you remove the small animals, you take food from larger animals.

Passage 3. Deserts are interesting places. Often a desert can become very rich farmland. All it needs is water. That's just what's happening in Israel. The desert is being changed into green, fertile farmland. The strategy that the people of Israel use is to irrigate the land and then plant vegetation that will grip the soil with strong roots. Irrigation brings water to the land. The vegetation prevents the wind from blowing the soil away.

1. Main idea A is: **A balance of food exists in the desert.** Which passage does main idea A best fit? *passage 2*
2. Main idea B is: **Humans change a desert into farmland.** Which passage does main idea B best fit? *passage 3*
3. Main idea C is: **Humans make a desert.** Which passage does main idea C best fit? *passage 1*

D Write **Part D** in the left margin of your paper. Rewrite the passage that follows using the words you have learned in place of the underlined words. Use the word **especially** one time. Remember to start every sentence with a capital letter and to punctuate each sentence correctly.

Student Book page 265 — Lesson 114

Lee is worried because most of the time her dog, Sammy, is noisy. There is a very sound reason for her fear—her landlord has a rule that does not allow tenants to have dogs. She doesn't want to get evicted, so she has made up a plan: as soon as she gets a chance, she is going to have Sammy changed into a cat.

E Write **Part E** in the left margin of your paper. Then number it from 1 to 8. The two passages below tell something about rats. Read both passages and find out which passage provides more real information about a rat's ability to survive.

Passage A. Rats eat one-fifth of the world's crops each year, destroying fields as well as invading storage silos. They carry dozens of diseases to humans and other animals. Under certain conditions, rats will attack animals hundreds of times their size, including humans. Although rats cause great damage, they have been used in laboratories to study different diseases. Through laboratory experiments, rats have contributed more to curing human illness than any other animal.

Passage B. For such a small animal, the rat performs incredible feats. The average rat can climb a brick wall as if it were a ladder, swim half a mile, and tread water for three days and nights. It can survive being flushed down the toilet, gnaw through lead pipes, or fall five stories to the ground and walk away unharmed. It's no wonder that rats feel at home almost anywhere.

Answer each question below. Some of the questions ask where you found an answer. Write **passage A, passage B,** or **passages A and B** for these questions.

1. Which passage tells more about a rat's ability to survive?
2. Which of the following main ideas fits passage A?

* **Rats are strong animals.**
* **Rats are both dangerous and helpful to humans.**
* **Rats carry many diseases.**

3. Name one way that rats are helpful.
4. Where did you find the answer to question 3?
5. Name two reasons that rats are dangerous to humans.
6. Where did you find the answer to question 5?
7. Name three things rats can do that seem incredible for such a small animal.
8. Where did you find the answer to question 7?

Workbook page 335

Lesson
114

A In each item that follows, the underlined sentence has two possible meanings. The sentence that follows the underlined sentence makes it clear which meaning is intended. Read the items and answer the questions.

• He set a ladder against the wall and broke it. He had to buy a new ladder.

1. What are the two possible meanings of the underlined sentence?

   Idea: He broke the ladder when he set it against the wall; he broke the wall when he set the ladder against it.

2. What is the intended meaning?

   Idea: He broke the ladder when he set it against the wall.

• When she added ice cubes to the glasses of hot tea, they broke. The tea ran all over the counter.

3. What are the two possible meanings of the underlined sentence?

   Idea: When she added ice cubes to the glasses of hot tea, the ice cubes broke; when she added ice cubes to the glasses of hot tea, the glasses broke.

4. What is the intended meaning?

   Idea: When she added ice cubes to the glasses of hot tea, the glasses broke.

• Let Mr. Fixit repair your house and save money. He charges less than anybody else in town.

5. What are the two possible meanings of the underlined sentence?

   Idea: You will save money if you let Mr. Fixit repair your house; Mr. Fixit will save money if you let him repair your house.

6. What is the intended meaning?

   Idea: You will save money if you let Mr. Fixit repair your house.

4. (Award points and direct students to record their points in Box **W.**)

0 errors	15 points
1–2 errors	12 points
3–5 errors	8 points
6–9 errors	5 points

5. (Award any bonus points. Direct the students to total their points and enter the total on the Point Summary Chart.)

6. Show me your work when you've finished correcting it. (When the students show you their corrected work, record their points on your Record Summary Chart.)

END OF LESSON 114

Workbook page 336

B After each statement, write a statement that is more general by using the name of a larger class for each underlined part.

1. Sweet, juicy grapefruits and oranges are grown in California, Texas, and Florida.

   Idea: Fruits are grown in the United States.

2. The short, red-haired typist likes chocolate, jelly beans, and red licorice.

   Idea: The person likes candy.

3. That collie eats orange peels, coffee grounds, and old food that's been thrown away.

   Idea: The dog eats garbage.

C You will be tested on a fact presented in this lesson. This fact is:

> The roots of plants help prevent the formation of a desert by holding down the soil.

Study this fact. Repeat it to yourself. Writing this fact may help you to remember it.

Lesson
115

Note: The circled letters indicate when you ask a question or when you direct the group to respond.

───────── **EXERCISE 1** ─────────

CONTRADICTIONS

Note: For this exercise, you will need a reference book that tells about the gold rush or John Sutter.

1. (Direct the students to find Lesson 115, part A, in the **Student Book**.)
2. (Call on individual students to read part A.)
   Ⓐ (Call on a student to name the point. Idea: *Passage 1 says that John Sutter went bankrupt, and passage 2 says that Sutter got rich.*)
   Ⓑ I'll read what it says in this reference book about the gold rush [or John Sutter]. (Read the relevant passages.) Which of the passages that you read earlier is accurate—passage 1 or passage 2? *Passage 1.*

───────── **EXERCISE 2** ─────────

INDEPENDENT WORK

1. **[Optional]** (Direct the students to read the instructions for part B to themselves. Then give them exactly two minutes to copy the paragraph. Count as errors any miscopied words and punctuation. Deduct these errors from the number of copied words, and mark the total on the Writing Rate Graph.)
2. Finish the Student Book and do the Workbook for Lesson 115. ✓

Lesson 115

| | **Student Book page 266** |

Ⓐ The two passages below contradict each other on an important point. Make sure you find the contradiction when you read the passages.

> **Passage 1.** The gold rush began in 1849, and that's why the people who flocked to California from different parts of the world were called "forty-niners." The first great gold deposits were discovered near Sacramento, but soon others were discovered, and California was teeming with people who believed "There's gold in them there hills!" John Sutter owned the mill where the first gold was found. He was plagued by people who stole his land and mined for themselves. He even called on Congress to help him protect his claim, but it refused. While others on his property were growing rich, Sutter went bankrupt. California finally offered Sutter a small monthly pension for his help in settling the West.

> **Passage 2.** On January 24, 1848, a worker at John Sutter's mill near Sacramento, California, discovered gold. Although Sutter tried to keep the discovery a secret, the news spread quickly. In the next year, thousands of people from all over the country packed up and headed for the hills of California. Many of them found gold, but many others found nothing at all. John Sutter successfully mined his land in the hills around Sacramento and built up one of the largest fortunes of the nineteenth century. Although many mining towns were destined to become ghost towns, Sacramento prospered and is now the capital of California.

The passages contradict each other on an important point. What is that point?

Let's look up the **gold rush** or **John Sutter** in an encyclopedia and find out which passage is accurate.

Ⓑ Write **Part B** in the left margin of your paper. You have two minutes to copy the paragraph below.

> **Australia imported some live rabbits from England. These rabbits soon multiplied into millions. The rabbits helped strip the vegetation from part of Australia. Without grass roots to hold down the earth, wind blew the earth away, and the area became a desert.**

| **Student Book page 267** | **Lesson 115** |

★ Ⓒ Write **Part C** in the left margin of your paper. In the passage below, the underlined words can be replaced with words you have learned. Rewrite the passage using the words you have learned. Use the word **especially** one time. Remember to start every sentence with a capital letter and to punctuate each sentence correctly.

> Kevin <u>argued</u> that girls should not be allowed to join the rowing team. He said that they are <u>almost never</u> strong enough. Everyone laughed at him, because his argument was not based on <u>sound facts</u>. He kept arguing, however, and the girls got tired of his <u>repetitive</u> nonsense. They <u>made up</u> a <u>really fitting plan</u> to <u>show</u> their strength. They picked him up and dunked him in the river.

Kevin contended that girls should not be allowed to join the rowing team. He said that they are rarely strong enough. Everyone laughed at him, because his argument was not based on valid data. He kept arguing, however, and the girls got tired of his redundant nonsense. They devised an especially appropriate strategy to exhibit their strength. They picked him up and dunked him in the river.

Student Book page 268

D Write **Part D** in the left margin of your paper. Then number it 1 and 2. Here are two main ideas:

> **Main idea A.** Schools are responsible for a student's education.
> **Main idea B.** Students are responsible for their own education.

Each main idea fits one of the passages below. After reading both passages, figure out which main idea goes with each passage.

> **Passage 1.** The school is being sued for damages because when Albert graduated, he couldn't read well enough to fill out a job application. But it's not the school's fault that Albert can't read. Albert was one of those students who are incapable of learning. The school gave Albert every opportunity to learn—the same opportunities it gave to other students. Albert didn't take advantage of those opportunities. That doesn't mean that the school is responsible.

> **Passage 2.** The school is being sued for damages because when Albert graduated, he couldn't read well enough to fill out a job application. The school's responsibility is to teach students how to read, write, and do arithmetic. We don't build schools and hire teachers to babysit kids until they are eighteen. If the schools aren't responsible for the education of children, then let's get rid of the schools.

1. Main idea A is: **Schools are responsible for a student's education.** Which passage does main idea A best fit? *passage 2*
2. Main idea B is: **Students are responsible for their own education.** Which passage does main idea B best fit? *passage 1*

Workbook page 337

Lesson 115

A In each deduction below, the rule is missing. Read each deduction and then answer the questions.

- Smoking is bad for you.
  Therefore, you shouldn't smoke.

1. What kind of statement is the conclusion? *statement of ought*

2. So, what do you know about the missing rule? *Idea: It must be a statement of ought.*

3. Write the missing rule. *Idea: You shouldn't do things that are bad for you.*

- If you exercise, you'll stay in good health.
  Therefore, you ought to exercise.

4. What kind of statement is the conclusion? *statement of ought*

5. So, what do you know about the missing rule? *Idea: It must be a statement of ought.*

6. Write the missing rule. *Idea: You ought to do things that keep you in good health.*

B After each statement, write a statement that is more general by using the name of a larger class for each underlined part.

1. Lions, wolves, dogs, and eagles eat mice, rabbits, and gophers. *Idea: Carnivores eat herbivores.*

2. Young boys, older boys, and grown men usually like football, baseball, soccer, swimming, bowling, golf, and all kinds of racing. *Idea: Males usually like sports.*

3. That strange-looking gentleman in the black suit and tie eats nothing but potato chips, corn chips, soft drinks, and ice-cream cones. *Idea: That man eats nothing but junk food.*

Workcheck

1. Get ready to check your answers starting with Student Book part C. Use a pen to make an **X** next to any item you miss.
2. (Call on individual students to read each item and its answer. Repeat for Workbook items.)
3. (Direct the students to count the number of errors and write the number in the **error** box at the top of the Workbook page.)
4. (Award points and direct students to record their points in Box **W**.)

0 errors	15 points
1–2 errors	12 points
3–5 errors	8 points
6–9 errors	5 points

5. (Award any bonus points. Direct the students to total their points and enter the total on the Point Summary Chart.)
6. Show me your work when you've finished correcting it. (When the students show you their corrected work, record their points on your Record Summary Chart.)

END OF LESSON 115

Lesson Objectives	LESSON 116 Exercise	LESSON 117 Exercise	LESSON 118 Exercise	LESSON 119 Exercise	LESSON 120 Exercise	Fact Game 8
Organization and Study Skills						
Main Idea	2	3, SB				
Outlining		SB				
Specific-General	SB	SB	SB	SB, WB	SB	FG
Writing Mechanics: Copying	3	4	3	3	1	
Reasoning Strategies						
Deductions	WB				WB	
Rules: Arguments		2	2	1, WB	WB	
Statements: Ought					WB	
Contradictions						FG
Information Sources/ Study Skills						
Basic Comprehension	SB	SB				
Reading Comprehension: Words or Deductions			WB	WB		
Interpretation: Maps/Pictures/Graphs	SB				SB	FG
Supporting Evidence	SB	SB			SB	FG
Vocabulary/Language Arts Skills						
Definitions	1, WB	1, WB	1, WB	WB	SB	FG
Usage	1, WB	1, WB	1, WB	WB	SB	FG
Sentence Combination	WB	SB		2		FG
Editing/Revising	SB, WB	SB, WB	WB	WB	SB	
Comprehension: Meaning from Context			WB		WB	
Information Application/ Study Skills						
Information Review				WB		
Assessment/Progress Monitoring						
Ongoing: Workcheck	Workcheck	Workcheck	Workcheck	Workcheck	Workcheck	
Formal: Mastery Test					MT12	

Student Book page 269

A

How do you make up statements that are more general? Ⓐ
To make up a statement that is more specific, you use the name of a smaller class.

Here's a picture:

Here's a statement about the picture:
 They went into a building.
Here's a more specific statement that uses the name of a smaller class for each underlined part:
 A woman and a man went into a restaurant.
Here's a statement that is even more specific:
 A curly-haired woman and a large man went into Harry's Restaurant.

• Here's a different statement about the picture:
 He carried something.
Make up a more specific statement by using the name of a smaller class for each underlined part. Ⓑ

• Here's a different statement about the picture:
 She was wearing something.
Make up a more specific statement by using the name of a smaller class for each underlined part. Ⓒ

Student Book page 270

B

The word **particularly** can often be used instead of the words **very, really,** and **especially.**
 Say these sentences with the word **particularly:**

• She was especially sad at dinnertime.
• His leg was very sunburned. Ⓔ
• He liked to cook, especially for large groups. Ⓕ
• She runs a lot, especially on Sundays. Ⓖ
• They were really glad to be home. Ⓗ
• Her shoes were especially dirty after the rain. Ⓘ
• His hair is very long. Ⓙ

C

Write **Part C** in the left margin of your paper. You have two minutes to copy the paragraph below.

 Rats eat one-fifth of the world's crops each year, destroying fields as well as invading storage silos. They carry dozens of diseases to humans and other animals. Under certain conditions, rats will attack animals hundreds of times their size, including humans.

Note: The circled letters indicate when you ask a question or when you direct the group to respond.

============ **EXERCISE 1** ============

MAIN IDEA

1. (Direct the students to find Lesson 116, part A, in the Student Book.)
2. (Call on individual students to read part A.)
 Ⓐ What's the answer? *By using the names of larger classes.*
 Ⓑ (Call on individual students. Idea: *The large man carried an umbrella.*)
 Ⓒ (Call on individual students. Idea: *The curly-haired woman was wearing a fur coat.*)

============ **EXERCISE 2** ============

DEFINITIONS

1. (Direct the students to find part B.)
2 (Call on individual students to read part B.)
 Ⓓ Say it with **particularly.**
 She was particularly sad at dinnertime.
 Ⓔ Say it with **particularly.**
 His leg was particularly sunburned.
 Ⓕ Say it with **particularly.**
 He liked to cook, particularly for large groups.
 Ⓖ Say it with **particularly.**
 She runs a lot, particularly on Sundays.
 Ⓗ Say it with **particularly.**
 They were particularly glad to be home.
 Ⓘ Say it with **particularly.**
 Her shoes were particularly dirty after the rain.
 Ⓙ Say it with **particularly.**
 His hair is particularly long.

EXERCISE 3

INDEPENDENT WORK

1. **[Optional]** (Direct the students to read the instructions for part C to themselves. Then give them exactly two minutes to copy the paragraph. Count as errors any miscopied words and punctuation. Deduct these errors from the number of copied words, and mark the total on the Writing Rate Graph.)

2. Finish the Student Book and do the Workbook for Lesson 116. ✓

Workcheck

1. Get ready to check your answers starting with Student Book part D. Use a pen to make an **X** next to any item you miss.

2. (Call on individual students to read each item and its answer. Repeat for Workbook items.)

Answer key for Student Book part D
1. *Passage A* **2.** *Idea: Sore throats* **3.** *Idea: Because garlic gets into your bloodstream, then into your lungs, and finally comes out with each breath* **4.** *Passage A* **5.** *Idea: It can dry the throat, making infection more likely.* **6.** *Passage A* **7.** *Idea: It can provide temporary relief from pain.* **8.** *Passage B* **9.** *No.* **10.** *Passage A* **11.** *Idea: If you stop taking the pills, a more powerful infection might result* **12.** *Passage B*

Answer key for Student Book part E (Ideas:)
1. *The train stopped to let the big ape out.*
2. *The woman wearing a shawl was playing a violin.* **3.** *The big, hairy ape was wearing a striped tie.*

3. (Direct the students to count the number of errors and write the number in the **error** box at the top of the Workbook page.)

★ **D** Write **Part D** in the left margin of your paper. Then number it from 1 to 12. The two passages below tell something about mouthwash. Read both passages and find out which passage gives more facts about mouthwash.

> **Passage A.** Mouthwashes that claim to stop bad breath by killing bacteria are useless. No amount of gargling could kill even one-tenth of the bacteria in the human mouth. Bad breath from eating garlic and onion does not come from your mouth at all. The digested garlic gets into your bloodstream, then your lungs, and finally comes out with each breath. Mouthwash cannot help this problem. Some kinds of bad breath come from throat infections that develop when the throat is too dry. Unfortunately, many mouthwashes contain alcohol, which actually dries the throat even more, making infection and bad breath more likely.

> **Passage B.** Most sore throats are due to virus infections, which cannot be stopped with mouthwash. Some sore throats are caused by bacteria alone, and they should be treated with antibiotics. The only way to determine what kind of organisms are causing a throat infection is to take a few drops from the infected area and examine them under a microscope. If the doctor prescribes an antibiotic for you when you have a sore throat, be sure to use all the pills prescribed. If you stop taking the pills in the middle of the treatment, a much more powerful infection may result. Treating a sore throat with mouthwash may provide temporary relief from pain, but it cannot cure serious throat infections.

Answer each question below. Some ask where you found an answer.
Write **passage A, passage B,** or **passages A and B** for these questions.
1. Which passage tells more about mouthwash?
2. The other passage gives more facts about something other than mouthwash. What does this passage tell more about?
3. Why doesn't mouthwash help bad breath that results from eating garlic?
4. Where did you find the answer to question 3?
5. How can mouthwash make a throat infection worse?
6. Where did you find the answer to question 5?
7. How can mouthwash help a sore throat?
8. Where did you find the answer to question 7?
9. Can mouthwashes kill all the bacteria in your mouth?
10. Where did you find the answer to question 9?
11. Why should you take all the antibiotic pills that a doctor prescribes for a throat infection?
12. Where did you find the answer to question 11?

E Write **Part E** in the left margin of your paper. Then number it from 1 to 3. Each item below tells about the picture. For each item, write a statement that is more specific by using the name of a smaller class for each underlined part.

1. The <u>vehicle</u> stopped to let the <u>animal</u> out.
2. The <u>woman</u> was playing a <u>musical instrument</u>.
3. The <u>ape</u> was wearing a <u>tie</u>.

4. (Award points and direct students to record their points in Box **W**.)

0 errors	15 points
1–2 errors	12 points
3–5 errors	8 points
6–9 errors	5 points

5. (Award any bonus points. Direct the students to total their points and enter the total on the Point Summary Chart.)

6. Show me your work when you've finished correcting it. (When the students show you their corrected work, record their points on your Record Summary Chart.)

Lesson 116 ERRORS W

Workbook page 338

★ **A** Select the right word for combining each pair of sentences. Then write the combined sentence. Remember to punctuate each sentence correctly.

1. The mechanic worked all morning on your car. Your car still will not start.   **so   but**

The mechanic worked all morning on your car, but your car still will not start.

2. The cement truck backed over the fire hydrant. Water was spraying all over the street.   **and   however**

The cement truck backed over the fire hydrant, and water was spraying all over the street.

3. We tease Mrs. Tremain. She is the school librarian.   **who   which**

We tease Mrs. Tremain, who is the school librarian.

4. The nurse told Kathleen that the shot wouldn't hurt. Kathleen's arm hurt all the next day.   **therefore   however**

The nurse told Kathleen that the shot wouldn't hurt; however, Kathleen's arm hurt all the next day.

5. Phyllis doesn't like to watch daytime television shows. She did enjoy that game show.   **and   but**

Phyllis doesn't like to watch daytime television shows, but she did enjoy that game show.

6. Mark got a haircut this afternoon. His father still thought that Mark's hair was too long.   **so   however**

Mark got a haircut this afternoon; however, his father still thought that Mark's hair was too long.

B In each item that follows, the underlined sentence has two possible meanings. The sentence that follows the underlined sentence makes it clear which meaning is intended. Read the items and answer the questions.

• She was looking for her glasses on her knees. She finally found them under the bed.

1. What are the two possible meanings of the underlined sentence?

Idea: She was looking for her glasses, which were on her knees; she was on her knees looking for her glasses.

---

2. What is the intended meaning?

Idea: She was on her knees looking for her glasses.

• My neighbor beat his dog. They often have races.

3. What are the two possible meanings of the underlined sentence?

Idea: My neighbor hit his dog; my neighbor raced his dog and won the races.

4. What is the intended meaning?

Idea: My neighbor raced his dog and won the races.

• She hung a picture on the wall and it fell down. She called a carpenter to put the wall back up.

5. What are the two possible meanings of the underlined sentence?

Idea: She hung a picture, but it fell off the wall; she hung a picture on the wall and the wall fell down.

6. What is the intended meaning?

Idea: She hung a picture on the wall and the wall fell down.

C Write each sentence below with the word **particularly**.

1. It was a very cold day.

It was a particularly cold day.

2. His feet look big, especially when he wears sandals.

His feet look big, particularly when he wears sandals.

3. It rains a lot in Seattle, especially in the winter.

It rains a lot in Seattle, particularly in the winter.

4. She was a very good student in high school.

She was a particularly good student in high school.

D In each deduction, the rule is missing. Read each deduction and then answer the questions.

• Photography interests you.
Therefore, you should learn more about photography.

1. What kind of statement is the conclusion?

statement of ought

2. So, what do you know about the missing rule?

Idea: It must be a statement of ought.

3. Write the missing rule.

Idea: You should learn more about what interests you.

• If you eat the right kinds of foods, you'll be healthier.
Therefore, you should eat the right kinds of foods.

4. What kind of statement is the conclusion?

statement of ought

5. So, what do you know about the missing rule?

Idea: It must be a statement of ought.

6. Write the missing rule.

Idea: You should do what makes you healthier.

END OF LESSON 116

Lesson 117

Note: The circled letters indicate when you ask a question or when you direct the group to respond.

━━━━━━━━━━ **EXERCISE 1** ━━━━━━━━━━

DEFINITIONS

1. (Direct the students to find Lesson 117, part A, in the **Student Book**.)
2. (Call on individual students to read part A.)
   Ⓐ Say it with **particularly**. *She likes to play tennis, particularly with Mary.*
   Ⓑ Say it with **particularly**. *The air smelled particularly clean after the storm.*
   Ⓒ Say it with **particularly**. *Ray plays the guitar particularly well.*

━━━━━━━━━━ **EXERCISE 2** ━━━━━━━━━━

ANALYZING ARGUMENTS

1. (Direct the students to find part B.)
2. (Call on individual students to read part B.)
   Ⓓ (Call on a student. Idea: *You shouldn't ride a bicycle blindfolded.*)
   Ⓔ (Call on a student. Idea: *Riding a bicycle blindfolded is too dangerous.*)
   Ⓕ Figure it out. (Wait. Call on a student. Idea: *You shouldn't do things that are too dangerous.*)
   Ⓖ (Call on a student.) *You shouldn't do things that are too dangerous* [or another acceptable rule]. *Riding a bicycle blindfolded is too dangerous. Therefore, you shouldn't ride a bicycle blindfolded.*
   Ⓗ (Call on a student. Idea: *You should do your homework.*)
   Ⓘ (Call on a student. Idea: *Your mother told you to do your homework.*)
   Ⓙ Figure it out. (Wait. Call on a student. Idea: *You should do what your mother tells you to do.*)
   Ⓚ (Call on a student.) *You should do what your mother tells you to do. Your mother told you to do your homework. Therefore, you should do your homework.*
   Ⓛ (Call on individual students.)
   Ⓜ (Call on individual students. Accept reasonable responses.)

━━━━━━━━━━━━━━━━━━━━━━━━━━━━━━

Ⓐ The word **particularly** can often be used instead of the words **very, really,** and **especially.** Say these sentences with the word **particularly:**
• She likes to play tennis, especially with Mary. ⓐ
• The air smelled really clean after the storm. ⓑ
• Ray plays the guitar very well. ⓒ

Ⓑ Sometimes the rule at the beginning of an argument is not stated in the argument. You have to figure it out.
   Here's an argument that has an ought statement for a conclusion.

> Nancy was teasing Brad and trying to get him to do silly things.
> "I'll bet you're too scared to jump out of that tree," Nancy said, pointing to a large oak tree in the yard.
> "I am not," replied Brad. He climbed the tree and then jumped.
> "I'll bet you wouldn't ride your bike blindfolded," Nancy said.
> "Riding a bicycle blindfolded is too dangerous," Brad replied. "Therefore, I shouldn't do it."

What conclusion does the author draw? ⓓ
What evidence is used to support this conclusion? ⓔ
   Here's the last part of the argument:
   Riding a bicycle blindfolded is too dangerous.
   Therefore, you shouldn't ride a bicycle blindfolded.
Figure out the missing rule. ⓕ
Say the whole deduction. ⓖ

   Here's another argument that has an ought statement for a conclusion.

> When Janet came home from the park, her father asked her to come into his study. "Janet," he said, "I'm concerned about your behavior lately. I know that it's spring, and the weather is getting warmer, but I don't think that's a good reason to abandon your responsibilities. Your mother told you to do your homework and you left for the park. When your mother tells you to do your homework, you should do it."

What conclusion does the author draw? ⓗ
What evidence is used to support this conclusion? ⓘ
   Here's the last part of the argument:
   Your mother told you to do your homework.
   Therefore, you should do your homework.
Figure out the missing rule. ⓙ
Say the whole deduction. ⓚ

━━━━━━━━━━━━━━━━━━━━━━━━━━━━━━

Do you agree with the rule that people should do what their mothers tell them to do? ⓛ
Can you think of any situations that would be unfair if people did what their mothers told them to do? ⓜ

Ⓒ How do you make up statements that are more general? ⓝ
To make up a statement that is more specific, you use the name of a smaller class.
   Here's a picture:

* Here's a statement about the picture:
   The <u>man</u> was sitting on a <u>chair</u>.
Make up a more specific statement by using the name of a smaller class for each underlined part. ⓞ
* Here's a different statement about the picture:
   The <u>children</u> walked out of the <u>store</u>.
Make up a more specific statement by using the name of a smaller class for each underlined part. ⓟ
* Here's a different statement about the picture:
   <u>He</u> was playing a <u>musical instrument</u>.
Make up a more specific statement by using the name of a smaller class for each underlined part. ⓠ

Student Book page 275

D Write **Part D** in the left margin of your paper. You have two minutes to copy the paragraph below.

> Most sore throats are due to viral infections, which cannot be cured with mouthwash. Some sore throats are caused by bacteria and should be treated with antibiotics. If a doctor prescribes an antibiotic for your sore throat, be sure to take all the pills.

★ **E** Write **Part E** in the left margin of your paper. Then number it from 1 to 3. Each item tells about the picture. For each item, write a statement that is more specific by using the name of a smaller class for each underlined part.

1. The <u>container</u> had <u>money</u> scattered around it.
2. The <u>dog</u> had <u>something</u> in its mouth.
3. <u>She</u> was juggling some <u>balls</u>.

Student Book page 276

F Write **Part F** in the left margin of your paper. Then number it from 1 to 14. The two passages below tell something about alfalfa. Read both passages and find out which passage gives more facts about the characteristics of alfalfa.

> **Passage A.** Alfalfa is one of the first crops that people grew to provide food for domestic animals such as horses or cows. Although alfalfa originally was grown in Asia, alfalfa is now an important source of hay throughout the world. Farmers often plant alfalfa in fields that have been overworked in previous years, because the alfalfa nourishes the soil with nitrogen. Although it is usually harvested before it flowers, farmers usually let one field bloom to provide nectar for honeybees. Alfalfa is sometimes added to ready-made foods to increase the vitamin content of those foods.

> **Passage B.** Alfalfa is one of the first crops that people grew to provide food for domestic animals. Alfalfa produces sweet hay, and the word **alfalfa** means **the best fodder.** Alfalfa grows quickly, and it grows in many types of soil. It endures well in hot, dry spells because its taproot extends two or three meters down into the ground, where it reaches moist soil. The plant smells sweet like clover, and it has yellow, blue, or purple flowers.

Answer each question that follows. Some of the questions ask where you found an answer. Write **passage A, passage B,** or **passages A and B** for these questions.

1. Which passage tells more about the characteristics of alfalfa?
2. Which of the following main ideas fits passage A?

   • **Alfalfa is grown to feed domestic animals.**
   • **Alfalfa has several uses.**
   • **Alfalfa contains nitrogen.**

3. Why do farmers plant alfalfa in overworked fields?
4. Where did you find the answer to question 3?
5. Why can alfalfa survive in dry climates?
6. Where did you find the answer to question 5?
7. Where was alfalfa originally grown?
8. Where did you find the answer to question 7?
9. Name one of the first crops that people grew to provide food for their animals.
10. Where did you find the answer to question 9?
11. What does the word **alfalfa** mean?
12. Where did you find the answer to question 11?
13. Why do farmers sometimes let alfalfa fields bloom?
14. Where did you find the answer to question 13?

EXERCISE 3

MAIN IDEA

1. (Direct the students to find part C.)
2. (Call on individual students to read part C.)
   - **N** What's the answer? *By using names of larger classes.*
   - **O** (Call on individual students. Ideas: *The old man was sitting on a rocking chair.*)
   - **P** (Call on individual students. Ideas: *Two children carrying ice-cream cones walked out of Mel's Drugstore.*)
   - **Q** (Call on individual students. Ideas: *The old man was playing a banjo.*)

EXERCISE 4

INDEPENDENT WORK

1. **[Optional]** (Direct the students to read the instructions for part D to themselves. Then give them exactly two minutes to copy the paragraph. Count as errors any miscopied word and punctuation. Deduct these errors from the number of copied words, and mark the total on the Writing Rate Graph.)
2. Finish the Student Book and do the Workbook for Lesson 117. ✓

Workcheck

1. Get ready to check your answers starting with Student Book part E. Use a pen to make an **X** next to any item you miss.
2. (Call on individual students to read each item and its answer. Repeat for Workbook items.)

> **Answer key for Student Book part E** (Ideas:)
> 1. *The empty can had coins scattered around it.*
> 2. *The spotted dog had a ball in its mouth.*
> 3. *The girl in the vest was juggling some striped balls.*

Answer key for Student Book part F
1. *Passage B* 2. *Alfalfa has several uses.*
3. *Idea: Because alfalfa nourishes the soil with nitrogen* 4. *Passage A* 5. *Idea: Because its roots extend deep into the ground to reach water*
6. *Passage B* 7. *In Asia* 8. *Passage A* 9. *Alfalfa*
10. *Passages A and B* 11. *The best fodder*
12. *Passage B* 13. *Idea: So honeybees can gather the nectar* 14. *Passage A*

Answer key for Student Book part G (Ideas:)
I took a train trip out to Washington state this summer. Trains are usually late, but the train I rode was right on time. The conductor took our tickets, which were purchased in the station. My brother hit his head on the top of the observation car; therefore, he wouldn't go in that car anymore.

Answer key for Student Book part H
I. *Animals communicate in different ways.*
  A. *Idea: Prairie dogs kiss.*
  B. *Idea: Dolphins, whales, and porpoises speak in high-pitched whistles and clicks.*
  C. *Idea: Male fiddler crabs wave their claws at female crabs.*
  D. *Idea: Cichlids change their color and the position of their fins.*

3. (Direct the students to count the number of errors and write the number in the **error** box at the top of the Workbook page.)
4. (Award points and direct students to record their points in Box **W**.)

0 errors	**15 points**
1–2 errors	**12 points**
3–5 errors	**8 points**
6–9 errors	**5 points**

5. (Award any bonus points. Direct the students to total their points and enter the total on the Point Summary Chart.)
6. Show me your work when you've finished correcting it. (When the students show you their corrected work, record their points on your Record Summary Chart.)

Student Book page 277 — Lesson 117

G Write **Part G** in the left margin of your paper. Rewrite the passage below in three or four sentences. Combine consistent sentences with **and** or **therefore.** Combine inconsistent sentences with **but** or **however.** Combine some sentences with **who** or **which.**

> I took a train trip out to Washington state this summer. Trains are usually late. The train I rode was right on time. The conductor took our tickets. The tickets were purchased in the station. My brother hit his head on the top of the observation car. He wouldn't go in that car anymore.

H Write **Part H** in the left margin of your paper.
Here are three main ideas:

> * **Animals communicate in different ways.**
> * **Communication among dogs or rattlesnakes is simpler than human communication.**
> * **Prairie dogs kiss.**

One of the main ideas fits the passage below. Read the passage.

> The whir of the rattlesnake, the bark of a dog, and thousands of other sounds and actions are used by animals to communicate. In order to live together, animals must be able to communicate. Compared with human speech, the language of most animals is simple, but these animals do communicate with each other. When prairie dogs want to be recognized, they exchange kisses. Dolphins, whales, and porpoises speak to each other in high-pitched whistles and clicks. When a male fiddler crab sees a female, he waves his claws to signal that he is ready to mate. The cichlid, which is a freshwater fish, has several ways of communicating. Cichlids will change their color and the position of their fins when they want to express their feelings.

Write the main idea that fits the passage. List the four points that fall under the main idea in outline form. Don't forget to indent and label the four points.

Workbook page 341 — Lesson 117

★ A Write each sentence that follows with the word **particularly.**

1. Fran's hair is curly, especially after she washes it.
   <u>Fran's hair is curly, particularly after she washes it.</u>

2. He is a very good writer.
   <u>He is a particularly good writer.</u>

3. She likes to watch football games, especially on Saturday afternoon.
   <u>She likes to watch football games, particularly on Saturday afternoon.</u>

4. Sam has a really well-trained dog.
   <u>Sam has a particularly well-trained dog.</u>

END OF LESSON 117

Student Book page 278

Lesson
118

A You've learned two words that can be used instead of the words **really** and **very**. What are those words? ⊖
Make up a sentence that uses the word **especially**. ⊖
Make up a different sentence that uses the word **particularly**. ⊖

B Sometimes the rule at the beginning of an argument is not stated in the argument. You have to figure it out.
　　Here's an argument that has an ought statement for a conclusion.

> "I understand your problem," his mother said. "You're interested in some things that are not taught at your school. I had a similar problem when I was in school. I was interested in astronomy. There was no way to study astronomy in my classes, so I studied on my own. You're interested in photography, so you should study photography on your own. Maybe you can enroll in a class at the Community Center."
> 　"You're right," Brian said. "I'll do that."

What conclusion does the author draw? ⊕
What evidence is used to support this conclusion? ⊖
　　Here's the last part of the argument:
　　Brian is interested in photography.
　　Therefore, Brian should study photography on his own.
Figure out the missing rule. ⊖
Say the whole deduction. ⊖

　　Here's another argument that has an ought statement for a conclusion.

> "Alvin, your sister tells me that you've been spending your lunch money on chocolate bars. You're not giving your body the nutrition it needs. If you eat the right kinds of foods, you'll be healthier. So, you ought to eat the right kinds of foods."

What conclusion does the author draw? ⊕
What evidence is used to support this conclusion? ⊖
　　Here's the last part of the argument:
　　Eating the right kinds of foods will make you healthier.
　　Therefore, you ought to eat the right kinds of foods.
Figure out the missing rule. ⊖
Say the whole deduction. ⊖

Do you agree that people should do things that will make them healthier? ⊖
Can you think of any situations where people shouldn't do things that would make them healthier? ⊖

Note: The circled letters indicate when you ask a question or when you direct the group to respond.

=========== **EXERCISE 1** ===========
DEFINITIONS

1. (Direct the students to find Lesson 118, part A, in the **Student Book**.)
2. (Call on individual students to read part A.)
   - Ⓐ (Call on two students to name one word each.) *Especially; particularly.*
   - Ⓑ (Call on individual students. Ideas: *The moon was especially bright last night. I like to go to movies, especially science-fiction movies.*)
   - Ⓒ (Call on individual students. Ideas: *Her car is particularly noisy when she races. He wants to take a vacation, particularly to the mountains.*)

=========== **EXERCISE 2** ===========
ANALYZING ARGUMENTS

1. (Direct the students to find part B.)
2. (Call on individual students to read part B.)
   - Ⓓ (Call on a student. Idea: *Brian should study photography on his own.*)
   - Ⓔ (Call on a student. Idea: *Brian is interested in photography, which is not taught at his school.*)
   - Ⓕ Figure it out. (Wait. Call on a student. Idea: *You should study subjects that interest you on your own.*)
   - Ⓖ (Call on a student.) *You should study subjects that interest you on your own [or another acceptable rule]. Brian is interested in photography. Therefore, Brian should study photography on his own.*

Ⓗ (Call on a student. Idea: *Alvin should eat the right kinds of foods.*)

Ⓘ (Call on a student. Idea: *If you eat the right kinds of foods, you'll be healthier.*)

Ⓙ Figure it out. (Wait. Call on a student. Idea: *You should do things that will make you healthier.*)

Ⓚ (Call on a student.) *You should do things that will make you healthier [or another acceptable rule]. Eating the right kinds of foods will make you healthier. Therefore, you ought to eat the right kinds of foods.*

Ⓛ (Call on individual students.)

Ⓜ (Call on individual students. Accept reasonable responses.)

═══════ **EXERCISE 3** ═══════

INDEPENDENT WORK

1. **[Optional]** (Direct the students to read the instructions for part C to themselves. Then give them exactly two minutes to copy the paragraph. Count as errors any miscopied words and punctuation. Deduct these errors from the number of copied words, and mark the total on the Writing Rate Graph.)

2. Finish the Student Book and do the Workbook for Lesson 118. ✓

A You've learned two words that can be used instead of the words **really** and **very**. What are those words? Ⓐ
Make up a sentence that uses the word **especially**. Ⓑ
Make up a different sentence that uses the word **particularly**. Ⓒ

B Sometimes the rule at the beginning of an argument is not stated in the argument. You have to figure it out.
Here's an argument that has an ought statement for a conclusion.

> "I understand your problem," his mother said. "You're interested in some things that are not taught at your school. I had a similar problem when I was in school. I was interested in astronomy. There was no way to study astronomy in my classes, so I studied on my own. You're interested in photography, so you should study photography on your own. Maybe you can enroll in a class at the Community Center."
> "You're right," Brian said. "I'll do that."

What conclusion does the author draw? Ⓐ
What evidence is used to support this conclusion? Ⓑ
Here's the last part of the argument:
Brian is interested in photography.
Therefore, Brian should study photography on his own.
Figure out the missing rule. Ⓒ
Say the whole deduction. Ⓓ

Here's another argument that has an ought statement for a conclusion.

> "Alvin, your sister tells me that you've been spending your lunch money on chocolate bars. You're not giving your body the nutrition it needs. If you eat the right kinds of foods, you'll be healthier. So, you ought to eat the right kinds of foods."

What conclusion does the author draw? Ⓔ
What evidence is used to support this conclusion? Ⓕ
Here's the last part of the argument:
Eating the right kinds of foods will make you healthier.
Therefore, you ought to eat the right kinds of foods.
Figure out the missing rule. Ⓖ
Say the whole deduction. Ⓗ

Do you agree that people should do things that will make them healthier? Ⓘ
Can you think of any situations where people shouldn't do things that would make them healthier? Ⓙ

C Write **Part C** in the left margin of your paper. You have two minutes to copy the paragraph below.

> Alfalfa is one of the first crops that people grew to provide food for domestic animals. Alfalfa produces sweet hay, and the word "alfalfa" means "the best fodder." Alfalfa grows quickly, and it grows in many types of soil and many types of climate.

★**D** Write **Part D** in the left margin of your paper. Then number it from 1 to 3. Each item below tells about the picture. For each item, write a statement that is more specific by using the name of a smaller class for each underlined part.

1. The <u>vehicle</u> landed <u>on the ground</u>.
2. <u>They</u> were playing <u>a game</u>.
3. The <u>animals</u> ran away.

1. Idea: *The spaceship landed on a hill near the picknickers.*
2. Idea: *The girls were playing checkers.*
3. Idea: *The horses and the dog ran away.*

Workbook page 342

★ **A** Read the passage and answer the questions. Circle **W** if the question is answered by words in the passage. Circle **D** if the question is answered by a deduction. If you circle **W** for an item, underline the words in the passage that give the answer.

Even though a cow does not eat animals the way a carnivore does, it receives much of its nourishment from very small animals that live in one of its stomachs. That's right, a cow has more than one stomach. Here's how a cow "eats animals."

The cow eats grass. <u>Grass is mostly cellulose</u>, a kind of woody material. If a carnivore ate only grass, the carnivore would not get much nourishment from the meal because the carnivore has no way to break the cellulose down into materials the body can use to build muscle or to provide energy.

Cows and some other grazing animals are different. They have a way of converting grass into a meal that is rich in protein. A cow eats grass, and the grass goes into the cow's first stomach. Inside this stomach are animals that can digest cellulose. These tiny organisms eat the grass.

While billions of these organisms are eating the grass, the organisms and the grass move to the next stomach. This stomach digests protein. The organisms that eat cellulose are rich in protein, so the stomach digests them. Although the cow is eating only grass, the cow is also digesting protein. This process continues as long as the cow lives. In the cow's first stomach, organisms digest the cellulose contained in plants. In the cow's second stomach, the organisms are digested. Without these organisms that eat cellulose, <u>the cow would not receive the nourishment that it needs, and it would soon die.</u>

1. What is grass mainly composed of?
<u>cellulose</u> (W) D

2. Why can't a lion get nourishment from eating only grass?
<u>Idea: because it has no way to break cellulose down to materials its body can use</u> W (D)

3. Explain what happens in the first stomach of a cow.
<u>Idea: Tiny organisms that can digest cellulose eat the grass.</u>

4. Explain what happens in the second stomach of a cow.
<u>Idea: The organisms, which are rich in protein, are digested.</u>

5. What would happen to a cow if it had no organisms that eat cellulose in its stomach?
<u>Idea: The cow would not receive the nourishment that it needs and it would soon die.</u> (W) D

Workbook page 343

B In each item that follows, the underlined sentence has two possible meanings. The sentence that follows the underlined sentence makes it clear which meaning is intended. Read the items and answer the questions.

• <u>Don laid the book on the table just as someone spilled coffee on it.</u> He wiped off the book before the coffee stained it.

1. What are the two possible meanings of the underlined sentence?
<u>Idea: Don laid the book on the table just as someone spilled coffee on the table; Don laid the book on the table just as someone spilled coffee on the book.</u>

2. What is the intended meaning?
<u>Idea: Don laid the book on the table just as someone spilled coffee on the book.</u>

• <u>Her dress was not fitting.</u> Everyone else at the party was wearing blue jeans.

3. What are the two possible meanings of the underlined sentence?
<u>Idea: Her dress did not fit her; her dress was not appropriate for the party.</u>

4. What is the intended meaning?
<u>Idea: Her dress was not appropriate for the party.</u>

• <u>The woman took out a cigarette, lit a match, and began to smoke.</u> The waiter poured some water on her to put out the fire.

5. What are the two possible meanings of the underlined sentence?
<u>Idea: The woman lit a cigarette and began to smoke it; the woman lit a match and she caught on fire.</u>

6. What is the intended meaning?
<u>Idea: The woman lit a match and she caught on fire.</u>

C Underline the redundant part in each sentence that follows. Then explain why the underlined part is redundant.

1. A car is a lethal object, <u>capable of killing living things.</u>
<u>Idea: If you know that something is lethal, you know that it is capable of killing living things.</u>

Workcheck

1. Get ready to check your answers starting with Student Book part D. Use a pen to make an **X** next to any item you miss.

2 (Call on individual students to read each item and its answer. Repeat for Workbook items.)

3. (Direct the students to count the number of errors and write the number in the **error** box at the top of the Workbook page.)

4. (Award points and direct students to record their points in Box **W**.)

0 errors	15 points
1–2 errors	12 points
3–5 errors	8 points
6–9 errors	5 points

5. (Award any bonus points. Direct the students to total their points and enter the total on the Point Summary Chart.)

6. Show me your work when you've finished correcting it. (When the students show you their corrected work, record their points on your Record Summary Chart.)

Lesson 118

2. The preceding event occurred earlier.

Idea: If you know that it was a preceding event, you already know it occurred earlier.

3. The bolts were made of metallic steel.

Idea: If you know that the bolts were metallic, you already know that they were made of steel.

D Each sentence that follows has two possible meanings. Read each sentence and answer the questions.

- The Tigers slaughtered the Buckeyes in tonight's game.

1. What's the intended meaning of the sentence?

Idea: The Tigers won tonight's game.

2. What's the unintended meaning?

Idea: The Tigers killed the Buckeyes in tonight's game.

3. Which word is involved in the two meanings?

slaughtered

- The headline read, "Stock market crashes."

4. What's the intended meaning of the sentence?

Idea: The price of stocks on the stock market declined rapidly.

5. What's the unintended meaning?

Idea: The stock market fell to the ground.

6. Which word is involved in the two meanings?

crashes

- They had a heated argument.

7. What's the intended meaning of the sentence?

Idea: They had a very emotional argument.

8. What's the unintended meaning?

Idea: They had an argument that was physically hot.

9. Which word is involved in the two meanings?

heated

Workbook page 345

E Copy each sentence that follows, using the word **especially** or **particularly** to fill in the blank. Use **especially** in two sentences and **particularly** in two sentences.

1. The sun is _____ hot today.

The sun is especially/ particularly hot today.

2. She likes to fix cars, _____ old convertibles.

She likes to fix cars, particularly/ especially old convertibles.

3. He reads a lot, _____ mystery novels.

He reads a lot, especially/particularly mystery novels.

4. They are building that house _____ fast.

They are building that house particularly/ especially fast.

F You will be tested on some facts presented in this lesson. These facts are:

1. In a cow's first stomach, organisms digest the cellulose contained in plants.
2. In a cow's second stomach, the organisms are digested.

Study these facts. Repeat them to yourself. Writing the facts may help you to remember them.

END OF LESSON 118

Note: The circled letters indicate when you ask a question or when you direct the group to respond.

=== **EXERCISE 1** ===

ANALYZING ARGUMENTS

1. (Direct the students to find Lesson 119, part A, in the **Workbook.**)
2. (Call on individual students to read part A.)
   Ⓐ Write the rule. ✓
   (Call on a student to say the rule. Idea: *You shouldn't do things that are against the law.*)
   Ⓑ Write the conclusion. ✓
   (Call on a student to say the conclusion. Idea: *Therefore, you shouldn't steal.*)
3. Do the next item. ✓
   Let's check your answers. Put an **X** next to any item you miss.
4. (Call on a student to read the whole deduction.)

=== **EXERCISE 2** ===

SENTENCE COMBINATIONS

1. (Direct the students to find Lesson 119, part A, in the **Student Book**.)
2. (Call on individual students to read part A.)
   Ⓒ What's the answer? *Change it to a comma.*
   Ⓓ What's the answer? *So.*
   Ⓔ What's the answer? *Change it to a comma.*
   Ⓕ What's the answer? *But.*
   Ⓖ What's the answer? *Change it to a comma.*
   Ⓗ What's the answer? *And.*

Lesson 119 ERRORS W **Workbook page 346**

A The arguments below have an ought statement for a conclusion. Complete the deductions after each argument by writing the missing rule and the conclusion. The evidence that the author uses in the argument is already written for you.

★ **B** Read the passage and answer the questions. Circle **W** if the question is answered by words in the passage. Circle **D** if the question is answered by a deduction. If you circle **W** for an item, underline the words in the passage that give the answer.

1. The judge leaned closer to the defendant. "You shouldn't steal, because stealing is against the law," the judge said. "Next time it happens, I'll see that you go to jail."

   Rule: Idea: You shouldn't do things that are against the law. Ⓐ
   Evidence: Stealing is against the law.
   Conclusion: Idea: Therefore, you shouldn't steal. Ⓑ

2. You're old enough to know better. Smoking is very bad for you, so you shouldn't smoke. That's the last time I'm going to tell you. From now on, it's up to you.

   Rule: Idea: You shouldn't do things that are bad for you.
   Evidence: Smoking is very bad for you.
   Conclusion: Idea: Therefore, you shouldn't smoke.

In Africa, there is a special partnership between tickbirds and large land animals such as the rhinoceros. Both the rhino and the tickbird benefit from this partnership.
   The tickbird is a medium-sized bird that gets food from the rhino's hide. The bird spends most of its life riding on the rhino's back, pecking away at the ticks that get into folds of the skin and ears. (Ticks are small parasites that dig into the skin and drink the host's blood.) The tickbird is well equipped for eating these ticks. It has special claws that enable it to walk upside down on the rhino's belly and pick lice and ticks from places that are hard to reach. One of the few times the tickbird leaves the rhino is when the rhino wallows and rolls in a muddy marsh.
   The tickbird benefits from the partnership because the rhino provides its food. The tickbird also gets free transportation. The rhino benefits because the tickbird gets rid of bothersome parasites. The rhino receives another benefit—a pair of sharp eyes. The rhinoceros cannot see very far, but the tickbird has keen eyes. When an animal (or hunter) approaches, the tickbird lets out a distinctive cry, a warning to the nearsighted rhino. If the rhino is sleeping or does not pay attention to the tickbird's warning, the tickbird will hop onto the rhino's head and give it a few brisk pecks on the top of the skull. The rhino usually responds to this second warning.

Lesson 119 **Student Book page 280**

A When you combine sentences with the word **so**, what do you do with the period of the first sentence? Ⓒ
What word follows the comma? Ⓓ
   When you combine sentences with the word **but**, what do you do with the period of the first sentence? Ⓔ
What word follows the comma? Ⓕ
   When you combine sentences with the word **and**, what do you do with the period of the first sentence? Ⓖ
What word follows the comma? Ⓗ

B Write **Part B** in the left margin of your paper. You have two minutes to copy the paragraph below.

   The fecundity of this soil is amazing. You can scatter corn seeds on top of the ground, and two months later you'll have cornstalks taller than you are. This ground grows everything from watermelons to strawberries as big as your fist.

Student Book page 281

Lesson 119

★ **C** Write **Part C** in the left margin of your paper. Then number it from 1 to 3. Each item below tells about the picture. For each item, write a statement that is more specific by using the name of a smaller class for each underlined part.

1. He was pounding with a <u>tool</u>.
2. <u>She</u> was carrying some <u>building materials</u> as she moved up an <u>object</u>.
3. <u>They</u> were working on a <u>building</u>.

1. Idea: The man on the roof was pounding with a hammer.
2. Idea: The woman was carrying some boards as she moved up the ladder.
3. Idea: The man and woman were working on a house.

Lesson 119 | ERRORS | W |

Workbook page 346

A The arguments below have an ought statement for a conclusion. Complete the deductions after each argument by writing the missing rule and the conclusion. The evidence that the author uses in the argument is already written for you.

1. The judge leaned closer to the defendant. "You shouldn't steal, because stealing is against the law," the judge said. "Next time it happens, I'll see that you go to jail."

   Rule: Idea: You shouldn't do things that are against the law.

   Evidence: Stealing is against the law.

   Conclusion: Idea: Therefore, you shouldn't steal.

2. You're old enough to know better. Smoking is very bad for you, so you shouldn't smoke. That's the last time I'm going to tell you. From now on, it's up to you.

   Rule: Idea: You shouldn't do things that are bad for you.

   Evidence: Smoking is very bad for you.

   Conclusion: Idea: Therefore, you shouldn't smoke.

★ **B** Read the passage and answer the questions. Circle **W** if the question is answered by words in the passage. Circle **D** if the question is answered by a deduction. If you circle **W** for an item, underline the words in the passage that give the answer.

In Africa, there is a special partnership between tickbirds and large land animals such as the rhinoceros. Both the rhino and the tickbird benefit from this partnership.

The tickbird is a medium-sized bird that gets food from the rhino's hide. The bird spends most of its life riding on the rhino's back, pecking away at the ticks that get into folds of the skin and ears. (Ticks are small parasites that dig into the skin and drink the host's blood.) The tickbird is well equipped for eating these ticks. It has special claws that enable it to walk upside down on the rhino's belly and pick lice and ticks from places that are hard to reach. One of the few times the tickbird leaves the rhino is when the rhino wallows and rolls in a muddy marsh.

The tickbird benefits from the partnership because the rhino provides its food. The tickbird also gets free transportation. The rhino benefits because the tickbird gets rid of bothersome parasites. The rhino receives another benefit—a pair of sharp eyes. The rhinoceros cannot see very far, but the tickbird has keen eyes. When an animal (or hunter) approaches, the tickbird lets out a distinctive cry, a warning to the nearsighted rhino. If the rhino is sleeping or does not pay attention to the tickbird's warning, the tickbird will hop onto the rhino's head and give it a few brisk pecks on the top of the skull. The rhino usually responds to this second warning.

━━━━━ **EXERCISE 3** ━━━━━

INDEPENDENT WORK

1. **[Optional]** (Direct the students to read the instructions for part B to themselves. Then give them exactly two minutes to copy the paragraph. Count as errors any miscopied words and punctuation. Deduct these errors from the number of copied words, and mark the total on the Writing Rate Graph.)
2. In Lesson 120, you'll have a test on story facts. The facts that will be tested appear in part G of your Workbook. Study them and make sure that you know them. Now, finish the Student Book and the Workbook for Lesson 119. ✓

Workcheck

1. Get ready to check your answers starting with Student Book part C. Use a pen to make an **X** next to any item you miss.
2. (Call on individual students to read each item and its answer. Repeat for Workbook items.)
3. (Direct the students to count the number of errors and write the number in the **error** box at the top of the Workbook page.)
4. (Award points and direct students to record their points in Box **W**.)

0 errors	15 points
1–2 errors	12 points
3–5 errors	8 points
6–9 errors	5 points

5. (Award any bonus points. Direct the students to total their points and enter the total on the Point Summary Chart.)
6. Show me your work when you've finished correcting it. (When the students show you their corrected work, record their points on your Record Summary Chart.)

Workbook page 347 — Lesson 119

1. Name two benefits the host receives from the partnership explained in the story.
   Ideas any 2: The tickbird gets rid of parasites; the tickbird acts as a set of eyes; the tickbird warns of danger. (W) D

2. Name two benefits the tickbird receives from the partnership.
   Idea: The rhino provides food and transportation. (W) D

3. How does the tickbird first signal danger?
   Idea: It lets out a distinctive cry.

4. What do the bird's special claws enable it to do?
   Idea: to walk upside down on the rhino's belly

5. What part of the host would not receive attention if the tickbird did not have these claws?
   Idea: places that are hard to reach (W) D

6. Why does the tickbird sometimes peck the host on the head?
   Idea: To give it a second warning that danger is approaching

7. Why would rhinos feel a lot worse if there were no tickbirds?
   Idea: They would be bothered constantly by parasites. (W) D

C Each argument below is faulty. Read the argument and answer the questions.

• Animals used to live much longer than they live today. I read that the brontosaurus lived for over five million years.

1. What does the writer want us to conclude?
   Idea: One brontosaurus lived for over five million years.

2. How could you show that the argument is faulty?
   Idea: Check an encyclopedia to find out whether there's any evidence that any one dinosaur lived for over five million years.

Workbook page 348 — Lesson 119

• Last winter, the city of Dayton used more electricity than the city of Memphis. It is quite apparent that every person in Dayton uses more electricity than every person in Memphis.

3. What does the writer want us to conclude?
   Idea: Every person in Dayton uses more electricity than every person in Memphis.

4. How could you show that the argument is faulty?
   Idea: Find one person in Memphis who uses more electricity than one person in Dayton.

• Don't be ridiculous. I have statistics to show that this prison is the most escape-proof prison in the country. On the average, it has less than one escape every five years. Compare this to Drearing State Penitentiary, which averages over eleven escapes every five years. The statistics show that the chances of escape are very low, so you're being ridiculous when you tell me that there has been a breakout in cell block 13.

5. What does the author want us to conclude?
   Idea: There can't have been a breakout in cell block 13.

6. How could you show that the argument is faulty?
   Idea: Go to cell block 13 and find out whether any prisoners are missing.

D Copy each sentence below, using the word **especially** or **particularly** to fill in the blank. Use **especially** in two sentences and **particularly** in two sentences.

1. She gets along well with her family, _____ with her brother.
   She gets along well with her family, especially/particularly with her brother.

2. He had a _____ good opportunity to get a job.
   He had an especially/particularly good opportunity to get a job.

3. Lynn goes to bed early, _____ on Sunday nights.
   Lynn goes to bed early, particularly/especially on Sunday nights.

Workbook page 349 — Lesson 119

4. These new regulations are _____ strict.
   These new regulations are especially/particularly strict.

E After each statement, write a statement that is more general by using the name of a larger class for each underlined part.

1. The little dark-eyed girl who served customers in the resturant carried a tray full of hamburgers, milkshakes, fries, hotdogs, and soft drinks.
   Idea: The waitress carried a tray full of food.

2. That half-grown colt rubbed against a thick-trunked black oak.
   Idea: The horse rubbed against a tree.

3. Spoons, forks, and knives were rattling around inside a dishwasher.
   Idea: Pieces of silverware were rattling around inside a machine.

F You will be tested on some facts presented in this lesson. These facts are:

> 1. A rhinoceros provides food and transportation for a tickbird.
> 2. A tickbird removes parasites from a rhinoceros and signals danger.

Study these facts. Repeat them to yourself. Writing these facts may help you to remember them.

G After you finish Lesson 120, you will be tested on facts you have learned. The test will include all of the facts presented in Lessons 114–119, and some of the facts from earlier lessons. These facts are:

1. The roots of plants help prevent the formation of a desert by holding down the soil.
2. In a cow's first stomach, organisms digest the cellulose contained in plants.
3. In a cow's second stomach, the organisms are digested.
4. A rhinoceros provides food and transportation for a tickbird.
5. A tickbird removes parasites from a rhinoceros and signals danger.

Workbook page 350 — Lesson 119

6. Study the chart below. Make sure that you can fill in this chart.

organisms
- plants
  - plants without chlorophyll
    - oak tree
    - rosebush
    - grass
    - and so forth
  - plants without chlorophyll are called decomposers
- animals
  - carnivores
    - carnivores that kill are predators
      - lions
      - tigers
      - wolves
      - coyotes
      - eagles
      - frogs
      - and so forth
    - carnivores that don't kill
      - scavengers
        - bears
        - vultures
        - and so forth
      - parasites that live on animal hosts
        - fleas
        - leeches
        - and so forth
  - herbivores

END OF LESSON 119

Lesson 120 — Student Book page 282

A Write **Part A** in the left margin of your paper. You have two minutes to copy the paragraph below.

> In Africa, there is a special partnership between tickbirds and large land animals such as the rhinoceros. The rhino provides the tickbird with food and with transportation. The tickbird frees the rhino of parasites and signals when danger is approaching.

★ B Write **Part B** in the left margin of your paper. In the passage below, the underlined words can be replaced with words you have learned. Rewrite the passage using the words you have learned. Use the word **particularly** at least one time. Use the word **especially** at least one time. Remember to start every sentence with a capital letter and to punctuate each sentence correctly.

> My roommate Jan is <u>really</u> honest, so I was surprised when she <u>showed</u> signs of <u>hiding</u> something from me. I had asked her who was coming to dinner, and she <u>paused</u> for a <u>very</u> long time. Then she gave me a <u>really</u> <u>unclear</u> answer. That night I found out that she had a <u>sound</u> <u>reason</u> for keeping the facts a secret: she was having a surprise birthday party for me!

Student Book page 283 — Lesson 120

C Write **Part C** in the left margin of your paper. Then number it from 1 to 3. One of the graphs is described below. Read the description and then answer the questions.

> The graph below shows how the average American family spends its income. As you can see, almost half of an average income is spent on food. Another large part of the income goes to taxes. The remaining money is spent on entertainment, house payments, clothes, and gasoline.

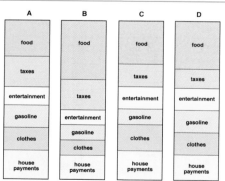

1. Which graph does the description tell about?
2. How do you know that the description does not tell about graph A?
3. How do you know that the description does not tell about graph D?

1. graph B
2. Idea: because almost half of an average income is spent on food
3. Idea: because another large part of the income goes to taxes

---

═══ EXERCISE 1 ═══
INDEPENDENT WORK

1. **[Optional]** (Direct the students to read the instructions for part A in the **Student Book** to themselves. Then give them exactly two minutes to copy the paragraph. Count as errors any miscopied words and punctuation. Deduct these errors from the number of copied words, and mark the total on the Writing Rate Graph.)

2. Finish the Student Book and Workbook for Lesson 120. ✓

Workcheck

1. Get ready to check your answers with Student Book part B. Use a pen to make an **X** next to any item you miss.

2. (Call on individual students to read each item and its answer. Repeat for Workbook items.)

3. (Direct the students to count the number of errors and write the number in the **error** box at the top of the Workbook page.)

4. (Award points and direct students to record their points in Box **W.**)

0 errors	**15 points**
1–2 errors	**12 points**
3–5 errors	**8 points**
6–9 errors	**5 points**

5. (Award any bonus points. Direct the students to total their points and enter the total on the Point Summary Chart.)

6. Show me your work when you've finished correcting it. (When the students show you their corrected work, record their points on your Record Summary Chart.)

Note: Before presenting Lesson 121, present Fact Game Lesson 8.

Student Book page 284

Lesson 120

D Write **Part D** in the left margin of your paper. Then number it from 1 to 3. Each item below tells about the picture. For each item, write a statement that is more specific by using the name of a smaller class for each underlined part.

1. <u>She</u> was washing clothes in an <u>appliance</u>.
2. <u>She</u> was licking <u>something sweet</u>.
3. <u>They</u> were in a <u>building</u>.

1. Idea: A woman was washing clothes in a washing machine.
2. Idea: A little girl was licking a big sucker.
3. Idea: The woman and the little girl were in a laundromat.

Workbook page 351

Lesson 120

A The arguments below have an ought statement for a conclusion. Complete the deduction after each argument by writing the missing rule and the conclusion. The evidence that the author uses in the argument is already written for you.

1. The Carlsons were trying to decide where to spend their next vacation. "Let's go someplace in the desert," Kathy said. "We've been there," her brother said. "Let's go camping in the woods instead." "We were there last year," their mother said. "How about Lake Gitchie Goomie?" "Yeah," said Kathy's brother. "We've never been to Lake Gitchie Goomie, so we should go there."

Rule: <u>Idea: You should go places that you've never been to.</u>
Evidence: The Carlsons have never been to Lake Gitchie Goomie.
Conclusion: <u>Idea: Therefore, the Carlsons should go to Lake Gitchie Goomie.</u>

2. Sharon sat next to Nancy in the cafeteria. "Sometimes the food in this place is just terrible," Sharon said. "Look here—canned peas again. Most kids hate canned peas. We shouldn't have to eat them."

Rule: <u>Idea: You shouldn't have to eat something you hate.</u>
Evidence: Most kids hate canned peas.
Conclusion: <u>Idea: Most kids shouldn't have to eat canned peas.</u>

Student Book page 285

Lesson 120

E Here are some words that will be in some editing activities. Test yourself to make sure that you know what the words mean.

extrovert—An extrovert is an outgoing person who likes to be with people and gets along well with people. Here's a sentence that uses the word **extrovert:**
  She is popular at school because she is such an extrovert.

genius—A genius is an extremely intelligent person. Here's a sentence that uses the word **genius:**
  She is a genius at arithmetic, but she has no plans to go to college.

miser—A miser is a person who is very stingy. Here's a sentence that uses the word **miser:**
  He is such a miser that he washes his used paper plates.

subsequent—A subsequent event is an event that follows another event. Here's a sentence that uses the word **subsequent:**
  The first act of the play is less boring than the subsequent act.

Workbook page 352

Lesson 120

B In each item that follows, the underlined sentence has two possible meanings. Read each item and answer the questions.

• The football star made a play for the <u>cheerleader.</u> She turned him down.

1. What are the two possible meanings of the underlined sentence?

<u>Idea: The football star made a football play for the cheerleader to see; the football star tried to get the cheerleader to go on a date with him.</u>

2. What is the intended meaning?

Idea: <u>The football star tried to get the cheerleader to go out on a date with him.</u>

• She put tuna on the lettuce before she <u>noticed it was moldy.</u> She threw out the tuna.

3. What are the two possible meanings of the underlined sentence?

<u>Idea: She put tuna on the lettuce before she noticed that the tuna was moldy; she put tuna on the lettuce before she noticed that the lettuce was moldy.</u>

4. What is the intended meaning?

<u>Idea: She put tuna on the lettuce before she noticed that the tuna was moldy.</u>

• They stopped the train near the truck so <u>they could load it more easily.</u> When they were done loading the truck, the train went on to the station.

5. What are the two possible meanings of the underlined sentence?

<u>Idea: They stopped the train near the truck so that they could load the truck more easily; they stopped the train near the truck so that they could load the train more easily.</u>

6. What is the intended meaning?

<u>Idea: They stopped the train near the truck so that they could load the truck more easily.</u>

END OF LESSON 120

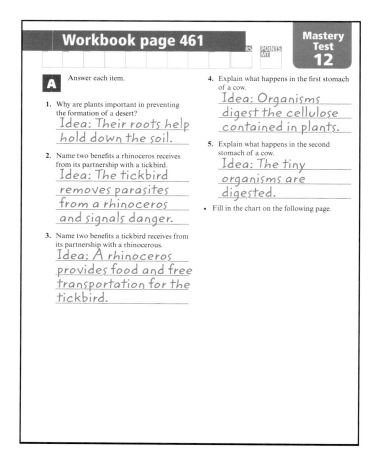

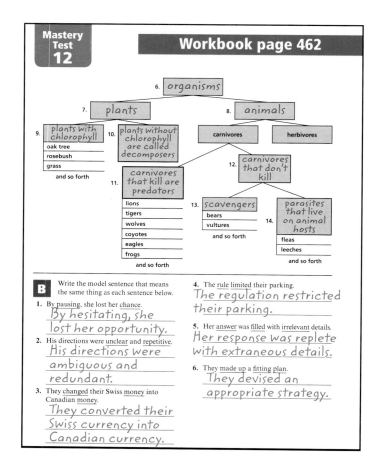

Mastery Test 12

════════════ **EXERCISE 1** ════════════

MASTERY TEST

1. Everybody, find page 461 in your workbook.

   • This is a test. If you make no mistakes on the test, you'll earn 20 points. Write the answers to the test items now using your pencil.

2. (After the students complete the items, gather the workbooks and grade the tests. As you grade each test, record the number of errors the student made on each part of the test in the appropriate box. Record the total number of errors in the **Error** box at the beginning of the test.)

3. (Return the workbooks to the students.) Raise your hand if you made _____ or more mistakes in part _____. (Record the number of students who raise their hand for the part.)

> **Key: Part A–4   Part B–3   Part C–2**
> **Part D–2   Part E–2   Part F–3**
> **Part G–1   Part H–1   Part I–1**

4. Raise your hand if you made no mistakes on the whole test. Great work. (Award 20 points to the students who made no errors. Award 5 points to students who made 1 or 2 errors.)

   • Record your bonus points in the box marked **MT** at the top of Mastery Test 12.

   • (Direct all students to enter their points on the Point Summary Chart.)

5. (Record test results on the Group Summary Sheet. Reproducible Summary Sheets are at the back of the Teacher's Guide.)

Workbook page 463

7. A strange <u>event</u> caused the <u>fear</u> that she <u>showed</u>.

A strange phenomenon caused the anxiety that she exhibited.

8. The major <u>argued</u> that he had <u>sound reasons</u> for hiding the <u>facts</u>.

The major contended that he had valid motives for concealing the data.

C The two passages that follow tell something about mouthwash. Read both passages and find out which passage gives more facts about mouthwash.

Passage A. Mouthwashes that claim to stop bad breath by killing bacteria are useless. No amount of gargling could kill even one-tenth of the bacteria in the human mouth. Bad breath from eating garlic and onion does not come from your mouth at all. The digested garlic gets into your bloodstream, then your lungs, and finally comes out with each breath. Mouthwash cannot help this problem. Some kinds of bad breath come from throat infections that develop when the throat is too dry. Unfortunately, many mouthwashes contain alcohol, which actually dries the throat even more, making the infection and bad breath more likely.

Passage B. Most sore throats are due to viral infections, which cannot be stopped with mouthwash. Some sore throats are caused by bacteria alone, and they should be treated with antibiotics. The only way to determine what kind of organisms are causing a throat infection is to take a few drops from the infected area and examine them under a microscope. If the doctor prescribes an antibiotic for you when you have a sore throat, be sure to use all the pills prescribed. If you stop taking the pills in the middle of the treatment, a much more powerful infection may result. Treating a sore throat with mouthwash may provide temporary relief from pain, but it cannot cure serious throat infections.

Answer each question below. If a question asks where you found an answer, write **passage A, passage B,** or **passages A and B** for that question.

1. Which passage tells more about mouthwash?

passage A

2. The other passage gives more facts about something other than mouthwash. What does this passage tell more about?

Idea: sore throats

3. Can mouthwashes kill all the bacteria in your mouth?

no

4. Where did you find the answer to the last question?

passage A

Workbook page 465

E In each item below, the underlined sentence has two possible meanings. The sentence that follows the underlined sentence makes it clear which meaning is intended. Read the items and answer the questions.

• <u>My neighbor beat his dog.</u> They often have races.

1. What are the two possible meanings of the underlined sentences?

Idea: My neighbor hit his dog; my neighbor raced his dog and won the race.

2. What is the intended meaning?

Idea: My neighbor raced his dog and won the race.

• <u>She hung a picture on the wall and it fell down.</u> She called a carpenter to put the wall back up.

3. What are the two possible meanings of the underlined sentence?

Idea: She hung a picture, but it fell off the wall; she hung a picture on the wall and the wall fell down.

4. What is the intended meaning?

Idea: She hung a picture on the wall and the wall fell down.

F In the passage below, the underlined words can be replaced with words you have learned. Rewrite the passage using the words you have learned. Remember to start every sentence with a capital letter and to punctuate each sentence correctly.

Rafael found a box full of <u>money</u> in the woods. He called up the man whose name was on the box. The man's <u>answer</u> was <u>very unclear</u>. He <u>argued</u> that he had a <u>very sound reason</u> for <u>hiding</u> it.

Rafael found a box full of currency in the woods. He called up the man whose name was on the box. The man's response was particularly ambiguous. He contended that he had a particularly valid motive for concealing it.

Workbook page 464

D Read the passage below and answer the questions. Circle **W** if the question is answered by words in the passage. Circle **D** if the question is answered by a deduction. If you circle **W** for an item, underline the words in the passage that give the answer.

In Africa, there is a special partnership between tickbirds and large land animals such as the rhinoceros. Both the rhino and the tickbird benefit from this partnership.

The tickbird is a medium-sized bird that gets food from the rhino's hide. The bird spends most of its life riding on the rhino's back, pecking away at the ticks that get into folds of the skin and ears. (Ticks are small parasites that dig into the skin and drink the host's blood.) The tickbird is well equipped for eating these ticks. It has special claws that enable it to <u>walk upside down on the rhino's belly and pick lice and ticks from places that are hard to reach.</u> One of the few times the tickbird leaves the rhino is when the rhino wallows and rolls in a muddy marsh.

The tickbird benefits from the partnership because the rhino provides its food. The tickbird also gets free transportation. The rhino benefits because the tickbird gets rid of bothersome parasites. The rhino receives another benefit--a pair of sharp eyes. The rhinoceros cannot see very far, but the tickbird has keen eyes. When an animal (or hunter) approaches, the tickbird lets out a distinctive cry, a warning to the nearsighted rhino. If the rhino is sleeping or does not pay attention to the tickbird's warning, the tickbird will hop onto the rhino's head and give it a few brisk pecks on the top of the skull. The rhino usually responds to this second warning.

1. How do the tickbird's keen eyes help the rhino?

Idea: The bird warns the rhino of any danger. (W) D

2. What part of the host would not receive attention if the tickbird did not have special claws?

Ideas: its belly; places that are hard to reach. (W) D

3. Why would rhinos feel a lot worse if there were no tickbirds?

Idea: They would be bothered constantly by parasites. W (D)

Workbook page 466

G Read the deduction and answer the questions.

• **You shouldn't do things that are bad for you.**
Eating fried food is bad for you. Therefore, you shouldn't eat fried food.

1. What kind of statement does the deduction begin with?

statement of ought

2. Is the deduction valid?

yes

3. Explain.

Idea: The deduction begins and ends with a statement of ought; therefore, it is a valid deduction.

H Write each sentence below with the word **especially.**

1. Anita was really tired after the meeting.

Anita was especially tired after the meeting.

2. He asked for a very large number of books.

He asked for an especially large number of books.

3. She had a really small meal for lunch.

She had an especially small meal for lunch.

I After each statement, write a statement that is more general by using the name of a larger class for each underlined part.

1. <u>Robins and owls</u> often fly into that <u>tall pine</u>.

Idea: Birds often fly into that tree.

2. The <u>small young boy</u> went into the <u>candy store</u> with a bagful of <u>pennies and nickels</u>.

Idea: The child went into the building with a bagful of change.

3. This <u>beagle</u> likes to eat <u>lettuce, carrots, and tomatoes</u>.

Idea: This dog likes to eat vegetables.

━━━━━━━━━━ **EXERCISE 3** ━━━━━━━━━━

TEST REMEDIES

1. (If more than 25% of the students failed a part of the test, provide the remedy specified for that part in the table below. The required Remedy Blackline Master worksheets can be found in Appendix H of the Teacher's Guide.)

2. (All remedies should be completed before beginning the next lesson in the program.)

Test Section	If students made this many errors	Present these tasks: Lesson	Exercise	Remedy Blackline Master	Required Student Book Parts
A	4 or more	Test remedy below		12–A, 12–B	
B	3 or more	Item 1: 19	1	12–C	Lesson 19–A
		Item 2: 22	1	12–C	Lesson 22–A
		Item 3: 28	3	12–D	Lesson 28–B
		Item 4: 34	2	12–D	Lesson 34–B
		Item 5: 57	1	12–E	Lesson 57–B
		Item 6: 63	1	12–E	Lesson 63–A
		Item 7: 86	1	12–F	Lesson 86–A
		Item 8: 101	3	12–F	Lesson 101–C
C	2 or more	107	2		Lesson 107–B
		108	3		Lesson 108–C
D	2 or more (Part D = 6 items)	109	—	12–G	Lesson 109–A
		118	—	12–H	
E	2 or more	113	1	12–I	Lesson 113–D
		114	—	12–J	Lesson 114–D
F	3 or more (Part F = 9 items)	108	1		Lesson 114–A
		109	2		Lesson 115–B
G	1 or more	114	—	12–K	Lesson 108–A
		115	—		Lesson 109–B
H	1 or more	111	1	12–K	Lesson 111–A
		112	1	12–L	Lesson 112–A
I	1 or more	112	2	12–L	Lesson 112–B
		113	3	12–M	Lesson 113–C

> **Note:** The teacher and each student who failed the test will need a copy of Remedy Blackline Master 12–A and 12–B. The Remedy Blackline Masters can be found in Appendix H of the Teacher's Guide.

PART A TEST REMEDY

1. We're going to go over some items from the test. I'll read the items. You'll say the answers. Then you'll write the answers.

2. (Read item 1 in part A of Remedy Blackline Master 12–A.) What's the answer? (Call on a student. Idea: *Tiny organisms are digested.*)

3. (Repeat step 2 for items 2–10.)

4. (Give each student a copy of Remedy Blackline Master 12–B.)
   This worksheet shows the chart that was on the test.

5. Touch box 11.
   Everybody, what goes in that box? (Signal.) *Organisms.*

6. (Repeat step 4 for each remaining box.)

7. Study the chart for a few minutes. Then you'll fill in the empty boxes.

8. (After several minutes:) Now you're going to write the answers to all the items in part A. Let's see who can get them all correct.

9. (After students complete the items:)
   Let's check your work. Use your pen to make an **X** next to any item you got wrong.

• (For items 11–17: Read the items. Call on individual students to answer each item.)

• (For the chart items:) What goes in box 11? (Call on a student.) *Organisms.*

• (Repeat for each remaining box.)

• Raise your hand if you got all the items correct. Nice work.

END OF MASTERY TEST 12

Note: Before beginning Lesson 121, present this Fact Game Lesson. You will need a pair of dice for every four or five students. Each student needs a pencil and Workbook.

EXERCISE 1

FACT GAME 8

1. (Divide the students into groups of four or five. Assign one player in each group to be the monitor. Seat the groups at different tables with a pair of dice.)
2. (Direct the players to open their Workbooks to page 353. Direct the monitors to open their Workbooks to page 481.)
3. You have 20 minutes to play the game. (Circulate as students play. Comment on groups that are playing well.)

Points for Fact Game

1. (At the end of 20 minutes, have all students who earned more than 12 points stand up. Award 5 bonus points to these players.)
2. (Award points to monitors. Monitors receive the same number of points earned by the highest performer in the group.)
3. (Tell the monitor of each game that ran smoothly:) Your group did a good job. Give yourself and each of your players 5 bonus points. ✓
4. Everybody, write your game points in Box FG on your Point Chart. Write your bonus points in the bonus box. ✓

Workbook page 353 — Fact Game 8

| 11 | 12 | 13 | 14 | 15 | 16 | 17 | 18 | 19 | 20 |
| 21 | 22 | 23 | 24 | 25 | 26 | 27 | 28 | 29 | 30 |

2. a. The teeth and eyes of many herbivorous mammals are well-designed for

   _____

   b. The teeth and eyes of many carnivorous mammals are well-designed for

   _____

3. Tell which rule this argument breaks.

   If that company makes good cars, it must make good lawn mowers.

4. The letter A on the graph shows the height for trees that are a certain age.
   a. What age?
   b. What height?

5. The letter B on the graph shows the height for trees that are a certain age.
   a. What age?
   b. What height?

6. Say each sentence with the word **especially.**
   a. The dog was really happy to see its owner.
   b. Summers in Arizona are very hot.

7. Make each statement more general by using the name of a larger class for each underlined part.
   a. The dogs, cats and goats ate the apples, steak and potatoes.
   b. The car and the truck stopped in front of the store and the theater.

Meters tall

8
7
6
5
4
3
2
1

1 2 3 4 5 6 7 8
Age (in years)

Fact Game 8 — Workbook page 354

8. Say each sentence with the word **particularly.**
   a. She is a very good singer.
   b. It rains a lot here, especially in the winter.

9. Tell which rule this argument breaks.

   If that class won the attendance award, every student in the class must have had excellent attendance.

10. a. What word comes from a Greek word that means **house?**
    b. What Greek word means **by the side of writing?**

11. Combine these sentences with **who** or **which.**

    She is going to the movies with Pete. Pete is her neighbor.

12. a. What are the only living things that manufacture their own food?
    b. The teeth of a carnivorous mammal

    are _____ and the teeth of a

    herbivorous mammal are _____.

Workbook page 353

2. a. The teeth and eyes of many herbivorous mammals are well-designed for

_____

b. The teeth and eyes of many carnivorous mammals are well-designed for

_____

3. Tell which rule this argument breaks.

If that company makes good cars, it must make good lawn mowers.

4. The letter A on the graph shows the height for trees that are a certain age.
   a. What age?
   b. What height?

5. The letter B on the graph shows the height for trees that are a certain age.
   a. What age?
   b. What height?

6. Say each sentence with the word **especially.**
   a. The dog was really happy to see its owner.
   b. Summers in Arizona are very hot.

7. Make each statement more general by using the name of a larger class for each underlined part.
   a. The <u>dogs, cats and goats</u> ate the <u>apples, steak and potatoes</u>.
   b. The <u>car and the truck</u> stopped in front of the <u>store and the theater</u>.

Meters tall

(bar graph: Age in years on x-axis 1–8, Meters tall on y-axis 1–8)

Workbook page 354

8. Say each sentence with the word **particularly.**
   a. She is a very good singer.
   b. It rains a lot here, especially in the winter.

9. Tell which rule this argument breaks.

If that class won the attendance award, every student in the class must have had excellent attendance.

10. a. What word comes from a Greek word that means **house?**
    b. What Greek word means **by the side of writing?**

11. Combine these sentences with **who** or **which.**

   She is going to the movies with Pete. Pete is her neighbor.

12. a. What are the only living things that manufacture their own food?
    b. The teeth of a carnivorous mammal

    are _____ and the teeth of a

    herbivorous mammal are _____.

FACT GAME 7

2. a. 1969
   b. 1869

3. a. Organism
   b. Any 3: Bears, porcupines, crows, vultures

4. a. By hiding it
   b. Could kill someone

5. a. Players on that team have practice every day.
   b. Nobody in those houses has a TV set.

6. a. He rarely likes to eat pizza.
   b. She goes to the movies occasionally.

7. The major contended that he had valid motives for concealing the data.

8. a. Statement of ought
   b. Statement of fact

9. a. Eohippus
   b. Endangered

10. He wants to buy a new bike, so he is saving all his money.

11. a. 5
    b. Brazil, Peru, Chile, Argentina, Paraguay

12. Peru, Bolivia, Paraguay, Argentina, Uruguay

FACT GAME 8

2. a. grazing
   b. hunting

3. Just because you know about a part doesn't mean you know about another part.

4. a. 5 years
   b. 3 meters

5. a. 7 years
   b. 6 meters

6. a. The dog was especially happy to see its owner.
   b. Summers in Arizona are especially hot.

7. a. The animals ate the food.
   b. The vehicles stopped in front of the buildings.

8. a. She is a particularly good singer.
   b. It rains a lot here, particularly in the winter.

9. Just because you know about a whole thing doesn't mean you know about every part.

10. a. Ecology
    b. Paragraphos

11. She is going to the movies with Pete, who is her neighbor.

12. a. Green plants
    b. pointed, flat

END OF FACT GAME 8

Lesson Objectives	LESSON 121	LESSON 122	LESSON 123	LESSON 124	LESSON 125
	Exercise	Exercise	Exercise	Exercise	Exercise
Organization and Study Skills					
Main Idea	2	1	2	2, SB	2, SB
Specific-General	SB	SB	SB	SB	
Writing Mechanics: Copying	3	3	3	3	3
Reasoning Strategies					
Deductions	WB	WB			WB
Rules: Arguments	WB	2, SB, WB	1	1, WB	1, WB
Statements: Ought	WB	WB			WB
Contradictions	1	SB	SB		
Information Sources/Study Skills					
Basic Comprehension				WB	WB
Reading Comprehension: Words or Deductions			WB	WB	
Interpretation: Maps/Pictures/Graphs	SB	SB	SB		
Supporting Evidence	SB	SB	SB	WB	WB
Vocabulary/Language Arts Strategies					
Definitions	SB	SB	SB		
Usage	SB	SB	SB		
Editing/Revising	SB	SB	SB, WB	WB	WB
Comprehension: Meaning from Context			WB		
Information Application/ Study Skills					
Information Review			WB		
Assessment/Progress Monitoring					
Ongoing: Workcheck	Workcheck	Workcheck	Workcheck	Workcheck	Workcheck

Note: The circled letters indicate when you ask a question or when you direct the group to respond.

═══ **EXERCISE 1** ═══

CONTRADICTIONS

Note: For this exercise, you will need a reference book about honeybees.

1. (Direct the students to find Lesson 121, part A, in the **Student Book.**)
2. (Call on individual students to read part A.)
   Ⓐ (Call on a student to name the point. Ideas: *Passage 1 says that honeybees have a language, and passage 2 says that they have no way of communicating with each other.*)
   Ⓑ I'll read what it says in this reference book about honeybees. **(Read the relevant passages.)** Which of the passages that you read earlier is accurate—passage 1 or passage 2? *Passage 1.*

═══ **EXERCISE 2** ═══

MAIN IDEA

1. (Direct the students to find part B.)
2. (Call on individual students to read part B.)
   Ⓒ (Call on individual students to name one event each. Ideas: *She watched the better jumpers. She listened to the coach teach techniques to other jumpers.*)
   Ⓓ (Call on individual students to name one event each. Ideas: *At the end of her first season, she was a better jumper. She placed second in the state.*)

Student Book page 286

A The two passages below contradict each other on an important point. Make sure you find the contradiction when you read the passages.

Passage 1. Honeybees seem to have a language, but their language is not much like human language. One very simple reason that the honeybee's language can't be like ours is that the brain of a honeybee is little more than a speck. It doesn't contain very many nerve cells. Honeybees don't actually learn language the way humans do. Honeybees are born with some sort of understanding and some types of responses. The first time they see another honeybee perform a particular dance, they respond and go to the place signaled by the dance. Honeybees also do other things they haven't been taught. If honeybees are raised in a place where they never see a beehive or see another bee build a beehive, the honeybees will still build a perfect hive the first time they try. Every cell inside the beehive will have six sides, even though the bees have never seen such cells before. Honeybees are like tiny computers that have been designed to do some very complicated things.

Passage 2. One of the most notable characteristics of honeybees is their ability to build a hive that is complete with places to store food and nurseries for raising young bees. The honeybees in the hive each have their own tasks to perform. Some collect pollen, others work on building the nest, and still others are responsible for looking after the helpless larvae. The complex organization of a beehive is all the more remarkable because honeybees have no way of communicating with each other. Each bee seems to know what it is supposed to do, or where it is supposed to go to gather nectar, without ever exchanging information with other honeybees. Honeybees seem to be born with a highly developed set of instincts that direct their activities during their entire lives.

The passages contradict each other on an important point. What is that point? Ⓐ

Let's look up **bee** or **honeybee** in an encyclopedia and find out which passage is accurate. Ⓑ

Student Book page 287

B Some passages present a main idea that is called a moral. When a passage presents a moral, the passage presents specific events. The moral is a general statement about those events.

The passage below presents this moral:
If you try, you'll succeed.

Irma started out as the poorest high jumper on the track team. Her best jump was slightly more than three feet. But Irma wanted to be a star high jumper. So she practiced, listened, and talked to herself. She watched the better jumpers—watched the way they approached the bar, how they tossed their arms when they started over the bar, and how they moved their legs. She listened to the coach when he explained jumping techniques to other jumpers. She arrived at practice early every day, and she worked and worked. At the end of her first season, she was better. She approached the bar faster, she had a better takeoff, and she tossed her arms with more force. She could now clear one and one-half meters, which isn't bad. But, by the end of the second season, Irma could clear six feet. She placed second in the state. You might say that she had the ability all along, but Irma also worked very hard.

Name the specific events in the story that show Irma tried. Ⓒ
Name the specific events in the story that show Irma succeeded. Ⓓ

C Write **Part C** in the left margin of your paper. You have two minutes to copy the paragraph below.

She tenaciously held on to her position in the argument. Everybody tried to attack what she said, but she would not give an inch. She was so tenacious that the people who tried to attack her argument finally got tired and gave up.

Lesson 121 — Student Book page 288

★ **D** Write **Part D** in the left margin of your paper. Then number it 1 and 2. One of the graphs is described below. Read the description and then answer the questions.

> The graph shows how Bernard spends his allowance. He puts 20 percent of it into his savings account. He divides half of it equally among clothes, entertainment, and food. A quarter of his allowance gets invested in his hobby, which is model-car racing.

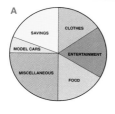 A

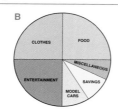 B

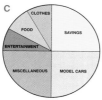 C

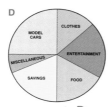 D

1. Which graph does the description tell about? *graph D*
2. How do you know that the description does not tell about graph A?

Idea: because a quarter of his allowance gets invested in model-car racing

Student Book page 289 — Lesson 121

E Write **Part E** in the left margin of your paper. Then number it from 1 to 4. Look at the picture. Then rewrite each sentence.

1. There was a <u>container</u> on the <u>table</u> with some <u>fruit</u> in it.
   Write a more specific statement.
2. The <u>big hairy ape</u> was breaking a <u>dining-room chair</u>.
   Write a more general statement.
3. The <u>boy</u> was crouching beside a <u>chair</u>.
   Write a more general statement.
4. The <u>boy</u> was crouching beside a <u>chair</u>.
   Write a more specific statement.

EXERCISE 3
INDEPENDENT WORK

1. **[Optional]** (Direct the students to read the instructions for part C to themselves. Then give them exactly two minutes to copy the paragraph. Count as errors any miscopied words and punctuation. Deduct these errors from the number of copied words, and mark the total on the Writing Rate Graph.)
2. Finish the Student Book and do the Workbook for Lesson 121. ✓

Workcheck

1. Get ready to check your answers starting with Student Book part D. Use a pen to make an **X** next to any item you miss.
2. (Call on individual students to read each item and its answer. Repeat for Workbook items.)

> **Answer key for Student Book part E** Ideas:
> **1.** *There was a bowl on the coffee table with some bananas in it.* **2.** *The animal was breaking a piece of furniture.* **3.** *The person was crouching beside a piece of furniture.* **4.** *The young boy was crouching beside an armchair.*

Answer key for Student Book part F *When an especially nasty dog appeared on the bike path, she exhibited anxiety. Occasionally she panics in a frightening situation, and this time, by hesitating, she lost her first opportunity to escape. Then she devised a particularly appropriate strategy and got away. Later, when she retold the story, some of the data seemed ambiguous. But she was especially glad to be safe.*

3. (Direct the students to count the number of errors and write the number in the **error** box at the top of the Workbook page.)

4. (Award points and direct students to record their points in Box **W.**)

0 errors	**15 points**
1–2 errors	**12 points**
3–5 errors	**8 points**
6–9 errors	**5 points**

5. (Award any bonus points. Direct the students to total their points and enter the total on the Point Summary Chart.)

6. Show me your work when you've finished correcting it. (When the students show you their corrected work, record their points on your Record Summary Chart.)

F Write **Part F** in the left margin of your paper. In the following passage, the underlined words can be replaced with words you have learned. Rewrite the passage using the words you have learned. Use the word **particularly** at least one time. Use the word **especially** at least one time. Remember to start every sentence with a capital letter and to punctuate each sentence correctly.

> When a <u>really</u> nasty dog appeared on the bike path, she <u>showed fear</u>. <u>Once in a while</u> she panics in a frightening situation, and this time, by <u>pausing</u>, she lost her first <u>chance</u> to escape. Then she <u>made up</u> a <u>very fitting plan</u> and got away. Later, when she retold the story, some of the <u>facts</u> seemed <u>unclear</u>. But she was <u>really</u> glad to be safe.

A Write whether each statement below is a **statement of ought** or a **statement of fact**.

1. He plans to go home after work.
   statement of fact
2. He ought to go home after work.
   statement of ought
3. We will elect a new governor next fall.
   statement of fact
4. Minimum attendance at school should be required for graduation.
   statement of ought

B The argument below has an ought statement for a conclusion. Complete the deduction after the argument by writing the missing rule and the conclusion. The evidence that the author uses in the argument is already written for you.

> First, there was ordinary cleanser. Then there was extra strength cleanser. Then there was Crud-Zip, and people all over the country thought that the perfect cleanser had finally arrived. But now there is something better. Scientists at the Crud-Zip laboratories have come up with a new, super strength formula. That's right. Crud-Zip is new and improved. You should buy yourself a can today.

Rule: Idea: You should buy things that are new and improved.

Evidence: Crud-Zip is new and improved.
Conclusion: Idea: You should buy Crud-Zip.

END OF LESSON 121

Student Book page 291
Lesson 122

A Some passages present a main idea that is called a moral. When a passage presents a moral, the passage presents specific events. The moral is a general statement about those events.

The passage below presents this moral:
If you do things right the first time, you can save time.

> Sid was trying to put up the jib sail on his boat when he noticed that there was a small tear in the sail. Sid was in a great hurry, so instead of taking time to sew the rip, he used a large safety pin to hold the sides of the rip together. The wind wasn't very stiff anyhow. Sid put up the sails and started across the lake. Suddenly, a great gust of wind hit the sails and tore the jib from top to bottom. Repairing the jib required three hours of sewing. It also caused two large blisters on Sid's fingers.

How could Sid have saved time by doing things right the first time? ⊙

B The argument below is faulty because it breaks this rule:

> **Just because events have happened in the past doesn't mean they'll always happen.**

Read the rule over to yourself and get ready to say it. ⊙

Here's an argument:
> I don't think we should hire Mr. Smith. Ten years ago, he was fired from his job because he was so lazy. We don't want to hire a lazy person.

What does the writer want us to conclude? ⊙
What evidence does the writer use to support this conclusion? ⊙
Say the rule the argument breaks. ⊙
Here's how you could show that Mr. Smith may not be a lazy person anymore. Find out who Mr. Smith has worked for recently. Ask those employers if Mr. Smith is still lazy.

C Write **Part C** in the left margin of your paper. You have two minutes to copy the paragraph below.

> Some passages present a moral. When a passage presents a moral, the passage presents specific events. The moral is a general statement about those events. Here is a moral that you may have heard: Don't count your chickens before they're hatched.

Lesson 122 **Student Book page 292**

★ D Write **Part D** in the left margin of your paper. Then number it from 1 to 4. Look at the picture. Then rewrite each sentence.

1. A <u>girl</u> was flying a <u>kite</u>.
   Write a more specific statement.
2. <u>They</u> were running toward a <u>tree</u>.
   Write a more specific statement.
3. A <u>spotted dog</u> was chasing after the <u>little girl</u>.
   Write a more general statement.
4. A <u>girl</u> was flying a <u>kite</u>.
   Write a more general statement.

1. Idea: A girl wearing shorts was flying a kite with a long tail.
2. Idea: The girl and the dog were running toward a big tree.
3. Idea: An animal was chasing after a person.
4. Idea: A person was flying something.

> **Note:** The circled letters indicate when you ask a question or when you direct the group to respond.

EXERCISE 1

MAIN IDEA

1. (Direct the students to find Lesson 122, part A, in the **Student Book**.)
2. (Call on individual students to read part A.)
   ⓐ (Call on individual students to name one opinion each. Ideas: *If he had sewn the small tear when he first discovered it, he would have saved time and avoided getting blisters. It wouldn't have taken him three hours to sew up the small tear, so he should have sewn it up right away.*)

EXERCISE 2

ANALYZING ARGUMENTS

1. (Direct the students to find part B.)
2. (Call on individual students to read part B.)
   ⓑ Do it. ✔
   (Call on individual students to say the rule.)
   ⓒ (Call on a student. Idea: *Mr. Smith is still lazy.*)
   ⓓ (Call on a student. Idea: *Mr. Smith was fired from his job ten years ago because he was lazy.*)
   ⓔ Say it. *Just because events have happened in the past doesn't mean they'll always happen.*

EXERCISE 3

INDEPENDENT WORK

1. **[Optional]** (Direct the students to read the instructions for part C to themselves. Then give them exactly two minutes to copy the paragraph. Count as errors any miscopied words and punctuation. Deduct these errors from the number of copied words, and mark the total on the Writing Rate Graph.)

2. Finish the Student Book and do the Workbook for Lesson 122. ✓

Workcheck

1. Get ready to check your answers starting with Student Book part D. Use a pen to make an **X** next to any item you miss.

2. (Call on individual students to read each item and its answer. Repeat for Workbook items.)

Student Book page 293

Lesson 122

E Write **Part E** in the left margin of your paper. Then number it 1 and 2. Here's an argument for why you should use White and Bright Toothpaste. Part of the argument is contradicted by the graph.

> The graph shows the percentage of cavities that our test group had before and after using White and Bright Toothpaste. In 1998, when we started examining our test group, about 12 percent of their teeth had cavities. By 2001, when our test group started using White and Bright, about 18 percent of their teeth had cavities. After the group used White and Bright, the percentage of cavities dropped. If you are tired of going to the dentist, consider White and Bright Toothpaste.

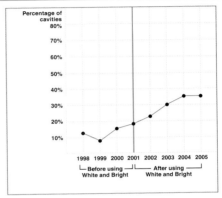

1. Part of the argument is contradicted by the graph. Which part is contradicted?
2. What does the graph show?

1. *After the group used White and Bright, the percentage of cavities dropped.*
2. *Idea: The number of cavities rose.*

Lesson
122

Student Book page 294

F Write **Part F** in the left margin of your paper. Then number it 1 and 2.

Here's a fact: **St. Louis is located near the junction of three rivers.**

1. In what kind of reference book would you look to find evidence to support this fact? *an atlas*
2. Look at the map below. Then write the names of the three rivers that join near St. Louis. *the Mississippi River, the Missouri River, the Illinois River*

Student Book page 295

G Write **Part G** in the left margin of your paper. Then number it from 1 to 3. The description below tells about one of the words shown below. Read the description and answer the questions.

> One root of this word is <u>dict</u>, which means say. A machine that records what you say is a <u>dictaphone</u>. If you say something is going to happen before it happens, you pre<u>dict</u> it.
> The other root of this word is <u>mal</u>, which means **evil** or **bad**. <u>Mal</u>nutrition is **bad nutrition**. <u>Mal</u>odorous means **evil-smelling**. The word made up of <u>dict</u> and <u>mal</u> means **an evil saying**, or **a curse**.

malicious	contradiction	malefactor	malediction

1. Which word does the description tell about?
2. How do you know that the description does not tell about the word **contradiction**?
3. How do you know that the description does not tell about the word **malicious**?

H Write **Part H** in the left margin of your paper. In the passage below, the underlined words can be replaced with words you have learned. Rewrite the passage using the words you have learned. Remember to start every sentence with a capital letter and to punctuate each sentence correctly.

> <u>Once in a while</u>, a <u>really</u> strange <u>event</u> happens in our town. Last week all the <u>money</u> in town was suddenly <u>changed</u> into fruit, and all the fruit was <u>changed</u> into <u>money</u>. Tourists <u>showed</u> a lot of confusion when they saw our bank <u>filled</u> with apples and plums. The tourists were <u>very</u> glad, however, to have a <u>chance</u> to pick from our <u>money</u> trees.

ERRORS W ## Workbook page 356

★ A The argument below has an ought statement for a conclusion. Complete the deduction after the argument by writing the missing rule and the conclusion. The evidence that the author uses in the argument is already written for you.

> In 1996, we began a careful study of different food products, concentrating on what is referred to as "junk food." The tests we did were designed to indicate how much nutritional value each product has. Among the products that we tested was a popular brand of cold cereal called Sugar Crunchos. Our studies showed that Sugar Crunchos have fewer important vitamins and minerals than any other cereal. Since Sugar Crunchos are worthless as a food, the public should stop buying them.

Rule: Idea: You shouldn't buy foods that are worthless in nutritional value.

Evidence: Sugar Crunchos are worthless as a food.

Conclusion: Idea: You shouldn't buy Sugar Crunchos.

Answer key for Student Book part G
1. *malediction* **2.** *Idea: because one root of the word is mal* **3.** *Idea: because one root of the word is dict*

Answer key for Student Book part H
Occasionally, a particularly strange phenomenon happens in our town. Last week, all the currency in town was suddenly converted into fruit, and all the fruit was converted into currency. Tourists exhibited a lot of confusion when they saw our bank replete with apples and plums. The tourists were especially glad, however, to have an opportunity to pick from our currency trees.

3. (Direct the students to count the number of errors and write the number in the **error** box at the top of the Workbook page.)
4. (Award points and direct students to record their points in Box **W.**)

0 errors	15 points
1–2 errors	12 points
3–5 errors	8 points
6–9 errors	5 points

5. (Award any bonus points. Direct the students to total their points and enter the total on the Point Summary Chart.)
6. Show me your work when you've finished correcting it. (When the students show you their corrected work, record their points on your Record Summary Chart.)

END OF LESSON 122

Note: The circled letters indicate when you ask a question or when you direct the group to respond.

EXERCISE 1

ANALYZING ARGUMENTS

1. (Direct the students to find Lesson 123, part A, in the **Student Book**.)
2. (Call on individual students to read part A.)
   Ⓐ Do it. ✓
   (Call on individual students to say the rule.)
   Ⓑ (Call on a student. Idea: *The Japanese are going to bomb Pearl Harbor again as soon as they have the money.*)
   Ⓒ (Call on a student. Idea: *The Japanese bombed Pearl Harbor in 1941.*)
   Ⓓ Say it. *Just because events have happened in the past doesn't mean they'll always happen.*

EXERCISE 2

MAIN IDEA

1. (Direct the students to find part B.)
2. (Call on individual students to read part B.)
   Ⓔ What's the answer? *Specific events.*
   Ⓕ What's the answer? *General.*
   Ⓖ (Call on a student.) *The Girls' Club.*
   Ⓗ (Call on a student.) *Jo.*
   Ⓘ (Call on a student.) *I tried going there once, but it seemed like nothing but a place for bullies.*

EXERCISE 3

INDEPENDENT WORK

1. **[Optional]** (Direct the students to read the instructions for part C to themselves. Then give them exactly two minutes to copy the paragraph. Count as errors any miscopied words and punctuation. Deduct these errors from the number of copied words, and mark the total on the Writing Rate Graph.)

A The argument below is faulty because it breaks this rule:

> **Just because events have happened in the past doesn't mean they'll always happen.**

Read the rule over to yourself and get ready to say it. Ⓐ

Here's an argument:

> **I don't think the United States should help support Japan's economy. The Japanese did bomb Pearl Harbor in 1941. As soon as they have the money, they'll do it again.**

What does the writer want us to conclude? Ⓑ
What evidence does the writer use to support this conclusion? Ⓒ
Say the rule the argument breaks. Ⓓ
Here's how you could show that the Japanese may not bomb Pearl Harbor again as soon as they have the money. Find out if the Japanese have had enough money to bomb Pearl Harbor since 1941 and if they have bombed it again.

B A passage that presents a moral tells about what kind of events? Ⓔ
The moral is a statement about those events that is more _____. Ⓕ
The passage below presents this moral:

> **Don't judge the whole by its parts.**

> It was the first time Tammy had been to the Girls' Club on Fifth Street, and it wasn't a very good introduction to the club. Tammy was fourteen at the time. A tall girl named Jo, who was sixteen and very tough, blocked Tammy's way as she tried to enter the club. "Hey, do you want me to punch you out?"
> At first Tammy didn't believe that Jo was talking to her. "Me?" she asked. "What did I do?"
> "I'm going to flatten you, you hear me?" Jo said and gave Tammy a little push.
> "Wait a minute," Tammy said. "I don't want to fight."
> "Well, if you stick around here, you will fight, and you'll fight me."
> Tammy went home and she never went back to the club. Three years later, Tammy was playing tennis with Linda Becker. Linda was terrific, and she easily beat Tammy. After the game, Tammy said, "I thought I could play pretty well, but you're the best I've seen."
> "Oh, I'm not very good," Linda said. "You should see some of the other girls at the club."

> "Which club is that?"
> "The Girls' Club on Fifth," Linda said. She went on to explain about the tennis program and the swimming program and all the outings that the club sponsored. After talking for about five minutes, Linda concluded, "It's the best club in the world."
> Tammy said, "I never would have thought that. I tried going there once but it seemed like nothing but a place for bullies."
> "I'll bet you met Jo. We kicked her out just about three years ago. She is one bad apple!"
> Tammy said, "Gee, maybe I should give the club another try."

Name the specific whole that is referred to in the story. Ⓖ
Name the specific part that is referred to in the story. Ⓗ
Tell what somebody said when she judged the whole by the part. Ⓘ

C Write **Part C** in the left margin of your paper. You have two minutes to copy the paragraph below.

> **Here's a rule that is sometimes broken in faulty arguments: Just because events have happened in the past doesn't mean they'll always happen. Some people never have a chance to escape the mistakes they've made because other people break this rule.**

Lesson
123
Student Book page 298

★ **D** Write **Part D** in the left margin of your paper. Then number it from 1 to 4. Look at the picture. Then rewrite each sentence.

1. She was riding a <u>horse</u>.
   Write a more specific statement.
2. It was jumping through a <u>hoop</u>.
   Write a more specific statement.
3. A <u>short clown in dotted pants</u> was <u>tossing three empty bottles into the air and catching them</u>.
   Write a more general statement.
4. He balanced on <u>something that is narrow</u>.
   Write a more specific statement.

1. Idea: A pretty young woman was riding a spotted horse.
2. Idea: A lion was jumping through a flaming hoop.
3. Idea: A person was doing tricks.
4. Idea: A man balanced on a tightrope.

Student Book page 299

Lesson
123

E Write **Part E** in the left margin of your paper. Then number it from 1 to 11. The two accounts below contradict each other on an important point. Make sure you find that contradiction when you read the accounts.

> **Passage 1.** A fire broke out in the Northside Apartments this morning. The fire was reported by Mr. James Monroe of 143 North Shore Road. Firefighters rushed to the six-story apartment building, where the fire was spreading rapidly. Thanks to some brave and prompt action by Fireman Foley, all the tenants escaped unharmed. Mrs. Fran Goode was trapped in a bedroom, and Fireman Foley dashed in and carried the unconscious woman to safety. Fire Chief Hanrahan says there is evidence to support the theory that the fire was set purposely. He is working with the firefighters on the investigation.

> **Passage 2.** Fireman Foley became a hero this morning when he rescued an unconscious woman from a smoke-filled room. The room collapsed in flames behind him as he emerged carrying Mrs. Fran Goode. The fire occurred in the Northside Apartments. The six-story building was already blazing when firefighters reached it. Fireman Foley suffered smoke inhalation and some burns on his hands. Mrs. Goode is reported in good condition. Fire Chief Hanrahan says that the fire started on the first floor, where a tenant had fallen asleep while smoking a cigar.

Answer each question below. Some of the questions ask where you found an answer. Write **passage 1, passage 2,** or **passages 1 and 2** for these questions.

1. These passages contradict each other on one big point. What point is that?
2. Where did the fire occur?
3. Where did you find the answer to question 2?
4. What kind of injuries did Fireman Foley have?
5. Where did you find the answer to question 4?
6. Who is investigating the cause of the fire?
7. Where did you find the answer to question 6?
8. Who rescued Mrs. Fran Goode?
9. Where did you find the answer to question 8?
10. Who reported the fire?
11. Where did you find the answer to question 10?

2. Finish the Student Book and do the Workbook for Lesson 123. ✓

Workcheck

1. Get ready to check your answers starting with Student Book part D. Use a pen to make an **X** next to any item you miss.
2. (Call on individual students to read each item and its answer. Repeat for Workbook items.)

> **Answer key for Student Book part E**
> **1.** *Idea: Whether or not the fire was set purposely* **2.** *Idea: In the Northside Apartments* **3.** *passages 1 and 2* **4.** *Idea: Smoke inhalation and burns on his hands* **5.** *passage 2* **6.** *Fire Chief Hanrahan* **7.** *passages 1 and 2* **8.** *Fireman Foley* **9.** *passages 1 and 2* **10.** *Mr. James Monroe* **11.** *Passage 1.*

3. (Direct the students to count the number of errors and write the number in the **error** box at the top of the Workbook page.)
4. (Award points and direct students to record their points in Box **W.**)

0 errors	**15 points**
1–2 errors	**12 points**
3–5 errors	**8 points**
6–9 errors	**5 points**

5. (Award any bonus points. Direct the students to total their points and enter the total on the Point Summary Chart.)
6. Show me your work when you've finished correcting it. (When the students show you their corrected work, record their points on your Record Summary Chart.)

Lesson 123 — Student Book page 300

F Write **Part F** in the left margin of your paper. In the passage below, the underlined words can be replaced with words you have learned. Rewrite the passage using the words you have learned. Remember to start every sentence with a capital letter and to punctuate each sentence correctly.

> Rafael almost never pauses before doing the fitting thing. When he found a box full of money in the woods, he called up the man whose name was on the box. The man's answer was very unclear. He argued that he had a very sound reason for hiding it, but he thanked Rafael anyway and gave him a reward. Rafael was glad to be helpful, and really glad to have some extra money.

Rafael rarely hesitates before doing the appropriate thing. When he found a box full of currency in the woods, he called up the man whose name was on the box. The man's response was particularly ambiguous. He contended that he had an especially valid motive for concealing it, but he thanked Rafael anyway and gave him a reward. Rafael was glad to be helpful, and particularly glad to have some extra currency.

Lesson 123 — Workbook page 358

- The captain made an innuendo at dinner. He hinted that he might quit his job. What he actually said was, "I won't be here much longer." He said it in a meaningful way. I'm fairly sure that his innuendo meant that he was quitting his job.

3. Circle the answer.

   Innuendo probably means:

   a story   (something said as a hint)
   something that is said very clearly

4. Write any sentence from the passage that contradicts the idea that **innuendo** means **something that is said very clearly.**
   Idea: He hinted that he might quit his job.

C Read the passage and answer the questions. Circle **W** if the question is answered by words in the passage. Circle **D** if the question is answered by a deduction. If you circle **W** for an item, underline the words in the passage that give the answer.

> There are over forty types of cleaner fish. These fish provide a special service to the larger ocean animals, and these animals often travel long distances to receive the cleaner fish's attention. The name "cleaner fish" describes this service. They clean other fish. Sharks covered with lice are often found near a cleaner fish station. Sometimes fish may actually wait in line while the cleaner fish works on other fish!

> The cleaner fish goes over the body of the shark or other fish like a vacuum cleaner, removing lice and other parasites. The cleaner fish removes rotten flesh from any injured areas. If a shark has mouth parasites, it will open its mouth and allow the cleaner fish to swim in and eat the parasites. When the parasites are removed from the shark's mouth, the cleaner fish swims out. No other fish could swim into the mouth of a shark and survive.

> Many large fish depend on the services of the cleaner fish. Sometimes cleaner fish follow whales and other extremely large ocean animals. A dozen whales can keep many cleaner fish busy.

1. What kind of water do cleaner fish live in?
   ocean water   W **(D)**
2. Would whales be followed by cleaner fish if the whales moved into deep water?
   yes
3. How many types of cleaner fish are there?
   Idea: over forty types
4. What do they eat?
   Idea: lice, other parasites, and rotten flesh from large fish

Lesson 123 — Workbook page 357

★ A Underline the redundant part in each sentence below. Then explain why the underlined part is redundant.

1. The organization hired a typist to type things.
   Idea: If the organization hired a typist, then the typist will type things.
2. I noted that all the events that followed were subsequent.
   Idea: If you know that all the events followed, you know that they were subsequent events.
3. Her brother, who had a sister, was the tallest person in the family.
   Idea: If he is her brother, then you know that he has a sister.

B Each passage that follows contains a word you may not know. Read each passage and answer the questions.

- He was exonerated from the charge of speeding through the city. His lawyer pointed out that he was the only doctor who could help a patient at the County Hospital and that the patient would have died if he had not been operated on within an hour. When the judge exonerated the doctor from the charge of speeding, the judge told the police officer to tear up the speeding ticket.

1. Circle the answer.

   Exonerated probably means:

   painted green   accused
   (freed from blame)   religious
2. Write any sentence from the passage that contradicts the idea that **exonerated** means **accused.**
   Idea: When the judge exonerated the doctor from the charge of speeding, the judge told the police officer to tear up the speeding ticket.

Lesson 123 — Workbook page 359

5. What would happen to the population of cleaner fish if no other fish visited their station?
   Idea: It would decline because they wouldn't have enough food.
6. Do parasites attack sea animals other than sharks?
   yes   W **(D)**
7. What does a shark do when a cleaner fish goes into its mouth?
   Idea: It allows the cleaner fish to eat parasites and then swim out again.

D You will be tested on some facts presented in this lesson. These facts are:

1. Cleaner fish eat parasites from larger ocean animals.
2. Sharks allow cleaner fish to eat things inside their mouths.

Study these facts. Repeat them to yourself. Writing these facts may help you to remember them.

END OF LESSON 123

A

Student Book page 301

Lesson 124

When you wish to find out information on a subject, you may consult a book or a person. You are using the book or the person you consult as a **source of information.**

Some sources of information are better than others. A doctor is a good source of information about medical and health problems. A doctor is not necessarily a good source of information about plumbing, raising corn, or building houses.

A car mechanic is a good source of information for answering some kinds of questions. Name some questions that could be answered best by a car mechanic. Ⓐ

A car mechanic is not necessarily a good source of information for answering other kinds of questions. Name some questions that could not be answered best by a car mechanic. Ⓑ

A lawyer is a good source of information for answering some kinds of questions. Name some questions that could be answered best by a lawyer. Ⓒ

A lawyer is not necessarily a good source of information for answering other kinds of questions. Name some questions that could not be answered best by a lawyer. Ⓓ

Lesson 124

Student Book page 302

B

A passage that presents a moral tells about what kind of events? Ⓔ
The moral is a statement about those events that is more _____. Ⓕ

The passage below presents this moral:
Never buy something you haven't seen.

Tom received a phone call from Doris on Saturday morning. Doris said, "Tom, I just talked to Marie, and she told me that there's a red bike down at the police station that you can buy for forty dollars. She says it's in really good shape and it has eighteen speeds and everything. I knew you'd been looking for a bike, so I thought I'd let you know about this one."

"Wow," Tom said. "It's in good shape, huh?"

"Oh yeah. Marie says it's spotless."

"Well, I can't get down to the police station until this afternoon because I've got an appointment with the dentist."

"That will be too late. They'll sell it this morning," Doris said. "Tell you what. Marie said she was going by that way. If I give her a call right now, she can buy it for you. Then all you have to do is pay her back."

"Good deal," Tom said. "Call her back and tell her to buy it."

So Marie bought the bike and later that day Tom went to the police station to get it. He looked around where the bikes were, but he couldn't locate a red eighteen-speed in spotless condition. The only red eighteen-speed was a complete mess, with bent wheels, a shift lever that didn't work, bald tires, bent handlebars, and a crooked frame. When Tom finally realized that the junky bike was the one that he had purchased, he said, "What have I done?"

Name what someone in the story bought without seeing. Ⓖ
Tell what was wrong with the thing. Ⓗ

C

Write **Part C** in the left margin of your paper. You have two minutes to copy the paragraph below.

There are over forty types of cleaner fish. These fish provide a special service to larger ocean animals by cleaning parasites and wounded flesh from the animals. Sometimes animals may actually wait in line while the cleaner fish work on other animals.

Note: The circled letters indicate when you ask a question or when you direct the group to respond.

━━━ EXERCISE 1 ━━━
ANALYZING ARGUMENTS

1. (Direct the students to find Lesson 124, part A, in the **Student Book.**)
2. (Call on individual students to read part A.)
   Ⓐ (Call on individual students. Ideas: *Does my car need a tune-up? What kind of oil should I use in my car?*)
   Ⓑ (Call on individual students. Ideas: *Do I need to have my tonsils removed? How much will it cost to have a garage built?*)
   Ⓒ (Call on individual students. Ideas: *Am I required by law to buy car insurance? Who's supposed to pay for house repairs in a rented house—the tenant or the landlord?*)
   Ⓓ (Call on individual students. Ideas: *Which manufacturer makes the best kind of refrigerator? When should I plant corn in my garden?*)

━━━ EXERCISE 2 ━━━
MAIN IDEA

1. (Direct the students to find part B.)
2. (Call on individual students to read part B.)
   Ⓔ What's the answer? *Specific events.*
   Ⓕ Finish the sentence. *General.*
   Ⓖ (Call on a student.) *A bike.*
   Ⓗ (Call on a student.) *It was a wreck.*

═══ EXERCISE 3 ═══
INDEPENDENT WORK

1. **[Optional]** (Direct the students to read the instructions for part C to themselves. Then give them exactly two minutes to copy the paragraph. Count as errors any miscopied words and punctuation. Deduct these errors from the number of copied words, and mark the total on the Writing Rate Graph.)

2. Finish the Student Book and do the Workbook for Lesson 124. ✓

Workcheck

1. Get ready to check your answers starting with Student Book part D. Use a pen to make an **X** next to any item you miss.

2. (Call on individual students to read each item and its answer. Repeat for Workbook items.)

3. (Direct the students to count the number of errors and write the number in the **error** box at the top of the Workbook page.)

4. (Award points and direct students to record their points in Box **W**.)

0 errors	**15 points**
1–2 errors	**12 points**
3–5 errors	**8 points**
6–9 errors	**5 points**

5. (Award any bonus points. Direct the students to total their points and enter the total on the Point Summary Chart.)

6. Show me your work when you've finished correcting it. (When the students show you their corrected work, record their points on your Record Summary Chart.)

Student Book page 303

★ **D** Write **Part D** in the left margin of your paper. Then number it from 1 to 4. Look at the picture. Then rewrite each sentence.

1. A <u>boy</u> was running toward the <u>boat</u>.
   Write a more specific statement.
2. A <u>boy with a hat</u> was sitting in a <u>rubber raft</u>.
   Write a more general statement.
3. A <u>volcano</u> was erupting on the <u>tropical island</u>.
   Write a more general statement.
4. A <u>bird</u> was following the <u>boy</u>.
   Write a more specific statement.

1. Idea: A boy with curly hair was running toward the rubber raft.
2. Idea: A boy was sitting in an object that floats.
3. Idea: A mountain was erupting on the island.
4. Idea: A parrot was following the boy who was running toward the raft.

Student Book page 304

E Write **Part E** in the left margin of your paper. Then number it from 1 to 3.
Here are three main ideas:

> Main idea A. **One kind of penguin mates during antarctic winters.**
> Main idea B. **Penguins have been around for millions of years.**
> Main idea C. **Penguins had to adapt to cold weather to survive.**

Each main idea fits one of the passages that follow. After reading all the passages, figure out which main idea goes with each passage.

> **Passage 1.** Penguins are one of the oldest kinds of birds. They have been on Earth for at least fifty million years. Some of the ancient penguins were more than five feet—taller than many people—and weighed about two hundred pounds. The tallest penguin today is the emperor penguin, which is only about three feet tall. Other kinds of penguins range from about a foot and a half to just less than three feet tall.

> **Passage 2.** Penguins have always made their home in Antarctica, which is a cold, ice-covered land. But Antarctica wasn't always cold. Millions of years ago, it was a green and pleasant land. Penguins thrived there because they had no predators. But Antarctica's climate slowly changed to one of icy winds and snow. Penguins had to find food in the sea. The strongest penguins learned to swim and survive the cold. Weak penguins died. Today, there are seventeen known kinds of penguins, and they all live in cold waters.

> **Passage 3.** The emperor penguin is the tallest and oddest of all penguins. It is the only animal that breeds in Antarctica during the winter. It mates and hatches its eggs in the coldest place on Earth! The emperor penguin sings to attract a mate. The female lays a large green egg that weighs about a pound. Then the male sits on the egg until it hatches several weeks later. The male is proud of the egg, and sings while he sits on it. Meanwhile, the female is off fishing. When the egg hatches, the female comes back. The parents take turns feeding the chick and sheltering it from the antarctic cold by sitting on it.

1. Which passage does main idea A best fit? passage 3
2. Which passage does main idea B best fit? passage 1
3. Which passage does main idea C best fit? passage 2

Lesson 124 — Workbook page 360

ERRORS W

★ **A** Read the passage and answer the questions. Circle **W** if the question is answered by words in the passage. Circle **D** if the question is answered by a deduction. If you circle **W** for an item, underline the words in the passage that give the answer.

Below is a picture of a crab. Crabs live in water and on beaches. The crab's hard shell is solid except for one small tender spot on the underside of its body.

Most smaller predators could not kill a crab by attacking its back or its front. Attacking a crab from the front is not a good idea, because the crab's pincers are so strong that they could snip off the end of a stick (or the end of your finger). But if a predator could reach the soft spot on the crab's underside, the predator could easily kill the crab.

Reaching that tender spot may seem like an easy thing to do. However, in addition to using their pincers, crabs have developed other methods of protection that make the predator's job very difficult.

The hermit crab hides itself whenever it can. It will hide in nearly anything that offers protection for its midsection—shells of other animals, tin cans, or anything else that can

serve as a hard overcoat. While wearing this borrowed covering, the hermit crab can move. It scoots along the sandy bottom of the ocean, looking like some sort of shellfish with crab legs sticking out of the bottom. This sight is not funny for the predators, however, because as long as the hermit crab stays inside the covering, the predators won't be able to eat it.

Some crabs get additional protection from small stinging animals called sea anemones. The crab pulls the sea anemones from a rock and places them on its shell. The stinging tentacles of sea anemones discourage predators from trying to dig into the shell. One type of crab carries a sea anemone in each claw. Whenever a predator approaches, the crab holds the anemones up, and the predator leaves.

Some crabs disguise themselves by attaching plants or other animals to their shells. Doing this makes the shells blend in with the surroundings. The spider crab attaches seaweed or other small animals to its shell. Other crabs protect the tender part of their shells by attaching a piece of sponge directly over the tender spot. Predators rarely eat sponges and, therefore, the sponge disguises the crab's tender spot. Another type of crab disguises itself to look like coral.

1. What part of their body do crabs have to protect?
   Idea: their underside
   W **D**

2. Does the sting of the sea anemone bother a crab?
   no
   W **D**

"soft spot"

pincers

Workbook page 361 — Lesson 124

3. How does the hermit crab protect its tender part?
   Idea: by hiding in anything that will offer its midsection some protection

4. Name a sea animal with a hard shell.
   Idea: the crab

5. Why do some crabs place a piece of sponge on the underside of their bodies?
   Idea: to protect the tender part of their shells

6. How do some crabs disguise themselves?
   Idea: by attaching plants or other animals to their shells

7. Fill in the chart below so that it tells four ways that crabs protect themselves.

how crabs protect themselves

- have strong pincers
- live inside hard objects
- carry sea anemones
- disguise themselves with plants and animals

Lesson 124 — Workbook page 362

B Read the argument below and answer the questions.

> We really can't accept you for this job, Ms. Lee. While reading over your job application, I noticed that you held your last job for only six months. I'm afraid we are looking for someone who will stay at this job for a much longer period of time.

1. What does the writer want us to conclude?
   Idea: Ms. Lee doesn't work at a job for more than six months.

2. What evidence does the writer use to support this conclusion?
   Idea: Ms. Lee held her last job for only six months.

3. What rule does the writer's argument break?
   Idea: Just because events happened in the past doesn't mean they'll always happen.

4. How could you show that the conclusion may not be valid?
   Idea: Show that Ms. Lee has worked somewhere for longer than six months.

C Ed sometimes has trouble using the words **who** and **which**. Following is a letter that he wrote to the Foodville Market. Cross out the words **who** and **which** if they are used incorrectly. Write the correct word above every crossed-out word.

Dear Foodville Market,

Chocolate-covered ants, which are the only things that I can eat, are out of stock at your store. I recently spoke with your manager, who promised me that she would order more ants right away. That was over three weeks ago, and now any girl ~~which~~ *who* looks at me thinks I'm sick because I'm so skinny. The doctor ~~which~~ *who* examined me told me that I must get some ants to eat soon or I will become even skinnier.

Which brings me to the point of this letter. Do you realize that there are many other people ~~which~~ *who* need to eat chocolate-covered ants? I have several other friends who have decided to shop at another market because they can't purchase ants at your store. I would like to know who hired your manager. Perhaps I could speak directly with this person, and he or she could order these ants, ~~who~~ *which* I need to keep up my strength. Please reply soon because I'm getting weaker every day.

Sincerely yours,
Edward Entomal

Workbook page 363 — Lesson 124

D Read each item and write the answers.

1. A car mechanic is a good source of information for answering some questions. Write three of those questions.
   Ideas: How often should you change the oil in a car? How can I improve my car's gas mileage? What is wrong with my car's engine when it begins to knock? etc.

2. A car mechanic is not necessarily a good source of information for answering some questions. Write three of those questions.
   Ideas: Is travel by car less hazardous than travel by plane? How can I save money on my income taxes? Who should finance highways? etc.

3. A farmer is a good source of information for answering some questions. Write three of those questions.
   Ideas: When is the best time to plant corn? What is the best fertilizer for wheat? Are cattle a good investment right now? etc.

4. A farmer is not necessarily a good source of information for answering some questions. Write three of those questions.
   Ideas: What's a good book on nuclear energy? Is this a good time to sell my house? What's a fair price for carpet? etc.

Workbook page 364

E In the passage below, the verbs **is** and **are** are used incorrectly five times. Cross out each incorrect word. Write the correct word above it.

There are two redundant parts in the passage below. Cross out each redundant part.

One of the best things you can do for yourself is learn a sport. Some of the more
are
popular sports ~~is~~ fishing, jogging, tennis,
_is_
and swimming. Each of these sports ~~are~~ guaranteed to keep you in shape both mentally and physically, ~~in your mind and in your body~~. Jogging, swimming, and
are
tennis ~~is~~ good for your circulatory system and your muscles. Fishing, since it often
_is_
involves hiking or canoeing, ~~are~~ also good
_is_
exercise. Fishing ~~are~~ a fine way to spend time outdoors, ~~out of the house~~. If you get a chance, buy yourself a fishing rod or a tennis racket and learn to use it.

F You will be tested on some facts presented in this lesson. These facts are:

Crabs have different ways to protect themselves from predators:

> 1. Crabs have strong pincers.
> 2. Hermit crabs live inside hard objects.
> 3. Some crabs carry sea anemones.
> 4. Some crabs disguise themselves with plants and other animals.

Study these facts. Repeat them to yourself. Writing these facts may help you to remember them.

END OF LESSON 124

Student Book page 305

A When you wish to find out information on a subject, you may consult a book or a person. You are using the book or the person you consult as a **source of information.**

> Some sources of information are better than others. A doctor is a good source of information about medical and health problems. A doctor is not necessarily a good source of information about plumbing, raising corn, or building houses.
>
> A secretary is a good source of information for answering some kinds of questions. Name some questions that could best be answered by a secretary. Ⓐ
>
> A secretary is not necessarily a good source of information for answering other kinds of questions. Name some questions that could not be answered best by a secretary. Ⓑ
>
> A dentist is a good source of information for answering some kinds of questions. Name some questions that could be answered best by a dentist. Ⓒ
>
> A dentist is not necessarily a good source of information for answering other kinds of questions. Name some questions that could not be answered best by a dentist. Ⓓ

Student Book page 306

B The passage below presents one of these morals:

- **What you have is better than a promise of something that you might get.**
- **You should always take advantage of opportunities that sound good.**
- **You should never listen to a man who talks about gold mines.**

Read the passage and figure out which moral fits.

> Jack had an office job that paid well. He liked his work, but he had been working there for seven years, and the routine had been getting on his nerves. Every day, five days a week, he got up at 7 A.M. After drinking his coffee, he drove to the office. He worked at the office for eight hours, then went home and watched television. He thought that life could be a bit more exciting than it was. Unfortunately, he owed around $5,000 to various department stores, and couldn't just quit his job. So Jack kept working.
>
> One day, a man came to the door when Jack was watching television. The man said that he represented a firm from Chicago. The firm owned gold mines in Africa and had just uncovered a big vein of gold. The man said that it was a sure bet. The man told Jack that he would be a millionaire overnight if he bought shares in the gold mine. It seemed a fine opportunity to make some money without even working for it. So Jack gave the man all his savings, which amounted to about $2,000. The next day, he resigned from his job because he knew that soon he would be rich.
>
> Unfortunately, Jack never heard from the man again. There was no gold mine. Jack's bills piled up, but he had no income. Finding another job was hard. He finally got hired at another office, but for much lower pay than what he had received before.

Which moral fits the passage? Ⓔ

C Write **Part C** in the left margin of your paper. You have two minutes to copy the paragraph below.

> Penguins have always made their home in Antarctica, which is a cold, ice-covered land. But Antarctica hasn't always been cold. Millions of years ago, it was a warm, green, pleasant land. Penguins thrived in that land because they had no predators.

Note: The circled letters indicate when you ask a question or when you direct the group to respond.

EXERCISE 1

ANALYZING ARGUMENTS

1. (Direct the students to find Lesson 125, part A, in the **Student Book.**)
2. (Call on individual students to read part A.)
   - Ⓐ (Call on individual students. Ideas: *What is the right format for a business letter? What is a good brand of typewriter to buy?*)
   - Ⓑ (Call on individual students. Ideas: *How do you make coffee in an electric coffeepot? What are the symptoms of measles?*)
   - Ⓒ (Call on individual students. Ideas: *How often should I brush my teeth? How many cavities do I have?*)
   - Ⓓ (Call on individual students. Ideas: *How do you stop a water faucet from dripping? How do you cook brussels sprouts?*)

EXERCISE 2

MAIN IDEA

1. (Direct the students to find part B.)
2. (Call on individual students to read part B.)
   - Ⓔ What's the answer? *What you have is better than a promise of something that you might get.*

EXERCISE 3

INDEPENDENT WORK

1. **[Optional]** (Direct the students to read the instructions for part C to themselves. Then give them exactly two minutes to copy the paragraph. Count as errors any miscopied words and punctuation. Deduct these errors from the number of copied words, and mark the total on the Writing Rate Graph.)

3. Finish the Student Book and do the Workbook for Lesson 125. ✓

Workcheck

1. Get ready to check your answers starting with Student Book part D. Use a pen to make an **X** next to any item you miss.

2. (Call on individual students to read each item and its answer. Repeat for Workbook items.)

3. (Direct the students to count the number of errors and write the number in the **error** box at the top of the Workbook page.)

4. (Award points and direct students to record their points in Box **W.**)

0 errors	**15 points**
1–2 errors	**12 points**
3–5 errors	**8 points**
6–9 errors	**5 points**

5. (Award any bonus points. Direct the students to total their points and enter the total on the Point Summary Chart.)

6. Show me your work when you've finished correcting it. (When the students show you their corrected work, record their points on your Record Summary Chart.)

Student Book page 307

★ **D** Write **Part D** in the left margin of your paper.
Here are three main ideas:

- Many marble games have interesting names.
- Many people enjoy playing marbles.
- Fatty Box is a marble game.

One of the main ideas fits the passage below. Read the passage.

There are many popular marble games with interesting names. One popular marble game is called Ringer. Ringer is played with thirteen marbles. It is the game that is played each year in the National Marbles Tournament. Another game with an interesting name is Old Bowler. Old Bowler involves a square shooting area and requires players to shoot marbles off the corners of the square. Variations of Old Bowler are played throughout the world. A game that is very similar to Old Bowler is a game called Fatty Box. Fatty Box is very popular in the Boston area.

Write the main idea that fits the passage. List the three points that fall under the main idea in outline form. Don't forget to indent and label the three points.

I. Many marble games have interesting names.
   A. Idea: Ringer is played with thirteen marbles.
   B. Idea: Old Bowler involves a square shooting area.
   C. Idea: Fatty Box is very popular in the Boston area.

Workbook page 365

★ **A** Underline the redundant part in each sentence below. Then explain why the underlined part is redundant.

1. He was a very intelligent genius.
   Idea: If you know that he was a genius, you know that he was very intelligent.

2. The giraffe she saw was tall and had four legs.
   Idea: If you know that she saw a giraffe, then you know that it was tall and had four legs.

3. That winter, which followed autumn, set five records for low temperatures.
   Idea: If you know that it was winter, then you know that it followed autumn.

B The argument below has an ought statement for a conclusion. Complete the deduction after the argument by writing the missing rule and the conclusion. The evidence that the author uses in the argument is already written for you.

"Look, Ralph, there's one of those Multipurpose Kitchen Wizards with fourteen interchangeable attachments. Give me the checkbook, will you, dear?"
"Oh, Martha, you shouldn't buy that thing."
"Why not?"
"Because we don't need it, that's why not."

Rule: Idea: You shouldn't buy things that you don't need.

Evidence: Martha and Ralph don't need the Multipurpose Kitchen Wizard.

Conclusion: Idea: Martha and Ralph shouldn't buy the Multipurpose Kitchen Wizard.

Workbook page 366

C Read each argument below and answer the questions.

- I doubt if we will be able to accept your application to this university, Joe. Your record from Smith State is very poor. You skipped classes and almost flunked out your first term. We don't want students like that here.

1. What does the writer want us to conclude?
   Idea: Joe won't be a good student.

2. What evidence does the writer use to support this conclusion?
   Idea: Joe's record from Smith State

3. What rule does the writer's argument break?
   Idea: Just because events have happened in the past doesn't mean they'll always happen.

4. How could you show that the conclusion may not be valid?
   Idea: Give Joe a chance to be a good student at this university.

- This guy is very qualified for the job. Unfortunately, he has a prison record. Once a crook, always a crook. He'll just have to find another sucker to hire him.

5. What does the writer want us to conclude?
   Idea: Because the man has been a crook, he'll always be a crook.

6. What evidence does the writer use to support this conclusion?
   Idea: The man has a prison record.

7. What rule does the writer's argument break?
   Idea: Just because events have happened in the past doesn't mean they'll always happen.

8. How could you show that the conclusion may not be valid?
   Idea: Give the man a chance to prove he's not a crook anymore.

Workbook page 367

D In each item that follows, the underlined sentence has two possible meanings. The sentence that follows the underlined sentence makes it clear which meaning is intended. Read each item and answer the questions.

- I leaned against the building to light my cigar just before it blew up. Bricks and boards flew all over the place.

1. What are the two possible meanings of the underlined sentence?
   Idea: I leaned against the building to light my cigar just before the building blew up; I leaned against the building to light my cigar just before the cigar blew up.

2. What is the intended meaning?
   Idea: I leaned against the building to light my cigar just before the building blew up.

- My neighbors make good hamburgers, but they're too cheesy. Last time I ate a burger at their house, all they did was talk about cheap schemes for making money.

3. What are the two possible meanings of the underlined sentence?
   Idea: My neighbors make good hamburgers, but their burgers are too cheesy; my neighbors make good hamburgers, but my neighbors are too cheesy.

4. What is the intended meaning?
   Idea: My neighbors make good hamburgers, but my neighbors are too cheesy.

Workbook page 368

- She tied the hat to her doll's head so it wouldn't blow away. The wind was too strong and blew the hat off anyway.

5. What are the two possible meanings of the underlined sentence?
   Idea: She tied the hat to her doll's head so its head wouldn't blow away; she tied the hat to her doll's head so its hat wouldn't blow away.

6. What is the intended meaning?
   Idea: She tied the hat to her doll's head so that the hat wouldn't blow away.

E Read each item and write the answers.

1. A truck driver is a good source of information for answering some questions. Write three of those questions.
   Ideas: How long should it take to drive from Witchita to Chicago? How do truckers use the CB radio? What's the maximum amount of time a person should drive without sleep? etc.

2. A truck driver is not necessarily a good source of information for answering some questions. Write three of those questions.
   Ideas: Should car racing be outlawed? Is professional football a good field to get into? When should I plant tulip bulbs? etc.

Workbook page 369

3. A telephone operator is a good source of information for answering some questions. Write three of those questions.
   Ideas: What time of day are long-distance rates cheapest? What's the charge for calling information? How do I place a collect call? etc.

4. A telephone operator is not necessarily a good source of information for answering some questions. Write three of those questions.
   Ideas: What do I need to hang wallpaper? What's the best brand of motor oil? How many eggs do robins usually lay in one season? etc.

5. A librarian is a good source of information for answering some questions. Write three of those questions.
   Ideas: Who wrote "Lord of the Flies"? What's a good magazine about coin collecting? How does the Dewey Decimal System work? etc.

6. A librarian is not necessarily a good source of information for answering some questions. Write three of those questions.
   Ideas: What will happen to General Motors stock? Should the National Football League go on strike? Will this be a cold winter? etc.

END OF LESSON 125

Lesson Objectives	LESSON 126	LESSON 127	LESSON 128	LESSON 129	LESSON 130
	Exercise	Exercise	Exercise	Exercise	Exercise
Organization and Study Skills					
Main Idea				2	
Morals	SB	SB	SB	SB	SB
Writing Mechanics: Copying	3	3	3	3	1
Reasoning Strategies					
Deductions	WB	WB	WB	WB	WB
Evidence			WB		WB
Rules: Arguments	2, WB	1, 2, WB	1, 2, WB	1, WB	WB
Statements: Ought	WB	WB	WB	WB	WB
Contradictions	1			WB	
Information Sources/Study Skills					
Basic Comprehension	WB				
Reading Comprehension: Words or Deductions		WB			
Interpretation: Maps/Pictures/Graphs	SB				SB
Supporting Evidence	SB, WB	WB	SB		SB
Vocabulary/Language Arts Strategies					
Definitions			SB		SB
Usage			SB		SB
Sentence Combination			WB		
Editing/Revising		WB		WB	
Comprehension: Meaning from Context			WB	WB	
Information Application/ Study Skills					
Information Review		WB		WB	
Assessment/Progress Monitoring					
Ongoing: Workcheck	Workcheck	Workcheck	Workcheck	Workcheck	Workcheck
Formal: Mastery Test					MT13

Note: The circled letters indicate when you ask a question or when you direct the group to respond.

═══════════ **EXERCISE 1** ═══════════

CONTRADICTIONS

Note: For this exercise, you will need a reference book that tells about the suffrage movement or about Susan B. Anthony.

1. (Direct the students to find Lesson 126, part A, in the **Student Book.**)
2. (Call on individual students to read part A.)
   Ⓐ (Call on two students to name one point each. Ideas: *Passage 1 says that women got the right to vote in 1940, and passage 2 says women got the right to vote in 1920. Passage 1 says that Susan B. Anthony gave up on trying to vote, and passage 2 says that she voted and got arrested*.)
   Ⓑ I'll read what it says in this reference book about Susan B. Anthony [or about suffrage]. (Read the relevant passages.) Which of the passages that you read earlier is accurate—passage 1 or passage 2? *Passage 2.*

═══════════ **EXERCISE 2** ═══════════

ANALYZING ARGUMENTS

1. (Direct the students to find part B.)
2. (Call on individual students to read part B.)
   Ⓒ (Call on a student. Idea: *The water level in the reservoirs is due to rainfall, and the amount of rainfall has decreased*.)
   Ⓓ (Call on a student. Idea: *The water commissioner cannot control the rainfall, so the lower water levels are not his fault*.)

A The two passages below contradict each other on two important points. Make sure you find those contradictions when you read the passages.

Passage 1. Suffrage means the right to vote. In the past, many countries, including the United States, allowed only men, landowners, or people from rich families to vote. Most countries today have laws that give all citizens over a certain age the right to vote. In the United States, women didn't have the right to vote until 1940. Suffrage was an issue for nearly fifty years, and the women who fought for the right to vote were called suffragettes. One of the most famous of these women was Susan B. Anthony. Ms. Anthony once tried to vote in a presidential election, but when a judge told her that she couldn't vote, she decided she didn't want to get in trouble and went home. She devoted the rest of her life to fighting for women's rights. She published her own newspaper, lectured around the United States, and wrote many magazine articles and a book.

Passage 2. Susan B. Anthony, who was born in 1820, taught school for fifteen years. She became a part of the antislavery movement and eventually began to struggle for women's rights. Today, we take for granted that the Constitution applies to all American citizens. In the 1800s, women were deprived of many constitutional rights, including the right to vote. In the election of 1872, Susan B. Anthony set out to change that. She turned up at the polls and voted. Later, she was arrested and sent to trial. The judge fined her $100, which she refused to pay. In 1920, fourteen years after Ms. Anthony's death, the Nineteenth Amendment was passed, granting women the right to vote.

The passages contradict each other on two important points. What are those points? Ⓐ

Let's look up **suffrage** or **Susan B. Anthony** in an encyclopedia and find out which passage is accurate. Ⓑ

B A biased argument is an argument that tells the truth, but it tells only part of the truth.

Study the graph below. Then read the biased argument that is based on the graph.

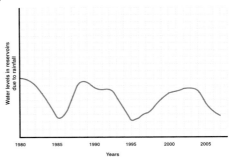

We are having a water shortage in 2007 because the water commissioner that we elected last year is irresponsible. Our reservoirs are at their lowest levels in ten years. Not since the droughts of 1985 and 1995 have we been so dry. It's time for a new water commissioner. Impeach Nad Honker!

This argument is biased because it doesn't take into account some important information. What information is that? Ⓒ

Let's say you wanted to attack the argument above. What would you say? Ⓓ

Student Book page 310

C Write **Part C** in the left margin of your paper. You have two minutes to copy the paragraph below.

> When you wish to find out information on a subject, you may consult a book or a person. You are using the book or the person you consult as a source of information. Some sources of information are better than others.

★ **D** Write **Part D** in the left margin of your paper. Then number it 1 and 2.

One of the graphs on the next page is described below. Read the description and answer the questions.

> The graph shows the amount of money spent on the United States space program during the years from 1960 to 1973. These were the early years of the space program. More money was spent in 1966 than in any other year. The graph also shows that the United States never spent more than six billion dollars on the space program in a single year during that time. Spending for the space program in the 1990s has been at least thirteen billion dollars each year.

Student Book page 311

1. Which graph does the description tell about? graph C
2. How do you know that the description does not tell about graph B?
   Idea: Graph B shows months, not years.

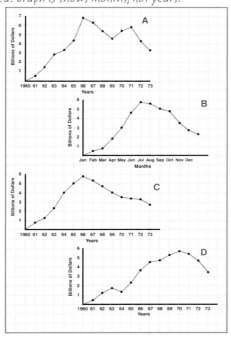

EXERCISE 3
INDEPENDENT WORK

1. **[Optional]** (Direct the students to read the instructions for part C to themselves. Then give them exactly two minutes to copy the paragraph. Deduct any errors from the number of copied words, and mark the total on the Writing Rate Graph.)
2. Finish the Student Book and do the Workbook for Lesson 126. ✓

Workcheck

1. Get ready to check your answers starting with Student Book part D. Use a pen to make an **X** next to any item you miss.
2. (Call on individual students to read each item and its answer. Repeat for Workbook items.)

> **Answer key for Student Book part F**
> **1.** *passage A* **2.** *Idea: Where to find water in the desert* **3.** *Idea: Because it doesn't rain often in the desert* **4.** *passages A and B* **5.** *Idea: They use them as sources of water.* **6.** *passage B* **7.** *Idea: Some desert plants have long roots that go down to where the sand is moist.* **8.** *passage A* **9.** *Idea: In the trunk or pulp, the leaves or the stems* **10.** *passages A and B*

3. (Direct the students to write the number of errors in the **error** box at the top of the Workbook page.)
4. (Award points and direct students to record their points in Box **W.**)

0 errors	15 points
1–2 errors	12 points
3–5 errors	8 points
6–9 errors	5 points

5. Show me your work when you've finished correcting it. (When the students show you their corrected work, record their points on your Record Summary Chart.)

Lesson 126 — Student Book page 312

E Write **Part E** in the left margin of your paper. The passage below presents one of these morals:

- You should never learn anything new.
- Sailing a boat can be dangerous.
- A little knowledge can be a dangerous thing.

Read the passage and figure out which moral fits.

> Carmen had been sailing a couple times with her brother. She loved the water, and she loved sailboats. Her brother, Francisco, let her hold the tiller when they sailed. Carmen loved to steer the boat so that it leaned over, low in the water. A couple times she even helped Francisco put up the sail. Carmen felt that she was beginning to know quite a bit about sailing. One sunny Saturday, when Francisco was in town, Carmen decided she wanted to go sailing. The sailboat was tied up to the dock by their summer cabin. She untied the ropes and got into the boat, put up the sail, and drifted away from the dock. Just then a very strong wind came up. When Carmen tried to steer into it, the boat tipped all the way over on its side, and she fell into the water. She grabbed the side of the boat and held on for what seemed like hours. Finally a boat came by, and a woman helped Carmen out of the water.

Write the moral that fits the passage.

A little knowledge can be a dangerous thing.

Lesson 126 — Workbook page 370

ERRORS W

A The argument below has an ought statement for a conclusion. Complete the deduction after the argument by writing the missing rule and the conclusion. The evidence that the author uses in the argument is already written for you.

> "Let's go to the store and get some Smackin' Goo. I heard it's the best bubble gum ever made."
> "Who told you that?"
> "That guy who dresses up like a clown on television."
> "That doesn't mean that it's really any good."
> "Why?"
> "The guy on television is just trying to sell you something. You shouldn't believe what he says."

Rule: *Idea: You shouldn't believe people who are trying to sell you something.*

Evidence: The guy on television is trying to sell you something.

Conclusion: *Idea: You shouldn't believe the guy on television.*

B Read each item and write the answers.

1. A doctor is a good source of information for answering some questions. Write three of those questions.
   Ideas: How often should I get a physical exam? What are the symptoms of a heart attack? What's the best way to treat the common cold?, etc.

2. A doctor is not necessarily a good source of information for answering some questions. Write three of those questions.
   Ideas: How do you put out a grease fire? What kind of accident insurance should I have? How much fabric do I need to make a coat?, etc.

Student Book page 313 — Lesson 126

F Write **Part F** in the left margin of your paper. Then number it from 1 to 10. The two passages below tell something about desert plants. Read both passages and find out which passage gives more facts about desert plants.

> **Passage A.** In the desert, rain comes only occasionally. The rain may either soak deep into the sand, or it may run off where there is a hard layer just below the surface of the desert. There may be no more rain for a whole year. Desert plants must have methods of storing water or reaching it. Some desert plants have deep roots that go down to where the sand is moist. Other desert plants, such as palm trees, have almost no roots at all. They store water in their trunks. Still other desert plants, such as cactus plants, are one big water-storage tank. If you slice open a cactus plant and squeeze the pulp that is inside, you will get large amounts of water.

> **Passage B.** Desert plants store moisture for use in the driest part of the year. Some plants store water in their leaves; others store water in their stems. Because the desert plants store water, they are ideal sources of water for animals that live in the desert. And people who are lost in the desert can often obtain enough water simply by cutting open particular desert plants.

Answer each question below. Some of the questions ask where you found an answer. Write **passage A**, **passage B**, or **passages A and B** for these questions.

1. Which passage tells more about desert plants?
2. The other passage gives more facts about something other than desert plants. What does it tell more about?
3. Why do many desert plants store water?
4. Where did you find the answer to question 3?
5. How do desert animals sometimes use desert plants?
6. Where did you find the answer to question 5?
7. How do some desert plants reach water?
8. Where did you find the answer to question 7?
9. In which parts of some desert plants can you find water?
10. Where did you find the answer to question 9?

Workbook page 371 — Lesson 126

3. A football star is a good source of information for answering some questions. Write three of those questions.
   Ideas: What exercises develop leg muscles? How important is teamwork in football? Is speed or strength more important in football?, etc.

4. A football star is not necessarily a good source of information for answering some questions. Write three of those questions.
   Ideas: What are the warning signs of cancer? When will the planet Venus be visible? How do you blacktop a driveway?, etc.

5. A plumber is a good source of information for answering some questions. Write three of those questions.
   Ideas: How do you fix a leaking faucet? Is it okay to pour grease down a kitchen drain? What causes a toilet to overflow?, etc.

6. A plumber is not necessarily a good source of information for answering some questions. Write three of those questions.
   Ideas: How long does it take bread dough to rise? How often should I mow the lawn? What color will help me feel relaxed?, etc.

END OF LESSON 126

Student Book page 314

Lesson 127

A

A biased argument is an argument that tells the truth, but it tells only part of the truth.

Study the graph below. Then read the biased argument that is based on the graph.

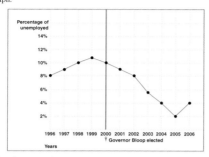

When Governor Bloop was elected in 2000, he promised the people of this state that he would reduce the unemployment rate. I don't see how we could possibly elect him to another term in office. Why, in the last year alone, the unemployment rate has **doubled** from 2 percent in 2005 to the current figure of 4 percent. We can't have this sloppy kind of economic management in our state. "Say no to Bloop, vote for Bleep."

This argument is biased because it doesn't take into account some important information. What information is that? ⊙

Let's say that you wanted to attack the argument above. What would you say? ⊙

B

Some arguments are faulty because they do not use good sources of information. They use people who are experts in one field to talk about another field.

Read this argument: Professor Deedee has been with the university for twelve years. He is the chairperson of the English department. He has received four awards for his work. All of us who have worked with him have marveled over how intelligent he is. So, when he tells us that our new storm sewers should be routed near the freeway, we should follow his suggestion.

Student Book page 315

Lesson 127

The argument uses Professor Deedee as a source for what kind of information? ⊙

Is Professor Deedee a good source for this information? ⊙

For what kind of information would Professor Deedee be a good source? ⊙

C

Write **Part C** in the left margin of your paper. You have two minutes to copy the paragraph below.

> Desert plants store moisture for use in the driest part of the year. Some plants store water in their leaves; others store water in their stems. This water storage makes desert plants ideal sources of water for animals that live in the desert.

★ D

Write **Part D** in the left margin of your paper. The passage below presents one of these morals:

> • **When you stay very close to something, you may not see it plainly.**
> • **When you work like mad, you will certainly fail.**
> • **When you shoot 50 percent on a twenty-foot jump shot, you're doing great.**

Read the passage and figure out which moral fits.

> John worked like crazy at basketball. He was weak on moving left and on his fadeaway jump shot. So hour after hour, he dribbled left, jumped, faded, and released the ball; however, he didn't hit many of those shots. But he kept trying and trying. After about two months of daily practice, he still wasn't hitting the shot every time. In fact, he was still missing it about half the time. John was discouraged.
>
> One day, John got into a game of one-on-one with Greg, the best player in the school. To John's surprise, he actually beat Greg in one of the three games they played and almost beat him in the other two. After the game, Greg said, "Man, you are something else. Where did you get that shot moving to the left?"
>
> "But I miss that shot nearly half the time I take it," John said, shaking his head.
>
> "Man," Greg said, "if you make that shot half the time, you're shooting 50 percent. That's a great percentage for a twenty-foot jump shot."

Write the moral that fits the passage.

When you stay very close to something, you might not see it clearly.

Note: The circled letters indicate when you ask a question or when you direct the group to respond.

═══════════ **EXERCISE 1** ═══════════

ANALYZING ARGUMENTS

1. (Direct the students to find Lesson 127, part A, in the **Student Book.**)
2. (Call on individual students to read part A.)
   - **Ⓐ** (Call on a student. Idea: *Unemployment has actually gone down since Governor Bloop was elected.*)
   - **Ⓑ** (Call on a student. Idea: *It is only in the last year that the unemployment rate has risen, and it is still lower than when Governor Bloop was elected. The unemployment rate has actually gone down since he was elected.*)

═══════════ **EXERCISE 2** ═══════════

ANALYZING ARGUMENTS

1. (Direct the students to find part B.)
2. (Call on individual students to read part B.)
   - **Ⓒ** (Call on a student. Idea: *Where storm sewers should be routed.*)
   - **Ⓓ** What's the answer? *No.*
   - **Ⓔ** (Call on individuals. Ideas: *Who wrote Moby Dick; what Mark Twain wrote.*)

═══════════ **EXERCISE 3** ═══════════

INDEPENDENT WORK

1. **[Optional]** (Direct the students to read the instructions for part C to themselves. Then give them exactly two minutes to copy the paragraph. Count as errors any miscopied words and punctuation. Deduct these errors from the number of copied words, and mark the total on the Writing Rate Graph.)
2. Finish the Student Book and do the Workbook for Lesson 127. ✓

Workcheck

1. Get ready to check your answers starting with Student Book part D. Use a pen to make an **X** next to any item you miss.
2. (Call on individual students to read each item and its answer. Repeat for Workbook items.)
3. (Direct the students to count the number of errors and write the number in the **error** box at the top of the Workbook page.)
4. (Award points and direct students to record their points in Box **W.**)

0 errors	**15 points**
1–2 errors	**12 points**
3–5 errors	**8 points**
6–9 errors	**5 points**

5. (Award any bonus points. Direct the students to total their points and enter the total on the Point Summary Chart.)
6. Show me your work when you've finished correcting it. (When the students show you their corrected work, record their points on your Record Summary Chart.)

Lesson 127 ERRORS W **Workbook page 372**

★ **A** The argument below has an ought statement for a conclusion. Complete the deduction after the argument by writing the missing rule and the conclusion. The evidence that the author uses in the argument is already written for you.

> Last weekend, I was out rafting on the river and I was shocked to see how much pollution was in the water. I passed one huge factory on the river, the Acme Company's textile mill. I could actually see the goop they were dumping in the river. The textile mill should be closed.

Rule: Idea: Companies that pollute the river should be closed.

Evidence: The textile mill is polluting the river.

Conclusion: Idea: The textile mill should be closed.

B Underline the redundant part in each sentence below. Then explain why the underlined part is redundant.

1. That act was followed <u>by a subsequent one.</u>
   Idea: If you know that something followed the act, you know that it was subsequent to the act.

2. He was a <u>stingy</u> miser.
   Idea: If you know that he was a miser, then you already know that he was stingy.

3. Her dog, <u>a canine</u> named Judy, was always barking.
   Idea: If you know that she had a dog, then you already know it was a canine.

Workbook page 373 **Lesson 127**

C Each argument that follows is faulty. Read each argument and answer the questions.

• Look at his entire record. He has entered that little number 35 racer in over 100 races, and he has the longest record of wins in the NASCAR. He's the biggest money winner in the history of stock-car racing. I haven't heard the results of last Saturday's race, but I don't have to hear. I know what must have happened—he won again.

1. What does the writer want us to conclude?
   Idea: The stock-car racer always wins.

2. How could you show that the argument is faulty?
   Idea: By finding evidence of a race he entered, but did not win.

• The increase in average wealth per person is causing the national debt to rise. The average wealth per person in the United States is now more than four times what it was in 1950. Since 1950, the national debt has also greatly increased. There is no doubt that the richer our people get, the more they put our country in debt. If we want to get rid of our national debt, we should all become poor.

3. What does the writer want us to conclude?
   Idea: The average wealth of a person influences the national debt.

4. How could you show that the argument is faulty?
   Idea: Show a time in our history when average wealth increased and the national debt decreased.

• The locks on the doors of Mazzo cars are the finest in the industry. They've outperformed the locks of all other cars. They're safer and more reliable. With the finest-engineered door locks in the world, you know that Mazzo cars must be the safest, best-engineered cars in the world.

5. What does the writer want us to conclude?
   Idea: Mazzo cars are the safest, best-engineered cars in the world.

6. How could you show that the argument is faulty?
   Idea: Find a make of car that has a better safety record than the Mazzo and whose engineering is as good as the Mazzo's.

Workbook page 374

D Read the passage and answer the questions. Circle **W** if the question is answered by words in the passage. Circle **D** if the question is answered by a deduction. If you circle **W** for an item, underline the words in the passage that give the answer.

Some trees do not need much sunlight to survive. These trees are called **tolerant**. A tolerant tree is tolerant of shade, which means it can get along in shade. Trees that are not tolerant can't survive in shade. They are called intolerant. The top of an intolerant tree must be in full sunlight. Some trees are fairly tolerant when they are young, but become very intolerant as they mature. Other trees are intolerant from the time they are tiny seedlings.

You can tell whether a tree is tolerant by its shape and by the pattern of leaves on the tree. Stand under a tree and look up. Can you see the sunlight or the sky? If not, the tree is probably intolerant. Intolerant trees usually try to shade everything beneath them. To do this, they put out lots of leaves on top—so many leaves that no sunlight can reach the ground beneath the tree. If there is no sunlight beneath the tree, no competing vegetation can spring up next to the tree to take water or to block the sunlight.

Find a tree whose lower branches are always shaded by its upper ones. If the lower branches are bare and the upper leaves are dense, the tree is probably an intolerant one. On an intolerant tree, leaves that are always shaded die.

Intolerant trees are usually fast growers. They have to grow fast to survive. If seeds from different trees fall on the bank of a river, the fastest-growing trees are going to get the sunlight. The slower-growing trees will be shaded by the faster-growing trees. If the intolerant trees were slow growers, they would be shaded and then die. Just as intolerant trees are usually fast growers, tolerant trees are usually slow growers. They can survive in the shade; therefore, they don't have to grow fast and be the first to reach for the sunlight.

1. A Douglas fir is a very intolerant tree. Is it probably a fast-growing tree or a slow-growing one?
   <u>Idea: fast-growing</u> W Ⓓ
2. In which of these places would you probably find a healthy, young Douglas fir growing—an open field, a forest, or a deep canyon?
   <u>Idea: an open field</u>
3. A Douglas fir is shaped like an upside-down ice-cream cone. Why would this shape help the bottom branches of the tree?
   <u>Idea: It would allow them to get light.</u>
4. What would happen to the bottom branches of a Douglas fir if the tree were shaped like a globe?
   <u>Idea: They would be bare.</u> W Ⓓ

Workbook page 376

E Use the rule in the box and the evidence to answer the questions.

> Every insect has six legs.

Tom has two insects in his pocket.

1. What's the conclusion?
   <u>Idea: Tom has 12 insect legs in his pocket.</u>
2. How do you know?
   <u>Idea: because every insect has 6 legs and he has 2 insects</u>

Rita's pet animal does not have six legs.

3. What's the conclusion?
   <u>Idea: Rita's pet is not an insect.</u>
4. How do you know?
   <u>Idea: because every insect has 6 legs</u>

There are forty-two insect legs in hill 1 and sixty insect legs in hill 2.

5. What's the conclusion?
   <u>Idea: There are 7 insects in hill 1 and 10 insects in hill 2.</u>
6. How do you know?
   <u>Idea: Because every insect has 6 legs</u>

F You will be tested on some facts presented in this lesson. These facts are:

> 1. Tolerant trees do not need much sunlight to survive.
> 2. Intolerant trees cannot survive in the shade.

Study these facts. Repeat them to yourself. Writing these facts may help you to remember them.

END OF LESSON 127

Workbook page 375

5. What are trees called that can't survive in shade?
   <u>intolerant trees</u> Ⓦ D
6. What are trees called that can survive in shade?
   <u>tolerant trees</u>
7. You can find young white oak trees growing beneath Douglas fir trees. What do you know about those white oaks?
   <u>Idea: They must be tolerant trees because they can grow in the shade.</u>
8. The picture shows eight trees that are the same age.

- Put an **F** on each fast-growing tree.
- Put an **S** on each slow-growing tree.
- Put a **T** on each tolerant tree.
- Put an **I** on each intolerant tree.

> **Note:** The circled letters indicate when you ask a question or when you direct the group to respond.

═══════ **EXERCISE 1** ═══════

ANALYZING ARGUMENTS

1. (Direct the students to find Lesson 128, part A, in the **Student Book.**)
2. (Call on individual students to read part A.)
   - Ⓐ (Call on a student. Idea: *What kind of fertilizer to buy.*)
   - Ⓑ What's the answer? *Yes.*

═══════ **EXERCISE 2** ═══════

ANALYZING ARGUMENTS

1. (Direct the students to find part B.)
2. (Call on individual students to read part B.)
   - Ⓒ What's the answer? *No.*
   - Ⓓ (Call on a student. Idea: *Four out of five doctors that we surveyed recommended Brand A aspirin.*)
   - Ⓔ What's the answer? *No.*
   - Ⓕ (Call on a student. Idea: *Professional exterminators use Knock-Em-Dead Bug Killer.*)

═══════ **EXERCISE 3** ═══════

INDEPENDENT WORK

1. **[Optional]** (Direct the students to read the instructions for part C to themselves. Then give them exactly two minutes to copy the paragraph. Count as errors any miscopied words and punctuation. Deduct these errors from the number of copied words, and mark the total on the Writing Rate Graph.)
2. Finish the Student Book and do the Workbook for Lesson 128. ✔

Lesson 128

Student Book page 316

Ⓐ Some arguments are faulty because they do not use good sources of information. They use people who are experts in one field to talk about another field.

> Read this argument: Mr. Leo Frank is a graduate of the University of Indiana School of Agriculture. He has done a number of field studies for leading seed and fertilizer manufacturers. Currently, he owns and manages over 6000 acres of farmland in central Illinois and Indiana. He has served on the Agricultural Advisory Board for three presidents. Mr. Frank is considered a leader in scientific farming, and here's what he says about Fliggo Steer Fertilizer: "It is the best fertilizer on the market. It goes farther and produces more, particularly on row crops. I don't think there's another fertilizer that can match it for performance or for cost."

The argument uses Mr. Frank as a source for what kind of information? Ⓐ
Is Mr. Frank a good source for this information? Ⓑ

Ⓑ The ads below tell the truth. But they don't actually say what they may seem to say.

Read this ad:

> Four out of five doctors that we surveyed recommended the pain reliever found in Brand A aspirin.

Does the ad actually say that the doctors recommended Brand A aspirin? Ⓒ
How would the ad be written if it said that the doctors recommended Brand A aspirin? Ⓓ

Read this ad:

> Use Knock-Em-Dead Bug Killer. It has the chemical that professional exterminators use. It kills bugs instantly, no matter where they are hiding.

Does the ad actually say that Knock-Em-Dead Bug Killer is used by professional exterminators? Ⓔ
How would the ad be written if it said that professional exterminators used Knock-Em-Dead Bug Killer? Ⓕ

Student Book page 317

Lesson 128

Ⓒ Write **Part C** in the left margin of your paper. You have two minutes to copy the paragraph below.

> **Some arguments are faulty because they do not use good sources of information. They use people who are experts in one field to talk about another field. Many television commercials use this trick. Don't be fooled by these kinds of commercials.**

Ⓓ Write **Part D** in the left margin of your paper. Then number it from 1 to 3. The description below tells about one of the words shown below. Read the description and answer the questions.

> One root of this word is <u>vor</u>, which means **eat**. An animal that eats plants is called an her<u>bivore</u>. Someone who eats a lot is <u>voracious</u>.
> The other root of this word is <u>omni</u>, which means **all**. A collection of all kinds of writing is an <u>omnibus</u>. Something that is all-powerful is <u>omnipotent</u>. This word, containing both roots, describes animals that will eat all things—meat and plants.

    omniscient   carnivore   omnivorous   omnifarious

1. Which word does the description tell about?
2. How do you know that the description does not tell about the word **omnifarious**?
3. How do you know that the description does not tell about the word **omniscient**?

1. omnivorous
2. Idea: because one root of the word is vor
3. Idea: because one root of the word is vor

Lesson 128

Student Book page 318

Lesson 128

E Write **Part E** in the left margin of your paper. The passage below presents one of these morals:

- **Rich people get richer.**
- **Don't question good luck when it comes your way.**
- **A person with $4.56 in his pocket should not turn down a gift of $1,000.**

Read the passage and figure out which moral fits.

> George Tiller was a perfect failure, and he was very poor. He had $4.56 in his pocket, and that was all the money he had in the world. He had almost no food in his shabby apartment, and he hadn't worked for nearly three weeks.
>
> He stuffed some bubble gum into his mouth and walked from the apartment, not quite knowing where he would go. He had no way of knowing that he was on his way to a very strange encounter. On the other side of town was a rich man who had decided on his sixtieth birthday to give some money to a needy person. That rich man, Arnold Glib, was driving toward George Tiller's neighborhood when George walked down the front steps of his apartment building.
>
> About ten minutes later, Arnold Glib parked his car near Tiller's apartment building and began looking for a needy person.
>
> George was just walking, not going anywhere in particular. He noticed a fancy car parked at the curb. The car was black and so expensive that George couldn't even afford the key to it. Then George noticed a man in a black coat. The man was standing by the car, and he was speaking to George. "Say there, I would like to talk to you for a moment."
>
> George noticed that the man was holding a pile of money. The man said, "Please take this money," and handed George $1,000.
>
> "Why should I?" George asked, staring at the pile of bills. "What kind of sucker do you think I am?"
>
> "You don't understand. I want to help you." Arnold smiled and shrugged. "Oh, forget it." Arnold put the money back into his pockets and walked away.
>
> George shook his head and reached into his own pocket, where he kept all his money: $4.56. As he stood there, he wondered if the money that Arnold had offered him was real.

Write the moral that fits the passage.

Don't question good luck when it comes your way.

Workbook page 377

Lesson 128

A Read the rule and each piece of evidence. Write a conclusion after each piece of evidence.

Rule. **Omnivorous animals eat plants and other animals.**

Evidence	Conclusion
1. Armadillos are omnivorous animals.	*Armadillos eat plants and other animals.*
2. Pandas do not eat plants and other animals.	*Pandas are not omnivorous.*
3. Pangolins do not eat plants and other animals.	*Pangolins are not omnivorous.*
4. Rats are omnivorous animals.	*Rats eat plants and other animals.*

B Here's what we know:

The regulation requires firefighters to wear uniforms.

For each item, combine one of the sentences with the sentence in the box.

- **Every firefighter owns at least two uniforms.**
- **They don't have to wear their jackets in the summer.**

1. Make a combined sentence with **but.**

The regulation requires firefighters to wear uniforms, but they don't have to wear their jackets in the summer.

2. Make a combined sentence with **and.**

The regulation requires firefighters to wear uniforms, and every firefighter owns at least two uniforms.

Workcheck

1. Get ready to check your answers starting with Student Book part D. Use a pen to make an **X** next to any item you miss.
2. (Call on individual students to read each item and its answer. Repeat for Workbook items.)
3. (Direct the students to count the number of errors and write the number in the **error** box at the top of the Workbook page.)
4. (Award points and direct students to record their points in Box **W.**)

0 errors	**15 points**
1–2 errors	**12 points**
3–5 errors	**8 points**
6–9 errors	**5 points**

5. (Award any bonus points. Direct the students to total their points and enter the total on the Point Summary Chart.)
6. Show me your work when you've finished correcting it. (When the students show you their corrected work, record their points on your Record Summary Chart.)

Lesson
128

Workbook page 378

C The arguments below have an ought statement for a conclusion. Complete the deduction after each argument by writing the rule, the evidence, and the conclusion.

1. Over 85 percent of the citizens of Ultuga believe that it is all right to eat another human being if the moon is full. Since most of the people believe that you may eat a person if the moon is full, we should let Ultugans eat people when the moon is full.

Complete the deduction:

Rule: Idea: We should let people do things they believe are all right.

Evidence: Idea: Most Ultugans believe that it is all right to eat another human if the moon is full.

Conclusion: Idea: We should let Ultugans eat people when the moon is full.

2. One man said, "I think that fool we call a president is doing everything completely wrong!"

"Listen, buddy," the other man said, "around here, we don't like to hear people talk like that. We ought to lock you up for what you said."

Rule: Idea: We ought to lock up people who say things we don't like.

Evidence: Idea: The first man said something we don't like.

Conclusion: Idea: We ought to lock up the first man.

D Each passage that follows contains a word you may not know. Read each passage and answer the questions.

- When the president was proven to be a cheater and a thief, the country was shocked at such ignominious behavior. Members of the president's staff were later suspected of behaving just as ignominiously and were brought to trial. Many of them went to jail.

1. Circle the answer.
   Ignominious probably means:
   (disgraceful)   bouncy
   praiseworthy   trusting

2. Write any sentence from the passage that contradicts the idea that **ignominious** means **trusting**.
   Idea: When the president was proven to be a cheater and a thief, the country was shocked at such ignominious behavior.

- The pain was so excruciating that he fainted. When he came to in the hospital, the pain was still excruciating, so he was given a shot to knock him out. The next morning, he could stand the pain. Later that day, the pain became excruciating again, and again he was given a drug to ease the pain.

3. Circle the answer.
   Excruciating probably means:
   (unbearable)   a tingling feeling
   praise   pleasant

4. Write any sentence from the passage that contradicts the idea that **excruciating** means **pleasant**.
   Idea: The pain was so excruciating that he fainted.

- The soldiers were camped in ice and snow for weeks at a time without food or warm clothes. They exhibited a great deal of fortitude. Although they were hungry and cold, no one complained. Some of them even joked about the weather. The commander was very proud of his people. He admired them for their great fortitude during these terrible times.

5. Circle the answer.
   Fortitude probably means:
   sorrow   fat
   (courage)   hunger

6. Write any sentence from the passage that contradicts the idea that **fortitude** means **sorrow.**
   Idea: He admired them for their fortitude during these terrible times.

END OF LESSON 128

Student Book page 319

A The ads below tell the truth. But they don't actually say what they may seem to say.

Read this ad:

Together, the people at Rammel's Real Estate Company have over 100 years of experience. Experience is the key word in real estate. See one of the people at Rammel's to help you buy or sell any kind of property.

Does the ad actually say that each person at Rammel's has a lot of experience? Ⓐ

How would the ad be written if it said that each person at Rammel's has a lot of experience? Ⓑ

Read this ad:

We have tested Blinko Car Batteries in cars entered in a demolition derby. After over forty hours of the most horrible abuse in head-on collisions, not one battery failed. If our batteries can stand up under this kind of abuse, you can imagine what they would do in your car.

Does the ad actually say that Blinko Batteries are better for your car? Ⓒ

How would the ad be written if it said that Blinko Batteries are better for your car? Ⓓ

B The passage below presents a moral. Read the passage. Then make up a moral that fits the passage.

Coro was a monkey who lived in New Guinea. Like all monkeys, Coro loved rice. One day Coro was in the jungle when he noticed a woman walk up to the tree in which he was perched. The woman put a heavy wooden box on the ground. Then she tossed several handfuls of rice on the ground. The rice formed a trail to the box.

As soon as the woman left, Coro scampered down the tree and began to eat the rice. He ate and ate, following the trail to the box. As he popped grains of rice into his mouth, he noticed that there was a hole in the box, just large enough for his hand to squeeze through. And inside the box was a huge pile of rice.

Coro reached in and grabbed the biggest fistful of rice his hand could hold. And then he tried to pull his hand out of the box. But the opening in the box was too small for his fist to go through. If Coro had tried to take a tiny handful, he probably could have forced his hand through the opening, but with his fist bulging with rice, there was no chance.

As he tugged and jerked, never letting go of the rice, he noticed that the woman was running toward him. But did Coro let go of the rice and escape? No. Coro just pulled harder, and before he realized what had happened, the woman had a rope around his neck. Coro had been tricked.

Student Book page 320

Make up a moral for the passage. Start the moral with the words, "If you _____." Ⓔ

C Write **Part C** in the left margin of your paper. You have two minutes to copy the paragraph below.

Crabs live in the oceans. A crab's shell is hard, and its armor is solid except for one small tender spot on the underside of the crab's shell. If a predator could reach that soft spot, the predator could easily kill the crab.

★D Write **Part D** in the left margin of your paper. The passage below presents a moral. Read the passage. Then make up a moral that fits the passage.

There once was a man who decided to build a house. Winter was approaching, so the man said to himself, "I'll do this house the fast way," and he did. He slapped up boards here and there. He didn't take the time to measure and fit. He pounded and slapped things together. Soon—very soon—his house was completed. "Not bad," he said to himself, until somebody came over to his house and slammed the front door, and down came the walls. In the end, the man had to rebuild his house the right way. It took him much longer this time, however, because he had to work in the cold, and he had to clear away the wreck of the old house.

Write a moral for the passage. Start the moral with the words, "If you _____."

Idea: If you do it the right way the first time, you will save time and money in the long run.

Note: The circled letters indicate when you ask a question or when you direct the group to respond.

EXERCISE 1
ANALYZING ARGUMENTS

1. (Direct the students to find Lesson 129, part A, in the **Student Book**.)
2. (Call on individual students to read part A.)
   - Ⓐ What's the answer? *No.*
   - Ⓑ (Call on a student. Idea: *Every person at Rammel's has had many years of experience.*)
   - Ⓒ What's the answer? *No.*
   - Ⓓ Call on a student. Idea: *Blinko batteries are better for your car.*)

EXERCISE 2
MAIN IDEA

1. (Direct the students to find part B.)
2. (Call on individual students to read part B.)
   - Ⓔ (Call on individual students. Idea: *If you are greedy, you may end up in trouble.*)

EXERCISE 3
INDEPENDENT WORK

1. [Optional] (Direct the students to read the instructions for part C to themselves. Then give them exactly two minutes to copy the paragraph. Count as errors any miscopied words and punctuation. Deduct these errors from the number of copied words, and mark the total on the Writing Rate Graph.)
2. In Lesson 130, you'll have a test on story facts. The facts that will be tested appear in part G of your Workbook. Study them and make sure that you know them. Now, finish the Student Book and do the Workbook for Lesson 129. ✓

Lesson 129

Workcheck

1. Get ready to check your answers starting with Student Book part D. Use a pen to make an **X** next to any item you miss.
2. (Call on individual students to read each item and its answer. Repeat for Workbook items.)
3. (Direct the students to count the number of errors and write the number in the **error** box at the top of the Workbook page.)
4. (Award points and direct students to record their points in Box **W**.)

0 errors	15 points
1–2 errors	12 points
3–5 errors	8 points
6–9 errors	5 points

5. (Award any bonus points. Direct the students to total their points and enter the total on the Point Summary Chart.)
6. Show me your work when you've finished correcting it. (When the students show you their corrected work, record their points on your Record Summary Chart.)

Lesson 129 · ERRORS W · Workbook page 380

★ **A** Each argument that follows breaks one of these rules:

Rule 1. Just because two things happen around the same time doesn't mean one thing causes the other thing.
Rule 2. Just because you know about a part doesn't mean you know about the whole thing.
Rule 3. Just because you know about a part doesn't mean you know about another part.
Rule 4. Just because you know about a whole thing doesn't mean you know about every part.
Rule 5. Just because words are the same doesn't mean they have the same meaning.
Rule 6. Just because the writer presents some choices doesn't mean there aren't other choices.
Rule 7. Just because events have happened in the past doesn't mean they'll always happen.

After each argument below, write the number of the rule the argument breaks.

1. When I asked if I should turn left at the stoplight, the man replied, "Right," so I went right. I went three miles out of my way just because that man gave me the wrong directions. _5_
2. We took dirt samples from the east side of the slope and from the south side. Both samples contained far too much ash. I think that it's safe to say that the north side of the slope has soil with too much ash. _3_
3. Sarah had a weakness for gambling. She bet on everything. She tried every game of chance. For a while, she made money gambling, but then her luck turned bad and she lost everything she and her husband owned: the house, the car, and the furniture.
   Although her husband, Bill, loved her, he finally decided to leave her. He felt that she had too much desire for taking a chance—a chance on which card would turn up or on which horse would win.
   As he left, he turned to Sarah and said, "You've always been a gambler and you'll never change." _7_
4. The principal of a large, city high school said this to a committee: "We have made a decision to permit students to attend only those classes that they wish to attend. We will not give students grades, and we will not require them to come to class every day. Of course, we will try to encourage them to come to class; however, attendance is not required. Our decision to change our school policies in this way is based on the fact that there has been a steady drop in enrollment. Students are not attending classes. They are doing things that are more interesting. So, it was a choice of making the classes easier for the students, or serving fewer and fewer students." _6_

B In each item that follows, the underlined sentence has two possible meanings. The sentence that follows the underlined sentence makes it clear which meaning is intended.

Workbook page 381 · Lesson 129

- She put rings in her doll's ears, but they fell off. So, she pasted the ears back on with glue.

1. What are the two possible meanings of the underlined sentence?
   Idea: She put rings in her doll's ears but the rings fell off; she put rings in her doll's ears, but the doll's ears fell off.
2. What is the intended meaning?
   Idea: She put rings in her doll's ears, but the doll's ears fell off.

- The car was on the bridge when it blew up. Fortunately, the only damage was to one end of the bridge.

3. What are the two possible meanings of the underlined sentence?
   Idea: The car was on the bridge when the car blew up; the car was on the bridge when the bridge blew up.
4. What is the intended meaning?
   Idea: The car was on the bridge when the bridge blew up.

- She put a spoon in the soup and it turned green. Nobody wanted green soup, so she threw it out.

5. What are the two possible meanings of the underlined sentence?
   Idea: She put a spoon in the soup and the spoon turned green; she put a spoon in the soup and the soup turned green.
6. What is the intended meaning?
   Idea: She put a spoon in the soup and the soup turned green.

C Underline the redundant part in each sentence below. Then explain why the underlined part is redundant.

1. Every time he purchased something, <u>he spent money.</u>
   Idea: If he purchased something, he spent money.
2. She was an <u>outgoing</u> extrovert.
   Idea: If you know that she was an extrovert, you know that she was outgoing.

Workbook page 382

3. All at once, there was a <u>sudden</u> burst of fire.

Idea: If you know that it happened all at once, you know that it was sudden.

D Read the argument and answer the questions on the next page.

My name is Giovanni Berlucci. You may not recognize me, because I am an Italian film actor. I've made thirty movies since I was twelve years old, some of which were released here in Canada. This is my first trip to your country, and while I'm here I'd like to tell you about a fine new car, the Distaray. It is tastefully designed to look expensive even though it really isn't. It has a smooth ride, even over bumpy roads. For a mid-sized car, the mileage is great. Just between you and me, let me tell you: The Distaray is the best designed and most expertly built car sold in Canada.

1. The argument uses Giovanni Berlucci as a source for what kind of information?

Idea: information about the Distaray

2. Is Giovanni Berlucci a good source for this information?

no

3. For what kind of information would Giovanni Berlucci be a good source?

Idea: information about acting in Italian films

E The argument below has an ought statement for a conclusion. Complete the deduction after the argument by writing the rule, the evidence, and the conclusion.

Lots of people feel that they just don't have enough time to do everything that they want to. Their problem is that they don't know how to do things efficiently. For example, some people walk or ride their bikes to work. Driving cars everywhere saves time. People should drive their cars everywhere.

Rule: *Idea: People should do whatever saves time.*

Evidence: *Idea: Driving cars everywhere saves time.*

Conclusion: *Idea: People should drive their cars everywhere.*

Workbook page 384

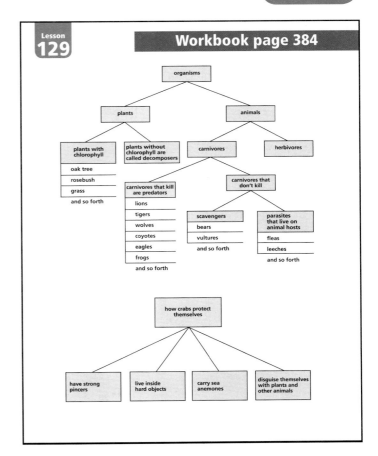

END OF LESSON 129

Workbook page 383

F Read the passage. Find a statement that contradicts an earlier statement.

- Underline the statement you assume to be true.
- Circle the contradiction.
- Make up an if-then statement that explains the contradiction.

We had suffered a drought of more than two years. <u>Our land was dry and dusty, and we couldn't grow anything on it.</u> For the first year, we lived by selling our cattle and chickens. We didn't have water for them either. One evening at dinnertime, my husband said, "I think we should sell the farm and move to the city."
"Let's enjoy our dinner and talk about it later," I said, trying to cheer him up. "Everything in the salad is fresh from the garden."
Well, as it turned out, we didn't have to talk about it. By the time we were eating dessert, it had started to rain.

Idea: If your land is dry and dusty and you can't grow anything on it, then you can't eat a salad made from things grown in your garden.

G Tomorrow you will be tested on facts you have learned. The test will include facts presented in Lessons 123–127 and some of the facts from earlier lessons. These facts are:

1. Cleaner fish eat parasites from larger ocean animals.
2. Sharks allow cleaner fish to eat things inside their mouths.
3. Tolerant trees do not need much sunlight to survive.
4. Intolerant trees cannot survive in the shade.
5. Study the two charts on page 384. Make sure that you can fill in both charts.

━━━━━━━━━━━━ **EXERCISE 1** ━━━━━━━━━━━━

INDEPENDENT WORK

1. **[Optional]** (Direct the students to read the instructions for part A in the **Student Book** to themselves. Then give them exactly two minutes to copy the paragraph. Count as errors any miscopied words and punctuation. Deduct these errors from the number of copied words, and mark the total on the Writing Rate Graph.)

2. Finish the Student Book and Workbook for Lesson 130. ✓

Workcheck

1. Get ready to check your answers starting with Student Book part B. Use a pen to make an **X** next to any item you miss.

2. (Call on individual students to read each item and its answer. Repeat for Workbook items.)

3. (Direct the students to count the number of errors and write the number in the **error** box at the top of the Workbook page.)

4. (Award points and direct students to record their points in Box **W**.)

0 errors	**15 points**
1–2 errors	**12 points**
3–5 errors	**8 points**
6–9 errors	**5 points**

5. (Award any bonus points. Direct the students to total their points and enter the total on the Point Summary Chart.)

6. Show me your work when you've finished correcting it. (When the students show you their corrected work, record their points on your Record Summary Chart.)

Student Book page 321

A Write **Part A** in the left margin of your paper. You have two minutes to copy the paragraph below.

> Tolerant trees do not need much sunlight to survive. They are usually slow growers. Tolerant trees can survive in the shade; therefore, they don't have to grow fast and be the first to reach for sunlight. A white oak is a tolerant tree.

★**B** Write **Part B** in the left margin of your paper. The passage below presents a moral. Read the passage. Then make up a moral that fits the passage.

> The Swedish exchange student called Rose for a date, and she turned him down. She just didn't think she'd like Gunnar. He wore funny clothes and had a strange way of talking. She didn't think they would have much in common.
> Sunday, when she took her clothes to the laundromat, Gunnar was there. She said hello and sat down to read the paper while her clothes were being washed. Gunnar came over and sat down beside her. "Do you come here often?" he said. He meant it as a joke. "Only to wash clothes," Rose said seriously. He laughed. Rose looked at him, and then she laughed too. Then they talked about baseball, which both of them liked a lot. By the time the clothes were washed, they had discovered that they liked a lot of the same things. This time, when Gunnar asked Rose if she'd like to see a movie, Rose accepted. She realized that Gunnar was fun to be with, and that she wanted to get to know him better.

Write a moral for the passage. Start the moral with the words, "If you _____."

Idea: If you judge people by the way they look or act, you might be making a big mistake.

Student Book page 322

C Write **Part C** in the left margin of your paper. Then number it 1 and 2. One of the graphs is described below. Read the description and then answer the questions.

> The circle graph is divided into seven sections, showing seven different sources of air pollution in the United States. The single largest cause of air pollution is road vehicles. The total pollution caused by power plants and by industry is about the same as pollution caused by road vehicles. Some people think that waste disposal is the major cause of air pollution. The graph shows that waste disposal causes only a small part of the problem.

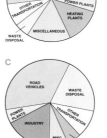

1. Which graph does the description tell about?
2. How do you know that the description does not tell about graph A?

1. graph B
2. Idea: because the total pollution caused by power plants and industry is about the same as pollution caused by road vehicles

Student Book page 323

D Here are some words that will be in some editing activities. Test yourself to make sure that you know what the words mean.

emphatically—When you say something emphatically, you say it as if you really mean it. Here's a sentence that uses the word **emphatically**:
His mother spoke emphatically when she told him to clean his plate.

independent—An independent activity is an activity that you do on your own. Here's a sentence that uses the word **independent**:
The teacher assigned an independent project to each student.

proximity—The proximity of an object is how close the object is to something. Here's a sentence that uses the word **proximity**:
He was in such proximity to the fire that his boots started smoking.

Workbook page 386

C The argument below has an ought statement for a conclusion. Complete the deduction after the argument by writing the rule, the evidence, and the conclusion.

"Turn that stereo down this minute. If I've told you once, I've told you a thousand times: You shouldn't listen to such loud music because you'll damage your ears."

Rule: Idea: You shouldn't do things that will damage your ears.
Evidence: Idea: Listening to loud music will damage your ears.
Conclusion: Idea: You shouldn't listen to loud music.

D Read the argument and answer the questions.

Ms. Smith has been counseling married couples for over twenty years. She is considered to be among the best five marriage counselors in Canada.
"Many people come to me because they are worried about their marriages," says Ms. Smith. "They are bored and blame their boredom on their partner. They think that the only way to overcome this boredom is to get a divorce. I tell them to take up a new hobby together. Any husband and wife who start climbing mountains or parachuting from a plane will not stay bored for long."
Ms. Smith has been married for thirty years and has three children and twelve grandchildren. If you are having problems with your marriage, I would recommend a visit to Ms. Smith.

1. The argument uses Ms. Smith as a source for what kind of information?
   Idea: information on marital problems
2. Is Ms. Smith a good source for this information? yes
3. For what kind of information would Ms. Smith be a good source?
   Idea: information on marital problems

END OF LESSON 130

Workbook page 385

A Read the ads and answer the questions.

- The combined experience of the ten salespeople at Frank's Car Lot is over 100 years. That means that the average salesperson at Frank's Car Lot has over ten years of experience. That's a lot of experience. Come down to Frank's and talk to one of our friendly and knowledgeable salespeople.
1. Does the ad actually say that each salesperson has over ten years of experience? no
2. Write a sentence that would be in the ad if the ad said that each of the salespeople had over ten years of experience.
   Idea: Each salesperson at Frank's Car Lot has over ten years of experience.

- Five people tried Slimmmm diet pills. Every single one of the people who tried Slimmmm lost over five pounds in one week. What about you? Wouldn't you like to lose some of that unattractive fat around your middle?
3. Does the ad actually say that Slimmmm will help **you** lose weight? no
4. Write a sentence that would be in the ad if the ad said that Slimmmm would help you lose weight.
   Idea: Slimmmm can help you lose weight.

B Read the evidence and write the conclusion for each item.

1. Here's the evidence:

High mountain peaks have cold weather.
Alaska has cold weather.

What's the conclusion?
Idea: Maybe Alaska has high mountain peaks.

2. Here's the evidence:

Good insulation retains heat.
Glass does not retain heat.

What's the conclusion?
Idea: Glass is not good insulation.

3. Here's the evidence:

A good soccer team must have a strategy that works. This school has a good soccer team.

What's the conclusion?
Idea: The school's soccer team has a good strategy.

━━━━━━━━━━━ **EXERCISE 1** ━━━━━━━━━━━

MASTERY TEST

1. Everybody, find page 467 in your workbook.

- This is a test. If you make no mistakes on the test, you'll earn 20 points. Write the answers to the test items now using your pencil.

2. (After the students complete the items, gather the Workbooks and grade the tests. As you grade each test, record the number of errors the student made on each part of the test in the appropriate box. Record the total number of errors in the **Error** box at the beginning of the test.)

3. (Return the Workbooks to the students.) Raise your hand if you made ____ or more mistakes in ____.
(Record the number of students who raise their hand for the part.)

> Key: Part A–8   Part B–3   Part C–1   Part D–2
> Part E–1   Part F–1   Part G–1

4. Raise your hand if you made no mistakes on the whole test. Great work. (Award 20 points to the students who made no errors. Award
5 points to students who made 1 or 2 errors.)

- Record your points in the box marked **MT** at the top of Mastery Test 13. Direct all students to enter their points on the Point Summary Chart.)

5. (Record test results on the Group Summary Sheet. Reproducible Summary Sheets are at the back of the Teacher's Guide.)

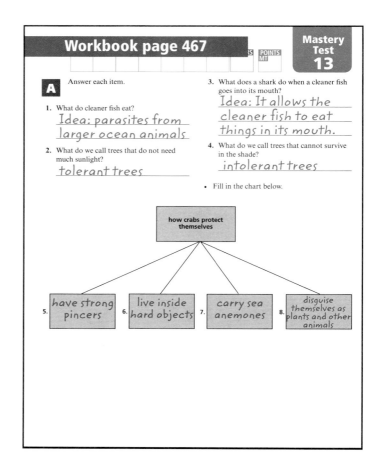

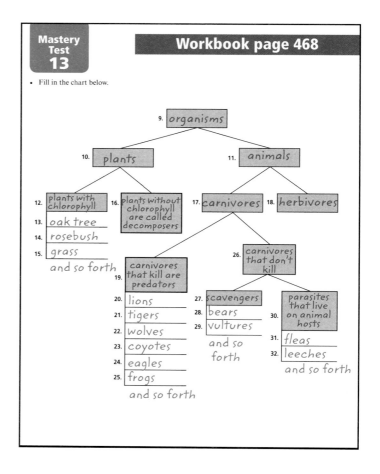

198   *Mastery Test 13*

Workbook page 469

B Write the model sentence that means the same thing as each sentence below.

1. His directions were <u>unclear</u> and <u>repetitive</u>.

   His directions were ambiguous and redundant.

2. The <u>rule</u> <u>limited</u> their parking.

   The regulation restricted their parking.

3. They <u>made up</u> a <u>fitting plan</u>.

   They devised an appropriate strategy.

4. The major <u>argued</u> that he had <u>sound reasons</u> for <u>hiding</u> the facts.

   The major contended that he had valid motives for concealing the data.

5. By <u>pausing</u>, she lost her <u>chance</u>.

   By hesitating, she lost her opportunity.

6. They <u>changed</u> their Swiss <u>money</u> into Canadian <u>money</u>.

   They converted their Swiss currency into Canadian currency.

7. Her <u>answer</u> was <u>filled</u> with <u>irrelevant</u> details.

   Her response was replete with extraneous details.

8. A strange <u>event</u> caused the <u>fear</u> that she <u>showed</u>.

   A strange phenomenon caused the anxiety that she exhibited.

C Write each sentence below with the word **particularly**.

1. His eyes look very blue when he wears a blue shirt.

   His eyes look particularly blue when he wears a blue shirt.

2. She likes to dance, especially on weekends.

   She likes to dance, particularly on weekends.

3. Jana has a really clear idea of what she wants to do.

   Jana has a particularly clear idea of what she wants to do.

Workbook page 471

F Look at the picture. Then rewrite each sentence.

1. The <u>vehicle</u> stopped to let the <u>animal</u> off. Write a more specific statement.

   Idea: The train stopped to let the gorilla off.

2. A <u>woman wearing a shawl</u> was playing a <u>violin</u>. Write a more general statement.

   Idea: A person was playing a musical instrument.

3. The <u>mammal</u> was wearing <u>some clothing</u>. Write a more specific statement.

   Idea: The ape was wearing a necktie and hat.

Workbook page 470

D Read the argument below and answer the questions.

> I don't think we should believe Joe's version of what happened. We know he lied about the missing book. Liars don't change.

1. What does the writer want us to conclude?

   Idea: Joe is a liar.

2. What evidence does the writer use to support this conclusion?

   Idea: Joe lied about the missing book.

3. What rule does the writer's argument break?

   Idea: Just because events have happened in the past doesn't mean they'll always happen.

4. How could you show that the conclusion may not be valid?

   Idea: Find someone else who could give their version to see if it is the same as Joe's.

E The description below tells about one of the organisms listed. Read the description and answer the questions.

> This thing is an organism that you can see without a magnifying glass. The organism is a carnivore, but it does not kill. The organism waits for an animal to die or be killed by a predator.

rose bush	flea	wolf
bear	cow	leech

1. Which organism does the description tell about?

   bear

2. How do you know that the description does not tell about a rose bush?

   Idea: A rose bush is not a carnivore.

3. How do you know that the description does not tell about a wolf?

   Idea: A wolf kills its prey.

Workbook page 472

G The argument below has an ought statement for a conclusion. Complete the deduction after the argument by writing the rule, the evidence, and the conclusion.

> One man said, "I think that fool we call a president is doing everything completely wrong."
> "Listen, buddy," the other man said. "Around here, we don't like to hear people talk like that. We ought to lock you up for what you said."

1. **Rule:** *Idea: We ought to lock up people who say things we don't like.*

2. **Evidence:** *Idea: The first man said something we don't like.*

3. **Conclusion:** *Idea: We ought to lock up the first man.*

Mastery Test 13

━━━━━━━ **EXERCISE 2** ━━━━━━━

TEST REMEDIES

1. (If more than 25% of the students failed a part of the test, provide the Remedy Blackline Master specified for that part in the table below. The required Remedy Blackline Master worksheets can be found in Appendix H of the Teacher's Guide.)

2. (All remedies should be completed before beginning the next lesson in the program.)

Test Section	If students made this many errors	Present these tasks: Lesson	Exercise	Remedy Blackline Master	Required Student Book Parts
A	8 or more	Test remedy below		13–A, 13–B	
B	3 or more	Item 1: 22	1	13–C	Lesson 22–A
		Item 2: 34	2	13–C	Lesson 34–B
		Item 3: 62	2	13–D	Lesson 62–B
		Item 4: 102	1	13–D	Lesson 102–A
		Item 5: 19	1	13–E	Lesson 19–A
		Item 6: 28	3	13–E	Lesson 28–A
		Item 7: 57	1	13–F	Lesson 57–B
		Item 8: 85	1	13–F	Lesson 85–B
C	1 or more	116	1	13–G	Lesson 116–A
		117	1	13–G	Lesson 117-Part A
D	2 or more	122	2	13–H	Lesson 122–B
		123	1		Lesson 123–A
E	1 or more	106	2		Lesson 106–B
		111	—		Lesson 111–E
F	1 or more	116	2		Lesson 116–B
		117	3		Lesson 117–C and F
G	1 or more	118	2		Lesson 118–B
		119	1	13–I	

> **Note:** The teacher and each student who failed the test will need a copy of Remedy Blackline Master 13–A. The Remedy Blackline Masters can be found in Appendix H of the Teacher's Guide.

PART A TEST REMEDY

1. We're going to go over some items from the test. I'll read the items. You'll say the answers. Then you'll write the answers.

2. (Read item 1 in part A of Remedy Blackline Master 13–A.) What's the answer? (Call on a student.) *Intolerant.*

3. (Repeat step 2 for items 2–9 in part A.)

4. (Give each student a copy of Remedy Blackline Master 13–A.)
   This worksheet shows the charts that were on the test.

5. Touch box 5.
   What goes in that box? (Call on a student. Idea: *Have strong pincers.*)

6. (Repeat step 5 for boxes 6–8.)

7. Touch box 9.
   Everybody, what goes in that box? (signal.) *Organisms.*

8. (Repeat step 7 for boxes 10–32.)

9. Study the charts for a few minutes. Then you'll fill in the empty boxes.

10. (After several minutes:)
    Now you're going to write the answers to all the items in part A. Let's see who can get them all correct.

11. (After students complete the items.)
    Let's check your work. Use your pen to make an **X** next to any item you got wrong.
    - (For items 1–4: Read the items. Call on individual students to answer each item.)
    - (For the chart items:) What goes in box 5? (Call on a student. Idea: *Have strong pincers.*)
    - Repeat for boxes 6–32.)
    - Raise your hand if you got all the items correct. Nice work.

END OF MASTERY TEST 13

Lesson Objectives	LESSON 131 Exercise	LESSON 132 Exercise	LESSON 133 Exercise	LESSON 134 Exercise	LESSON 135 Exercise	Fact Game 9
Organization and Study Skills						
Morals	SB				SB	
Writing Mechanics: Copying	3	3	2	2	2	
Reasoning Strategies						
Deductions	2	2, WB	1		WB	
Evidence		WB	WB			FG
Rules: Arguments	1, WB	1, WB		WB	1, WB	FG
Statements: Ought					WB	
Contradictions		SB	WB	SB		
Inference				WB	WB	
Information Sources/ Study Skills						
Basic Comprehension				WB	WB	
Reading Comprehension: Words or Deductions				WB		
Interpretation: Maps/Pictures/Graphs	WB	SB	WB	SB, WB		FG
Supporting Evidence	WB	SB, WB		SB	WB	FG
Vocabulary/Language Arts Skills						
Definitions	WB		SB			
Usage	WB		SB			
Sentence Combination			WB	1, SB	WB	FG
Editing/Revising	WB	WB	SB, WB	SB		
Comprehension: Meaning from Context				WB	WB	
Information Application/ Study Skills						
Directions: Writing	WB					
Directions: Filling Out Forms		WB				
Assessment/Progress Monitoring						
Ongoing: Workcheck	Workcheck	Workcheck	Workcheck	Workcheck	Workcheck	
Formal: Mastery Test						

Lesson
131

Student Book page 324

A

A biased argument is an argument that tells the truth, but it tells only part of the truth.

Study the description below. Then read the biased argument that is based on the description.

Name: Lisa Bennett
Age: 26
Height: 6 feet 3 inches
Weight: 150 pounds
Occupation: Model
Experience in occupation: Five years of modeling
Education: High school graduate, two years of college
Marital status: Married, one child
Hobbies: Skiing, photography

I'll grant you that most of her qualifications are very good—in fact, they're probably better than any of the other candidates that we're considering for the job. However, I would like to point out one fact. Mrs. Bennett is not a good candidate because she weighs 150 pounds. We all know that women who weigh 150 are far too heavy to model. Let's face it; they're fat. So I vote against hiring Mrs. Bennett.

This argument is biased because it doesn't take into account some important information. What information is that? Ⓐ

Let's say that you wanted to attack the argument above. What would you say? Ⓑ

B Read the paragraph below.

The people of Sipple had gone to the lake outside their city ever since the city was formed. They swam, fished, and canoed. Then, in 1979, a large factory was built near the lake. After 1979, nobody went to the lake.

The paragraph gives a clue about what caused the people to stop going to the lake. What caused them to stop? Ⓒ

Name two ways that it could cause people to stop going to the lake. Ⓓ

Student Book page 325

Lesson
131

C Write **Part C** in the left margin of your paper. You have two minutes to copy the paragraph below.

Intolerant trees cannot survive in the shade. They usually try to shade everything beneath them by putting out lots of leaves on top. If there is no sunlight beneath the tree, no competing vegetation can spring up next to the tree.

★D Write **Part D** in the left margin of your paper. The passage below presents a moral. Read the passage. Then make up a moral that fits the passage.

When Fran was eleven, she collected pennies. She loved to skateboard. Almost every day after school, she played with Dizzy and Deb. She did great imitations of her teachers, particularly Mr. Briggs. And she was starting to learn to play the guitar.

Then she entered the gymnastics program at the Academy for Perfection. Her daily schedule called for her to be at the academy every day—even Sundays—at 7:30 A.M. On all days except Sundays, she worked on the parallel bars for two hours, the vaulting horse for two hours, the balance beam for two hours, and the floor exercises for two hours. Later in the day, she had a one-hour dancing lesson. On Sundays she had a light workout for about three hours. In addition to the gymnastic work, Fran did schoolwork—reading, arithmetic, science, social studies, writing, and special projects. For some subjects, she attended regular classes. For other subjects, she was taught by teachers at the academy between the periods of work in various areas of gymnastics.

Fran is now seventeen, and they say that she may make the Olympic team. She's obviously a good gymnast, but she's not much fun anymore. She never talks about anything but gymnastics. I don't think she collects pennies, goes skateboarding, or does any of the other things she used to do. She spends most of her time doing gymnastics.

Write a moral for the passage. Start the moral with the words, "If you _____."

Idea: if you concentrate on just one thing, you might miss a lot of other things.

Note: The circled letters indicate when you ask a question or when you direct the group to respond.

EXERCISE 1
ANALYZING ARGUMENTS

1. (Direct the students to find Lesson 131, part A, in the **Student Book.**)
2. (Call on individual students to read part A.)
   Ⓐ (Call on a student. Idea: *Lisa Bennett is 6 feet 3 inches tall.*)
   Ⓑ (Call on a student. Idea: *For a person who is 6 feet 3 inches tall, 150 pounds is not too heavy to be a model.*)

EXERCISE 2
DEDUCTIONS

1. (Direct the students to find part B.)
2. (Call on individual students to read part B.)
   Ⓒ (Call on a student. Idea: *A large factory was built near the lake.*)
   Ⓓ (Call on individual students. Ideas: *The smoke from the factory polluted the air. The factory's waste polluted the lake.*)

EXERCISE 3
INDEPENDENT WORK

1. **[Optional]** (Direct the students to read the instructions for part C to themselves. Then give them exactly two minutes to copy the paragraph. Count as errors any miscopied words and punctuation. Deduct these errors from the number of copied words, and mark the total on the Writing Rate Graph.)
2. Finish the Student Book and do the Workbook for Lesson 131. ✓

Workcheck

1. Get ready to check your answers starting with Student Book part D. Use a pen to make an **X** next to any item you miss.

2. (Call on individual students to read each item and its answer. Repeat for Workbook items.)

3. (Direct the students to count the number of errors and write the number in the **error** box at the top of the Workbook page.)

4. (Award points and direct students to record their points in Box **W**.)

0 errors	15 points
1–2 errors	12 points
3–5 errors	8 points
6–9 errors	5 points

5. (Award any bonus points. Direct the students to total their points and enter the total on the Point Summary Chart.)

6. Show me your work when you've finished correcting it. (When the students show you their corrected work, record their points on your Record Summary Chart.)

Lesson 131 | **Workbook page 388**

B For each item, write a sentence that means the same thing by changing the underlined words.

1. The <u>rule</u> <u>limited</u> their parking.

   The regulation restricted their parking.

2. She had an excellent <u>chance</u> to <u>show</u> her paintings.

   She had an excellent opportunity to exhibit her paintings.

3. He <u>hid</u> his true feelings by presenting <u>irrelevant</u> facts.

   He concealed his true feelings by presenting extraneous data.

4. The frightening <u>event</u> <u>changed</u> their excitement into <u>fear</u>.

   The frightening phenomenon converted their excitement into anxiety.

C Write the instructions for this diagram.

③ ambiguous
②
①
④ strategy

1. (what) *Idea: Draw a circle.*

2. (what and where) *Idea: Draw a triangle to the left of the circle.*

3. (what and where) *Idea: Write the word ambiguous above the circle.*

4. (what and where) *Idea: Write the word strategy below the circle.*

Workbook page 387 | **Lesson 131**

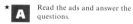

★ **A** Read the ads and answer the questions.

• Professional tennis players are very critical about the equipment they use. Among the fussiest of all is Gron Grog, the current Wibley champion. Shortly before the Wibley tournament, Grog switched to the Neilson tennis racket, with the patented vulcanized handle. Here's what Grog said about this racket.

   "My game improved perhaps 25 percent with the Neilson racket. It's amazing. In the finals, I beat Trebling, a player I have never defeated before."

   Wouldn't you like to play 25 percent better? Try the Neilson racket.

1. Does the ad actually say that the Neilson racket will improve your game?

   no

2. Write a sentence that would be in the ad if the ad said that the Neilson racket would improve your game.

   Idea: The Neilson racket is guaranteed to improve your game.

• The Ascender is the toughest jeep on the road. This jeep has been tested for traction over muddy mountain roads, sand dunes, and rocky trails. It has been driven over the roughest terrain we could find, and it keeps its traction better than any other leading jeep. Since the Ascender can perform in rough country, think of what an easy time it will have doing everyday driving chores, such as taking you to the grocery store.

3. Does the ad actually say that the Ascender is the best jeep for **you**?

   no

4. Write a sentence that would be in the ad if the ad said that the Highlander is the best jeep for you.

   Idea: The Ascender is the best jeep for you.

Workbook page 389 | **Lesson 131**

D Read the arguments and answer the questions.

• Professor Johnson has been with the University of Idaho for twelve years and is chairperson of the history department. He has received awards for his outstanding research in the field of nineteenth-century bonnets and hats. All those who have worked with him have the highest respect for his keen, inquiring mind. Now Professor Johnson is urging that the city close four junior high schools. Surely it is foolish to ignore the wisdom this most worthy man is offering us.

1. The argument uses Professor Johnson as a source for what kind of information?

   Idea: information about whether four junior high schools should be closed

2. Is Professor Johnson a good source for this information?

   no

3. For what kind of information would Professor Johnson be a good source?

   Idea: information on history and nineteenth-century bonnets and hats

• Don is an auto mechanic. Don never watched television until about a year ago, when someone gave him an old Stella television set. It must be five years old, but he's never had a problem with it. If you are thinking of buying a television set, Don definitely recommends a Stella. He says it will last forever.

4. The argument uses Don as a source for what kind of information?

   Idea: information on the Stella television set

5. Is Don a good source for this information?

   no

6. For what kind of information would Don be a good source?

   Idea: information about auto maintenance and repairs

END OF LESSON 131

Lesson 132

Lesson 132 — Student Book page 326

A

> A biased argument is an argument that tells the truth, but it tells only part of the truth.

Study the graphs below. Then read the biased argument that is based on the graphs.

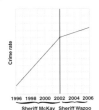

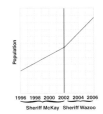

1996 1998 2000 2002 2004 2006
Sheriff McKay Sheriff Wazoo

1996 1998 2000 2002 2004 2006
Sheriff McKay Sheriff Wazoo

Sheriff Wazoo was elected in 2002. At that time, the crime rate in the county was forty crimes per day. These included crimes against property, murders, other violent crimes, and other forms of disorder. When we look at the crime rate now, four years later, we see that the rate has risen to over forty-seven crimes per day. Imagine that! Although Sheriff Wazoo has spent more money than his predecessor, Sheriff McKay, the crime rate has gone up by more than seven crimes per day. If this is the best Sheriff Wazoo can do, I say let's get somebody in the office who can do the job. Let's put McKay back in office and put a stop to this rising crime rate.

This argument is biased because it doesn't take into account some important information. What information is that? ⓐ

Let's say that you wanted to attack the argument above. What would you say? ⓑ

B

Read the paragraph below.

> I lived on a farm in Pennsylvania and worked in a nearby town. I had four goats, a horse, two dogs, and three kittens. Two weeks ago I got a new job. I don't have any animals now.

The paragraph gives a clue about why the writer doesn't have animals anymore. Why doesn't the writer have animals anymore? ⓒ
Name two ways that it could cause the writer not to have animals anymore. ⓓ

Student Book page 327 — Lesson 132

C

Write **Part C** in the left margin of your paper. You have two minutes to copy the paragraph below.

> The captain made an innuendo at dinner. He hinted that he might quit his job. What he actually said was, "I won't be here much longer." But I'm fairly sure that his innuendo meant that he was quitting his job.

★ D

Write **Part D** in the left margin of your paper. Then number it from 1 to 5. Assume that the picture below is accurate. Examine the picture carefully. Then read the statements below the picture. Some of the statements contradict what the picture shows.

- Write **contradictory** or **not contradictory** for each statement.
- If a statement contradicts the picture, write what the picture shows.

1. The man is leaning over the speaker's stand as he delivers his speech.
2. A pitcher of water is on the table beside the speaker.
3. The man is wearing a suit and a hat.
4. The man has his left hand on the speaker's stand, and he is reaching for a glass of water with his right hand.
5. The curtain behind the speaker is concealing him from the crowd.

Note: The circled letters indicate when you ask a question or when you direct the group to respond.

EXERCISE 1
ANALYZING ARGUMENTS

1. (Direct the students to find Lesson 132, part A, in the **Student Book.**)
2. (Call on individual students to read part A.)
   - ⓐ (Call on a student. Idea: *The population has increased since Sheriff Wazoo was elected.*)
   - ⓑ (Call on a student. Idea: *If you compare the crime rate to the population, Sheriff Wazoo is keeping crime down better than McKay did. The population increase also accounts for Wazoo spending more money.*)

EXERCISE 2
DEDUCTIONS

1. (Direct the students to find part B.)
2. (Call on individual students to read part B.)
   - ⓒ (Call on a student. Idea: *The writer got a new job.*)
   - ⓓ (Call on individual students. Ideas: *The writer had to move to a city. The writer doesn't have time to take care of the animals anymore.*)

EXERCISE 3
INDEPENDENT WORK

1. **[Optional]** (Direct the students to read the instructions for part C to themselves. Then give them exactly two minutes to copy the paragraph. Count as errors any miscopied words and punctuation. Deduct these errors from the number of copied words, and mark the total on the Writing Rate Graph.)
2. Finish the Student Book and do the Workbook for Lesson 132. ✓

Workcheck

1. Get ready to check your answers starting with Student Book part D. Use a pen to make an **X** next to any item you miss.

2. (Call on individual students to read each item and its answer. Repeat for Workbook items.)

> **Answer key for Student Book part D**
> **1.** not contradictory **2.** not contradictory
> **3.** contradictory; Idea: the man is not wearing a hat. **4.** contradictory; Idea: the man's right hand is balled up into a fist. **5.** contradictory; Idea: he is standing in view of the crowd and is in front of the curtain.

3. (Direct the students to count the number of errors and write the number in the **error** box at the top of the Workbook page.)

4. (Award points and direct students to record their points in Box **W.**)

0 errors	**15 points**
1–2 errors	**12 points**
3–5 errors	**8 points**
6–9 errors	**5 points**

5. (Award any bonus points. Direct the students to total their points and enter the total on the Point Summary Chart.)

6. Show me your work when you've finished correcting it. (When the students show you their corrected work, record their points on your Record Summary Chart.)

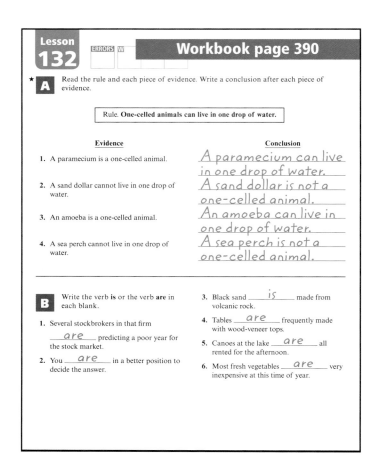

Lesson 132 ERRORS W **Workbook page 390**

★ **A** Read the rule and each piece of evidence. Write a conclusion after each piece of evidence.

Rule. One-celled animals can live in one drop of water.

Evidence	Conclusion
1. A paramecium is a one-celled animal.	A paramecium can live in one drop of water.
2. A sand dollar cannot live in one drop of water.	A sand dollar is not a one-celled animal.
3. An amoeba is a one-celled animal.	An amoeba can live in one drop of water.
4. A sea perch cannot live in one drop of water.	A sea perch is not a one-celled animal.

B Write the verb **is** or the verb **are** in each blank.

1. Several stockbrokers in that firm _are_ predicting a poor year for the stock market.

2. You _are_ in a better position to decide the answer.

3. Black sand _is_ made from volcanic rock.

4. Tables _are_ frequently made with wood-veneer tops.

5. Canoes at the lake _are_ all rented for the afternoon.

6. Most fresh vegetables _are_ very inexpensive at this time of year.

Workbook page 391

C Use the facts to fill out the form.

> **Facts:** Your name is Sarah Liebmann and you are applying for a National Direct Student Loan with the Financial Aid Office of the University of New Orleans. You are a second-year student. Your major subject is biology. Your social security number is 556-56-7090. Your campus address is 1416 Summer Drive, and your campus phone number is 868-6364. Your parents now reside in Monroe, Louisiana. Your father is a building contractor in Monroe, and your mother is an interior designer. Their combined income for the year is $85,000. They live at 4350 Highland Road in Monroe. You are single and were born June 5, 1986. The loan amount you want is $3,000 to cover your expenses for a year. Mr. Nick Boudreaux is the person who knows you best. His address is 1418 Perkins Road in Monroe, Louisiana, and his phone number is 322-4567. The bank in your hometown—where you have both a checking and a savings account—is the Monroe Federal Bank, 123 Lake Ave., in Monroe, Louisiana.

Office of Student Financial Aid
University of New Orleans, New Orleans, Louisiana

Student's name __Liebmann_____ __Sarah_____
             Last   First
Telephone number (campus) __868-6364__ Social Security number __556-56-7090__
Home address __4350 Highland Road, Monroe, Louisiana__
Campus address __1416 Summer Drive__
Father's occupation __building contractor__
Mother's occupation __interior designer__
Parents' combined income for the year __$85,000__
Your year in school: 1 ② 3 4 (Circle one) Major subject __biology__
Amount of the loan you are requesting __$3,000__
List the name and address of a reference: Name __Mr. Nick Boudreaux__
Address __1418 Perkins Road, Monroe, Louisiana__
Name of the bank in your home city __Monroe Federal Bank__
Address of bank __123 Lake Ave., Monroe, Louisiana__
Type of account: Savings ⟨yes⟩ no   Checking ⟨yes⟩ no

Workbook page 393

• Here's another conclusion:

> **Christmas should probably be a summer holiday.**

3. Does the passage contain evidence to support this conclusion or evidence to refute this conclusion?

__evidence to support this conclusion__

4. Which sentence contains the evidence?

__Actually, many people believe that Christ was probably born sometime in June or July.__

END OF LESSON 132

Workbook page 392

D Read the ads and answer the questions.

• All Miter toys are totally nontoxic. That means that we use paint and other materials that are nonpoisonous. Children playing with Miter toys are totally safe from any possible poisoning caused by paint or glue. If we go to the trouble of making sure that there is no possible way that our toys can poison your children, you can imagine the care we take with every other detail of our toys.

1. Write a sentence that would be in the ad if the ad said that the toys were completely safe.

__Idea: Miter toys have been laboratory tested and are completely safe for children to use.__

• Here's some good news for those who suffer from bad breath. Pure and Fresh mouthwash has been designed to fight the germs that cause mouth odor. Pure and Fresh is made from the purest spring waters, and it contains active chemical ingredients that fight ugly bad breath. Available now at your local drugstore.

2. Write a sentence that would be in the ad if the ad said that Pure and Fresh mouthwash gets rid of bad breath.

__Idea: Pure and Fresh mouthwash gets rid of bad breath.__

E Read the passage below.

> In early civilizations, people used to celebrate when the shortest day of the year passed and the days started getting longer again. In the Northern Hemisphere, the shortest day comes late in December, which is when the celebration would occur. Many people believe that the Christian celebration of Christmas at this same time of year is really a holdover from the earlier custom of celebrating the return of the sun. Actually, many people believe that Christ was probably born sometime in June or July.

• Here's a conclusion:

> **People in early times were indifferent to the changing seasons.**

1. Does the passage contain evidence to support this conclusion or evidence to contradict this conclusion?

__evidence to contradict the conclusion__

2. Which sentence contains the evidence?

__In early civilizations, people used to celebrate when the shortest day of the year passed and the days started getting longer.__

Lesson 133

Note: The circled letters indicate when you ask a question or when you direct the group to respond.

EXERCISE 1

DEDUCTIONS

1. (Direct the students to find Lesson 133, part A, in the **Student Book.**)
2. (Call on individual students to read part A.)
   ⓐ (Call on a student. Idea: *Ted began working for High Saddle Riding School in August.*)
   ⓑ (Call on individual students. Ideas: *Ted is very grumpy now that he has to work. Ted smells like a horse now that he works in the stables.*)

EXERCISE 2

INDEPENDENT WORK

1. **[Optional]** (Direct the students to read the instructions for part B to themselves. Then give them exactly two minutes to copy the paragraph. Count as errors any miscopied words and punctuation. Deduct these errors from the number of copied words, and mark the total on the Writing Rate Graph.)
2. Finish the Student Book and do the Workbook for Lesson 133. ✓

Workcheck

1. Get ready to check your answers with Student Book part C. Use a pen to make an **X** next to any item you miss.
2. (Call on individual students to read each item and its answer. Repeat for Workbook items.)

Lesson 133 — Student Book page 328

A Read the paragraph below.

> Before August, Ted had a lot of friends. Whenever you would see Ted, you would almost always see a group of people around him, talking and laughing. In August, Ted began working for High Saddle Riding School. Now, whenever Ted is in public, there aren't any people around him. Sometimes a person will come up and say a few words to Ted, but that person will quickly leave.

The paragraph gives a clue about what caused people to stop being around Ted. What caused them to stop? ⓐ
Name two causes for Ted's not having lots of friends anymore. ⓑ

B Write **Part B** in the left margin of your paper. You have two minutes to copy the paragraph below.

> **In early civilizations, people used to celebrate when the shortest day of the year passed and the days started getting longer again. In the Northern Hemisphere, the shortest day comes late in December, which is when the celebration would occur.**

★ **C** Write **Part C** in the left margin of your paper. In the passage below, the underlined words can be replaced with words you have learned. Rewrite the passage using the words you have learned. Remember to start every sentence with a capital letter and to punctuate each sentence correctly.

> "Your answer is unclear and filled with very irrelevant facts. You know that the rules forbid the sort of thing you did. I'm not at all sure you had really sound reasons for hiding your action, but we will give you one more chance to prove yourself here. You should be very careful about acting in a fitting manner in the future."

Lesson 133 ERRORS W — Workbook page 394

★ **A** Underline the redundant part in each sentence below. Then explain why the underlined part is redundant.

1. His extraneous remarks were irrelevant to the discussion.
   Idea: *If his remarks were irrelevant, then they were extraneous.*
2. She was an average person, like most other people.
   Idea: *If she was an average person, then she was like most other people.*
3. She permitted the children to work alone by allowing independent activities.
   Idea: *If she permitted the children to work alone, then she allowed independent activities.*

B In each item below, the underlined sentence has two possible meanings. The sentence that follows the underlined sentence makes it clear which meaning is intended. Read the items and answer the questions.

- My friends told me to eat eggs, but I can't stand them. Eggs always make me sick.

1. What are the two possible meanings of the underlined sentence?
   Idea: *My friends told me to eat eggs, but I can't stand eggs; my friends told me to eat eggs, but I can't stand my friends.*
2. What is the intended meaning?
   Idea: *My friends told me to eat eggs, but I can't stand eggs.*

- The goat took a pear out of the basket and then ate it. It got straw all over its whiskers.
3. What are the two possible meanings of the underlined sentence?
   Idea: *The goat took a pear out of the basket and then ate the pear; the goat took a pear out of the basket and then ate the basket.*
4. What is the intended meaning?
   Idea: *The goat took a pear out of the basket and then ate the basket.*

Workbook page 395

- She took the cake from the oven and it collapsed. She fed the cake to the dog and made another one.
5. What are the two possible meanings of the underlined sentence?

Idea: She took the cake from the oven and the cake collapsed; she took the cake from the oven and the oven collapsed.

6. What is the intended meaning?

Idea: She took the cake from the oven and the cake collapsed.

C Look at this diagram:

(chance)   (chance)

[opportunity]   [   ]

opportunity

The diagram contradicts part of these instructions:
1. Draw a circle.
2. Write the word **chance** inside the circle.
3. Draw a rectangle under the circle.
4. Write the word **opportunity** under the rectangle.

Circle the instruction that the diagram contradicts.
Draw a new diagram that follows the instructions.

D Read the facts and the items. If an item is relevant to fact A, write **relevant to fact A**. If an item is relevant to fact B, write **relevant to fact B**. If an item is irrelevant to both facts, write **irrelevant**.

Fact A. **Allen hates to travel in airplanes.**
Fact B. **Allen doesn't know how to drive a car.**

1. Allen hesitated when he was asked to fly to the meeting in Los Angeles.
relevant to fact A

2. Allen rides a ten-speed bicycle to work.
relevant to fact B

3. Allen doesn't have a driver's license.
relevant to fact B

4. Allen refused to fly to Hawaii for a vacation that he won.
relevant to fact A

E Select the right word for combining each pair of sentences that follow. Then write the combined sentence. Remember to punctuate each sentence correctly.

1. Five boys ran after the robber. The robber had stolen fifty-five glazed donuts.
who which
Five boys ran after the robber, who had stolen fifty-five glazed donuts.

Workbook page 396

2. The bus ran through a red light. The police officer gave the bus driver a traffic ticket. **therefore but**
The bus ran through a red light; therefore, the police officer gave the bus driver a traffic ticket.

3. George ate a candy bar. The candy bar was on the shelf. **who which**
George ate a candy bar, which was on the shelf.

4. Aaron was supposed to go to bed early. He stayed up late listening to the radio. **and however**
Aaron was supposed to go to bed early; however, he stayed up late listening to the radio.

5. Marlene is working her way through college. She works as a waitress three nights a week. **so but**
Marlene is working her way through college, so she works as a waitress three nights a week.

6. It rained for five days in a row. The stream did not overflow its banks. **therefore however**
It rained for five days in a row; however, the stream did not overflow its banks.

F Read the passage below. Find a statement that contradicts an earlier statement.
- Underline the statement you assume to be true.
- Circle the contradiction.
- Make up an if-then statement that explains the contradiction.

It was one of those rare winter days high in the mountains of Colorado. As sometimes happens, a hot wind called the chinook began to blow down the valley. Within three hours, the temperature had risen more than thirty degrees Celsius. Snow that had accumulated on the ridges was melting, as were the icicles hanging from bare tree limbs.
It was so warm outside that Jan and Eddie went into their backyard and sat on a blanket under the maple. Hearing the warm chinook rustling the oak leaves above her head, Jan said, "This feels just like summer."

Idea: If the tree limbs were bare, then there would not be any oak leaves rustling above Jan's head.

---

3. (Direct the students to count the number of errors and write the number in the **error** box at the top of the Workbook page.)
4. (Award points and direct students to record their points in Box **W.**)

0 errors	**15 points**
1–2 errors	**12 points**
3–5 errors	**8 points**
6–9 errors	**5 points**

5. (Award any bonus points. Direct the students to total their points and enter the total on the Point Summary Chart.)
6. Show me your work when you've finished correcting it. (When the students show you their corrected work, record their points on your Record Summary Chart.)

END OF LESSON 133

Student Book page 329

Lesson 134

A

When you combine sentences with the word **but,** what do you do with the period of the first sentence? Ⓐ

What word follows the comma? Ⓑ

When you combine sentences with the word **therefore,** what do you do with the period of the first sentence? Ⓒ

What follows the semicolon? Ⓓ

What follows the word **therefore?** Ⓔ

When you combine sentences with **who** or **which,** what punctuation comes before **who** or **which?** Ⓕ

B

Write **Part B** in the left margin of your paper. You have two minutes to copy the paragraph below.

> He was exonerated from the charge of speeding through the city. At the trial, his lawyer pointed out that he was the only doctor who could help a patient at County Hospital; the patient would have died unless he was operated on within an hour.

C

Write **Part C** in the left margin of your paper. Rewrite the passage below in three or four sentences. Combine consistent sentences with **and** or **therefore.** Combine inconsistent sentences with **but** or **however.** Combine some sentences with **who** or **which.**

> Charges were brought against Mr. Jones by the FTC. FTC stands for Federal Trade Commission. Mr. Jones had advertised that his product contained lots of vitamins and minerals. It really contained only chemicals. Many people had spent money on food that was nutritionally worthless. These people were angry. Mr. Jones knew he was in big trouble if he got Judge Lawson. Judge Lawson gave stiff penalties for false advertising.

Lesson 134

Student Book page 330

D

Write **Part D** in the left margin of your paper. Then number it 1 and 2. Read the argument below and study the map. Part of the argument is contradicted by the map.

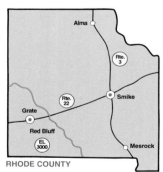

RHODE COUNTY

The symbol ○ means that the city has between 5,000 and 10,000 people.
The symbol ◉ means that the city has between 10,000 and 20,000 people.

The symbol (Rte. 22) means that the name of the road is Route 22.

The symbol (EL 3000) means that the mountain is 3,000 meters high.

> There are several good reasons for routing the new interstate highway through Alma, Smike, and Mesrock.
> - Smike is one of the larger towns in Rhode County.
> - There are no mountains in the way.
> - Right now, there is no road that connects these three towns.
> - The new interstate would cross Route 22.
> - There are no rivers or creeks to build bridges over.

1. Part of the argument is contradicted by the map. Which part is contradicted?
2. What does the map show?

Note: The circled letters indicate when you ask a question or when you direct the group to respond.

EXERCISE 1
SENTENCE COMBINATIONS

1. (Direct the students to find Lesson 134, part A, in the **Student Book.**)
2. (Call on individual students to read part A.)
   Ⓐ What's the answer? *Change it to a comma.*
   Ⓑ What's the answer? *But.*
   Ⓒ What's the answer? *Change it to a semicolon.*
   Ⓓ What's the answer? *Therefore.*
   Ⓔ What's the answer? *A comma.*
   Ⓕ What's the answer? *A comma.*

EXERCISE 2
INDEPENDENT WORK

1. **[Optional]** (Direct the students to read the instructions for part B to themselves. Then give them exactly two minutes to copy the paragraph. Count as errors any miscopied words and punctuation. Deduct these errors from the number of copied words, and mark the total on the Writing Rate Graph.)
2. Finish the Student Book and do the Workbook for Lesson 134. ✓

Workcheck

1. Get ready to check your answers starting with Student Book part C. Use a pen to make an **X** next to any item you miss.
2. (Call on individual students to read each item and its answer. Repeat for Workbook items.)

Answer key for Student Book part C (Ideas:)
Charges were brought against Mr. Jones by the FTC, which stands for Federal Trade Commission. Mr. Jones had advertised that his product contained lots of vitamins and minerals; however, it really contained only chemicals. Many people had spent money on food that was nutritionally worthless, and these people were angry. Mr. Jones knew he was in big trouble if he got Judge Lawson, who gave stiff penalties for false advertising.

Answer key for Student Book part D
1. *Right now, there is no road that connects these three towns.* **2.** *Idea: Route 3 connects the three towns.*

3. (Direct the students to count the number of errors and write the number in the **error** box at the top of the Workbook page.)
4. (Award points and direct students to record their points in Box **W.**)

0 errors	**15 points**
1–2 errors	**12 points**
3–5 errors	**8 points**
6–9 errors	**5 points**

5. (Award any bonus points. Direct the students to total their points and enter the total on the Point Summary Chart.)
6. Show me your work when you've finished correcting it. (When the students show you their corrected work, record their points on your Record Summary Chart.)

Workbook page 397 | B | T |

A Each argument that follows is faulty.

- The senator said, "Mr. Jenkins says that my bill is absurd. Is this the same Mr. Jenkins who made a $30,000 mistake in the 2000 audit? Is this the same Mr. Jenkins who made a false statement before a committee in 2003? Need I say more about Mr. Jenkins?"

1. What does the writer want us to conclude?
   Idea: Mr. Jenkins doesn't have credibility.

2. How could you show that the argument is faulty?
   Idea: Find someone who does have credibility and who also thinks the senator's bill is absurd.

- I don't know why my dad got so mad at me. Before I left on the date, he said, "You must be home by a quarter of twelve."
  I told him I would, and I went out on the date. When I got home, you should have heard him. He yelled and screamed about how late I got in. I don't know what he was so excited about. He said to get home by a quarter of twelve, and I did. Three is a quarter of twelve, and I got home at 3 A.M.

3. What does the writer want us to conclude?
   Idea: Her father got mad at her without a good reason.

4. How could you show that the argument is faulty?
   Idea: Show that her father meant for her to be home by 11:45 P.M. and not by 3:00 A.M.

- Don't tell me about that mountain. I've flown over it a hundred times. I know just how it's shaped. I know where the glacier on it is, and how it runs. You tell me there's a big cave in that mountain, and I say you're wrong. I've observed that mountain quite carefully.

5. What does the writer want us to conclude?
   Idea: There isn't a big cave in the mountain.

6. How could you show that the argument is faulty?
   Idea: Find a big cave in the mountain.

Workbook page 398

B Read the argument and answer the questions.

We interviewed three chefs concerning our new product, Hamburger-Yumm. These people are featured at some of the finest hotels in Europe. We just mixed a little Hamburger-Yumm with tomatoes, onions, and hamburger (so easy even **you** can do it) and asked these fine chefs to taste the results. "Remarkable," said the first chef. "Amazing," said the second chef. "Fantastic," said the third chef.
If it pleases these experts, it's bound to please you. Run down to your local grocery and buy some today—but don't be surprised if you can't find it! Hamburger-Yumm is selling too fast for grocers to keep it in stock!

1. The argument uses three chefs as a source for what kind of information?
   Idea: a new food product called Hamburger-Yumm

2. Are these chefs a good source for this information?
   yes

3. For what kind of information would the chefs be a good source?
   Idea: any information that deals with food or food preparation

C Read the paragraph below.

Sue worked in a restaurant and rented a room in a nearby boardinghouse. Sue got a new job installing telephones. She moved to a house on Llewellyn Avenue.

1. The paragraph gives a clue about what caused Sue to move to a house on Llewellyn Avenue. What caused her to move?
   Idea: her new job

2. Name two ways that your answer to question 1 could cause Sue to move.
   Idea: She could have received more money in her new job; she could have moved to be closer to her new job.

D Read the passage and answer the questions. Circle **W** if the question is answered by words in the passage. Circle **D** if the question is answered by a deduction. If you circle **W** for an item, underline the words in the passage that give the answer.

Graph A shows how a population cycle works. The broken line shows the food supply for an area. The solid line shows the number of animals that live in the area. When the food supply goes up, the number of animals goes up. When the food supply goes down, the number of animals goes down.

Lesson 134

Workbook page 399

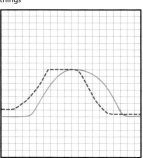

Number of living things

Years

Graph A

You won't become confused about population cycles if you remember that the population of animals depends on the food supply. When the supply goes up, more animals can eat and live. If too many of them eat, they will reduce the food supply. When the food supply goes down, the population of the animals will go down also.

1. When the food supply goes up in an area, what happens to the number of animals in that area?
   <u>Idea: It goes up.</u> Ⓦ D

2. Let's say that the number of predators that eat squirrels increased. What would happen to the squirrel population?
   <u>Idea: It would go</u> w Ⓓ
   <u>down.</u>

3. Let's say that the number of insects that woodpeckers eat decreased. What would happen to the woodpecker population?
   <u>Idea: It would</u> w Ⓓ
   <u>decrease.</u>

4. Write what would happen next in the population cycle for sparrows and their predators:

   The number of predators that eat sparrows decreases.

   The population of sparrows increases.

   The number of predators that eat sparrows increases.

   Then what happens?
   <u>Idea: The population</u>
   <u>of sparrows decreases.</u>

Here's an example of how the population cycle works. Let's say that the number of prairie rats increases. These rats are food for other animals. When the number of rats increases, the food supply for other animals, such as coyotes and owls, increases. As their food supply increases, so does the number of coyotes and owls—until there are too many predators for the food supply. When this happens, too many rats get eaten and the number of rats goes down. This means that the food supply for the predators goes down, and many of them starve. When there are fewer predators to eat the rats, more and more rats survive. This increase in the rat population means an increase in the food supply for certain predators, and so the number of those predators also increases.

Workbook page 400

5. Look at graph B. The dotted line shows how much grass there is in an area. The solid line shows how many herbivores are in that area. If the solid line is below the dotted line, there is more than enough grass for the herbivores. But if the solid line goes above the dotted line, there is not enough grass for the herbivores.

- Complete the dotted line using these facts:
  In 2003, the amount of grass drops to 30.
  In 2004, the amount of grass stays at 30.
  In 2005, the amount of grass rises to 50.
- Answer these questions:
  In 2001, is there enough grass for the herbivores?
  <u>yes</u>
  In 2003, is there enough grass for the herbivores?
  <u>no</u>
  In 2004, is there enough grass for the herbivores?
  <u>yes</u>
  What happens to the number of herbivores in 2005?
  <u>Idea: It increases.</u>
  Why?
  <u>Idea: because there's</u>
  <u>plenty of grass to eat</u>

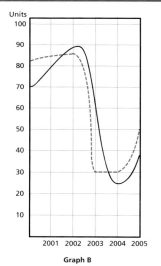

Units

Graph B

Workbook page 401

E Each sentence that follows has two possible meanings. Read each sentence and answer the questions.

- **Our team quickly jumped ahead of the other team.**
  1. What's the intended meaning of the sentence?
     <u>Idea: Our team's</u>
     <u>score quickly</u>
     <u>increased over the</u>
     <u>other team's score.</u>
  2. What's the unintended meaning?
     <u>Idea: Our team</u>
     <u>physically jumped in</u>
     <u>front of the other</u>
     <u>team.</u>
  3. Which words are involved in the two meanings?
     <u>jumped ahead</u>

- **Buffy is a spoiled child.**
  4. What's the intended meaning of the sentence?
     <u>Idea: Buffy is selfish</u>
     <u>and always wants her</u>
     <u>own way.</u>
  5. What's the unintended meaning?
     <u>Idea: Buffy is no</u>
     <u>longer fresh.</u>
  6. Which word is involved in the two meanings?
     <u>spoiled</u>

- **When their eyes met, sparks flew.**
  7. What's the intended meaning of the sentence?
     <u>Idea: When their</u>
     <u>eyes met, they were</u>
     <u>attracted to each</u>
     <u>other.</u>
  8. What's the unintended meaning?
     <u>Idea: When their</u>
     <u>eyes met, sparks of</u>
     <u>fire burst into the air.</u>
  9. Which words are involved in the two meanings?
     <u>sparks flew</u>

END OF LESSON 134

Student Book page 331
Lesson 135

A A biased argument is an argument that tells the truth, but it tells only part of the truth.

Study the graph below. Then read the biased argument that is based on the graph.

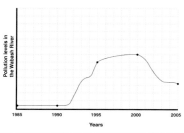

Pollution levels in the Wabash River

Years
1985 1990 1995 2000 2005

Over the last five years, the Dino factory has cut pollution in the Wabash River to half of what it was in 2000. The environmentalists are being unfair when they conclude in their report, "The Dino plant is the biggest problem for the river." Actually, the Dino factory is part of the solution! Ever since the plant opened in 1990, management has done everything possible to be a constructive, helpful part of this community. The recent program to cut waste levels in half is just one example of Dino's good will toward its neighbors and the river.

This argument is biased because it doesn't take into account some important information. What information is that? Ⓐ

Let's say that you wanted to attack the argument above. What would you say? Ⓑ

B Write **Part B** in the left margin of your paper. You have two minutes to copy the paragraph below.

The population of animals depends on the food supply. When the supply goes up, more animals can eat. If too many animals eat, they will reduce the food supply. When the food supply goes down, the population of the animals will go down also.

Lesson 135   ### Student Book page 332

★ **C** Write **Part C** in the left margin of your paper. The passage below presents a moral. Read the passage. Then make up a moral that fits the passage.

Glenda visited her friend Carla, who lived in a town in southern Texas. Most of the families who lived in this town were Mexican, like Carla's family. Carla and her father met Glenda at the bus station and drove her home. They arrived just before supper. Carla's mother explained that she had fixed beef enchiladas for dinner. "I have two kinds—one for Glenda and one for us."

"What's the difference?" Glenda asked.

Carla's mother laughed and then said, "How hot it is. We like things hot—probably too hot for you."

"I don't know," Glenda said. "I've had hot chili and I like it."

"The hot enchiladas are quite hot," Carla said. "If you're not used to really hot food, you should try the mild one."

"Oh, come on," Glenda said. "Let me take a taste of a hot one." She took her fork and cut off a piece from one end of an enchilada. The piece was mostly tortilla, which is not very hot.

Glenda ate it and said, "Oh, that's nothing." She cut a large piece from the center of the enchilada and popped it into her mouth. A moment later, her eyes filled with tears and she gasped, "Oh, oh!" She drank a lot of water and walked around with ice cubes in her mouth for the rest of the evening, but her tongue was still sore.

Write a moral for the passage. Start the moral with the words, "If you _____."

Idea: If you judge a whole by a part, you might be sorry.

Note: The circled letters indicate when you ask a question or when you direct the group to respond.

EXERCISE 1

ANALYZING ARGUMENTS

1. (Direct the students to find Lesson 135, part A, in the **Student Book**.)
2. (Call on individual students to read part A.)
   Ⓐ (Call on a student. Idea: *Pollution in the Wabash River increased greatly as soon as the factory opened.*)
   Ⓑ (Call on a student. Idea: *The Dino factory has not reduced river pollution to the level it was before the factory opened. There is still a lot of polluting going on.*)

EXERCISE 2

INDEPENDENT WORK

1. **[Optional]** (Direct the students to read the instructions for part B to themselves. Then give them exactly two minutes to copy the paragraph. Count as errors any miscopied words and punctuation. Deduct these errors from the number of copied words, and mark the total on the Writing Rate Graph.)
2. Finish the Student Book and do the Workbook for Lesson 135. ✓

Workcheck

1. Get ready to check your answers starting with Student Book part C. Use a pen to make an **X** next to any item you miss.

2. (Call on individual students to read each item and its answer. Repeat for Workbook items.)

3. (Direct the students to count the number of errors and write the number in the **error** box at the top of the Workbook page.)

4. (Award points and direct students to record their points in Box **W.**)

0 errors	15 points
1–2 errors	12 points
3–5 errors	8 points
6–9 errors	5 points

5. (Award any bonus points. Direct the students to total their points and enter the total on the Point Summary Chart.)

6. Show me your work when you've finished correcting it. (When the students show you their corrected work, record their points on your Record Summary Chart.)

END OF LESSON 135

Note: Before presenting Lesson 136, present Fact Game 9.

Lesson
135 ERRORS W **Workbook page 402**

★ **A** Read the argument and answer the questions.

> I'm Alvin Cleats, first baseman for the Tule Lake Tubes. Maybe you remember that great play I made in the World Series. Yes, baseball has been a great life for me. I've had as many thrills as you have had watching me. If you want to keep watching me, let me recommend this PDZ-440 color television. It's made by the folks at Power Drain Enterprises. And I can tell you, they know how to make them so that they last and last. Get the PDZ-440, and I'll see you in next year's World Series. PDZ-440: It's the best, like me!

1. The argument uses Alvin Cleats as a source for what kind of information?
   Idea: information on the PDZ-440

2. Is Mr. Cleats a good source for this information?
   no

3. For what kind of information would Mr. Cleats be a good source?
   Idea: information about baseball

B Write whether each statement below is a **statement of ought** or a **statement of fact**.

1. A regulation should be made to restrict smoking to certain areas of this restaurant.
   statement of ought

2. A regulation restricts smoking to certain areas in this restaurant.
   statement of fact

3. Those schools shouldn't be so competitive.
   statement of ought

4. Most people should drive their cars less.
   statement of ought

C Read the paragraph below.

> Old Mr. Jones could always be seen on summer days kneeling on his lawn, digging out dandelions. Ever since that day a long, black car was parked in front of his house, we haven't seen Mr. Jones.

1. The paragraph gives a clue about why Mr. Jones has not been seen. What is the clue?
   Idea: A long, black car parked in front of his house.

2. Name two reasons for Mr. Jones not being seen.
   Idea: He might have died; he might have been kidnapped.

Workbook page 403 Lesson **135**

D Read each deduction and write the answers to the questions.

• We should do what is necessary to have a good school program.
   In a good school program, students attend classes all day.
   Therefore, we should make sure that students attend classes all day.

1. What kind of statement does the deduction begin with?
   statement of ought

2. Is the deduction valid?
   yes

3. Explain.
   Idea: The deduction begins and ends with a statement of ought.

• This machine will keep very old people alive for ten years or more.
   There are thousands of old people who would like to live longer.
   Therefore, we should use this machine to keep these old people alive.

4. What kind of statement does the deduction begin with?
   statement of fact

5. Is the deduction valid?
   no

6. Explain. *Idea: The deduction does not begin and end with a statement of ought.*

E Here's what we know:

> The police officer's directions were ambiguous.

For each item, combine one of the sentences below with the sentence in the box.

• We found the correct street without too much trouble.
• We got lost on our way to the meeting hall.

1. Make a combined sentence with **but**.
   The police officer's directions were ambiguous, but we found the correct street without too much trouble.

2. Make a combined sentence with **so**.
   The police officer's directions were ambiguous, so we got lost on our way to the meeting hall.

Note: Before beginning Lesson 136, present this Fact Game Lesson. You will need a pair of dice for every four or five students. Each student needs a pencil and Workbook.

━━━━━ **EXERCISE 1** ━━━━━

FACT GAME

1. (Divide the students into groups of four or five. Assign one player in each group to be the monitor. Seat the groups at different tables with a pair of dice.)
2. (Direct the players to open their Workbooks to page 404.
   Direct the monitors to open their Workbooks to page 482.)
3. You have 20 minutes to play the game. (Circulate as students play. Comment on groups that are playing well.)

Points for Fact Game

1. (At the end of 20 minutes, have all students who earned more than 12 points stand up. Award 5 bonus points to these players.)
2. (Award points to monitors. Monitors receive the same number of points earned by the highest performer in the group.)
3. (Tell the monitor of each game that ran smoothly:) Your group did a good job. Give yourself and each of your players 5 bonus points. ✓
4. Everybody, write your game points in Box FG on your Point Chart. Write your bonus points in the bonus box. ✓

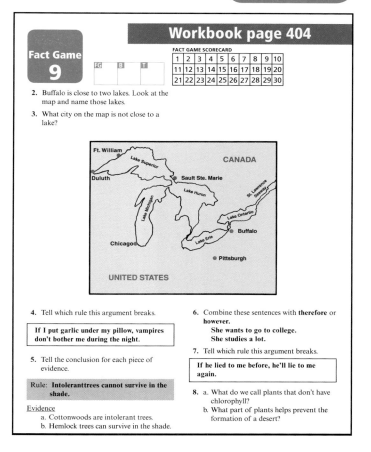

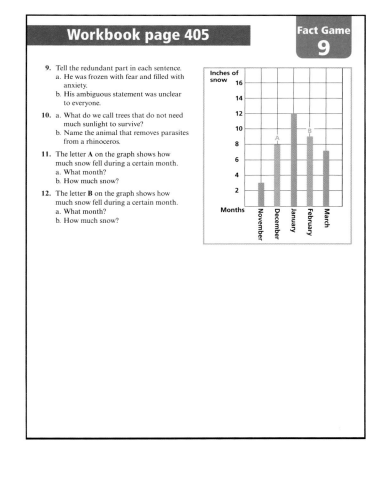

Workbook page 404

FG [ ] B [ ] T [ ]

FACT GAME SCORECARD

1	2	3	4	5	6	7	8	9	10
11	12	13	14	15	16	17	18	19	20
21	22	23	24	25	26	27	28	29	30

2. Buffalo is close to two lakes. Look at the map and name those lakes.

3. What city on the map is not close to a lake?

4. Tell which rule this argument breaks.

> If I put garlic under my pillow, vampires don't bother me during the night.

5. Tell the conclusion for each piece of evidence.

> **Rule: Intoleranttrees cannot survive in the shade.**

Evidence
  a. Cottonwoods are intolerant trees.
  b. Hemlock trees can survive in the shade.

6. Combine these sentences with **therefore** or **however**.
> She wants to go to college.
> She studies a lot.

7. Tell which rule this argument breaks.

> If he lied to me before, he'll lie to me again.

8. a. What do we call plants that don't have chlorophyll?
  b. What part of plants helps prevent the formation of a desert?

Workbook page 482

FACT GAME 9

2. Lake Ontario, Lake Erie

3. Pittsburgh

4. Just because two things happen around the same time doesn't mean one thing causes the other thing.

5. a. Cottonwoods cannot survive in the shade.
  b. Hemlock trees are not intolerant trees.

6. She wants to go to college; therefore, she studies a lot.

7. Just because events have happened in the past doesn't mean they'll always happen.

8. a. Decomposers
  b. Roots

9. a. And filled with anxiety
  b. Was unclear to everyone

10. a. Tolerant
  b. Tickbird

11. a. December
  b. 8 inches

12. a. February
  b. 9 inches

END OF FACT GAME 9

Workbook page 405

9. Tell the redundant part in each sentence.
  a. He was frozen with fear and filled with anxiety.
  b. His ambiguous statement was unclear to everyone.

10. a. What do we call trees that do not need much sunlight to survive?
  b. Name the animal that removes parasites from a rhinoceros.

11. The letter **A** on the graph shows how much snow fell during a certain month.
  a. What month?
  b. How much snow?

12. The letter **B** on the graph shows how much snow fell during a certain month.
  a. What month?
  b. How much snow?

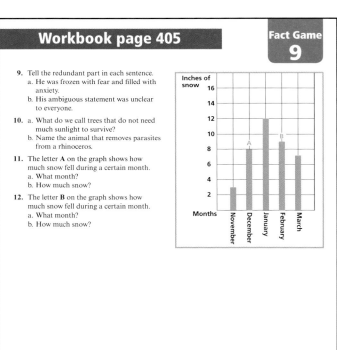

Lesson Objectives	LESSON 136	LESSON 137	LESSON 138	LESSON 139	LESSON 140
	Exercise	Exercise	Exercise	Exercise	Exercise
Organization and Study Skills					
Main Idea	SB	SB			SB
Outlining		SB			
Writing Mechanics: Copying	2	2	2	2	1
Reasoning Strategies					
Deductions	WB	1	1, WB		WB
Evidence	WB		WB		
Rules: Arguments	1, WB	WB	WB	1, WB	WB
Contradictions	SB	WB		SB	
Inference	WB			WB	WB
Information Sources/Study Skills					
Basic Comprehension	WB			WB	WB
Reading Comprehension: Words or Deductions			WB		
Interpretation: Maps/Pictures/Graphs		WB		SB, WB	WB
Supporting Evidence			SB	SB, WB	
Vocabulary/Language Arts Strategies					
Definitions			SB		WB
Usage			SB		WB
Sentence Combination					WB
Editing/Revising	WB	WB	SB	WB	WB
Comprehension: Meaning from Context		WB			
Information Application/ Study Skills					
Directions: Writing		WB			
Directions: Filling Out Forms				WB	
Information Review			WB	WB	
Assessment/Progress Monitoring					
Ongoing: Workcheck	Workcheck	Workcheck	Workcheck	Workcheck	Workcheck
Formal: Mastery Test					MT14

Student Book page 333

A

A biased argument is an argument that tells the truth, but it tells only part of the truth.

Study the graph below. Then read the biased argument that is based on the graph.

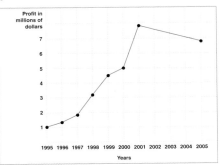

To our customers:

No one likes to see the price of our products go up. You end up paying more, and we always end up losing some customers. But, as this graph shows, our profits have been declining steadily over the last four years. There's no way for us to continue operating this way. Every business has to make a profit. That's why we are announcing this price increase for our products.

This argument is biased because it doesn't take into account some important information. What information is that? Ⓐ

Let's say that you wanted to attack the argument above. What would you say? Ⓑ

Student Book page 334

B

Write **Part B** in the left margin of your paper. You have two minutes to copy the paragraph below.

The soldiers were camped in ice and snow for weeks at a time without warm clothes and with little food. They exhibited a great deal of fortitude. Although they were cold and hungry, no one complained. Some even joked about the weather.

★ **C**

Write **Part C** in the left margin of your paper. Then number it from 1 to 11. The two accounts below contradict each other on an important point. Make sure you find that contradiction when you read the accounts.

Passage 1. The small country of Murk has reportedly attacked its neighbor, the kingdom of Smoo. According to reports wired in by Dave Finch, our foreign reporter, Murkian jets bombed Smoo last night, and Murkian soldiers moved into the city of Gona, capital of Smoo. All the details of this attack are not yet known. Over 100 Smoo citizens have been killed. Our president said last night that we will not get involved.

Passage 2. The age-old war between Murk and Smoo flared up again yesterday when Murk launched a full-scale attack on Gona, capital of Smoo. Without warning, Murkian bombers flew over Gona and dropped bombs at about 8 P.M. About 200 Smoos are believed to be dead. The Smoo army is still fighting Murkian soldiers in the streets. The king of Murk has made no comments about the attack. Our president told reporters that this could mean world war and that he was ready to give Smoo whatever help it needs.

Answer each question. Some questions ask where you found an answer. Write **passage 1, passage 2,** or **passages 1 and 2** for these questions.

1. These passages contradict each other on one big point. What is that?
2. Which country was attacked?
3. Where did you find the answer to question 2?
4. What is the capital of Smoo?
5. Where did you find the answer to question 4?
6. At what time did Murk attack Gona?
7. Where did you find the answer to question 6?
8. Who sent in the reports of the attack?
9. Where did you find the answer to question 8?
10. What reasons does the king of Murk give for this attack?
11. Where did you find the answer to question 10?

Note: The circled letters indicate when you ask a question or when you direct the group to respond.

EXERCISE 1
ANALYZING ARGUMENTS

1. (Direct the students to find Lesson 136, part A, in the **Student Book.**)
2. (Call on individual students to read part A.)
   Ⓐ (Call on a student. Idea: *Profits are still higher than at any time before 1992.*)
   Ⓑ (Call on a student. Idea: *Even though profits have been declining for the past four years, profits are still higher than they were five years ago.*)

EXERCISE 2
INDEPENDENT WORK

1. **(Optional)** (Direct the students to read the instructions for part B to themselves. Then give them exactly two minutes to copy the paragraph. Count as errors any miscopied words and punctuation. Deduct these errors from the number of copied words, and mark the total on the Writing Rate Graph.)
2. Finish the Student Book and do the Workbook for Lesson 136. ✓

Workcheck

1. Get ready to check your answers starting with Student Book part C. Use a pen to make an **X** next to any item you miss.
2. (Call on individual students to read each item and its answer. Repeat for Workbook items.)

Answer key for Student Book part C
1. *Idea: Whether or not the president will get his country involved in the war* **2.** *Smoo*
3. *passages 1 and 2* **4.** *Gona* **5.** *passages 1 and 2*
6. *8 P.M.* **7.** *passage 2* **8.** *Dave Finch*
9. *passage 1* **10.** *Idea: None* **11.** *passage 2*

3. (Direct the students to count the number of errors and write the number in the **error** box at the top of the Workbook page.)
4. (Award points and direct students to record their points in Box **W.**)

0 errors	15 points
1–2 errors	12 points
3–5 errors	8 points
6–9 errors	5 points

5. (Award any bonus points. Direct the students to total their points and enter the total on the Point Summary Chart.)
6. Show me your work when you've finished correcting it. (When the students show you their corrected work, record their points on your Record Summary Chart.)

Lesson 136 ERRORS W **Workbook page 406**

A ★ Underline the redundant part in each sentence below. Then explain why the underlined part is redundant.

1. He was sad, and he wasn't very happy.
Idea: If you know he was sad, then you already know he wasn't happy.

2. The cabin was in proximity to the riverbank, near the water's edge.
Idea: If you know the cabin was in proximity to the riverbank, then you already know it was near the water's edge.

3. Their infant, not yet an adult, had black hair and brown eyes.
Idea: If you know that it was their infant, then you already know it was not yet an adult.

B Read the ads and answer the questions.

- If you have ever suffered from dandruff, you know how embarrassing it can be. It messes your clothing, and it itches. Well, here's some good news. Feel Free dandruff shampoo is now available in all drugstores. Feel Free is a shampoo that contains powerful chemicals that will help control those ugly white flakes. Mary Morse, star of *Starship*, says: "This is the shampoo that makes my hair shine." Why not try some today?

1. Write a sentence that would be in the ad if the ad said that Feel Free gets rid of dandruff.
Idea: Feel Free shampoo gets rid of dandruff.

- Five people have driven the Hodo moped around New York City for a week. Their average gas mileage was 132.8 miles per gallon. In this day of rising gas prices, shouldn't you consider a Hodo moped?

2. Write a sentence that would be in the ad if the ad said that you would get 132.8 miles per gallon on the Hodo moped.
Idea: You will be able to get 132.8 miles per gallon on your Hodo moped.

Student Book page 335 **Lesson 136**

D Write **Part D** in the left margin of your paper. Then number it from 1 to 3.
Here are three main ideas:

> **Main idea A. You pay for more than you eat.**
> **Main idea B. There are ways to make your food dollar go further.**
> **Main idea C. Inflation is eating into the American dollar.**

Each main idea fits one of the passages below. After reading all the passages, figure out which main idea goes with each passage.

> **Passage 1.** Inflation is a serious problem in many countries of the world. Inflation means that prices keep going up. Ever since you were born, prices have been increasing. Every year, food costs more. In the United States, over one-third of the average wage is spent on food. If inflation continues in the United States, close to one-half of the average wage will be spent on food!

> **Passage 2.** Because of rising food costs, people have become interested in stretching their food money. Some ways of saving on food are: use powdered milk for baking; mix hamburger with cereal for a bigger meat loaf; buy the cheaper cuts of meat and tenderize them yourself by cooking them longer or marinating them. Eggs are still one of the cheapest forms of protein and can be made into many interesting dishes.

> **Passage 3.** With food prices soaring, you might think that the farmers in the United States are making a big profit. That is not true. In fact, many farmers are going broke and are selling out to big companies. Who, then, is making the money? Shipping food by truck costs a lot. Processing food—such as canning or freezing—costs a lot. You also pay for the colorful packaging of a box of breakfast cereal and for television advertisements of a product. Actually, most of the money you pay for a can of tuna or a can of beans goes to the "middle men"—the ones who ship and process the food before it reaches your table.

1. Main idea A is: **You pay for more than you eat.** Which passage does main idea A best fit? *passage 3*
2. Main idea B is: **There are ways to make your food dollar go further.** Which passage does main idea B best fit? *passage 2*
3. Main idea C is: **Inflation is eating into the American dollar.** Which passage does main idea C best fit? *passage 1*

Workbook page 407 **Lesson 136**

C In the passage below, the verbs **was** and **were** are used incorrectly five times.
Cross out each incorrect word. Write the correct word above it.
There are three redundant parts in the passage below. Cross out each redundant part.

> In the 1930s and 1940s, it ~~were~~ *was* common to see hitchhikers ~~hitching rides~~ on the road. However, these people ~~was~~ *were* not kids traveling for fun. These hitchhikers ~~was~~ *were* adults who were heading west. They had hopes of getting jobs in California ~~and finding work~~. The homes they ~~was~~ *were* coming from had been destroyed by great dust storms. They ~~was~~ *were* poor and homeless, ~~without money or a home.~~

D Read the paragraph below and answer the questions..

> Anne went outside dressed in her shorts and carrying a picnic basket. She stood in front of her house and looked around. "Darn it," she said, and went back inside.

1. The paragraph gives a clue about what caused Anne to go back inside the house. What caused her to go back?
Idea: what she saw outside

2. Name two causes for Anne going back inside the house.
Idea: There were rain clouds in the sky; someone had stolen her car.

E Read each item. Cross out the irrelevant words in the second piece of evidence, and write the conclusion for each item.

1. All ships have drag.
A submarine is a ~~submersible~~ ship.
A submarine has drag.

2. Some fruit seeds contain poisonous chemicals.
Apples contain ~~dark, bitter~~ seeds.
Maybe apple seeds contain poisonous chemicals.

END OF LESSON 136

Lesson
137
Student Book page 336

A Read the paragraph below.

Five people went into that house over there. A woman met each of them at the door. Then she took them into the living room. They have been very quiet, but every now and then I see one of them peeking out the front window.

The paragraph gives a clue about what the people are doing inside the house. What is the clue? Ⓐ
Name two things they could be doing. Ⓑ

B Write **Part B** in the left margin of your paper. You have two minutes to copy the paragraph below.

With food prices soaring, you might think that farmers are making big profits. That is not true. In fact, many farmers are going broke. Most of the money that you pay for food goes to the people who ship and process the food.

Note: The circled letters indicate when you ask a question or when you direct the group to respond.

EXERCISE 1

DEDUCTIONS

1. (Direct the students to find Lesson 137, part A, in the **Student Book**.)
2. (Call on individual students to read part A.)
   Ⓐ (Call on a student. Idea: *The woman was wearing fancy clothes.*)
   Ⓑ (Call on individual students. Ideas: *They are having a meeting and waiting for the last person. They are having a surprise party and waiting for the guest of honor.*)

EXERCISE 2

INDEPENDENT WORK

1. **[Optional]** (Direct the students to read the instructions for part B to themselves. Then give them exactly two minutes to copy the paragraph. Count as errors any miscopied words and punctuation. Deduct these errors from the number of copied words, and mark the total on the Writing Rate Graph.)
2. Finish the Student Book and do the Workbook for Lesson 137. ✓

Workcheck

1. Get ready to check your answers with Student Book part C. Use a pen to make an **X** next to any item you miss.

2. (Call on individual students to read each item and its answer. Repeat for Workbook items.)

Answer key for Student Book part C

I. *Exploration of the ocean depths is a fairly recent phenomenon.*

   A. *Idea: In 1818, Sir John Ross brought up samples of mud from the ocean floor.*

   B. *Idea: In 1872, a vessel hauled up nets of organisms never seen before.*

   C. *Idea: In 1934, William Beebe and Otis Barton observed sea creatures 3,027 feet beneath the sea.*

---

3. (Direct the students to count the number of errors and write the number in the **error** box at the top of the Workbook page.)

4. (Award points and direct students to record their points in Box **W.**)

0 errors	**15 points**
1–2 errors	**12 points**
3–5 errors	**8 points**
6–9 errors	**5 points**

5. (Award any bonus points. Direct the students to total their points and enter the total on the Point Summary Chart.)

6. Show me your work when you've finished correcting it. (When the students show you their corrected work, record their points on your Record Summary Chart.)

Student Book page 337

C Write **Part C** in the left margin of your paper. Here are three main ideas:

- The world is covered by large amounts of water.
- Exploration of the ocean depths is a fairly recent phenomenon.
- Sir John Ross and William Beebe explored the ocean.

One of the main ideas fits the passage below. Read the passage.

> Exploring deep in the oceans presents several problems: for example, the lack of light and the severe water pressure. These problems prevented deep-sea exploration for many years. Finally, in 1818, Sir John Ross brought up samples of mud from the ocean floor. He discovered worms in this mud, which had come from over 6,000 feet below. Other explorers searched for life below the sea. In 1872, a vessel used strictly for exploring the ocean used nets to investigate the depths of the ocean. The organisms hauled up in these nets had never been seen by people before. This proved that life existed in spite of the darkness and the tremendous pressure. In 1934, William Beebe and Otis Barton actually went down to a depth of 3,027 feet. These people used a deep-sea diving vessel called a bathysphere. They had the opportunity to observe many kinds of sea creatures.

Write the main idea that fits the passage. List the three points that fall under the main idea in outline form. Don't forget to indent and label the three points.

I. Exploration of the ocean depths is a fairly recent phenomenon.
   A. Idea: In 1818, Sir John Ross brought up samples of mud from the ocean floor.
   B. Idea: In 1872, a vessel hauled up nets of organisms never seen before.
   C. Idea: In 1934, William Beebe and Otis Barton observed sea creatures 3,027 feet beneath the sea.

Workbook page 408

A Ray sometimes has trouble using the words **who** and **which.** Below is a letter that he wrote to his friend Slim. Cross out the words **who** and **which** if they are used incorrectly. Write the correct word above every crossed-out word.

Dear Slim,

I used our money to buy a company, ~~who~~ (which) has invented some interesting products. Our company, ~~which~~ (which) is named Knot-So-Brite, is sure to be a success. The people ~~which~~ (who) work for us are very smart. They have invented a machine that uses milk instead of oil for fuel. Some of our employees, ~~which~~ (who) are famous scientists, are working on a machine that will convert mud into chocolate pudding. Guess ~~which~~ (who) works in our art department? The same men who painted our house! You'll be pleased to know that the men who sold us this company are the same men ~~which~~ (who) sold us the swampland in Florida.

Your pal,

Ray

B Read the ads and answer the questions.

- We have put this engine through a torture test. First, we filled the crankcase with Nu-Lube oil, with the patented graphite base. This is the famous black oil that has been revolutionizing motoring. Then, while the engine ran, we drained out the oil. But did the engine freeze up? No. Did the metal parts begin to grind each other into piles of metal filings? No. Has there been any sign of wear on this engine in the hour that it has run without oil? No. Imagine how Nu-Lube will save the life of your engine. Buy it now at leading gas stations.

1. Write a sentence that would be in the ad if the ad said that Nu-Lube is the best oil for your car.

Idea: Nu-Lube is the best oil on the market for your car.

- Come Hither is a new perfume from the makers of the world-famous Aroma No. 9. Some of the richest and most beautiful women in the world wear Come Hither. This perfume costs a little more—but then, it's only for special people. Would you like to be like those women who wear Come Hither? Remember to buy some soon.

2. Write a sentence that would be in the ad if the ad said that Come Hither will make you a special person.

Idea: Come Hither perfume will make you a special person.

Workbook page 409

C Each argument that follows breaks one of these rules:

Rule 1. Just because two things happen around the same time doesn't mean one thing causes the other thing.

Rule 2. Just because you know about a part doesn't mean you know about the whole thing.

Rule 3. Just because you know about a part doesn't mean you know about another part.

Rule 4. Just because you know about a whole thing doesn't mean you know about every part.

Rule 5. Just because words are the same doesn't mean they have the same meaning.

Rule 6. Just because the writer presents some choices doesn't mean there aren't other choices.

Rule 7. Just because events have happened in the past doesn't mean they'll always happen.

After each argument that follows, write the number of the rule the argument breaks.

1. If the National Food Corporation is earning a huge profit, you can bet that every employee of that company is rich.
   _4_

2. Sharon is on the witness stand.
   District Attorney: "Isn't it true that you were a car thief when you were a teenager?"
   Sharon: "Yes, it's true."
   District Attorney: "Why shouldn't we believe that you still commit crimes?"
   _7_

3. A survey of families who started out poor and became rich has been completed. This survey shows that the number of telephones in a house is related to the achievement of the children living in the house. When the families had no phones, the achievement of the children was very low. When the families had an average of one phone, the achievement level of the children went up greatly. When these families had an average of 2.3 phones, the achievement level of the children was the highest. This survey shows that we can improve the achievement of children by putting more phones in the house.
   _1_

4. Cars, trucks, and buses make noise, pollute the atmosphere, use up gasoline or diesel fuel, and cause many accidents. Cars and trucks and buses are vehicles. The bicycle is also a vehicle. So, the bicycle must have the same faults as cars and trucks and buses. We should outlaw all these vehicles.
   _3_

Workbook page 410

D Read the passage below. Find a statement that contradicts an earlier statement.
- Underline the statement you assume to be true.
- Circle the contradiction.
- Make up an if-then statement that explains the contradiction.

> Garlic is a wonderful herb. Perhaps because of its powerful smell (and the telltale breath it leaves), people used to think it could ward off vampires and give soldiers courage. In truth, garlic will take the sting out of insect bites if you crush a clove and apply it to your skin. Planted near certain crops, it will keep insects away. Garlic provides protection against certain germs. The next time you feel a cold coming on, try chewing a few cloves of garlic—they may help your cold. Garlic is also a good breath freshener because of its mild odor. It can be used in almost any dish—casseroles, vegetables, even meat. Powdered garlic can be used, but fresh cloves are much better.

Idea: If garlic has a powerful smell, then it can't have a mild odor.

E Write the instructions for this diagram.

② currency ① ③
④

1. (what) Idea: Draw a triangle.
2. (what and where) Idea: Write the word currency to the left of the triangle.
3. (what and where) Idea: Draw a square to the right of the triangle.
4. (what and where) Idea: Draw a horizontal line below the triangle and the square.

Workbook page 411

F Each passage below contains a word you may not know. Read each passage and answer the questions.

- Her mind had <u>obliterated</u> all memory of that terrible night. She no longer remembered the flames and the smoke. Unfortunately, the memory of her childhood also was obliterated. She couldn't even recognize her mother and father.
1. Circle the answer.
   Obliterated probably means:
   recognized   increased
   saved   (destroyed)

2. Write any sentence from the passage that contradicts the idea that **obliterated** means **saved**.
   Idea: She no longer remembered the flames and the smoke.

- She is very <u>diligent</u>. She carefully attends to details and checks everything twice to make sure it is correct. This diligence may slow her down a little, but she keeps plugging away and never makes a mistake. Sometimes she spends an hour or two double-checking her figures and outlining her next job.
3. Circle the answer.
   Diligent probably means:
   (careful)   dopey   quick   careless

4. Write any sentence from the passage that contradicts the idea that **diligent** means **quick**.
   Idea: She carefully attends to details and checks everything twice to make sure it is correct.

- I've never met a person with a better <u>aesthetic</u> sense than Mildred. Have you seen what she's done to her house? It's magnificent inside. The colors, the arrangement of pictures, and the choice of plants are all very tasteful. Also, the lighting is very impressive. Mildred's aesthetic abilities simply amaze me.
5. Circle the answer.
   Aesthetic probably means:
   vulgar   sleepy   (artistic)   writing

6. Write any sentence from the passage that contradicts the idea that **aesthetic** means **vulgar**.
   Idea: The colors, the arrangement of pictures, and the choice of plants are all very tasteful.

END OF LESSON 137

Note: The circled letters indicate when you ask a question or when you direct the group to respond.

━━━━━ EXERCISE 1 ━━━━━

DEDUCTIONS

1. (Direct the students to find Lesson 138, part A, in the **Student Book.**)
2. (Call on individual students to read part A.)
   - **Ⓐ** (Call on a student. Idea: *His parents put in a new furnace last year.*)
   - **Ⓑ** (Call on individual students. Ideas: *Tom doesn't have to chop wood anymore for the old wood stove. Tom's house is warmer now so he doesn't go out and get much exercise. Tom is allergic to the new furnace.*)

━━━━━ EXERCISE 2 ━━━━━

INDEPENDENT WORK

1. **[Optional]** (Direct the students to read the instructions for part B to themselves. Then give them exactly two minutes to copy the paragraph. Count as errors any miscopied words and punctuation. Deduct these errors from the number of copied words, and mark the total on the Writing Rate Graph.)
2. Finish the Student Book and do the Workbook for Lesson 138. ✓

Workcheck

1. Get ready to check your answers starting with Student Book part C. Use a pen to make an **X** next to any item you miss.
2. (Call on individual students to read each item and its answer. Repeat for Workbook items.)

Lesson 138 — Student Book page 338

A Read the paragraph below.

> Tom was one of the strongest boys in school. He was very active and happy. His parents took out their old wood stove and installed a new gas furnace last year. Since that time, he has become weaker, unhappy, and less active.

The paragraph gives a clue about what caused Tom to become weaker and less active. What caused him to get weaker and less active? Ⓐ
Name two ways that it could cause him to get weaker and less active. Ⓑ

B Write **Part B** in the left margin of your paper. You have two minutes to copy the paragraph below.

> **The Norwegian lemming has a strange way of handling overpopulation. About every five years, the lemming population increases greatly. The lemmings then march out of the mountains where they usually live. They keep marching until some die, which reduces the population.**

★ **C** Write **Part C** in the left margin of your paper. In the passage below, the underlined words can be replaced with words you have learned. Rewrite the passage using the words you have learned. Remember to start every sentence with a capital letter and to punctuate each sentence correctly.

> The writer's article was <u>unclear</u> and <u>repetitive</u>, filled with <u>very</u> boring jokes and <u>irrelevant facts</u>. When he showed it to his editor, she <u>argued</u> that he would have to <u>make up</u> a different <u>plan</u> for the article. Then she told him, "<u>Most of the time</u> your articles are <u>very</u> well written. I think you can <u>change</u> this poorly written article into one that people will <u>really</u> want to read."

D Write **Part D** in the left margin of your paper. Then number it from 1 to 14. The two passages on the next page tell something about hailstorms. Read both passages and find out which passage gives more facts about the damage that hailstorms cause.

Student Book page 339

Lesson 138

Passage A. Hailstorms can cause more property damage than tornadoes. The falling ice destroys crops and kills livestock. Animals as large as horses are occasionally killed in hailstorms. Leaves and fruit are knocked off trees in orchards. Fields of grain, such as wheat or corn, suffer the most. A hailstorm can flatten a ripe field of wheat or corn in a few minutes.

Passage B. Hail is formed in clouds that have strong air currents going up and down. These clouds may be seven or eight kilometers from top to bottom. The air at the top of the clouds is very cold, while the air near the bottom is warm. Rain starts falling in these clouds. But air currents take the raindrops up to the top of the cloud, where they freeze into tiny balls. Then they drop down inside the cloud, and as they do, they are covered with water. Again, the air currents take them up to the top, where the water freezes. Again, they drop down, gathering another coating of water. This process goes on until the hailstone becomes so heavy that it drops from the clouds. Sometimes, these stones are as big as baseballs. If you want to see how many times a hailstone has gone up and down through a cloud, break it open and count the layers, or rings. Every time the stone went up through the cloud, it gathered one layer.

Answer each question below. Some of the questions ask where you found the answer. Write **passage A, passage B,** or **passages A and B** for these questions.

1. Which passage tells more about the damage that hailstorms cause?
2. The other passage gives more facts about something else. What does it tell more about?
3. How can you figure out how many times a hailstone has gone up and down through a cloud?
4. Where did you find the answer to question 3?
5. When does a hailstone finally fall from a cloud?
6. Where did you find the answer to question 5?
7. What is the temperature like at the top of a cloud?
8. Where did you find the answer to question 7?
9. What is the temperature like at the bottom of a cloud?
10. Where did you find the answer to question 9?
11. Name two reasons that farmers don't like hailstorms.
12. Where did you find the answer to question 11?
13. What carries a hailstone up and down in a cloud?
14. Where did you find the answer to question 13?

Workbook page 412

Lesson 138

ERRORS W

★ **A** Read the evidence and write the conclusion for each item.

1. Here's the evidence:

   All immersible appliances are waterproof.
   Toasters are not waterproof.

   What's the conclusion?
   Toasters are not immersible appliances.

2. Here's the evidence:

   Broccoli is a plant with chlorophyll.
   Chlorophyll makes plants green.

   What's the conclusion?
   Broccoli is a green plant.

3. Here's the evidence:

   Some banks exchange currency.
   The American is a bank.

   What's the conclusion?
   Maybe the American exchanges currency.

B Read the argument and answer the questions.

Joe Block led the New York Bullets basketball team to a victory over the Minnesota Pugs last season. The Bullets were predicted to lose by at least twenty points, but the Bullets won. So, when Joe says, "Light and Fluffy popcorn is the best popcorn on the market," you can bet that he is right again! Put a little Light and Fluffy in your life—tonight!

1. The argument uses Joe Block as a source for what kind of information?
   Idea: information about Light and Fluffy popcorn
2. Is Joe Block a good source for this information?
   no
3. For what kind of information would Joe Block be a good source?
   Idea: information about basketball

Answer key for Student Book part C *The writer's article was ambiguous and redundant, filled with particularly boring jokes and extraneous data. When he showed it to his editor, she contended that he would have to devise a different strategy for the article. Then she told him, "Usually your articles are especially well written. I think you can convert this poorly written article into one that people will particularly want to read."*

Answer key for Student Book part D
1. *passage A*   2. *Idea: How hail is formed*
3. *Idea: Break it open and count the layers.*
4. *passage B*   5. *Idea: When it becomes too heavy to be carried upward by air currents*
6. *passage B*   7. *Idea: It is very cold.*   8. *passage B*
9. *Idea: It is warm.*   10. *passage B*   11. *Idea: They destroy crops and kill livestock.*   12. *passage A*
13. *Idea: Air currents*   14. *passage B*

3. (Direct the students to count the number of errors and write the number in the **error** box at the top of the Workbook page.)
4. (Award points and direct students to record their points in Box **W**.)

0 errors	**15 points**
1–2 errors	**12 points**
3–5 errors	**8 points**
6–9 errors	**5 points**

5. (Award any bonus points. Direct the students to total their points and enter the total on the Point Summary Chart.)
6. Show me your work when you've finished correcting it. (When the students show you their corrected work, record their points on your Record Summary Chart.)

Workbook page 413

C Read the passage and answer the questions. Circle **W** if the question is answered by words in the passage. Circle **D** if the question is answered by a deduction. If you circle **W** for an item, underline the words in the passage that give the answer.

The population cycle depends on the food supply. When the food supply is large in an area, the area can support many animals. When the number of animals becomes so great that they eat most of the food supply, animals starve. Now there aren't as many animals to eat the food, so the food supply grows again. Soon the supply is large, so the area can once more , support a large number of animals.

Predators control the population of many animals. Predators keep the number of these animals from becoming too great. However, some animals have no natural enemies, so predators do not hold down their population growth. The Norwegian lemming is one of these animals. The lemming is a furry cousin of the rat that is about five inches long. Normally, lemmings live in the mountains. About every five years, the lemming population increases greatly. The number of lemmings is greater than the food supply. But the lemmings do something about this problem. They begin to march from the mountains into the lowlands, where many predators live. Hundreds of thousands of lemmings join the march, moving steadily in the same direction. Nothing seems to stop them. If a lake is in their way, they try to swim across, and many drown. With each mile, hundreds of lemmings die. Sometimes the march continues all the way to the ocean. The lemmings continue

their journey into the sea, where most of them drown. A few lemmings survive, and these lemmings return to the mountains. Now there is ample food for the lemmings, and the population begins to grow and grow. Five years later, the lemming population will again be very large, and the lemmings will start another march into the lowlands.

1. What does the population cycle of animals depend on?

   <u>Idea: the supply</u> Ⓦ D
   <u>of food</u>

2. Write what would happen next in the population cycle for rabbits and predators that eat rabbits:

   The number of predators that eat rabbits decreases.

   The population of rabbits increases.

   The number of predators that eat rabbits increases.

   Then what happens?

   <u>Idea: The population</u>
   <u>of rabbits decreases.</u>

3. Where do lemmings normally live?
   <u>in the mountains</u> Ⓦ D

4. Why does the lemming population sometimes get too big?
   <u>Idea: because they</u>
   <u>have no natural</u>
   <u>enemies</u> Ⓦ D

5. How do lemmings reduce their population?
   <u>Idea: by going on a</u>
   <u>march to the sea</u>

Workbook page 414

D Read the ads and answer the questions.

- The Lakeview lawn mower has an adjustable blade that lets you cut your grass with a minimum of effort. In the spring, your grass is long and hard to cut. With the Lakeview, you simply adjust the blade to a higher position, which makes the grass much easier to mow. In the summer, adjust the blade to a lower position. Your lawn will be as smooth as any lawn in your neighborhood. This adjustable blade is only one of the many features on the Lakeview mower. Don't you think that we take as much care with all of these features as we do with the adjustable blade? Lakeview, the premium lawn mower!

1. Write a sentence that would be in the ad if the ad said that all the features were as carefully designed as the special blade.

   <u>Idea: We take as</u>
   <u>much care with all</u>
   <u>the other features of</u>
   <u>the Lakeview lawn</u>
   <u>mower as we do with</u>
   <u>its special blades.</u>

- The Hammon Moto 600 is the fastest motorcycle on the road today. It can accelerate up to 100 miles per hour in ten seconds. The Hammon Moto gets about 50 miles per gallon of gasoline—almost twice as much mileage as you get from an old-fashioned car. When you consider speed performance and mileage, it's no wonder that over 10,000 people switched from old-fashioned cars to the Hammon Moto 600. These people are convinced that the Hammon is the best vehicle on the road today.

2. Write a sentence that would be in the ad if the ad said that the Hammon Moto 600 is the best vehicle on the road today.

   <u>Idea: The Hammon</u>
   <u>Moto 600 is the best</u>
   <u>vehicle on the road</u>
   <u>today.</u>

E Read the facts and the items. If an item is relevant to fact A, write **relevant to fact A.** If an item is relevant to fact B, write **relevant to fact B.** If an item is irrelevant to both facts, write **irrelevant.**

Fact A. **Susan and Michael are excellent cooks.**
Fact B. **Susan is trying to quit smoking.**

1. Because they both studied oriental art, Susan and Michael enjoyed their visit to the Art Institute of Chicago.
   <u>irrelevant</u>

2. Susan knows that smoking cigarettes can be harmful to her health.
   <u>relevant to fact B</u>

3. All of their friends enjoy the dinner parties Susan and Michael give.
   <u>relevant to fact A</u>

4. Neither Michael nor Susan can decide whose omelettes are better.
   <u>relevant to fact A</u>

Workbook page 415

F You will be tested on some facts presented in this lesson. These facts are:

1. Lemmings normally live in the mountains.
2. The lemming population sometimes gets too big because there are not many predators in the mountains.
3. Lemmings reduce their population by marching to the sea.

Study these facts. Repeat them to yourself. Writing these facts may help you to remember them.

END OF LESSON 138

Lesson 139

Student Book page 340

A A biased argument is an argument that tells the truth, but it tells only part of the truth.

Study the graph below. Then read the biased argument that is based on the graph.

> Since 2000, there has been a constant rise in the number of war toys that have been purchased for children. I think we should enlarge the war-toy department in our store. After all, more and more people are buying war toys.

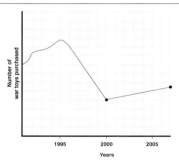

This argument is biased because it doesn't take into account some important information. What information is that? Ⓐ

Let's say that you wanted to attack the argument above. What would you say? Ⓑ

B Write **Part B** in the left margin of your paper. You have two minutes to copy the paragraph below.

> Hailstorms can cause more property damage than tornadoes. Animals as large as horses are occasionally killed in hailstorms. Leaves and fruit are knocked off trees in orchards. A hailstorm can flatten a ripe field of wheat or corn in a few minutes.

Student Book page 341

Lesson 139

★ C Write **Part C** in the left margin of your paper. Then number it from 1 to 5. The graph below shows the divorce rate for some years between 1970 and 2005. Assume that the graph is accurate. Examine the graph carefully and then read the statements below it. Some of the statements contradict what the graph shows.

* Write **contradictory** or **not contradictory** for each statement.
* If a statement contradicts the graph, write what the graph shows.

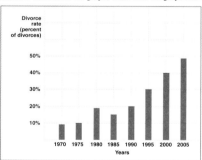

1. Of the years shown on the graph, 1970 had the lowest divorce rate.
2. Between 1975 and 1995, the divorce rate doubled.
3. The divorce rate in 1980 was lower than the divorce rate in 1985.
4. The divorce rate has been increasing since 1990.
5. The divorce rate in 2005 was almost 40 percent.

1. not contradictory
2. not contradictory
3. Contradictory; the divorce rate in 1980 was higher than the divorce rate in 1985.
4. not contradictory
5. Contradictory; the divorce rate in 2005 was almost 50 percent.

Note: The circled letters indicate when you ask a question or when you direct the group to respond.

═══════════ **EXERCISE 1** ═══════════
ANALYZING ARGUMENTS

1. (Direct the students to find Lesson 139, part A, in the **Student Book.**)
2. (Call on individual students to read part A.)
   Ⓐ (Call on a student. Idea: *The sales of war toys have decreased since 1995.*)
   Ⓑ (Call on a student. Idea: *Even though sales of war toys have increased since 2000, sales have decreased since 1995.*)

═══════════ **EXERCISE 2** ═══════════
INDEPENDENT WORK

1. **[Optional]** (Direct the students to read the instructions for part B to themselves. Then give them exactly two minutes to copy the paragraph. Count as errors any miscopied words and punctuation. Deduct these errors from the number of copied words, and mark the total on the Writing Rate Graph.)
2. In Lesson 140, you'll have a test on story facts. The facts that will be tested appear in part G of your Workbook. Study them and make sure that you know them. Now, finish the Student Book and do the Workbook for Lesson 139. ✓

Workcheck

1. Get ready to check your answers starting with Student Book part C. Use a pen to make an **X** next to any item you miss.
2. (Call on individual students to read each item and its answer. Repeat for Workbook items.)

3. (Direct the students to count the number of errors and write the number in the **error** box at the top of the Workbook page.)
4. (Award points and direct students to record their points in Box **W**.)

0 errors	15 points
1–2 errors	12 points
3–5 errors	8 points
6–9 errors	5 points

5. (Award any bonus points. Direct the students to total their points and enter the total on the Point Summary Chart.)
6. Show me your work when you've finished correcting it. (When the students show you their corrected work, record their points on your Record Summary Chart.)

Workbook page 417
Lesson 139

C Read the paragraph below.

> I was watching a biography of Edna St. Vincent Millay on television when a big thunderstorm started. I missed the end of the show.

1. The paragraph gives a clue about what caused the writer to miss the end of the show. What caused the writer to miss it?

Idea: a big thunderstorm

2. Name two ways that your answer to question 1 could cause the writer to miss the end of the show.

Idea: The noise of the storm drowned out the television's sound; the writer was so frightened of the storm that he/she wasn't able to concentrate on the program.

D Read the arguments and answer the questions.

- Mike Hanney has worked as an engineer for twenty years. He has completed skyscrapers in New York and built many bridges in Peru and Central America. He says we should build a floating bridge between the mainland and Strawberry Island. If he says the bridge should be a floating bridge, I think we should seriously consider building that type of bridge.

1. The argument uses Mike Hanney as a source for what kind of information?

Idea: information about bridge building

2. Is Mike Hanney a good source for this information? *yes*

3. For what kind of information would Mike Hanney be a good source?

Idea: information about building bridges and buildings

- The University of Washington spends more money on its science departments than on any other department. The oceanography and fisheries departments are excellent. Teachers and students take boats out on the ocean to study sea life. These boats are equipped with the most modern devices for studying life under the sea. The University of Washington receives millions of dollars from the government for research. Its professors and students are carefully selected. This group of people agrees that the salmon season should be cut short this year. I think we should follow their advice.

4. The argument uses the University of Washington as a source for what kind of information?

Idea: information about shortening the salmon season

5. Is the University of Washington a good source for this information? *yes*

6. For what kind of information would the University of Washington be a good source?

Idea: information about sea life

Workbook page 416
Lesson 139 ERRORS W

A Underline the redundant part in each sentence below. Then explain why the underlined part is redundant.

1. "That's it!" he exclaimed emphatically.

Idea: If you know that he exclaimed it, then you already know that he said it emphatically.

2. She drew a four-cornered rectangle.

Idea: If you know that she drew a rectangle, then you know that it had four corners.

3. By the time a year was over, twelve months had passed.

Idea: If you know that a year was over, then you know that twelve months had passed.

B Look at diagram 1.

Diagram 1

You can see the dots and the triangle, but you can't see the circle.
1. Complete the deduction:

All the dots are in the triangle.
Part of the triangle is in the circle.

So, *maybe all the dots are in the circle.*

2. Draw a circle in diagram 1.

- Look at diagram 2.

Diagram 2

You can see the dots and the triangle, but you can't see the circle.
3. Complete the deduction:

All the dots are in the triangle.
None of the triangle is in the circle.

So, *none of the dots are in the circle*.

4. Draw a circle in diagram 2.

Workbook page 418
Lesson 139

E Read the passage below.

> For generations, people all over the world have watched horse races and horse shows. Many others have enjoyed riding or hunting or the game of polo. Horses are also a popular theme in pictures, beginning centuries ago with paintings and continuing through modern times with photographic stories.
> It wasn't until the camera was invented that a startling discrepancy was discovered. Popular paintings up to the nineteenth century showed horses flying over the ground with all four legs outstretched. When the camera was perfected in the 1870s, snapshots showed that horses never run that way. As a horse's front legs leave the ground, its back legs come down for the next stride. No horse could extend all four of its legs without falling on its stomach!
> When painters applied this new knowledge to their work and began painting horses as they actually run, everyone complained that their pictures looked wrong.

- Here's a conclusion:

Some paintings of horses are more than 100 years old.

1. Does the passage contain evidence to support this conclusion or evidence to refute this conclusion?

evidence to support this conclusion

2. Which sentence contains the evidence?

Horses are also a popular theme in pictures, beginning centuries ago with paintings and continuing through modern times with photographic stories.

- Here's another conclusion:

People don't like art unless it is realistic.

3. Does the passage contain evidence to support this conclusion or evidence to refute this conclusion?

evidence to refute this conclusion

4. Which sentence contains the evidence?

When painters applied this new knowledge to their work and began painting horses as they actually run, everyone complained that their pictures looked wrong.

Workbook page 419

- Here's another conclusion:

  Horseback riding and hunting are unpopular.

  5. Does the passage contain evidence to support this conclusion or evidence to refute this conclusion?

  evidence to refute this conclusion

  6. Which sentence contains the evidence?

  Many others have enjoyed riding or hunting or the game of polo.

- Here's another conclusion:

  There are horses in many countries.

  7. Does the passage contain evidence to support this conclusion or evidence to refute this conclusion?

  evidence to support this conclusion

  8. Which sentence contains the evidence?

  For generations, people all over the world have watched horse races and horse shows.

Workbook page 421

G Tomorrow you will be tested on facts you have learned. The test will include all of the facts presented in Lessons 123–138, and some of the facts from earlier lessons. These facts are:

1. Lemmings normally live in the mountains.
2. The lemming population sometimes gets too big because there are not many predators in the mountains.
3. Lemmings reduce their population by marching to the sea.
4. Tolerant trees do not need much sunlight to survive.
5. Intolerant trees cannot survive in the shade.
6. When an animal hibernates, it curls up in a safe place and sleeps for a long period of time.
7. Inflation means that prices keep going up.
8. Study the chart below. Make sure that you can fill in this chart.

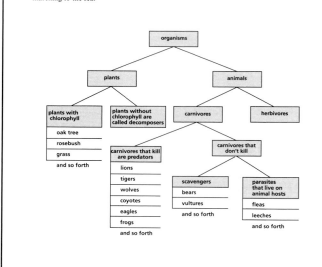

Workbook page 420

F Read this: A title is a piece of paper that tells who owns something. When you buy a car, for example, you take title to the car. When you apply for license plates, you must show that you have title to the car. You must also show that you have title to the car when you sell it. Use the facts to fill out the form.

Facts: **Your name is Rebecca Lynn. You are applying for a new driver's license in Vancouver, British Columbia. You are eighteen years old and were born April 22, 1988, in Butte, Montana. You are 5 feet 4 inches tall, you weigh about 115 pounds, your hair is black, and your eyes are brown. You live with your parents, John and Mary Lynn, at 1230 Stapleton in Vancouver. You passed both the written and driving tests given by the province. Your score on the road-signs test was 85 percent correct, and your score on the driver-information test was 98 percent correct. You drive a 1998 Ford. The license plate number is BC 2356. The car's title is in your name. The title number is 3945-84-87. The car's serial number is A543-4HL2-450. You must use your glasses to drive because, without them, your eyesight is poor. The car is insured by Safeink Insurance Company.**

Province of British Columbia
Driver's License Application Form

Name _Rebecca Lynn_

Date of birth _April 22, 1988_ Place of birth _Butte, Montana_

Present address _1230 Stapleton Vancouver, British Columbia_
Street City State/Province

Is this application for a new license or for a renewal of an old one? New _√_ Old ___

Eyesight without glasses good ___ poor _√_

Eyesight with glasses good _√_ poor ___

Height _5 feet 4 inches_ Weight _115 pounds_

Hair color _black_ Eye color _brown_

Percent correct on driver-information test _98_ Percent correct on road-signs test _85_

What is the license plate number of the vehicle you own? _BC 2356_

What is the title number of the vehicle? _3945-84-87_

Whose name is on the title? _mine_

What is the serial number of the vehicle? _A543-4HL2-450_

Name of your insurance company _Safeink Insurance Company_

Workbook page 422

9. Study the chart below. Make sure that you can fill in this chart.

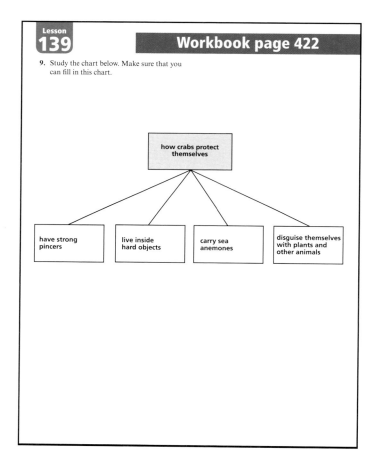

END OF LESSON 139

EXERCISE 1

INDEPENDENT WORK

1. **[Optional]** (Direct the students to read the instructions for part A in the **Student Book** to themselves. Then give them exactly two minutes to copy the paragraph. Count as errors any miscopied words and punctuation. Deduct these errors from the number of copied words, and mark the total on the Writing Rate Graph.)

2. Finish the Student Book and Workbook for Lesson 140. ✓

Workcheck

1. Get ready to check your answers starting with Student Book part B. Use a pen to make an **X** next to any item you miss.

2. (Call on individual students to read each item and its answer. Repeat for Workbook items.)

3. (Direct the students to count the number of errors and write the number in the **error** box at the top of the Workbook page.)

4. (Award points and direct students to record their points in Box **W**.)

0 errors	**15 points**
1–2 errors	**12 points**
3–5 errors	**8 points**
6–9 errors	**5 points**

5. (Award any bonus points. Direct the students to total their points and enter the total on the Point Summary Chart.)

6. Show me your work when you've finished correcting it. (When the students show you their corrected work, record their points on your Record Summary Chart.)

Lesson 140 — **Student Book page 342**

A Write **Part A** in the left margin of your paper. You have two minutes to copy the paragraph below.

> Last Christmas I got a job decorating windows for the department store downtown. My boss criticized me for putting too many details in the decorations. Finally I devised a strategy for some window scenes that she liked: Santa Claus stuffing stockings with gifts.

★ **B** Write **Part B** in the left margin of your paper. Here are three main ideas:

> - Many people enjoy mountain climbing.
> - There are many dangers in mountain climbing.
> - Climbers have to be careful when they cross glaciers.

Mountain climbers face many dangers. Rockfall is a common danger in mountain climbing. Rockfall is often caused when water enters the fine cracks in rocks and then freezes. When the water freezes in cracks, it expands and often causes the rocks to crack open and fall on climbers below. Climbers also have to be careful when they cross glaciers. The movement of ice can cause giant cracks called crevasses. These cracks may be covered with fresh snow, and a climber who is unroped may fall into one. Bad weather can also be dangerous to climbers. Mist or blowing snow can prevent climbers from seeing their route. Even a little mist or blowing snow may cause climbers to become lost. Winds can become so strong in mountains that climbers may be blown off ridges. Many climbers have been killed in avalanches. Avalanches are sudden snow or rock slides that bury everything in their path.

Write the main idea that fits the passage. List the four points that fall under the main idea in outline form. Don't forget to indent and label the four points.

I. There are many dangers to mountain climbing.
   A. Idea: Rocks crack and fall on climbers.
   B. Idea: Climbers might fall into crevasses.
   C. Idea: Wind or snow can blind climbers or blow them off mountains.
   D. Idea: Avalanches can bury climbers.

Workbook page 423 — **Lesson 140**

★ **A** Select the right word for combining each pair of sentences below. Then write the combined sentence. Remember to punctuate each sentence correctly.

1. Jeff forgot to feed his dog last night. His dog was very hungry today. **and but**
Jeff forgot to feed his dog last night, and his dog was very hungry today.

2. Jackie has always wanted to learn to play the guitar. She has never had enough money to buy one. **so however**
Jackie has always wanted to learn to play the guitar; however, she has never had enough money to buy one.

3. We wanted to see both movies. We arrived at the theater almost an hour after the first movie began. **therefore but**
We wanted to see both movies, but we arrived at the theater almost an hour after the first movie began.

4. The auditor found many mistakes in the books. The books were kept in the safe. **who which**
The auditor found many mistakes in the books, which were kept in the safe.

5. People frequently talk with George. He is very open and friendly. **who which**
People frequently talk with George, who is very open and friendly.

6. The librarian told me that I still had six books checked out. He wouldn't let me check out any more. **so however**
The librarian told me that I still had six books checked out, so he wouldn't let me check out any more.

B For each item, write a sentence that means the same thing by changing the underlined words.

1. The principal made up a rule that was based on the facts about school attendance.
The principal devised a regulation that was based on the data about school attendance.

---

2. He caused a great misunderstanding by giving an <u>unclear answer</u>.

He caused a great misunderstanding by giving an ambiguous response.

3. The manager has a <u>sound plan</u> for increasing production.

The manager has a valid strategy for increasing production.

4. In her proposal, Dr. Martin <u>argued</u> that she was not <u>hiding</u> the <u>reasons</u> for doing her research.

In her proposal, Dr. Martin contended that she was not concealing the motives for doing her research.

C Read the paragraph below.

When Jim arrived at work in the morning, his boss was in a foul mood. The next day Jim started work at another store.

1. The paragraph gives a clue about what caused Jim to start work at another store the next day. What caused him to start work at another store?

Idea: his boss's foul mood

2. Name two ways that your answer to question 1 could cause Jim to start work at another store.

Idea: His boss chewed him out; his boss's foul personality depressed Jim, so he wanted to work elsewhere.

D Look at diagram 1.

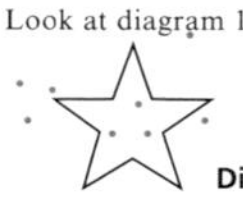

Diagram 1

You can't see the dots in the picture, but **some dots are in the star.**

1. We're looking for a dot. What's the conclusion about where that dot is?

Maybe the dot is in the star.

2. Draw dots in diagram 1.

• Look at diagram 2.

Diagram 2

You can see the rectangle and the oval, but you can't see the squares.

3. Complete the deduction.
All the squares are in the oval.
None of the oval is in the rectangle.

So, *none of the squares are in the rectangle*

E Each argument that follows is faulty. Read each argument and answer the questions.

• I thought I knew Charley really well. We've gone fishing together, and I can't tell you how many times I've visited his place. We used to play baseball together every weekend. As I say, I thought I knew him really well. You can't imagine how surprised I was to find out that he had a nervous breakdown. That doesn't sound like the Charley I know.

1. What does the author want us to conclude?

Idea: He couldn't imagine the Charley he knew having a nervous breakdown.

2. How could you show that the argument is faulty?

Idea: Point out to the writer that he obviously didn't know Charley as well as he thought he did.

• The building repairer tried to tell me that our house has a crack in the foundation. Do you realize that the beams in our house are made from lumber imported all the way from northern British Columbia? And the windows are made of a special high-lead Italian glass. The roof is the best you can buy—red cedar shakes. How could there be a crack in the foundation?

3. What does the writer want us to conclude?

Idea: There can't be a crack in the house's foundation.

4. How could you show that the argument is faulty?

Idea: Ask the building supervisor to take photos of the crack and show them to the owners.

• We know that it rains an average of more than twenty-five inches during the winter in Drinmo, Washington. This means that during the winter season it rains nearly a quarter of an inch every day. When I go to Drinmo on February 8, I know that it will rain nearly a quarter of an inch that day.

5. What does the writer want us to conclude?

Idea: It rains nearly a quarter of an inch every day during the winter in Drinmo, Washington.

6. How could you show that the argument is faulty?

Idea: Invite him to Drinmo on a winter day during which it doesn't rain.

END OF LESSON 140

EXERCISE 1

MASTERY TEST

1. Everybody, find page 473 in your workbook.

- This is a test. If you make no mistakes on the test, you'll earn 20 points. Write the answers to the test items now using your pencil.

2. (After the students complete the items, gather the Workbooks and grade the tests. As you grade each test, record the number of errors the student made on each part of the test in the appropriate box. Record the total number of errors in the **Error** box at the beginning of the test.)

3. (Return the Workbooks to the students.) Raise your hand if you made _____ or more mistakes in _____.
(Record the number of students who raise their hand for the part.)

> Key: Part A–8   Part B–3   Part C–2
>   Part D–1   Part E–1   Part F–1

4. Raise your hand if you made no mistakes on the whole test. Great work. (Award 20 points to students who made no errors. Award 5 points to students who made 1 or 2 errors.)

- Record your points in the box marked **MT** at the top of Mastery Test 14.

- (Direct all students to enter their points on the Point Summary Chart.)

5. (Record test results on the Group Summary Sheet. Reproducible Summary Sheets are at the back of the Teacher's Guide.)

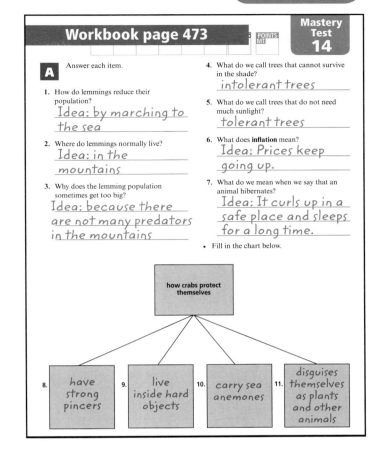

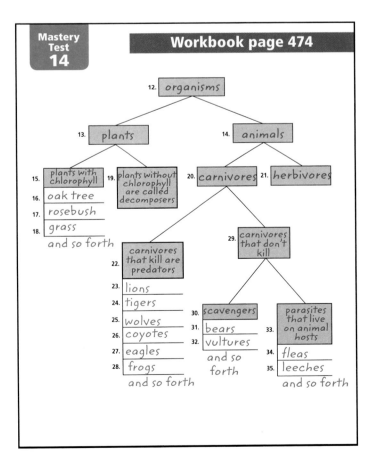

Workbook page 475

B Write the model sentence that means the same thing as each sentence below.

1. A strange event caused the fear that she showed.

   A strange phenomenon caused the anxiety that she exhibited.

2. Her answer was filled with irrelevant details.

   Her response was replete with extraneous details.

3. They changed their Swiss money into Canadian money.

   They converted their Swiss currency into Canadian currency.

4. By pausing, she lost her chance.

   By hesitating, she lost her opportunity.

5. His directions were unclear and repetitive.

   His directions were ambiguous and redundant.

6. The rule limited their parking.

   The regulation restricted their parking.

7. They made up a fitting plan.

   They devised an appropriate strategy.

8. The major argued that he had sound reasons for hiding the facts.

   The major contended that he had valid motives for concealing the data.

C Read the ads and answer the questions.

> Four out of five doctors that we surveyed recommended the pain reliever found in Brand X aspirin.

1. Does the ad actually say that the doctors recommended Brand X aspirin?

   no

2. Write a sentence that would be in the ad if the ad said that the doctors recommended Brand X aspirin.

   Idea: Four out of five doctors that we surveyed recommended Brand X aspirin.

Workbook page 477

E Read the paragraph below.

> The people of Sipple had gone to the lake outside their city ever since the city had been formed. They swam, fished, and canoed. Then, in 1994, a large factory was built near the lake. After 1994, nobody went to the lake.

1. The paragraph gives a clue about what caused the people to stop going to the lake. What caused them to stop?

   Idea: A large factory was built near the lake.

• Name two ways that it could cause people to stop going to the lake.

2. *Ideas: The factory polluted the water. The factory made the air smell too bad.*

3. *Idea: The factory owned the lake and wouldn't let people use it.*

F The passage below presents a moral. Read the passage. Then make up a moral that fits the passage.

> There once was a man who decided to build a house. Winter was approaching, so the man said to himself, "I'll do this house the fast way," and he did. He slapped up boards here and there. He didn't take the time to measure and fit. He pounded and slapped things together. Soon–very soon–his house was completed. "Not bad," he said to himself, until somebody came over to his house and slammed the front door, and down came the walls. In the end, the man had to rebuild his house the right way. It took him much longer this time, however, because he had to work in the cold, and he had to clear away the wreck of the first house.

Write a moral for the passage. Start the moral with the words "If you

Idea: do things right the first time, you'll save time."

Workbook page 476

> The combined experience of the ten salespeople at Frank's Car Lot is over 100 years. That means that the average salesperson at Frank's Car Lot has over ten years of experience. That's a lot of experience. Come down to Frank's and talk to one of our friendly and knowledgeable salespeople.

3. Does the ad actually say that each salesperson has over ten years of experience?

   no

4. Write a sentence that would be in the ad if the ad said that each of the salespeople had over ten years of experience.

   Idea: Each salesperson at Frank's car Lot has over ten years of experience.

D Read the argument and answer the questions.

> Professor Davis has been with the college for fifteen years. She is the chairperson of the science department. She has written three books that are used in colleges around the country. All of us who have worked with her are very impressed with how intelligent she is. So, when she tells us where we should build the new gym, we should follow her suggestion.

1. The argument uses Professor Davis as a source for what kind of information?

   Idea: information about where a new gym should be built

2. Is Professor Davis a good source of information?

   no

3. For what kind of information would Professor Davis be a good source?

   Idea: information about science

━━━ **EXERCISE 2** ━━━

TEST REMEDIES

1. (If more than 25% of the students failed a part of the test, provide the remedy specified for that part in the table below. The required Remedy Blackline Master worksheets can be found in Appendix H of the Teacher's Guide.)

2. (All remedies should be completed before beginning the next lesson in the program.)

Test Section	If students made this many errors	Present these tasks: Lesson	Exercise	Remedy Blackline Master	Required Student Book Parts
A	8 or more	Test remedy below		14–A, 14–B	
B	3 or more	Item 1: 86	1	14–C	Lesson 86–A
		Item 2: 57	1	14–C	Lesson 57–A
		Item 3: 28	3	14–D	Lesson 28–B
		Item 4: 19	1	14–D	Lesson 19–A
		Item 5: 22	1	14–E	Lesson 22–A
		Item 6: 34	2	14–E	Lesson 34–B
		Item 7: 63	1	14–F	Lesson 63–B
		Item 8: 102	1	14–F	Lesson 102–A
C	2 or more	128	2		Lesson 128–A
		129	1		Lesson 129–A
		131	—	14–G	
D	1 or more	127	1		Lesson 127–B
		128	—		Lesson 129–A
		131	—	14–H	
E	1 or more	133	1		
		134	—	14–I	
F	1 or more	129	2		Lesson 129–B and D
		130	—	14–J	Lesson 130–D

Note: The teacher and each student who failed the test will need a copy of Remedy Blackline Master 14–A. The Remedy Blackline Masters can be found in Appendix H of the Teacher's Guide.

PART A TEST REMEDY

1. We're going to go over some items from the test. I'll read the items. You'll say the answers. Then you'll write the answers.

2. (Read item 1 in part A of Remedy Blackline Master 14–A.) What's the answer? (Call on a student. Idea: *Prices keep going up*.)

3. (Repeat step 2 for items 2–9 in part A.)

4. (Give each student a copy of Remedy Blackline Master 14–A.)
   This worksheet shows the charts that were on the test.

5. Touch box 10.
   What goes on that box? (Call on a student. Idea: *Have strong pincers*.)

6. (Repeat step 5 for boxes 11–13.)

7. Touch box 14.

8. (Repeat step 7 for boxes 15–37.)

9. Study the charts for a few minutes. Then you'll fill in the empty boxes.

10. (After several minutes:)
    Now you're going to write the answers to all the items in part A. Let's see who can get them all correct.

11. (After students complete the items:)
    Let's check your work. Use your pen to make an **X** next to any item you got wrong.
    - (For items 1–9: Read the items. Call on individual students to answer each item.)
    - (For the chart items:) What goes in box 10? (Call on a student. Idea: *Have strong pincers*.)
    - (Repeat for boxes 11–37.)
    - Raise your hand if you got all the items correct. Nice work.

END OF MASTERY TEST 14

GLOSSARY

aesthetic A building that has aesthetic value is one that has artistic value.

affirm When you affirm something, you agree with it.

ambiguous An ambiguous statement is an unclear statement.

appropriate An appropriate idea is a fitting idea.

Arabian horse An Arabian horse is a light, fast horse that is bred to produce more intelligent horses.

atlas An atlas is a reference book that has maps and gives facts about places. It shows the size of cities and countries, how far it is from one place to another, and the number of people who live in different places.

audibly When you say something audibly, you say it loud enough for people to hear you.

boar A boar is a wild pig with large tusks.

boycott A boycott takes place when people stop buying from a business or selling to a business. When a business is successfully boycotted, it can either change its practices or go out of business.

braille Braille is the system of reading and writing that blind people use. Braille is read by running your fingers across patterns of bumps.

carnivorous Carnivorous animals eat other animals. If there were no herbivorous animals, carnivorous animals would become extinct. The teeth and the eyes of carnivorous animals are well designed for hunting. The teeth of carnivorous mammals are pointed. Their right eyes and their left eyes see nearly the same things.

catastrophe A catastrophe is a terrible event that results in death and destruction. Earthquakes, fires, and floods are catastrophes.

cautious When you are cautious, you are very careful.

clarity Something that has clarity is very clear. A diamond with great clarity is a very clear diamond.

cleaner fish Cleaner fish eat parasites from larger ocean animals. Sharks allow cleaner fish to eat things inside their mouths.

clewe In Middle English, **clewe** was the word for thread.

clue A clue is a hint that helps you find your way out of a puzzle.

coast-to-coast railroad The first coast-to-coast railroad in the United States was completed in 1869.

cold war A cold war happens when two countries are close to being in a shooting war with each other.

conceal When you conceal something, you hide it.

consistent Things that are consistent are things that you expect to happen together.

contend When you contend that something is true, you argue that it is true.

convert When you convert something, you change it.

cow A cow is an herbivorous animal that has several stomachs. In a cow's first stomach, organisms digest the cellulose contained in plants. In the second stomach, the organisms are digested.

crab A crab is an animal that has a hard shell. Crabs have different ways to protect themselves from predators: crabs have strong pincers; some crabs live inside hard objects; some crabs carry sea anemones; some crabs disguise themselves with plants and other animals.

currency Currency is money.

data Data are facts.

decomposers Plants that do not have chlorophyll are decomposers.

deprecate When you deprecate someone, you express disapproval of that person.

devise When you devise something, you make it up.

dictionary A dictionary is a reference book that gives facts about words. It shows how to spell a word and how to pronounce it. It tells which part of speech a word is and what the word means. A dictionary also tells the history of words.

diligent A diligent person is a careful person.

donkey A donkey is an animal that descended from equus. Two other names for a donkey are a burro and an ass.

ebullient An ebullient person is a joyful person.

ecology The word **ecology** comes from a Greek word that means **house.** The study of ecology is the study of living things in the world and how they affect each other.

emphatically When you say something emphatically, you say it as if you really mean it.

encyclopedia An encyclopedia is a reference book that gives facts about nearly everything. It tells about planets and plants, about animals and buildings, and about history and famous people.

endangered species An endangered species is one that is nearly extinct. There are more than 1,000 species of animals that are currently endangered.

eohippus Eohippus was the earliest-known close relative of the modern horse. We know that eohippus was related to the horse because its skeleton resembles that of a modern horse. Eohippus defended itself by outrunning its enemies. The feet of eohippus changed over the centuries to make it a better runner.

equus Modern horses and other similar animals belong to a group called equus. Some types of equus became large and others became slender, depending on what climate they lived in.

excruciating An excruciating pain is an unbearable pain.

exonerate When you exonerate someone, you free that person of blame.

extinct A type of animal becomes extinct when there are no more animals of that type. A hundred years ago, people were not concerned with ecology because they believed there was no end to different types of wildlife.

extol When you extol something, you praise it.

extraneous An extraneous comment is an irrelevant comment.

extrovert An extrovert is an outgoing person who likes to be with people and gets along well with people.

fallacious A fallacious argument is an argument that is full of error.

fecund Fecund soil is fertile soil.

fenestration The fenestration of a room is the arrangement of windows in the room.

financial aid When people receive financial aid for their schooling, they get the money they need to pay their tuition or living expenses.

fortitude Someone who has fortitude has courage.

fubsy A fubsy person is a fat person.

genius A genius is an extremely intelligent person.

haze When you haze people, you torment them.

herbivorous Herbivorous animals eat plants. If there were no plants, herbivorous animals would become extinct. The teeth and the eyes of many herbivorous mammals are well designed for grazing. The teeth of a herbivorous mammal are flat. Many herbivorous mammals can eat and watch out for enemies at the same time. Their right eye and their left eye don't see the same things.

hesitate When you hesitate, you pause.

hibernate When an animal hibernates, it curls up in a safe place and sleeps for a long period of time.

Houston, Texas Houston is a large city in the southern part of the United States. The two things that stimulated Houston's growth were a railroad and a canal.

ignominious An ignominious person is a disgraceful person.

illusion An illusion is something that doesn't exist.

imitation Something that is fake is an imitation.

inconsistent Things that are inconsistent are things that you don't expect to happen together.

independent An independent activity is an activity that you do on your own.

indolent An indolent person is a lazy person.

inflation Inflation means that prices keep going up.

innuendo An innuendo is something that is said as a hint.

inquiries Inquiries are questions.

interrogation An interrogation session is a questioning session.

intolerant trees Intolerant trees cannot survive in the shade.

irrelevant Information that does not help explain a fact is irrelevant to the fact.

lease A lease is an agreement to pay for an apartment or house for a set period of time.

lemming A Norwegian lemming is a furry, ratlike animal that normally lives in the mountains. The lemming population sometimes gets too big because there aren't many predators in the mountains. The lemmings reduce their population by marching to the sea.

Leonardo da Vinci Leonardo da Vinci was an inventor, a painter, a musician, and a scientist. He was an Italian, and he lived from 1452 to 1519.

lethal Something that is lethal is capable of killing living things.

loquacious A loquacious person is a talkative person.

magnanimous A magnanimous person is a generous person.

main-idea sentence The main-idea sentence of a paragraph is the sentence that tells what the paragraph is about. The main idea of a paragraph is the most important idea.

malaise A malaise is a feeling of depression.

malapropos A malapropos comment is an inappropriate comment.

malign When you malign someone, you speak badly about that person.

marital status Your marital status tells whether you are married, single, widowed, or divorced.

maverick A maverick can be a person who isn't a part of the group.

Millard Fillmore Millard Fillmore was moderate in his views, which means he didn't take a strong stand on anything. He became president of the United States when President Taylor died.

miser A miser is a person who is very stingy.

monthly expenses Your monthly expenses are how much you pay out each month for things such as rent, food, and car maintenance.

monthly income Your monthly income is how much money you make each month.

motive When you have a motive for doing something, you have a reason for doing it.

niggling Niggling details are petty or small details.

nook A nook is a small place.

notorious A notorious person is a well-known person. A notorious person usually has become famous as a result of having done something bad.

obliterated When something is obliterated, it is destroyed.

opportunity An opportunity is a chance.

organism Any living thing is an organism.

overpopulated When a place is overpopulated, too many things are living there.

panache When you have panache, you have a dashing charm.

paragraphos The Greek word **paragraphos** means **by the side of writing.**

parasite A parasite is one kind of carnivore that does not kill. It gets its nourishment from animal hosts. Fleas, ticks, mosquitoes, and leeches are parasites that live on animals.

penurious A penurious person is a stingy person.

plants Green plants are the only living things that manufacture their own food. For plants to manufacture food, they must have sunlight, water, and carbon dioxide. Plants are different from animals in several ways. Plants "breathe in" carbon dioxide, they "exhale" oxygen, and they make their own food.

Pony Express The Pony Express delivered mail from St. Joseph, Missouri, to Sacramento, California, in eight days instead of the twenty days that mail delivery had taken before. The Pony Express was faster because fresh horses were stationed along the route.

preceding A preceding event is an event that happened before another event.

predator A predator is a carnivorous animal that kills.

proximity Proximity to an object is how close the object is to something.

qualifications for a job Your qualifications for a job are the things that you have done that would make you good at the job.

redundant A redundant sentence is a repetitive sentence.

reference for a job When you name somebody as a reference, that person is supposed to give evidence about what kind of worker you are and how reliable you are.

regulation A regulation is a rule.

relevant Information that helps explain a fact is relevant to that fact.

remote A remote area is an area that is far from towns or cities. Very few people live in remote areas.

replete A speech that is replete with jokes is filled with jokes.

response A response is an answer.

restrict When you restrict something, you limit it.

robot A robot is a machine that looks and does some things like a human.

rogue An animal that is a rogue is an animal that travels by itself and is usually mean.

roots The roots of plants help prevent the formation of a desert by holding down the soil.

sanction When you sanction something, you approve of it.

scavenger A scavenger is one kind of carnivore that does not kill. It eats the remains of animals that are already dead. Bears, porcupines, crows, and vultures are scavengers.

scrupulous A person who is scrupulous is a person who pays a lot of attention to details.

siblings Siblings are people who have at least one parent in common.

somnolent When you are somnolent, you are sleepy.

sorrow Sorrow is sadness. When you are filled with sorrow, you are very sad.

spoonerism A spoonerism is made by exchanging the first parts of words.

statement of fact A statement of fact tells what is or what happens.

statement of ought A statement of ought tells what we should do or what ought to happen.

strategy A strategy is a plan.

subsequent A subsequent event is an event that follows another event.

tantalize When you tantalize someone, you tease that person by putting something just out of reach.

temporary Situations that are temporary do not last forever. They change.

tenacious A tenacious person is a stubborn person.

tickbird A tickbird removes parasites from a rhinoceros and signals danger. The rhinoceros provides food and transportation for the tickbird.

title for property A title is a piece of paper that tells who owns something.

tolerant trees Tolerant trees do not need much sunlight to survive.

tuition Tuition is the fee that people pay to attend a school.

uncouth An uncouth remark is a vulgar remark.

unctuous An unctuous liquid is an oily liquid.

valid A valid excuse is a sound excuse.

vital Something that is vital is necessary.

wildlife Wildlife is made up of plants and animals that are wild.